History in Person

M000238100

**Publication of the Advanced Seminar Series
is made possible by generous support from
The Brown Foundation, Inc., of Houston, Texas.**

School of American Research
Advanced Seminar Series

Douglas W. Schwartz
General Editor

History in Person

Contributors

Begoña Aretxaga
Department of Anthropology, University of Texas at Austin

Steven Gregory
Department of Anthropology, New York University

Dorothy Holland
Department of Anthropology
University of North Carolina at Chapel Hill

Michael Kearney
Department of Anthropology, University of California at Riverside

Jean Lave
Social and Cultural Studies in Education
University of California at Berkeley

Daniel T. Linger
Department of Anthropology, University of California at Santa Cruz

Liisa H. Malkki
Department of Anthropology, University of California at Irvine

Debra Skinner
Department of Anthropology and Frank Porter Graham Child Development Center, University of North Carolina at Chapel Hill

Kay B. Warren
Department of Anthropology, Harvard University

Paul Willis
Social and Cultural Studies, University of Wolverhampton, UK Centre for Cultural Research, University of Växjö, Sweden

History in Person

Enduring Struggles, Contentious Practice,
Intimate Identities

Edited by Dorothy Holland and Jean Lave

School of American Research Press
Santa Fe

James Currey
Oxford

School of American Research Press

Post Office Box 2188
Santa Fe, New Mexico 87504-2188

James Currey Ltd

73 Botley Road
Oxford OX2 0BS

Editors: Joan K. O'Donnell and Jane Kepp
Designer: Context, Inc.
Indexer: Nancy Bennett
Typographer: Cynthia Welch
Printer: Sheridan Books

Library of Congress Cataloging-in-Publication Data:
History in person : enduring struggles, contentious practice, intimate identities / edited by Dorothy Holland and Jean Lave.
    p. cm. — (School of American Research advanced seminar series)
    Includes bibliographical references and index.
    ISBN 1-930618-00-X (cloth) — ISBN 1-930618-01-8 (paper)
    1. Social conflict—History. 2. Group identity—History. 3. Culture—History. 4. Social stratification—History. I. Herring, Dorothy Holland, 1937– II. Lave, Jean. III. Series.
HM1221 .H57 2000
305.5—DC21   00-052651
                                                 CIP

British Library Cataloguing in Publication Data:
History in person : enduring struggles, contentious practice, intimate identities. -
  (A School of American Research advanced seminar)
  1. Identity (Psychology) 2. Ethnology
  I. Holland, Dorothy II. Lave, Jean III. School of American Research
  305.8

  ISBN 0-85255-929-1 (cloth) 0-85255-924-0 (paper)

Library of Congress Catalog Card Number 00-052651.
International Standard Book Numbers 0-930618-00-X (cloth) and 0-930618-01-8
(paper).
First edition 2001.

1 2 3 4 5 05 04 03 02 01

Cover illustration: "History in Person" by Dr. Hysse Forchhammer, neuropsychologist. Pastel and water color on paper. Copyright © 2000 Dr. Hysse Forchhammer, Copenhagen, Denmark.

Contents

CONTENTS

Illustrations

History in Person

1

History in Person

An Introduction

Dorothy Holland and Jean Lave

In October 1995, the School of American Research in Santa Fe, New Mexico, hosted an advanced seminar titled "History in Person."[1] As co-chairs of the seminar, we began with the proposition that pervasive, long-term, transformative struggles are telling sites for the study of "history in person." Our topic was the mutually constitutive nature of long and complex social, political, and economic struggles and the historically fashioned identities-in-practice and subjectivities that they produce. Long and overwhelming situations of conflict in Northern Ireland and South Africa and the contested rise of powerful multinational corporations are obvious examples of long-term struggles, but there are other, more circumscribed, yet equally persistent and riveting conflicts in workplaces, households, and academic fields. Whatever the circumstances, we cannot understand enduring struggles as crucibles for the forging of identities unless our accounts encompass the working creativity of historically produced agents and the interconnected differences among their interests, points of view, and ways of participating in the production of ongoing struggles. During the seminar we brought our ethnographic research on enduring struggles together with our attempts to address practices of identity in those struggles. Nine participants were involved in this project: Begoña Aretxaga, Steven Gregory, Dorothy Holland, Michael Kearney, Jean Lave, Dan Linger, Liisa Malkki, Kay Warren, and Paul Willis.[2]

In the following chapters, which are revised versions of the papers discussed during the seminar, Aretxaga writes about the politically sexualized transformation of identities of women who were political prisoners in Northern Ireland; Warren, about the changing character of political activism across generations in a Mayan family in Guatemala; Holland and Debra Skinner, about the changing fields of struggle of Hindu women in Nepal and their effects on the divisiveness of women's identities; Gregory, about struggles between state and grass-roots activists over the exploitation of local communities in New York for the sake of more powerful class constituencies elsewhere; Willis, about cultural forms generated in and mediating struggles of working-class men on shop floors in England; Linger, about the everyday struggles over identities of nationality of Brazilians of Japanese descent living in Japan; Kearney, about enduring, contradictory struggles between class- and ethnicity-based transnational communities and the Mexican state; Lave, about the struggles of British wine merchant families, long-term residents of Portugal, to sustain their enclave as a living monument to their version of the past and themselves as the masters of its future; and Malkki, about the social consequences of Central African violence among Hutu exiles in Montreal and their social imagination of the future.

The seminar developed from the organizers' shared theoretical perspective, which is grounded in a theory of practice that emphasizes processes of social formation and cultural production. We began with the tenet that the political-economic, social, and cultural structuring of social existence is constituted in the daily practices and lived activities of subjects who both participate in it and produce cultural forms that mediate it. Claims that such relations lie at the heart of social investigation are at the same time claims that they are historical processes—that both the continuity and the transformation of social life are ongoing, uncertain projects. For us, one central analytical intention of social practice theory lies in inquiry into historical structures of privilege, rooted in class, race, gender, and other social divisions, as these are

4

brought to the present—that is, to local, situated practice. In practice, material and symbolic resources are distributed disproportionally across socially identified groups and generate different social relations and perspectives among participants in such groups. With their impetus from the past, historical structures infuse and restrain local practices, whether they be—to take examples from this volume—shop-floor relations (Willis), community meetings with the Port Authority of New York and New Jersey (Gregory), or activities that go under the rubric of the Tij festival in Nepal (Holland and Skinner). Historical structures also provide resources for participants and their practices and leave traces in their experience.

Nonetheless, as Willis (1977) and Bourdieu (1977, 1990), among others, have elaborated, history in institutional structures and history in person are never simple equivalents. Nor are they related to each other in unmediated, symmetrical, or predictable ways. Instead, especially in cases of obvious struggle, the two come together, again and again, in conflicted practice undertaken not only in the face of changing material and social circumstances but also in the changing terms of culturally produced forms. The two histories come together with the result that local practice always has the unfinished quality of an experiment for the future of these structures.

We proposed to the seminar participants that we explore enduring struggles and the cultural production of identity, beginning from situated participation in explicit local conflict. Employing such a starting point directs attention to social life in relational and dialogic or dialectical terms, especially to the generative, conflictual participation of persons in practice—where subjects are in part fashioned and yet also fashion themselves in historically and culturally specific ways. Further, this starting point sets terms for the discussion of the cultural production of identities. We wanted to concentrate on culturally "hot," or intensely generative, aspects of identities and their existence under urgent contention.

Like the seminar itself, this book is focused on a constellation of relations between subjects' intimate self-making and their participation in contentious local practice—what we refer to as "history in person." The contributors explore the innermost, generative, formative aspects of subjects as social, cultural, and historical beings. These aspects, being relational, are always but never only "in" the person, never entirely a matter of autobiography nor, on the other hand, entirely reducible to membership (voluntary or involuntary) in culturally, politically distinctive groups or social categories. This view of identities as historical and contested in practice is intended to set the terms for the discussion of structure as process—as produced in struggles or as struggles and never captured in global terms alone. Indeed, there is a second principal constellation of relations under discussion here— relations between contentious local practice and broader, more enduring (historical, processual, and open-ended) struggles. We must ask how the latter are locally realized, how they shape subjectivities, and how they are shaped in practice if we are also to address relations between contentious local practice and the production of subjectivities.

We have tried, then, to raise serious questions about specific long-term conflicts and sustained identities in the world today, as these are realized in specific ways in local settings and through particular occasions of social practice. It is important for our broader project that both enduring struggles and history in person be seen as realized in contentious local practice rather than in direct relation with each other. Diagrammatically, we envision "history in practice" as encompassing the two constellations of relations—what we call "history in person" and "enduring struggles." The diagram shown as figure 1.1 is intended to show that they are both given in, and mediated through, contentious local (i.e., situated) practice.

There is an asymmetry in the work of the seminar, however. Questions about durable, long-term struggles and the complex relations by which they are taken up in local struggles set the terms of debate for exploring processes of cultural production of identities. Although we debate the ways in which history in person constrains and enables broad structuring relations, we problematize and pursue more intently the relations of local struggle to identity and subjectivity. This emphasis reflects a desire to contribute, however modestly, to the redress of a broad asymmetry in anthropology more generally. It should be the case that studies of social formations in historical terms (including in practice) would at the same time be studies of "history in person." But, as Maurice Bloch made clear some years ago in his summary of the social practice tradition in anthropology, analyses of social

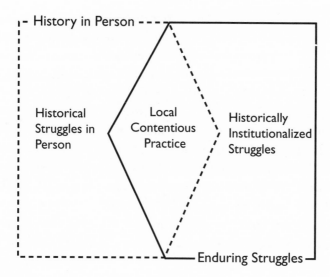

FIGURE 1.1.

Relations between history in person and enduring struggles.

formations have been moving toward greater historical sophistication yet retaining an ahistorical conception of the person (Bloch 1989). The tradition has not addressed, in equivalently historical terms, social agents, their interrelations in practice, their identities, their life trajectories, and their changing understandings. This cannot be easy to do (as Bloch warned). The challenge in this project has been to devise ways to go about it. Theorizing that begins with social practice offers a perspective for the endeavor. It requires careful theoretical attention to relational conceptions of history in person (for which the work of M. Bakhtin has provided clues and possibilities for us and several of the other contributors), and then ethnographic efforts to explore history in person (in this case, in the context of long-term struggles).

Not all of us who participated in the seminar made our way into the problem from the same point of departure. The theoretical perspective that is articulated in this introduction and that shaped the project of the seminar did not animate all participants in the same way. Dissent there is and was—debate during the seminar was lively, indeed, sometimes vociferous. Produced as they were in contentious practice, we believe the ideas and themes that emerged from discussions of participants' papers are novel just in their analytical focus on ongoing contentious practice as they trace out the relations of local conflicts and durable structuring forces and the relations between local practice and the intimate constitution of historical identities in person.

What sorts of local practices are to be found in this book? Liisa Malkki takes Hutu weddings and other social gatherings in Montreal as occasions on which divisions over envisioned political and social futures are played out in people's relations with each other, especially around the divided vision of the meaning of exile and political alternatives for "the Hutu" as a discrete categorical subject of history. Steven Gregory describes practices of local mobilization against the encroachment of state public works projects, especially a series of meetings between neighborhood groups in Queens and the state port authority. Paul Willis works through a long interview between himself and a working-class shop-floor veteran about how old-timers treat newcomers, "hardening" them through veteran cultural forms such as the "put-on" and the "piss take." Daniel Linger focuses on the ethnically charged relations that occur in the everyday encounters of Japanese-Brazilians in Japan, whether in work practices or in workplace rituals of sociability. Begoña Aretxaga concentrates on the traumatic practice of strip-searching and how it turned from the policing of convicts to specific forms of terrorizing women political prisoners in a Northern Irish prison in the early 1990s.

Altering prisoner search procedures, negotiating the complications of multinational identities in Japan, fighting the building of a light rail line through a New York neighborhood, hazing newcomers on the shop floor, negotiating the political dance of imagination and anticipation in refugee weddings—these are the kinds of local practices our authors chose as starting points. It seems to us neither immediately obvious how history in person should relate to these everyday goings-on nor self-evident how those local practices, in the context of enduring struggles, are structured by and structuring of state and civil institutions, the reaches of which extend far beyond the immediate circumstances. In the next sections we take up these issues, beginning with an introduction to the formation of historical subjectivities in local struggles. We then discuss relations between enduring struggles (as structural processes) and the realizations of such struggles in local practice. Finally, we return to the notion of history in person.

HISTORICAL SUBJECTIVITIES AND LOCAL CONTENTIOUS PRACTICE

Our project brings us to dilemmas familiar in the last several decades of social and cultural theory: How can we conceptualize history in person in a way that does not in the end underwrite ahistorical, asocial, essentialist perspectives on identity? How can we avoid sacrificing the obvious generativity of local, on-the-ground human agents? Both persons and lived struggles are unfinished and in process. Rather than beginning from conceptions of already formed persons who are "affected" by already formed institutions, or vice versa, our approach has been to start with local struggles—that is, struggles in particular times and places—and trace out practices of identification, the relation of these practices to broader structural forces, and, within that relational context, the historical production of persons and personhood. Still, along with our insistence that identities are always in process, we must also address the durable dimensions of history in person. Set within the context of enduring struggles, the question for our project is, How can we conceptualize the interplay between the local historical formation of persons in practice and the (mediated) place of historical subjectivities in the creation and undoing of enduring struggles?

Dialogism

Michael Holquist (1990) used the term "dialogism" to label a central organizing theme in Bakhtin's seminal contributions to literary analysis and criticism, to linguistics, and to anthropology (Bakhtin 1981, 1986, 1990 [1929]; Volosinov 1986 [1929]). "Dialogism" attends to the social complexity, history, and generativity of human actors and thus resonates with our project. It begins from social practice, emphasizes the existence of persons in time, attributes an open-endedness to identity, attends in great detail to the distribution of the social in, over, and through persons, and insists upon the generativity of the cultural genres through which people act upon themselves and others (cf. Holland et al. 1998 and Lachicotte n.d. on "the space of authoring").

Four themes in Bakhtin's writings help illuminate ways in which local struggles and historical subjectivities are mutually constitutive. One theme, especially of his early work, resolutely places persons in practice. Dialogism begins from the premise that sentient beings—

9

alone and in groups—are always in a state of active existence; they are always in a state of being "addressed" and in the process of "answering." Holquist (1990:47) provided a helpful exposition:

> Dialogism begins by visualizing existence as an event, the event of being responsible for (and to) the particular situation existence assumes as it unfolds in the unique (and constantly changing) place I occupy in it. Existence is addressed to me as a riot of inchoate potential messages, which at this level of abstraction may be said to come to individual persons much as stimuli from the natural environment come to individual organisms. Some of the potential messages come to me in the form of primitive physiological stimuli, some in the form of natural language, and some in social codes or ideologies. So long as I am in existence, I am in a particular place, and must respond to all of these stimuli either by ignoring them or in a response that takes the form of making sense, of producing—for it is a form of work—*meaning* out of such utterances [emphasis Holquist's].

Judging from the ethnographic accounts in this volume, struggles produce occasions on which participants are "addressed" with great intensity and "answer" intensely in their turn. Gregory's description of a meeting between port authority officials and a coalition of mostly African-American neighborhood associations certainly gives this sense. So, too, does Aretxaga's chapter on a disciplinary procedure carried out by prison officials on a group of IRA women political prisoners in their charge. Moreover, these addresses and answers take shape in the cultural genres at hand.

Cultural Genre and "Self"-Authoring

In the making of meaning—a second dialogical theme—we "author" the world and ourselves in that world. But the "I" is by no means a freewheeling agent, authoring worlds from springs of meaning and insight within. Instead, in answering the other, a collective language must be used. Like Lévi-Strauss's (1966) *bricoleur*, the "I" builds, and so is built, opportunistically with preexisting materials. In authoring local conflicts, in applying words to the contentious others who address it, the "I" draws upon the languages, dialects, genres, and words of others to which she has been exposed. Because the self is the nexus of an ongoing flow of social activity and necessarily participates in this activity, it cannot be finalized or defined in itself, in its own terms. "In order to be known, to be perceived as a figure that can be 'seen,' a person or thing must be put into the categories of the other, categories that [for the moment, despite the self's open-endedness] reduce, finish, consummate" (Holquist 1990:84). This necessity of using the language of the other is but one aspect of Bakhtin's recognition of the collective nature of the "author." His conceptualization takes us far from the notion of the centered Western "individual" or "self," no matter whether the actor in question is overtly a group or not.

The making of meaning, self-authoring, and self-identification in the categories of the other all focus attention on the centrality of cultural forms in the formation of the acting subject, and so they open up a range of possibilities cross-culturally, cross-historically, and across lifetimes. The impetus for Holland and Skinner's study of activities associated with the Tij festival in central Nepal came from Skinner's (1990) earlier interviews with girls and young women. Expecting a narrative, a life story, when she asked them to tell her about their lives, she was surprised when they sang songs for her instead, especially ones that had been collaboratively produced by groups of local women for the Tij festival. These Tij songs, with their accounts of women's positions in households and politics, were, it turned out, a medium of imagination by which the young women authored their senses of self.

Of particular value to our project is the complexity of Bakhtin's view of cultural productions such as Tij songs. As we elaborate in greater detail later, his appreciation of cultural forms allowed for their liberatory possibilities, including altered subjectivities. Yet at the same time he maintained a thoroughly social perspective and therefore equally stressed the social constraints of their production. Tij songs have long been a major component of central Nepali women's "answers" to societal messages about their social position. As with any cultural resource, whether used for political ends or not, the making of the songs and their content are constrained by conventions wrought over the years in response to the conditions of their production. Although at certain historical moments the groups producing the songs break these conventions and begin to reconceptualize them-selves as different sorts of agents, it is always clear that self-authoring through cultural forms is tested in social venues, not just in personal imagination.

The chapters in this volume make it clear that the same self-authoring occurs with all manner of cultural forms. Bakhtin's dialogic approach and Vygotsky's (1971, 1978a, 1978b, 1987) related perspec-tive emphasize the importance of words and verbal genres as the media through which senses of self and group are developed. We see a need to go beyond these limits. The field of cultural studies, especially the intel-lectual tradition identified with the Centre for Contemporary Cultural Studies (e.g., Johnson 1987; Lave et al. 1992; Willis 1981a, 1981b), leads us to augment dialogism's emphasis on verbal forms by moving to the more encompassing category of "cultural forms" as the significant media through which identities are evoked in social practice and in intimate dialogue.

Paul Willis's chapter is especially vivid in showing the power of practices in self-authoring. He reports a conversation with Percy, a working-class man, about a practice that Percy and his friends on the shop floors of the English midlands in the late 1970s called a "piss take." A piss take is a practical joke usually played on neophytes. They are tricked into running a fool's errand, in this case the errand of a fooled worker. In Willis's analysis, piss-taking involves creating a double reality and drawing one's unsuspecting mate or coworker into it; the double reality lies over the top of that proposed (or imposed) by man-agement, and it significantly alters the subjective experience of factory work. In the conversation, Willis tries to engage Percy in analytical talk about the critical impulse behind the jokes—that is, something like the experiential instruction of the newcomer in the relationship between owners and workers. Percy resists his interlocutor's efforts and stead-fastly stays with the richness of his own practice. In Percy's reluctance, Willis finds reason. The practice both creates a double reality, home to a rich subjective sense of self and labor, and identifies practitioners as those with whom Percy finds kindred spirit. Both sorts of identification give him a delight and a more pleasurable workday that would be miss-ing were the critical practice to be reduced to a more economical, explicit discourse.

Identities as Configurations of Self and Other

The third theme of dialogism stresses the sociality of the intimate self: just as local struggles are dialogic, the self-process is dialogic. It incorporates the others of its social world. As Holquist (1990:22, 28) put it, the self-process relates, in inner speech and inner activity, the "I-for-itself" (the center) and the "not-I-in-me" (the noncenter). As the dialogic self is always already decentered, its gravity lies not within a psychological being already replete with essential characteristics (and to that extent independent of its social and cultural world), but in the dynamic tension of a socially given constellation of self (selves) and others, identified and interpreted through culturally given discourses and practices.

From a Bakhtinian perspective, all dialogic engagements of self (or selves, for there is no single self) are struggles across and about differences between self and others. In the chapters in this volume, however, we find a more specific set of circumstances: dialogic selves engaged with others in local struggles animated at least in part by the power, if not by the representatives, of pervasive translocal institutions and by discourses widely circulating locally and beyond. In these chapters, the energy of enduring struggles—carried out for and against societal institutions and discourses that disproportionally distribute symbolic and material resources to favored racial, ethnic, class, and gendered groups—has been realized in local practice and brought from there into the intimate.

Dan Linger's chapter provides a vivid example of self-identification as forming in and through dialogic encounters. Linger describes Eduardo Mori, a man of Japanese ancestry who is a second-generation immigrant to Brazil. When Linger encounters him, Mori has moved to Japan after growing up in Brazil. For him, the broader struggle in Japan over racial and ethnic relations is mediated through everyday practices of identification, such as the way people stare or do not stare at him on the street and the treatment he receives from his coworkers at a going-away party held for him before he returns to Brazil. Mori is clearly engaged in dialogic relations with others, combining his assessment and feelings about the positions offered him in those situations with his feelings about what seem to him generic differences between Japanese and Brazilians. At one point, for example, he claims that in Brazil (that is, in relation to Brazilians) he is Japanese; in Japan (in relation to Japanese), he is Brazilian. In the terms of "dialogism," Mori's senses of his ethnic and racial identity are built around histories of his relations to particular others.

Boundaries

A fourth theme problematizes the boundaries of self and other and the hardness of the differences that mark such divides. The cultural productions through which people act also provide the media through which persons live the boundaries between themselves and those identified as others. Through embracing their words and practices, socially marked others can be incorporated into "us." Through being forced or seduced into using their words, we can be colonized by others. On the other hand, we can become more and more distant from others and their words and practices. We can break radically from the other. We can sneer at their words and practices and stop attending seriously to them.

For Bakhtin, the incorporation of the voices and words of others was set off in a fundamental way from "internalization." His insistence on the sociality of the self made the self simply another site for configuring the social. Thus, he did not envision persons as metaphorical recorders designed for faithful reproduction of the discourses or texts to which they were exposed. Instead, persons take *active stances* toward others and the dialects they use, the speeches they give, the films they make, and the other cultural forms they produce. Bakhtin conceived of several possibilities for drawing others into ourselves or, rather, drawing upon their words (and other practices) for the authoring and identification of ourselves in relation to others. At one extreme, some words, those of accepted authorities, may be kept apart in inner speech, treated with reverence, repeated verbatim, never purposely varied, never put into our own words, and never treated as vulnerable to inspection or playful treatment. Or, perhaps, the words of an other—an other who is distant because of animosity or presumed inferiority or the perception of a marked difference or a suspect category—may be treated as though they are wooden and fixed, of no depth, certainly not bespeaking any subjectivity with which we would care to become familiar. All these remain the "not-I-in-me," a source of lively and not so lively interlocutors and fantasized antagonists in inner speech. In contrast, there are those with whom we identify and sense a commonality. In those cases, the words of the other may eventually become personalized into one's own. One gains a feeling for their complexity and life, their meaning for one's self. In these cases, the other becomes indistinguishable from the "I for myself," or rather part of one's self becomes an incorporation of the other.

Again, we make an extension from Bakhtin's emphasis on language. One can relate oneself to the practices (more generally) of another. In an account of an incident in Nicaragua, Roger Lancaster (1997) specifically developed the potential of copying practices of the other for refiguring the self. He described what he calls "transvestism." Lancaster was visiting the home of friends when one of the women of the family unwrapped a frilly blouse sent to her from abroad. Her brother, a young man, grabbed up the blouse and began a performance in which he and the others present participated. He assumed the postures, movements, and behaviors associated in Nicaragua with a particular culturally imagined, socially constructed person, a type of homosexual man. Lancaster treated in depth the issue of the man's relation to his actions. Even if the performance was "only" a play at being a homosexual, how much of a boundary, if any, was being maintained between the author of the performance and the character he was enacting? If we can play at being another, as this man did, or even fantasize about playing at being another, we are on our way to incorporating another. Although this incident did concern a case of crossdressing, Lancaster sees "transvestism" as a useful term for the initial steps of taking on any new identity. Just as we author ourselves by repeating the words of others, we are frequently in the process of enacting ourselves through enacting the culturally identified activities of others.

In short, the self is an orchestration of the practices of others, but we do not relate to all such practices in the same way. This emphasis on problematic boundaries and varying stances provides a suitably nuanced appreciation of the possibilities that arise in local struggles. Aretxaga discusses the penal practice of strip-searching as a punitive mechanism used against female political prisoners in Northern Ireland. She examines the history of the use of strip searches, in which the practice became transformed from a security routine into a disciplinary punishment. She shows how prison officers attempted to use strip searches to break the political identity of IRA women prisoners through a bodily invasive practice that reduced women to objectified femininity. The prisoners, however, refused to take the position of subdued femininity assigned to them. Instead of divesting IRA women prisoners of political identity, the use of strip searches had the effect of radicalizing them. Although the punitive strip searches left deep emotional traces in the women subjected to them, they also transformed their political subjectivity into a more nuanced and complex form of political identity that included their position as women and distanced them even more than before from the institutional practices of the British state.

Bakhtin's focus on practices and discourses as the means through which we build or tear down boundaries between ourselves and others opens up other subtleties of identification as well. "Heteroglossia," the simultaneity of different languages, as well as of different cultural genres and practices, is the rule in social life (Bakhtin 1981; see Clark and Holquist 1984 and Holquist 1990 for discussion). Yet these genres, words, practices are not used by just anyone. Instead, genres are collectively associated with particular persons or groups of people identified in social space and historical time. Practices and discourses become markers of their "owners" and evoke their social image. They carry with them the aura or, to use more sensuous metaphors, the images and the odors of the particular others, particular professions, particular social groups, particular individuals with which they are associated.

Practices, including discursive practices, may evoke class, gender, or other associations of general currency. But the same process of inscription can mark valuations that may be specific to a particular family or a particular neighborhood. A stance, a position, a practice may bespeak, in inner speech, a particular person—one's mother, for example. In this way—to the extent that the practice invokes that other— one's feelings and associations with the practice become thoroughly entangled in one's relationship to that other. All the chapters in this book are testimony to the importance of ethnographies of enduring struggle, but Kay Warren's piece is especially striking in uncovering the ways in which larger, more widespread struggles can be unexpectedly complicated by meanings accruing from more particular ones.

Warren's research with a family of activists involved in the Mayan struggles in Guatemala examines intergenerational differences over ways of carrying on the struggle. Fathers and sons, brothers, uncles and nephews differ in their evaluations of the morality and effectiveness of guerrilla fighting, identification with Ladinos of the same class, and celebration of Mayan ethnicity. In their conversations with Warren, they fashioned dialogues between themselves and other members of the family. These specific familial valuations across sites produced crosscurrents within the larger conflicts between Maya-identified peoples and those non-Maya groups holding power in Guatemala. As persons, the activists were caught up in intersecting dialogues that were not dictated by the larger struggle. Rather, the practices of struggle, whether guerrilla fighting or developing educational materials about a Mayan language, had become associated for them with the voices and actions of particular family members, family members with whom they had a history of relations underdetermined with respect to the larger political arena.

Because history is made in person, registered in intimate identities as well as in institutions, there is every reason to expect that age cuts across people's experiences and creates intergenerational differences. As a more general feature of social life, intergenerational and age-associated struggles, genres, and identities are likely to divide persons. Opportunities are often open to those of a particular age; they bypass those who are too old or too young. It is even the case that younger members of a radicalized group, for example, come into a context already layered with owned forms of radical expression. Younger actors' dialogue with the struggle at hand—in Warren's chapter, the Mayas' struggle against institutional and symbolic structures that disadvantage and discredit them—is formed not only with opponents who may well have changed their tactics over the years, and to that extent their identities, but also with other Mayan political actors who developed their views in earlier years and under different alliances. Warren's chapter is important in bringing out the significance of generational differences for history in person and thus helps account for impulses to reconfigure struggles drastically from one generation to the next. Moreover, older identities can lose their dialogic partners and become stranded. Perhaps the "uneducated" women described in Holland and Skinner's chapter are receding from the points of contestation that are alive and "hot"; perhaps the British gentleman wine exporter of Porto, Portugal, in Jean Lave's chapter has fallen out of the serious dialogues of the day and lives on not because he is a relevant character on the stage of the multinational corporations that have purchased the port export businesses but because he has become an icon for a brand of port wine.

Dialogism and Generativity

The dialogic selves formed in local contentious practice are selves engaged with others across practices and discourses inflected by power and privilege. They are selves formed in and against uncomfortable practices that they cannot simply refuse (e.g., in Aretxaga's chapter, the practices of the prison guards and officials who physically overpower the IRA prisoners, or in Linger's, the actions of the Japanese in Japan who stare at Mori). Or they are selves formed in and against practices that afford them privilege (e.g., in Lave's chapter, British practices that exclude from full participation in British institutions the Portuguese with whom the British have shared a city for three hundred years).

Often a consumer, sometimes a co-producer, of cultural forms and practices, or at least a spectator, a person is vulnerable to being identified by others. Enmeshed in dialogues across difference, often sharply contentious ones, over which they lack total "say," persons are ever open to radicalization and the experience of heightened structural apprehension, or to its partial opposite, incorporation of the other into the "I for myself." Especially for the weak, it seems that one is probably always being pushed and pulled, positioned first this way and then that, drawn into one transvestism and then another—willingly or not, into describing one's self or enacting one's self in the words and behaviors of another. It would appear that dialogism offers little possibility for accounting for durability. But this would follow only if "the person" is taken as separate from others.

History in person can in no way be confined to discrete persons. Durable intimate formations result from practices of identification in historically specific times and places. Dialogism insists upon the always-engaged-in-practice, always-engaged-in-dialogue, unfinished character of history in person. The person is necessarily "spread" over the social environment, becoming in substance a collection point of socially situated and culturally interpreted experience. And herein lie important sources of stability and thickening. Weaker parties to struggles, as well as the strong, can durably create their own discourses, practices, and emblems of struggle.

Given the uneven playing fields of power depicted in this volume, it is important that dialogism provides a way to think about a generativity that "fills up the space between transgression and reproduction" (to borrow Willis's borrowing of Aretxaga's phrase from the seminar). In the course of local struggles, marginalized groups create their own practices. Participants in these groups both are identified by these practices and often identify themselves as "owners" of them. These practices thus provide the means by which subjectivities in the margins of power thicken and become more developed and so more determinant in shaping local struggles.

Holland and Skinner's chapter, for example, emphasizes the importance of cultural production in developing alternative subjectivities. Tij festival songs depict the practices to which women are subjected; they picture women put in their place by the speech and behavior of different participants (e.g., husbands, mothers-in-law, fathers) in the imagined world, or the chronotope (Bakhtin 1981), or in what Holland and colleagues (1998) called the figured world of Nepali domestic relations. A second type of song, which came to predominate in a later political period, moves women into another figured world: no longer that of the household and local neighborhood but rather that of party politics. In these songs, listeners hear the voices and learn about the actions of party officials, government officials from the discredited one-party system, and "educated" and "uneducated" women. Both types of songs depict an imagined future in which women are accorded more respect and resources. Holland and Skinner argue that Tij songs have figured in the formation of a critical political consciousness that women express and act upon, especially following the successful Pro-Democracy Movement in 1990.

The generativity of cultural practices and their importance in establishing and developing alternative subjectivities introduce uncertainty—wild cards of a sort—into the careers of local contentious practice and through them into struggles over national institutions and widespread cultural discourses. The creation and development of subjectivities, even those marginal to power, is made possible, even likely, because cultural forms are not only tools for positioning the other but also tools for positioning the self. They are a means of re-identifying self.

Discourse theory's focus on subject positioning leads us to attend to the power of state and other hegemonic discourses and cultural forms to objectify social position as behavior, to inscribe state categories in the body's habits, and to make subjectivities of those they define. The ethnographic studies in this book emphasize that the powers of inscription that cultural forms possess are not solely the tools of the state. Groups in civil society—women's groups in Nepal, working-class men on the shop floors of England, or community leaders in Queens, New York—also create cultural forms as means to gain some limited control over their own construction (Holland et al. 1998). And, as Kearney, Warren, Willis, and others pointed out repeatedly during the seminar, the postmodern conditions of the current era are such that local cultural production has a tremendous array of images and texts from all over the world to draw on in constructing new local practices. People are reworking this wealth of symbols at the same time that, as Kearney argues, the forces we call transnationalism reduce the state's ability to intercede in, and so control, the practices of identity. People from the Mixtec area in southern Mexico moving back and forth in a labor circuit between Mexico and the United States cannot be controlled as closely as the citizen or subject of state apparatuses. People positioned by the state as laborers and peasants who are also moving transnational subjects have become ethnically identified groups demanding an improved place in the nation.

ENDURING STRUGGLES IN LOCAL AND HISTORICAL RELATIONS

We have discussed the complex dialogic traffic between local practice and the historical subjectivities that are formed in practice, furnishing a living edge to change. There are complex relations between the struggles in which people are caught up in the everyday world and the broader struggles that encompass many localities and longer periods of time. Local contentious practices are the sites of complex mediations between intimate, interiorized practices of identity, on the one hand, and, on the other, three hundred years of conflict in Northern Ireland, genocidal civil war in Rwanda, earlier genocides in Burundi, civil war in Guatemala, race and class relations, the rights and oppression of nationally marginalized ethnic populations, gender inequalities, and competing forms of capitalism.

Social, cultural, economic, and political relations at their broadest are enduring, high-stake struggles, perhaps "Struggles" with a capital *S*. As these struggles are concretely realized and specifically appropriated or thrust into everyday practice, some involve sustained violence, whereas others are ubiquitously low-key. Some are struggles over state oppression through local representatives; some are among participants with similar resources but different stakes who are connected beyond local settings and events by institutional relations of various kinds (regional agencies, corporations, subnational ethnarchies, actor networks, etc.). Still others are among participants who are connected through widely extended, heterogeneous structuring relations such as contentious relations of gender.

There are certain things we do not mean in this conception of the constellation of relations that bind local conflicts to broad enduring struggles. We refrain from terms such as "ideological struggle" that conventionally omit a dialogic view of the I/other relations involved. Likewise, we have tried not to single out the efforts of a group to get something it wants apart from the relations of struggle in which it is embedded. Such a focus would bracket out the practices of struggling *with* others and the significance of the opponents' differing perspectives, resources, and power. Reciprocal relations among enduring struggles and the cultural production of identities present a complex problem for analysis because they are mediated through local conflicts and perspectives in the practices of daily existence.

Our focus encompasses struggles of large scope in space and time in part because of the riveting force of such struggles and their undoubtedly urgent impact on practices that affect the authoring of local lived identities. Further, the fashioning of cultural forms and identities as intimate furnishings are high-stake, salient issues for those involved. Participants gradually become just that—they take the standpoints, personalize the dialogues and other cultural forms salient to their lives—as they answer to burning issues and interests that may or must be vital. The structuring effects in practice of long-term struggles are inescapable, and other aspects of life tend to bear durable, well-felt relations to them—to be enmeshed in, cordoned off from, masked by, or confused with such struggles—because they are deeply significant to the limits and possibilities of social existence.

Part of the significance of enduring struggles lies in their scope in time, space, and political-economic relations, and part lies in their life-and-death, indelible impact on everyday lives. We concentrate here, as in the discussion of dialogic practices, on how long-term struggles are appropriated and lived in practice. With rare exceptions, broad, enduring struggles are not addressed directly in people's lives. They are lived as they are concretely realized, as they rudely or routinely intrude, or as they are appropriated into local social practice. This leads to the original problem of the seminar: We suppose that enduring struggles unleash and shape the social production of local cultural forms in local contentious practice—the very social, collective, and contested forms by which historical selves are made. At the same time, enduring struggles that extend into and are appropriated by (and that partially structure) local struggles are themselves changed in the process. The reciprocal character of this relation between local practices of struggle and global, structuring struggles means that each can change the other—theirs is a two-way generative traffic (locally mediated) that reminds us of the constant movement and countermovement between the social and the intimate. Indeed, many of the chapters in this volume capture local struggles and other cultural practices *as they are undergoing transformation*. This seems remarkable; it is perhaps the most unusual accomplishment of the seminar and the book.

To talk of far-reaching struggles that appropriate (and are appropriated into) participants' local contentious practice calls attention to a range of questions somewhat different from theories of "resistance" or "reproduction." Much of what is contested in local struggles is the very meaning of "what's going on." The world is not "given" in this perspective, in contrast to the familiar scenario of resistance theory, that of a massive but passive condition of political domination and an active but impotent local resistance. The powerful in the following chapters not only win, but act (the British port shippers resist, actually), and the less powerful act, too—differently. To talk of "struggles" is in part to argue for including in our analyses all of the parties to the struggle, with their different perspectives on and stakes in their interdependent lives. There is one further consideration: beginning with local contentious practice leaves the extension of relevant connections among practical settings open-ended and the boundaries of the relevant participants reconfigurable. To talk of hegemony and resistance presumes nation-states or something like them as units of social existence and turns attention to relations between the powerful and the oppressed *pre-categorized* as such, rather than defined in terms of the characteristics of the struggles in which they are engaged: multiple, diverse, and interconnected. Resistance theory tends to preordain the boundaries and characteristics not only of the struggle but of the participants as well.

There are other considerations that led us to characterize the enterprise in terms of enduring struggles, contentious practice, and history in person. "Struggling" suggests active engagement and avoids static notions of conflicts as stable or self-contained things in themselves. The notion of long-term struggles offers a view of structure as process, as a matter of relations in tension. Indeed, we are trying to give special attention to moving struggles, those with the same sort of live, generative force Bakhtin described—not dead, done deals (assuming there are any).

A focus on history in person and how practices of identification are appropriated and transformed in local articulations of long-term struggles leads to questions about relations among ongoing, apparently quite disparate struggles. We have found ourselves asking, Of what more far-reaching struggles are local struggles a partial realization? The question seems useful to ask, given that local struggles are not merely nested within, or a reflection of, larger struggles but are partial in different ways and can be interconnected in ways that have the potential to generate varied cultural forms and social alliances. For the British enclave in Porto, local struggles over where to place the church altar and whether the Oporto British School should offer the International Baccalaureate degree reflect divisions over religious and educational practice within the Anglican church and between families with school-age children. But the altar and the IB degree are also stakes in conflicts over forms of corporate organization that for the moment coexist within the port trade, just as they are part of struggles over the continuing social domination of "old port shipping families."

Multi-Idiom Struggles

In practice, multiple social divisions and struggles are given together—they co-occur in space and time. Contention surely rivets attention, resources, and participants' sense of historical identification selectively on some issues rather than others. Local conflicts, then, are interpreted through cultural forms that simplify, conceal, suppress, and give salience and priority to some ways of comprehending and participating in ongoing practice, in terms of some relevant subjectivities but not others. For instance, "old port wine" families in Porto struggle to sustain their "British" identity against British contract managers who are struggling for a less conservative community in thoroughly gendered ways. But the struggle over national identity and social conservatism precludes, and is invoked to suppress, active struggle over issues of gender at the same time.

Gregory's chapter on community responses to the port authority's proposal for a light rail project offers another example of the kind of social work that can deflect possible identifications in practice. When their spokespersons took up the discourse of "environmental justice" and cast themselves and those they represented as sharing an identity in common, residents of several neighborhoods forged what was for them a novel identity as claimants of common rights to a beneficial environment, regardless of neighborhood. Gregory describes how, over the ensuing weeks, the neighborhood groups were divided by the machinations of the port authority, which then leveled charges of parochial selfishness against the now reduced and divided groups. There are many reasons why the port authority was able to re-identify the participants and undermine their cross-neighborhood unity. Community members' relationship to the selves afforded by a discourse of environmental justice was tenuous. Gregory's research suggests that this discourse failed to become a tool for neighborhood residents to use in authoring selves, a tool with personal significance over and beyond that of the strategic moment. It did not provide a stable orchestration of self and others in the residents' intimate lives, in inner speech. Identities form and develop in and through cultural practices that divide and identify the social world—in Gregory's case, through discourses in the public sphere. But their generativity depends upon whether they have sedimented as durable positions in social struggles *and* in persons.

The focus on history in person in mediated relations with long-term struggles is intended to underline the significance of political differentiation among identities and to generate discussion of the relative valuation and salience of action in the name of some relations of identity rather than others. In exploring conceptions of multiple identities, we have moved away from conceptions of undifferentiated, equal, equally ephemeral, "fragmented" identities that somehow miss the politics of identity, the contested salience of different identity-generated ways of participating in differently situated practices, including local struggles.

Relations among identities-in-practice are serious political issues. Michael Kearney writes about enduring struggles between the government of Mexico and its marginal and poor indigenous populations. At the turn of the last century, the latter were characterized officially as, and acted on their own behalf in the name of, "peasants" or "workers." More recently, political projects have changed relations among identities. Old ones have been suppressed in favor of new ones. This is occurring, Kearney argues, in a dialogic process in which the state attempts to contain indigenous movements but in doing so also reifies them in unintended ways. Meanwhile, marginal, impoverished indigenous movements unite many disparate groups across the nation but thereby create new dangers of ethnic ghettoization and continued impoverishment. Thus, engaging in struggles in the name of specific identities means that other possible identities and struggles are crowded out. They are not equally available, not equally high-priority on community and personal agendas, and not equally powerful at mustering resources and mobilizing people. Some struggles suppress others, silence others, make shared traditions of opposition impossible. It is as if, in the contentious politics of relations among identities and struggles, only one or a few emerge to stand as the important struggles (and identities), and so they disentitle, silence, or suppress others or turn them into "merely" parochial battles. There are well-known examples, not unlike the one Kearney describes, in which class or national identities take on priorities that suppress ethnic, racial, and gender struggles (see Lave and others in this volume).

At the same time, identities are institutionally given together in practice. This implies that people struggling in the name of one identity are doing so in ways that at the same time involve other kinds of identities. Examples include ethnic and gendered nationalist identities in the United States and Ireland and kin/religious/gendered political activism in Guatemala. We can ask how people act so as to foreground one kind of identity over others in local contentious practice, and at the same time act in ways saturated with other identity practices.

The chapters that follow are unusual in throwing into high relief moments of such transformations of long-term struggles. For example, in Nepal, the lifting of repressive state controls had a fortuitous effect on possible new dialogic dimensions of identity. In day-to-day struggling to bring political changes into village life, the local character of struggle changed, too. Holland and Skinner's analysis of Tij songs shows a change from domestic divisions and women's antagonistic authoring of themselves vis-à-vis their husbands and affines to an emerging prospect of division along the line between "educated" and "uneducated" women. Bakhtin did, of course, argue that any given struggle is partially formed in the taking up of the idiom of others (e.g., gendered ethnic and national conflicts), offering obvious possibilities for transformation of the terms of struggling. The Nepali case provides a good example.

There are other examples of multi-idiom struggles and their transformations in this book. Thus, in an important sense, long-term struggles are traditions shared by those joined in opposition. A broadly shared understanding of what struggling is about is in some sense a victory for the proponents of some version of a struggle (Kearney, Malkki). In many of these chapters, people struggle to win a battle to define the situation, to produce new versions of old conflicts. Historical contingencies set and reset the stage. Lave's chapter on the British enclave in Portugal argues that the social and economic foundations of the enclave and its contested relations with citizens of the host country have been reconfigured by changes that take the form of competing modes of international capital. New resources, new opportunities are also crucial in the situations described by Gregory and Kearney.

Presumably, people also fight over their different perspectives on what they are struggling about. A number of chapters present startlingly clear accounts of contention over changing struggles. Warren's distinctive analysis of ways to engage in Mayan political activism reveals differences generation by generation. The civil war in Guatemala has had phases, has changed character. Strategies for leadership and authority, creating tensions between "being traditional" and "being modern" and between different religious, cultural, and linguistic ways of doing both, are enacted in the life trajectories, in the ways of participating, of each generation—always, however, in tension with each other.

This approach argues against Hobbesian understandings of struggle as a war of all against all, as being reduced to competition and violence and its formal corollary, "cooperation." Conflicts locally and globally produced are historically complex and multiply contradictory in their actual relations. Struggles do not occur as universal processes through which participants race single-mindedly toward a goal or join general stampedes for a particular exit. This book offers rich evidence that enduring struggles and practices of identity are heatedly contradictory and, not surprisingly, transformative, and they create new objectifications—for example, across generations within a Mayan family, for whom conjunctures of religion, cultural nationalism, and revolution sponsor changing cultural practices, or among Mixtec Indians who, squeezed out of their villages by economic forces and out of Mexican nationhood by state political strategies, make transnational communities that now offer new challenges to state categorization and control.

Struggles over Futures

One version of an enduring struggle—what might be called the "struggle over the future"—surely helps to furnish cultural practices and genres in later iterations (Aretxaga, Holland and Skinner, Kearney, Warren). It is part of the locally mediated historical traffic between the long-term and the day-to-day. It may be useful to consider day-to-day struggles over community identities as in part staking claims into the future. If people fight with and over versions of history (recent anthropology gives rich testimony to this), they are also fighting *for* particular versions of the future. We are impressed by the compelling motivation

of conflicting historical claims as urgent attempts to secure future possibilities. In practice, participants struggle to affect the implications of
different versions and meanings of ongoing practice for their future
lives, especially for their children and for their own future place in history. To look at enduring struggles and local contentious practice as
they mutually inform each other offers one way to trace processes by
which present efforts to give birth to the past shape and obtain advantages for some futures over others.

Historical struggles of long endurance that cast local conflicts as
fights over the future are undoubtedly ubiquitous. But Malkki points
out "the theoretical invisibility of the future" in studies of national consciousness undertaken by researchers in anthropology, history, and cultural studies. The future is relegated to the unknowable or, worse, to
the utopian fantasies of the theorist. And yet, she argues, "futures, like
histories, are constrained and shaped by lived experience…. Discourses
of the past and discourses of the future feed off of each other; indeed,
they are often only different chapters of the same narrative story."

Malkki describes the fear and profound pessimism of recent Hutu
immigrant exiles in Montreal, who are struggling to imagine futures
with and without the terrible enmity and convulsive violence between
Hutu and Tutsi in Rwanda and Burundi and now the broader Great
Lakes region of Central Africa. Political-moral divisions of the two sides
into good and evil generate scenarios of endless war or partition of the
two countries into Hutu and Tutsi zones. Other stances with respect to
the future, articulated by groups and individuals within the urban Hutu
refugee community in Montreal, focus on possibilities for the coexistence of Hutu and Tutsi in Central Africa or, in some cases, the future
irrelevance of the now deadly division. Those who espouse the latter
seem to be predominantly women, and strong, articulate women to
boot. But their views are not universally shared. All of this occurs within
Hutu speculative discourses about partially hidden relations between
the West and Africa and between Francophone and Anglophone interests in Africa.

The issues articulated in Malkki's paper and in Warren's analysis of
intergenerational changes in political activism in Guatemala led to
seminar discussions in which every participant pointed to the importance in her or his analysis of understanding how futures as well as tra-

ditions and histories are constituted in and constitutive of present struggles, identities, lives, communities, and social formations. There could be no better recommendation for a close historical, ethnographic reading than the heterogeneity of relations documented in these chapters about new struggles at stalemate, old ones enduring too, struggles over new issues continuing in the name of old social divisions, and intentions to preserve the past that create novel futures while intentions to create the new fail. A close ethnographic look at struggles in practice takes their heterogeneity as an invitation to inquire into relations among struggles and their interconnected consequences.

HISTORY IN PRACTICE, HISTORY IN PERSON

The chapters in this book richly illustrate constellations of relations between enduring struggles and local contentious practice. They focus closely on relations between contentious practice and changing subjectivities. Yet the chapters all begin, by design, from historically situated practice. They give substance to our argument that relations between enduring struggles and historical subjectivities are mediated through local, situated practice.

A major objective of the book is to extend social practice theory to the historical formation of persons. The double constellations of relations discussed here are integral to a broad conception of history in practice. Our more specific topic of history in person must be read as a *facet* of this complex set of changing relations.

History is constituted in the space that encompasses both social participation and self-authoring. Dialogically constituted identities are always re-forming somewhere between positions institutionalized on social terrain and their habitation as it is made meaningful in intimate terms. Identities live through practices of identification. Subjectivities are neither simple reflexes of social position, as Gregory phrases it, nor simply the meaning that individuals give to these positions. Subjectivities and their more objectified components, identities, are formed in practice through the often collective work of evoking, improvising, appropriating, and refusing participation in practices that position self and other. They are durable not because individual persons have essential or primal identities but because the multiple contexts in which dialogical, intimate identities make sense and give meaning are re-created in contentious local practice (which is in part shaped and reshaped by enduring struggles).

All of the multiply authored and positioned selves, identities, cultural forms, and local and far-reaching struggles, given together in practice, are bound up in making "history in person." "History in person" thus indexes a world of identity, action, contentious practice, and long-term transformative struggles. On the one hand, history in person is usefully illuminated by Bakhtin's "dialogism." We have posited subjectivities as always forming in dialogues across difference—for the ethnographic studies in this volume, in *struggles* across difference—where "answers" to "addresses" made by the contentious others are authored in the cultural discourses and practices at hand. Persons-as-agents thus are always forming themselves in collective terms as they respond to the social situations they encounter locally and in their imaginations. Social forms and cultural resources produced in these situations are made personal in the arrangement or orchestration of the voices enmeshed in them. Consequently, social struggles become personified, so that their forces assimilate the "character" of the people from and by whom they are reproduced. Thus, history is made in persons and by persons.

On the other hand, history in person partakes not only of the lived dialogues close at hand but also of enduring struggles that extend in larger reaches of time and space. Local contentious practice is produced in persons and by persons under changing material and symbolic conditions occasioned by major political-economic and political-ecological transformations. So, too, participants in local conflicts are likely to appropriate resources from other sites of these enduring struggles.

"History in person" is not a simple idea, but it is amenable to more specifically focused inquiries, of which two stand out in the method of the present project: to approach history as something that is in part made in and by persons, and to approach the study of persons as historically fashioned. Both require that ethnographic study begin and end in a differentiated, wide-ranging analysis of everyday, local, conflictual social practice. Further, the shifting inflections of identity in the day-to-day practice of historical persons must be appreciated as part of the hard reality of political domination and enduring struggles that keep certain identities in practice non-negotiable and others instrumentally salient in those struggles (even as they change).

Our search for more adequate concepts of history in person has emphasized the importance of socially powerful, conflict-driven cultural forms as crucial in local-level practices of identification. We initiated the seminar discussion with a dual focus on relations running across intimate terrain, through situated local struggles, and between the latter and struggles of broader scale that durably produce multi-institutional, multi-discursive constraints and resources. The project sought to employ ethnographic inquiry in order to understand the relations between practices of identification and participation as they interconnected in this complex landscape of relations.

This view also implies more specific dimensions of analysis: In the book we have emphasized the dense and contentious relational traffic between persons in practice and the same persons as made in practice. Local struggles-in-practice have required investigation in their own right. Questions about how they mediate enduring, broad-scale struggles and how they inform and transform one another are common themes. We also ask how struggles-in-practice are diverse in themselves, and how they take in, exchange, and act through historical cultural forms. This approach recommends other questions as well. How are enduring struggles produced, how do they travel, and how are they appropriated locally and on intimate terrain? How does the "living out" of contesting identities at a particular historical moment relate to the production and contestation of previously durably produced, translocal partial coherencies that link institutions, discourses, and other widespread practices of struggle across international, national, regional, and subregional, as well as local, arenas of action? How do these relations affect which of the identities given together in local contentious practice are suppressed while others are given play? How are the futures over which people struggle a part of enduring struggles?

We hope the view of history-in-practice developed here illuminates the benefits of understanding history in person. Local struggles—in a Northern Ireland prison, in "ethnic" festivals in Oaxacalifornia, in tensions among the life trajectories of members of a Mayan activist family, at Hutu exile weddings, on the British factory floor, in the Nepali Tij festival, on the streets of Japan where Mori walked, in a public meeting

organized by the port authority, or in those held by the Oporto British
School's governing committee—were not just keyholes conveniently
placed for spying on the connections of these particular events to large-
scale, multi-institution, multi-practice enduring struggles. They were
also—crucially—places where significant social valuations of futures
were being produced, where the social work of identification was ongoing, where persons were being positioned by practices and becoming
suppressed or radicalized, where powerful cultural forms were being
produced and were altering subjectivities, and where coherencies
across local sites were being (re)produced or disrupted. They were
places where persons were replenished with histories, thickening
already existing subjectivities.

In elaborating here a complex view of history in person, we have
tried to do justice to the density of the essays that compose this book.
The first three chapters, those by Aretxaga, Warren, and Holland and
Skinner, capture moments of transformation of broad struggles in
which, in practice, identities also are undergoing transformation.
Gregory's, Willis's, and Linger's chapters are especially intense
accounts of deepening practices of identity in relation to local contentious practice. They have much to tell us about the generation of
cultural forms that support and bind those practices. Finally, the last
three essays, by Kearney, Lave, and Malkki, focus on struggles over "the
future" for contending persons in history.

Notes

1. We wish to thank the School of American Research for this wonderful
opportunity for intellectual exchange. Generous support also came from the
National Endowment for the Humanities and the Luso-American Foundation
for Development. We have worked together in a close and balanced collaboration on all aspects of this project, from developing the seminar proposal for
SAR and chairing the seminar to preparing this book and writing its introduc-
tory chapter. Two anonymous reviewers, along with William S. Lachicotte, SAR's
editor-in-chief Joan O'Donnell, and freelance editor Jane Kepp, provided very
helpful comments on drafts of the introduction, as did participants in the
seminar. Although we did not always do what they wanted, their comments
helped our thinking enormously. We especially thank Amy Mortensen and

Susan Shepler, who contributed their considerable skills to helping edit the book and whose humor made the whole process much more fun.

2. Because of a family tragedy, Brackette Williams was unable to attend the seminar.

Part One

Struggles in Transformation

2

Engendering Violence

Strip-Searching of Women in Northern Ireland

Begoña Aretxaga

On the second of March, 1992, men and women prison officers dressed in riot gear and armed with helmets, shields, batons, and dogs entered the wing of Maghaberry Prison that housed 21 IRA female prisoners. After physically immobilizing the prisoners, female guards forcefully stripped them naked in their own cells. The strip searches lasted the whole day and were conducted in the midst of screams, insults, and physical violence. This "security procedure," as the governor of the prison called it, failed to produce any evidence of a potential security threat. Instead, what it produced was an intense public controversy about the nature of institutional practices used in the Northern Ireland women's prison. The event triggered a surge of discourses about the relationship between state power and sexuality—the body politic and women's bodies—and thrust into action new practices by republican activists and civil rights organizations to end the use of strip searches in the women's prison. In doing so, the event endowed an occluded penal practice with political visibility, making strip searches a site in which histories and structures of ethnic and gender domination in Northern Ireland converged to reformulate identities and political practices.

For women prisoners, the redefinition of political subjectivities triggered by the strip search of 1992 was not an effect of discourse or disembodied structures of power. Such redefinition began as an effect of power on the women's own bodies, which were subjected to the violence of forced exposure and examination by hostile loyalist guards. The political significance of this violence, embedded as it was in a long history of British colonial scrutiny of things Irish—Irish land and Irish bodies particularly (Bondi 1990; Cairns and Richards 1988; Jones and Stallybrass 1992)—and in a recent history of intense state surveillance in Northern Ireland, was experienced personally by women prisoners as the embodiment in their own flesh of a history of British domination of Irish Catholics and a history of male domination of women.

The mass strip search of 1992 brings into relief the gender and sexual character of the struggles that took place in the political theater of Northern Ireland. On the institutional stage of the women's prison, the state attempted to control IRA female prisoners and break their political identity by subjecting them to the violence of random strip searches. Such practices aimed at inscribing the bodies of women prisoners with the meanings of both gender and ethnic subordination, effectively making gender and ethnicity inextricable from one another.[1]

The concrete battles for identity and control that took place in the women's prison did not occur in a historical vacuum. They were overdetermined by long-standing colonial and state forms of domination, as well as by struggles against them. Within the colonial history of Northern Ireland, the body has long been a site for the production of ethnic identities (Burton 1978; Feldman 1991), and the bodies of women, symbolic terrain for colonial and nationalist struggles (Aretxaga 1997). A good number of anthropological studies of ethnic and political violence have theorized the body as the symbolic and material locus for the creation of identities and the deployment of power struggles (Appadurai 1998; Feldman 1991; Malkki 1995; Nordstrom and Martin 1992; Nordstrom and Robben 1995; Tambiah 1996; Taussig 1987; Warren 1993). Yet while many cases of ethnic and political violence are characterized by various forms of sexual violence against ethnicized others, few anthropological studies of ethnic violence take sexual difference into account in their theorizing of the body. More often than not, the universal "body" of studies of political violence is in practice a male body.

A theoretically undifferentiated "body" tends to produce accounts of identity and political agency that mask forms of sexual and gender subjection, as well as masking women's political agency. This has been the case in studies of identity and political conflict in Northern Ireland dominated by a "tribalist" conception focused on the "feuds" between male Protestants and Catholics (Curtin, Donnan, and Wilson 1993). In these studies, as well as in mass media representations, women either remain passive bystanders (or victims) in a basically male conflict or they become replicas of men (a common representation of terrorist women) (Elshtain 1987; Meinhof 1986). In either case, women's subjectivity and agency are obliterated. Despite the heterogeneous gender struggles that have permeated the unfolding of ethnic violence and the emergence of feminism as a site for contested definitions of both femininity and ethnic nationalism, gender has been taken for granted by the majority of theorists of the Northern Ireland conflict.

The body that enters the circuit of violence in Northern Ireland, as anywhere else, cannot escape the operations of sexual difference. Such difference not only gives different signifying valence to bodies identified as female and male but also complicates the formation of ethnic identity and the structure of political violence. This has become more than clear in the Balkans, where rape has been systematically used as an instrument of "ethnic cleansing." Yet to see the political use of sexual violence only in an instrumental light runs the risk of obscuring the ways in which it reconfigures not only ethnic but also gender identities and the ways in which personal as well as collective histories are affected by it. As Judith Butler (1993) has noted, the ways in which bodies are constituted within normative systems of gender and sexual difference matter. And it matters, too, how subjects disrupt those normative systems in the very process of being constituted by them. The political operativity of "the body" depends precisely on the interconnection of collective and personal histories that play on the differentiation of bodies—a differentiation in which or through which ethnic and sexual markers are used to construct or deconstruct each other.

The strip search analyzed in this essay was a "critical event" (Das 1995), an event that "triggered the emergence of new forms of action, the redefinition of traditional categories" (Das 1995:5–6). In discussing it, I attempt to show, first, the mutual constitution of gender and ethnic identities; second, the sexualization of state forms of control embedded in histories of colonial surveillance; and third, the ways in which violence on the bodies of women creates specific kinds of political subjectivities. I situate my analysis within the convergence of different histories: the narratives of women prisoners, the history of strip searches as a punitive practice used by the state against women, the history of sexualized state violence, the history of women's political activism, and the history of feminism. The bodies of the prisoners emerge as the sediment of histories that make their manipulation politically possible but also make the effects of this manipulation unpredictable. Political subjectivity, I argue, is not only gendered but also contingent, at once the product and the force of history.

STRIP SEARCHES: HISTORY OF A PRACTICE

Strip searches were one of the first things I heard about during my first visit to Belfast in the summer of 1987, when I told republican women that I wanted to write a book about their experiences of the violent conflict in Northern Ireland. At the time, women ex-prisoners and their relatives had formed a committee to campaign against the random use of strip searches, which was for them a degrading and deeply hated practice of power. While the Northern Ireland Office insisted that strip-searching was a routine security procedure, women prisoners strongly contended that its character was not purely procedural but punitive.

Throughout my stay in Northern Ireland, the issue of strip searches surfaced repeatedly during discussions about violence. Discussions among feminists seemed to be particularly prone to confrontations over the issue of strip searches. Whenever IRA violence was under attack by feminists, republican women brought up strip searches as an example of state violence against women that did not receive the same condemnation. Was it less morally condemnable because the violence of strip searches was inflicted on the bodies of women? they asked. Strip searches seemed to be the site of a moral aporia concerning violence, an aporia embodied in IRA women prisoners. As IRA members, these women were for some mainstream feminists complicit in a climate of violence that oppressed women's lives. On the other hand, they were also subjected to a very specific form of state violence that was not inflicted, at least in the same way, on male prisoners. The twin elements of agency and subjection that are inherent in practices of violence and that may in fact form its paradoxical dimension, were condensed and signified in the body of the IRA woman prisoner. To separate strip searches from the political identity of the prisoners was a difficult operation that amounted to splitting a subject whose agency and subjection in relation to state power were in a constant interplay in the prison theater. Whatever else it was and from whatever angle one chose to look at it, strip-searching was a practice that exceeded routine procedure by being clearly enmeshed in long-standing political struggles. If strip searches were situated within the various histories of struggle for recognition and domination that marked the political climate of the 1970s and early 1980s in Northern Ireland—histories of which the prisons were a part—they also had a history within the prisons themselves.

Strip searches were introduced in Armagh Prison in 1982 after a dramatic hunger strike ended a prolonged conflict in the prisons of Northern Ireland. The conflict was triggered by the British government's decision to refuse political recognition to incarcerated members of paramilitary organizations such as the IRA. The decision eliminated the prisoners' organizational autonomy and the right to wear their own clothes. Most importantly, it divested them and their struggle of political meaning by reducing them to the status of common criminals. This was a sensitive issue for members of the IRA who had fought for acknowledgment of the political character of their activities at different stages. Historically, prisons in Ireland have been key battlegrounds for the colonial state and nationalist rebels. During the late nineteenth century and throughout the twentieth century, many nationalist campaigns were launched from the prisons, creating a distinctive political tradition of struggle that was tapped ideologically during the prison conflict that marked the late 1970s in Northern Ireland. For the prisoners, accepting criminal status amounted to criminalizing the history of Irish struggles against British colonization and renouncing their own identity. The struggle against this policy of criminalization led to dramatic forms of resistance involving prisoners' refusal to wear uniforms, covering themselves only with blankets, their refusal to wash, living amid their own excrement, and hunger strikes that led to the deaths of 10 prisoners (Aretxaga 1993, 1995, 1997; Feldman 1991).

Like their male comrades, republican women prisoners, who were then housed at Armagh Prison, struggled against the divestment of their political identity. But the women's no-wash protest involved the additional hardship of contending with menstrual periods. As I have argued elsewhere (Aretxaga 1995, 1997), the imagery of women forced to live amid their own excrement and menstrual blood gave the protest of women prisoners unusual political visibility. Women prisoners abandoned the "dirty protest" in 1981 when men republican prisoners embarked on the hunger strike in which 10 men died. It was after this period of enormous political tension inside and outside the prisons that strip searches began to be used with unjustified frequency in the women's prison. Strip searches were not conducted in an unusual way in the Maze, the prison housing the majority of male political prisoners, and strip searches of men had not become a political issue.[2]

Before 1982, women were strip-searched when they first came into jail as part of a ritual of committal that also included a bath. The usual procedure when women left the prison was a routine rubdown search accompanied by a metal detector. In October 1982, two remand prisoners (prisoners awaiting trial) were found in possession of two keys, which they apparently had picked up in the courthouse and brought with them into Armagh Prison (National Council for Civil Liberties [NCCL] 1986:7). This incident was the single justification offered by the secretary of state and the prison governor for a change of policy that substituted random strip searches for rubdown searches. The rationale was the maintenance of security at the prison. It should be noted that the number of women prisoners at Armagh had rarely surpassed 40, and in 1985 the ratio of prison officers to prisoners there was as high as two to one.

The form in which strip searches have been conducted since November 1982, and their frequency, has not followed a consistent pattern. Initially, women were strip-searched every time they went into or out of jail, whether on parole or to attend a court hearing. For women on remand, strip-searching was a frequent occurrence because they were required to visit the courthouse weekly. Strip searches could also be conducted before and after visits with relatives or friends.

In March 1983, the searches changed from a relatively stable pattern to a "random" pattern, and they were concentrated especially on unsentenced prisoners, the most vulnerable subgroup.[3] Prisoners could be called for a strip search at any moment, for no particular reason, which triggered great anxiety and distress among women prisoners. In discussing the randomness of strip searches, the National Council for Civil Liberties found that the searches were conducted on the basis of personal decisions made by prison officers, who would act on anything they considered to be suspicious behavior, such as a prisoner's being sick (NCCL 1986:15). Between November 1992 and the beginning of 1995, more than 2,000 strip searches were conducted in Armagh Prison (Brownlee 1985). In a single month in 1983, three prisoners were strip-searched 8 times each, one prisoner was strip-searched 31 times, and another was strip-searched once (NCCL 1986:8).

The new policy of strip searches attracted widespread condemnation by political and civic organizations that considered the practice deeply damaging psychologically and totally unnecessary for the security of the prison (Community for Justice 1987; NCCL 1986). Moreover "the 'random' nature of the searches makes it possible for strip searches to be used (consciously or unconsciously) as a means of punishing certain prisoners" (NCCL 1986:30).

In 1986, women prisoners were transferred to a newly built high-security prison, Maghaberry. The old Victorian prison of Armagh was closed. Maghaberry was equipped with state-of-the art surveillance technology that made any breach of security practically impossible. There was, then, no justification for frequent strip searches. However, although they seemed to become less random, according to the prisoners, strip searches continued to be performed, despite the prison's panoptic surveillance and its advanced technology of control. Neither in modern Maghaberry nor in the former decaying prison of Armagh was anything that might have compromised the prison's security ever found in a strip search.

A CHANGING BATTLEGROUND

Strip searches had been conducted since their introduction in 1982 in a special room with cubicles. Women were supposed to undress in the cubicles, hand the items of clothing to the officers for inspection, and cover themselves with a sheet. Once every piece of clothing had been inspected, the officers turned to the prisoners, opened the sheet, and visually inspected the women's bodies, first in a general way and then in detail: hair, hands and soles of feet, armpits. There is little doubt about the reifying effect of this practice. Prisoners were ritually transformed into objects of scrutiny and optic appropriation. They were stripped not only of clothes but of personhood. It was indeed a woman's person that was reconstituted during and through the strip search. One former prisoner whom I interviewed, Carol, expressed to me this sense of objectification when, in describing the procedure of the strip search, she said that she had felt like "cattle in a market."

The constant surveillance of the prisoner culminates in the naked body of the stripped woman, bringing to maximum expression what Allen Feldman (1991:156) has called the "optics of domination." Brenda, another ex-prisoner, preferred to be beaten than to be stripped: "You feel so vulnerable when you are naked. You don't feel like fighting back when you are naked because you expose yourself in every way. You were nearly crying when you knew you were going to be stripped-searched. It made you very angry and very violent too." Carol's humiliating sense of objectification and Brenda's vulnerability reveal the character of strip searches as a technique of domination rather than a neutral security regulation.

When strip searches were intensified as a punitive technique by being increased in frequency and randomness, women prisoners decided to physically resist them. What happened then, in Brenda's words, was that "they literally had to pull the clothes off you. That was embarrassing because you were kicking and struggling and they were ripping the clothes completely off you and you feel...I cannot describe the way I used to feel. You felt as if you were nothing, you feel degraded. It's like a rape of some kind. They are ripping the bra and the panties off you [sigh], you felt like crying, you felt like rolling back in a ball and getting into the corner and never coming out of there again!"

After a prolonged campaign against strip searches by civic and religious organizations, the frequency and randomness of the searches diminished, and prisoners' tactics again changed. Jennifer, the leader of the women prisoners in 1989, told me that physical resistance had been taking an enormous psychological toll on the prisoners. Not only was it deeply distressing to be forcefully undressed and even injured in the process, but prisoners were also punished afterward for disobedience with solitary confinement and loss of good-conduct days discounted from their sentences.

From 1984 onward, the prisoners undressed in their cubicles but refused to put on a sheet, remaining naked and silent while looking directly into the eyes of the stripping officers with a sardonic smile. The prisoners said that the officers often made remarks about their bodies. According to Brenda, women prisoners sometimes would answer the guards with rhetorical questions such as "Do you enjoy it?" or "Would you do this to your daughter?" These gestures were aimed at redirecting the embarrassment and humiliation from the prisoner to the guards.

Although strip searches clearly engaged the subjectivity of those involved, they were surrounded by an appearance of impersonality, neutrality, and sanitary distance. The cubicles, the sheets, and the ritualized sequencing of the search disguised the appropriation of the prisoner's body as a detached institutional procedure. This dissociation between the intersubjective dynamic of hostility, humiliation, and control that pervaded the strip search and its institutional rationalization as an aseptic and necessary procedure, allowed prison officers to negate the actual power relation in which they were engaging, and to shield themselves under the cover of professional duty. An inquiry into the strip-searching of Armagh prisoners conducted by the National Council for Civil Liberties (1986:8) reported that prison officers were firmly convinced that strip searches were an effective deterrent against security breaches, saying that they preferred to conduct the searches themselves than trust mechanical instruments of surveillance. This personal involvement in the dynamic of control was further revealed when the officers admitted that any kind of "suspicious" behavior—behavior that they did not fully control, such as a prisoner's getting sick—would warrant a search (National Council for Civil Liberties 1986:14). As Foucault noted, "power is tolerable on condition that it masks a substantial part of itself" (1980:86). This negation of power was particularly injuring to the prisoners, who were thus stripped not only of their clothes but also of their experience of violation, with its concomitant feelings of humiliation and powerlessness.

Because of the shattering impact of a violence that disguises itself as a "normal" form of existence, prisoners struggled to make manifest the power pervading the strip searches. At first they refused to undress themselves, obligating prison officers to engage physically in the violence of stripping them. Later, they engaged in tactics of passive resistance, such as refusing to use the sheet. Such refusal was important because the sheet functioned in this context as a masquerade of propriety. It was there not to cover but to be opened, which constituted a second act of forced disclosure, a double strip that masked the visual invasion of the body with the aseptic meanings of a medical examination.[4] The refusal to use the sheet was a refusal to collaborate in this fiction of power. By remaining naked while silently looking the officers in the eyes and smiling sardonically, female prisoners were doing what Judith Butler has called "a parodic inhabiting of conformity that subtly calls into question the legitimacy of the command" (1993:122). This parody of conformity countered the sanitation of strip searches—their rational, utilitarian appearance—by directly addressing the persons shielded behind uniforms and forcing them to confront their own engagement in a power relation. According to the investigation conducted by the National Council for Civil Liberties, some prison officers did indeed find this attitude disturbing (NCCL 1986:12).

In January 1993, when I went back to Belfast, women ex-prisoners told me a harrowing tale about the strip searches conducted in Maghaberry Prison in 1992. The story of this strip search was substantially different from any I had heard before.

The material for the analysis that follows comes from two fundamental sources: the narrative statements written by women prisoners immediately after the mass strip search of 1992, and interviews with ex-prisoners. One of the women who suffered the search provided me with copies of all handwritten statements. I conducted open-ended interviews with prisoners released after that date, as well as with prisoners who had experienced strip searches prior to 1992. I have also consulted a variety of communiqués and other documents published since 1982 on the issue of strip searches. Let me turn, then, to the events of March 1992, which I will describe through extensive quotations from the prisoners.

STRIP SEARCH 1992: WOMEN'S NARRATIVES

I woke at 8:00 am as usual to the signs of screws [this is how

prison officers are called by prisoners] coming on to the wing
that signals the morning unlock of cells. There seemed to be a
longer delay than usual. I glanced at my watch that showed 8:20
am and I thought that the lock up was getting later every morning. Just then I heard foot steps and the sound of jingling keys,
however the screws passed my cell and stopped next door at
Rosie's cell. I heard them telling her that we would not be
unlocked that morning due to a search being conducted
throughout the jail. Just as I was settling down to write some letters a shout from Rosie told us that something was wrong, she
explained that one of the PO [prison officers] had informed
her that as each cell was being searched individually so too
would the occupants be subjected to a "full search" that is a
"strip search."—Theresa Browne

Around 10:00 am I heard that they were going to strip all of us.
I couldn't believe it because we had jail searches before but they
never involved us being stripped. Then I saw the search team
coming in with full riot gear and I heard one of the men screws
singing "happy days are here again."—Bernie Reilly

They came into the wing, a lot of screws, both male and female,
all dressed in black, with shields, helmets, visors in the helmets,
padding in elbows and knees, you couldn't distinguish men
from women, there were carrying dogs.—Carol

I saw a stream of screws in full riot gear entering the front gate
of the jail and advance towards our wing. They were all dressed
in navy-blue, boiler suit type of outfits with helmets and carried
shields and batons, I don't know if they were all females as it was
difficult to see their faces. I felt bewildered and frightened. I
couldn't understand why the riot squad had been brought in
since we had just awakened and all prisoners were still in their
cells. Within a few minutes someone shouted "what is going
on?" and the reply came "the riot squad is in with Theresa, they
are stripping her." I felt totally shocked and horrified. It was difficult to believe that they were going to strip me in my cell.
When someone shouted that they were barricading themselves

in I did the same by pushing my bed against the door. Another
team of screws arrived and I heard them working on the outside
of the doors taking the frame off so that the doors would open
out onto the landing. Then I realized that my barricade was no
longer any use.—Louise

In the women's description of events, men and women officers appeared
from afar, indistinguishable from each other. Their riot uniform had the
effect of blurring gender lines. Women prisoners did in fact worry that
male officers were present while they were being forcefully stripped.
This indistinguishability was accentuated by the fact that the officers
used numbers rather than names to refer to themselves, thus accentu-
ating the anonymity, hierarchical distance, and antagonism between
prisoners and officers (both male and female): prisoners were the ones
stripped; officers were the strippers. The prisoners' isolation in their
cells and their reliance on hearing and fragmentary seeing for knowledge of the situation accentuated the terror.

The forced strip-searching of women began at approximately
10:30 A.M. and lasted until 9:00 P.M. with two breaks for lunch and dinner (an incongruent fiction of routine). I continue with the narratives:

The riot squad entered the cell of Marie. I could hear a lot of
commotion and Marie shouting at them to leave her alone.
This went on for quite some time before they moved on to
Louise in the cell next door. Again there came the sound of
things being knocked over and Louise screaming. Everything
went quiet for a few minutes and the only sound was made by
Louise gasping for breath.—Ailish Carroll

All day long these screams of anguish came from the cells and I
had to sit and listen to what the women were going through and
helpless to do anything about it. The male screws stood laughing and taunting the women and were in the wing while these
women were being raped. It was nerve wracking waiting and
knowing that they would eventually get to me.—Karen Quin

During most of the attacks I saw and heard both male and
female screws laughing and jeering while women were being

pinned down and stripped naked. At one stage I watched a
male screw making sick and disgusting sexual remarks. I cannot
describe what it is really like to watch women being trailed off
the window bars to be sexually assaulted and to listen to their
cries and screams—it's a nightmare.—Shaureen Baker

All prisoners affirmed that hearing the screams of other women
produced a feeling of impotence and anxious waiting that was almost
worse than the assault itself.[5] Many women described officers (men and
women) laughing with each other; Carol heard male officers outside
her cell laughing and coaching the women officers who were stripping
her. Ailish Carroll described how, "when the screams of women began,
male officers in the wing laughed and shouted, held up their middle
fingers and stuck out and wiggled their tongues." Another prisoner
heard a male officer saying, "We are going to fuck you all." In addition,
several prisoners reported that sexual remarks were interspersed with
anti-Catholic abuse. Prison officers are overwhelmingly Protestant and
often strongly prejudiced against Catholics. The waiting time, filled
with the screams and cries of women, the laughter and sexual joking of
officers, the barking of dogs, and shouting by everybody, produced a
heightened state of terror among the women locked in their cells, a terror associated in the women's accounts with the threat of rape. Carol
expressed this association when, apropos of describing the atmosphere
in the jail that day, she said suddenly, "The worst nightmare of any
woman is being sexually abused, and…it was terrifying!"

Prisoners barricaded themselves inside their cells by pushing their
beds against the doors. Officers counteracted by unhinging the doors
and removing them from their frames. Prisoners clung to the bars of
windows and kicked prison officers whenever they could. They also
shouted encouragement to one another. In the process of being immobilized, prisoners were bruised and injured in more or less severe ways.

The actual strip search, to which I turn now, followed a consistent
pattern of militarized sexual assault. Prisoners were reduced by force to
the floor or the bed. Officers (sometimes women, sometimes men and
women) held the prisoners in painful locks, or body holds, that were
changed at command. The actions performed on the bodies of the
women followed military codes such as "change lock" or "lock four" or

"reverse position." Four officers (sometimes five) immobilized the body of each woman while two undressed her and searched her clothes. They began with the shoes, working their way up the body and finishing with the bra. After the strip, the officers left or stood by watching while the prisoner gathered her clothes. In some cases they dressed the prisoners. Let me quote some narratives:

> Throughout the day I listened as one woman after another was attacked in her cell, I can still clearly hear the screams and shouts. When the riot squad entered our cell Theresa and I [two sisters who share a cell] sought to protect ourselves the best we could. Ten screws entered the cell dressed in riot gear complete with shields helmets and batons. We held on to each other and at the same time clung to the bars on the window. I was aware of the sound of the other women on our wing shouting at the screws to leave us alone. One screw was hammering at my fingers on the bars with a baton while the rest were pulling at my legs and one grabbed me by the hair and pulled my head back. On my right hand side I could see Theresa being roughly dragged out and she was screaming to the screws to leave me alone. I am not exactly sure at which point we became separated but I could constantly feel screws pulling and clapping at me. When my body was trailed back by the head, one screw was digging her baton into my neck and the next thing I was being thrown to the floor, my face pushed into the corner, arms twisted up my back and a screw standing on the joints at the back of my knees. As I was lying on the floor I could hear Theresa calling my name from the cell they had taken her to. One screw was pulling at my track shoes, she took off my socks also before proceeding to take off my track bottoms, leggings and my panties. When I was naked from the waist down with screws twisting my arms and legs my jumper, tee-shirt and then my bra was removed.—Mary McArdle

The narrative of Mary's sister, Theresa, is the same until the point when they became separated by guards:

> They were kicking at my legs and had my arms behind my back

in a painful lock as they dragged me towards the door of the cell. Once outside the cell I was ordered to lie down on the floor, even as I was refusing to do so I was slammed face down on to the wing where I was held by at least four screws. The screw pressing my face on to the floor yelled at me to bend my legs and for one moment I thought I was going to be strip searched on the wing [there were male officers on the wing]. I was panic stricken and struggled even harder. After a few minutes of violent struggle the screws managed to carry me in to an empty cell. Once in the cell I was again slammed face down onto the floor and held there for 10 minutes before the sexual assault on me began. During this time and in between my own screams I could hear the assault on Mary going on in the other cell. After a seemingly endless wait, the attack began. My shoes and socks were removed first, then my leggings. At this point a sheet folded into a ridiculously small shape was thrown across the lower half of my body. I still don't know why this was done because once my panties were removed it was lifted. Once I was naked from the waist down a screw sat on my legs while the others eased their grip slightly to remove the clothes from the top half of my body. When I was totally undressed they told me to get dressed as they left me lying on the floor. I then insisted that they dress me. The four screws who had held me down and the two who had stripped me reentered the cell and stood looking everywhere but at me. The same two screws who had torn the clothes from my body seconds earlier now stood fumbling and avoiding my angry glare as they gathered my clothes which were all over the floor and put them on my body.—Theresa Browne

All 21 prisoners described the assault in very similar terms, suggesting that underneath the appearance of instrumental rationality lay a highly ritualized event. For Carol, the feelings of violation and humiliation produced by the violent assault were compounded by the fact that she was having her period:

They came into my cell and threw me to the floor, they held me between four screws and two others removed my clothes forcefully. I was taking my period. They took the sanitary towel and

> threw it to a corner as if I was shit! They had the door open and
> the male screws were outside, I don't know how much they
> could see. They were coaching the female screws and could
> hear everything. Then they told me to dress and I refused. I was
> lying there naked on the floor and they had to dress me. Then
> they tramped me out of the cell into the association room.—
> Carol[6]

The forced appropriation and visibility of the body and its most
intimate physiological functions produced feelings not only of humiliation and impotence but also of personal degradation—feelings of
being "treated like shit," in Carol's words—against which all the women
prisoners had to struggle. Ann Cavanagh said, "One screw was watching
me while I started to dress. I have never felt more humiliated and
degraded in my life." Geraldine Ferrity wrote, "They all left the cell
leaving me lying on the floor with no clothes while the screws laughed.
It was very humiliating." The humiliation was deepened by the seeming
enjoyment of the officers, who were laughing and joking. "They
laughed and looked at me, enjoying every minute of it," Maureen
Delaney wrote.

The statements written by women prisoners, as well as their interviews, speak above everything else of an "excess" that pervaded the
implementation of security practices within the prison. There is an
excess in the way in which strip searches have been used as an "instrument of security" in Northern Ireland, an excess that cannot be contained by the rational discourse that justifies them as necessary
procedures (Scarry 1985). Such excess, particularly spectacular in the
case of 1992, exposes strip searches as a practice of power aimed at the
transformation of "souls" (Foucault 1979), rather than the impersonal
procedure claimed by prison authorities.

Women prisoners had complained about strip searches as a
degrading invasion of privacy. But in 1992 they were openly speaking of
rape and sexual abuse. This change can be linked to a discursive space
opened by feminism and the social recognition of sexual harassment as
a specific form of power against women. In talking of strip searches as
rape, republican women were challenging narrow legal definitions that
restricted rape to a category of violence involving penile penetration.

Legal definitions of rape ignore the violence of other forms of bodily invasion and the political character of it "as an attack on the core constructions of identity and ontological security in its most personal and profound sense" (Nordstrom 1996:151). While prisoners' insistence on the political meaning of strip searches as targeting especially republican women encountered resistance from civil rights activists who opposed strip searches, everyone agreed that strip searches were akin to rape (Stryker 1998). The Christian Response to Strip Searches (CRSS), a nondenominational, heterogeneous group involving members of the clergy, community workers, and counselors, wrote a report after the events of 1992 in which strip searches in Northern Ireland were considered "rape without penetration" (Stryker 1998) and a form of punishment specifically targeted at women. While prisoners agreed that their sexuality was used as a weapon against them, they were also adamant that what happened in 1992 could not be understood *only* from a feminist perspective as an attempt to subordinate women. Carol was insistent in telling me that the attack was also aimed at weakening their identity as Irish political prisoners. To prisoners, their identity as women and republicans (members of the IRA) was indissoluble.

After the searches, the women were charged with disorderly behavior. All of them were sentenced to punishment cells, loss of recreation, and several other disciplinary measures for disobeying prison orders. Within the rationale of the prison, the sentences acted as the legitimating force for the guards' assault, making it the women's fault for not complying with the order of undressing. The sentences *produced* the "act of rebellion" rather than resulting from it. It is the very act of punishment by the law that makes the refusal to be stripped into a criminal act, a breach of order. The logic is similar to that summoned by perpetrators of sexual violence, who often rationalize their violence as a response to some previous act of provocation on the part of the victim. Indeed, in a clear example of the contorted way in which the paranoid logic of security was suffused with the delusional logic of rape, the Northern Ireland Office claimed that the women had orchestrated the whole event by letting out a rumor about a gun in order to provoke a mass strip search so they could get publicity for International Women's Day (Stryker 1998:7). (The searches occurred the second of March, and International Women's Day took place on the eighth.)

The inanity of the excuse and the excess permeating the 1992 performance suggest that the prolonged strip searches were orchestrated as a display of state power that was deployed in the arena of sexuality—a mise-en-scène of (military) mass rape aimed at producing a maximum effect of terror. Sexuality, Foucault wrote, "is not the most intractable element in power relations but rather one of those endowed with the greater instrumentality: useful for the greatest number of maneuvers and capable of serving as a point of support, a linchpin for the most varied strategies" (1980:103). Sexuality was, in the case described, the support point for a strategy of subjugation whereby the penetration of the prisoners' bodies enacted the penetration of their rebellious political identities, thus giving the governor full control of the prison space. The control of prisoners' bodies must be interpreted not so much as a show of force but more as an attempt to reconfigure the prisoners' subjectivity—from political prisoners to conforming prisoners but also, and equally importantly, from rebellious to submissive women. This was clearly understood by the prisoners themselves, who claimed that sexuality was being used as a political weapon against them.[7]

The subjection of the republican women was organized as a reinscription of identity within the normative bounds of a hierarchical gender system that attempted to transform the bodies of militants into the subjugated bodies of sexualized women. Such transformation was attempted through a violation of the (collective) political body of the prisoners by the male body politic, represented by the prison officers. Inasmuch as the bodies of women prisoners were ethnically marked as Irish Catholic, and inasmuch as the body politic was represented by British authorities, the subjection of women had the added meaning of dominating the Catholic-nationalist community. It was inscribed within a colonial history of optic appropriation and a history of representation that often cast Anglo-Irish relations in the idiom of sexual violence.[8] Although a discussion of this history is beyond the bounds of this chapter, I feel compelled at least to outline some of its implications.

THE STRIPPING COLONIAL GAZE

It is difficult to separate the practice of strip searches of female political prisoners from the long-running British colonial obsession with "stripping" the people they colonized. A reading of British colonial texts on Ireland shows an intense fascination with the land and people of Ireland coupled with a deep anxiety about their unreadability. This anxiety was fixated on the mantles worn by the native Irish, which English colonizers suspected of concealing weapons. For early colonizers such as Edmund Spenser, the conquest of the country entailed a fundamental act of "stripping" the Irish of their mantles in order to render their dangerous bodies "transparent," readable, and thus unthreatening. Not only could the mantle hide weapons of rebellion, but in the case of women it also betrayed a sexual laxness, an unruliness that could only be guessed at but that represented a threat to social order. The transformation of Irish bodies—from wearing mantles to wearing trousers; from the opaque to the known—was for the early colonizers the materialization of a more profound reconfiguration of the subjectivity of the wild Irish into a civilized, Anglicized form (Cairns and Richards 1988; Jones and Stallybrass 1992). Such colonial strippings represent not only an epistemic act of violence but a physical one as well, sanctioned with laws that punished people for wearing native apparel.

Such attempts to impose order on an unreadable body were projected onto the geography of the land, which the British perceived as chaotic and disordered, with loughs and bogs crowning mountains and dense forests filling valleys. The major undertaking at mastering the land was the First Ordinance Survey of Ireland, lasting from 1824 to 1846. Never before had a country been surveyed in such detail. The body of Ireland was stripped of the significance attached to Irish place-names and reconfigured into English topography. It would be interesting to trace in all the detail that it deserves the stubborn persistence of this anxious colonial gaze in Ireland, a gaze which, the more it penetrated, the more it seemed to lose its object. But I want to trace this appropriating gaze to the recent history of Northern Ireland and the ways in which it has manifested itself in the practices of surveillance hovering over the Catholic-nationalist communities in the form of constant military patrols and technologies of control (Faligot 1983; Feldman 1991; Sluka 1989).

At the height of the conflict in the early seventies, the threat of terrorism focused British attention upon the bodies of women, who were required to open their coats at army checkpoints to show that they were not carrying weapons. To Catholic women, the act of opening their coats to the intent gaze of strange men amounted to an act of undressing, a "stripping," with concomitant feelings of embarrassment, degradation, and guilt. Frequently women refused to open their coats even if it meant risking arrest. The optic penetration of women's bodies was most routinized in the form of sexual harassment by security forces (McVeigh 1994:124–134).

But it is perhaps the house searches that offer the closest analogy to optic and physical violence on the body of the Catholic-nationalist community. Thousands of house searches have been carried out in the tightly knit working-class communities of Irish Catholics, including a search of the house in which I lived. Almost no one has been unaffected by a house search, either directly or through the search of a relative or friend's house. Often these searches involved physical violence, humiliation, and unnecessary destruction of property. Like strip searches, their only justification was security; like the actions of the early colonizers, they manifested an anxiety about the opaqueness of the community-scape. The more it was surveyed, the more impenetrable this space seemed to appear. Like strip searches, house searches consistently failed to yield significant findings. For these reasons, nationalist people understand house searches as rituals of punishment against the community as a whole (Feldman 1991). Such rituals of punishment were often allegorized in the nationalist press through photographs of distressed women in the midst of their devastated houses. The feelings of violation and dirtiness described by women who had undergone strip searches were often echoed by women in describing a house search. For them the humiliation, destruction, feelings of impotence, and anxiety accompanying a house search were as defiling as a sexual assault. The strip searches and other rituals of body disclosure performed by the security forces constituted a literalization of such an allegory (Aretxaga 1997).

In prison, the cell becomes women's only private space, the equivalent of the house as a space of security and intimacy. The stripping of women prisoners in their own cells instead of in the usual space of the cubicle represents a double violation that deprives women of a secure psychological space. There is nowhere to go after the assault; the cell is transformed into an estranged space that acts as a constant reminder of the prisoner's vulnerability. The double stripping of body and space inflicted on the women prisoners at Maghaberry in 1992 metaphorically condensed the optic penetration of the community of prisoners, the nationalist community, and the space of the Irish nation as a whole.

FINAL REMARKS

Maghaberry women prisoners have sued the prison governor for sexual harassment, a collective measure as unprecedented as the type of strip search the governor orchestrated.[9] During my interviews with them, ex-prisoners talked about the terrifying effects of the forced strip. They had all suffered, to varying degrees, sleeplessness, nightmares, fear, and nervousness. The women I interviewed pointed out that there was still fear inside Maghaberry Prison that it might happen again. The terror was triggered, said Louise (who was released a few months before I interviewed her in January 1995), by any deviation from institutional routine: "a delay in opening a door or serving a meal becomes very upsetting because you think that they are up to something." To some degree, the governor had accomplished his purpose of making the prison a thoroughly ordered and regulated space. His terrorism had the effect of institutionalizing women to the point of leaving them vulnerable to small variations of routine. There have been no strip searches since 1992, but in a way they are not needed, for the same effect can be accomplished with more discrete moves.

At the same time, prisoners also emphasized that they had become "more political" as a consequence of the violence. What women like Carol and Anne Mary meant by this was that the violence had made them think more deeply about the connections between different forms of domination. For some of these women, who had become involved in the IRA as a gut reaction to the militarized repression of nationalist communities, the new consciousness meant an understanding of how domination was structurally organized to subdue them as both women and Catholic-nationalists. For the ex-prisoners I spoke to, being a woman took on a politicized dimension that it did not have before. What became problematized by this politicization was what being a woman meant.

For the prisoners, their identity as women was linked to their active involvement in a nationalist struggle against the British government. Their subjectivity, of which the prisoners became particularly aware after the stripping, was an obstacle to the male governor's total control of the prison. It was also a challenge to socially dominant norms of femininity that had long seen "terrorist" women as gender deviations, that is, as not quite women. The stripping can be understood as the use of bodily violence to subdue the prisoners into conforming not only to the norms of the prison but also to the colonial hierarchy of Northern Ireland, within which Catholics had to be put in their (subjugated) place. Yet strip-searching is not "just" another kind of violence but, in Northern Ireland, one specifically targeted toward women. It is not only violence but the form violence takes that matters in the formation of subjectivities and political discourse, as Das and Nandy (1985) astutely noted.[10] Inasmuch as the resisting prisoners were women, the stripping was aimed at subduing them into the norms of passive femininity by transforming an autonomous feminine political subject into a male-dependent sexual one, stripped, so to speak, of political agency.

Modern mechanisms of punishment, Foucault (1979) observed, are aimed at transforming souls, at reconfiguring identity. Yet such transformation is a tricky process. Subject itself to the contingency of collective and personal histories, the transformation of "souls" is unpredictable and often backfires. The attempt at bending the politically radical republican identity of the prisoners by sexualizing their bodies into "possessable" femininity did not produced tamed subjects but subjects marked by a coexistence of terror with radicalized definitions of femininity and Irish identity.

If practices of bodily violence are capable of engendering specific identities, these cannot be disengaged from specific histories. The strip searches of 1992 suggest that identity should be conceived of as a permutation of difference embedded in social and political practices. Ethnic identity is constituted through historical practice, but history cannot be represented as a single narrative, nor is ethnic identity constituted in the same way for everybody. The focus on the play of difference (and continuities) between Catholic and Protestant identities has obliterated the shifting mechanisms in which sexual difference constitutes ethnic identity in Northern Ireland. I do not mean to claim visibility for an eclipsed gender identity, although some Irish critics (and of course feminists) have argued for a feminist identity as a third alternative to the polarized opposition of Protestant and Catholic identities (Foster 1991). Yet the political history of feminism in Northern Ireland and outside of it has made it impossible to think of gender as a unified political identity operating independently of ethnic, political, or other differences.

By questioning the unified character of identity, I do not intend to minimize the importance of the politics of identity. I do not think of identity as an object of free choice, but neither do I think it is a product of cultural determinism. Nor is identity in my view purely situational, either. Identity is, after all, the effect of differences that are political— that is, differences in resources, in rights, in power, which are often quite independent of people's will. In other words, identity is often imputed by practices of power rather than inherited or chosen. What I have argued in this essay is that as much as identity is also constituted by practices of violence, such practices function in a symbolic order marked already with difference, notably sexual difference. Attention to the operations of sexual difference in the formation of ethnic and national identities in Ireland indicates that these, like gender identity, are not unified and fixed but rather split and shifting. On the other hand, the practices and feelings linked to the politics of identity emerge less as a result of identity than as a result of the historical contestation of it.

Notes

I am indebted to Dorothy Holland and Jean Lave for their suggestions, encouragement, and editorial work on this chapter. It also benefited greatly from insightful comments made by the other participants at the seminar "History in Person." I am also indebted to colleagues at Harvard University who read this chapter at various stages in its development: Michael Herzfeld, Kenneth George, Stanley Tambiah, Arthur Kleiman, Byron Good, and Mary Jo DelVechio Good. A version of the chapter was presented at the University of Massachusetts at Amherst as the Annual Distinguished Lecture in European Anthropology in 1997. I am grateful to the participants and especially to Jacqueline Urla for her intellectual generosity and insight. My greatest debt is to the women in Northern Ireland who generously provided documentary material and oral narratives in spite of the emotional distress that such retelling often entailed. The research for this chapter was made possible by grants from the Social Sciences Research Council, the American Council for Learned Societies, and the MacArthur Foundation, and by a Tozzer research grant from Harvard University.

1. In the context of Northern Ireland, the categories Protestant and Catholic designate different "'imagined communities" with their own historical narratives, social networks, spatial enclaves, political organizations, expressive culture, and semiotics of identification. Here I follow scholars of Northern Ireland in seeing the two categories as signifiers of ethnic identity and not just as indicators of religious ascription.

2. Women ex-prisoners with whom I talked said that random strip searches as they began to be used in 1982 were a practice specifically targeted at breaking women politically. They emphasized that men were not strip-searched randomly but in specific situations such as upon leaving prison. Even then, women say that men were not asked to strip fully but to open their shirts and their pants. This does not mean, however, that men were not subjected to sexualized forms of bodily scrutiny. During the dirty protest of the 1970s, men were frequently subjected to violent body searches that included internal exploration, a practice hated and strongly resisted by male prisoners (Aretxaga 1995; Feldman 1991). But such forms of bodily violence have not been used with male prisoners since the end of the prison conflict. Male prisoners have not, in fact, complained about strip searches.

3. Prisoners awaiting trial lived in a kind of existential limbo pervaded by the anxiety of not knowing when they would be sentenced and for how long they would be in prison. This anxious uncertainty made them especially vulnerable to institutional pressure, because they wondered whether resisting that pressure might have a negative effect when they came up for trial. Sentenced prisoners, on the other hand, were less susceptible to the possibility of institutional blackmail.

4. See also Feldman 1991 on the use of medical metaphors during interrogation and in the subculture of violence of some paramilitary groups (e.g., Shankill butchers).

5. Crapanzano (1986) has written insightfully about the meaning of waiting as a situation that erases historical time and is thoroughly predicated on anguish. See also Das and Nandy 1985. Scarry (1995) has elaborated on the power of sounds to create terror. See Feldman 1991 and Aretxaga 1995 for use of sounds in Northern Ireland prisons.

6. I have analyzed elsewhere the deep feelings of vulnerability and shame

produced by the forced disclosure of menstruation, especially in a situation of utter powerlessness such as incarceration or interrogation. For most young women in Northern Ireland, as in many other places, it is embarrassing to talk about menstruation in public and deeply distressing to have the blood exposed—the more so to people known to be hostile and in a position of control. Police authorities know this and frequently use menstruation and sexual harassment as psychological weapons against women detainees during interrogation (Aretxaga 1995, 1997).

7. At the time of the assault there were 21 female prisoners and 300 male prisoners in Maghaberry Prison. The women had retained their political identity as members of the IRA, maintaining their own organizational structure, whereas the men were nonpolitical or had renounced their political identity and conformed fully with prison regulations. Women prisoners claim that they have been subjected to sexual discrimination by the governor of the prison in matters of prison life such as visits, association, and education. They attribute this discrimination to the fact that they are women and to their political identity. Republican women prisoners believe that they are the governor's only obstacle to full control of the prison.

8. See, for example, Aretxaga 1997, Herr 1990, Nash 1993, Kilfeather 1989, and Lloyd n.d. See also the poetry of Seamus Heaney, particularly *An Open Letter* (1983).

9. The individual reports of what happened that March second were written primarily as testimonies for the case. I have no reason to doubt the truth of the stories. Anybody who knows the social culture of Northern Ireland knows that women do not speak easily or lightly about sexual harassment. While sexual harassment has been an ongoing part of security forces' repartee, it is more the silence about it than the vocalization of it that has been the norm during most of the conflict. Some civil rights activists, such as members of the Christian Response to Strip Searches, found the language of the prisoners' reports too propagandistic. Yet the quibble seems to have been over the prisoners' self-identification as prisoners of war rather than over the claim of sexualized violence (see Stryker 1998).

10. See also Das 1995 on the way in which violence to the bodies of women reconfigures political discourse.

3

Indigenous Activism across Generations

An Intimate Social History of Antiracism Organizing in Guatemala

Kay B. Warren

How is political struggle reproduced over time in indigenous communities? How do succeeding generations of activists see the process? This essay examines these issues by retracing lifetimes of antiracism activism in a Guatemalan community that has produced nationally prominent leaders in the current Pan-Mayan Movement.[1] Rather than beginning with the Mayan movement for cultural rights—which captured national attention in the late 1980s and early 1990s with its denunciations of Guatemalan racism and calls for the restructuring of national culture and the state—the analysis starts with the localized struggles of earlier generations as a preface to the current movement.

My focus is on the social history of individuals as protagonists in tension with the structured social worlds they inhabit. I am interested, on the one hand, in the continuities of tacit knowledge that inform Kaqchikel family life and, on the other, in self-conscious disjunctures in cultural transmission. To paraphrase from Holland and Lave's introduction to this volume, my analysis pursues contestations and oppositions that arise historically yet—as they are reproduced across generations—become conventions that inform a variety of spheres of life. Identity, in this account, becomes a shifting composite, complexly influenced by individual protagonists, the transnational discourses they appropriate, and the shifting arenas of their activism.

The irony of an "across generations" framing of activism and cultural transmission is that it forces anthropologists to double back on the discipline's conventional method for ethnographic production. Anthropological writing seeks to bring social institutions and events into focus, yet much of the data for our general images of social life comes through personal encounters with specific people who recount their autobiographical experiences in ways that catch our attention. Writing becomes the process of effacing the personal encounter of fieldwork to achieve the appearance of a higher level of abstraction. Recent ethnographic experiments have attempted to remind us of the intimacy of cultural production for those we study and of the dialogical method of knowing central to anthropological research.[2] What I attempt to retain in this chapter is the initial autobiographical dimension from the accounts of Mayan activists and institution builders.

An "across generations" inquiry also raises the issue of how anthropologists conceptualize generations and how Mayas inevitably confound analysts' reified expectations with social practices that draw in issues far beyond "Western" conceptions of generation.[3] Central to this formulation is the issue of Mayan family dynamics and the ways social relations and patrilocal kinship ideologies constitute individual experiences and are transformed in the unfolding of actual lives. That *intra*generational relations turn out to be as important for activists as relations across generations should not surprise us; the question is how individuals instantiate particular social forms, with their inevitable tensions, and how social forms in all their variety shape the process. Further implicated in the consideration of kinship relations is the issue of *historical* generation in the sense of the formative political and economic conditions that create similar experiential environments and existential dilemmas for individuals in the same cohort. Moreover, one cannot really talk about the practice of kinship, community authority, or historical generations without dealing with Mayan constructions of the person (Warren 1998) and the complications this cultural formation creates for all sorts of social relations.

The ethnographic element of this analysis illustrates the ways Mayas have employed and transformed their culture to challenge social arrangements that have historically subordinated and marginalized the indigenous sector, which makes up about 60 percent of the national population. Throughout this essay, I juxtapose Mayan imaginaries of the relations between generations—drawn from rituals, fantasy, and social critiques—with the political biography of a prominent Kaqchikel Maya activist family in San Andrés, whom I will call the Ixims. The constant in this family has been social activism, first local and regional and most recently national. But their tactics, their sense of indigenous identity, and their ways of moralizing continuity versus discontinuity have often put members of this extended family at odds with each other. It is in this intimate family context that I examine cultural transmission and political action.

Before engaging these issues ethnographically, however, I want to revisit current anthropological framings of indigenous identity in Guatemala. My goal is to introduce a reflexive element to this analysis. That is, we need to identify an anthropological level on which oppositions arise historically, become conventionalized, and are reproduced through the interventions of particular individuals.

NARRATING IDENTITY POLITICS: A CLASH OF ANTHROPOLOGIES

Mayan identity—as the product of self-other contrasts and mutual constructions—has always been multifaceted. Before the Spaniards instituted their sixteenth-century colonial social order, trade and invasions had brought waves of central Mexican culture to Guatemala, and a centralized Mayan empire had given way after A.D. 900 to decentralized states struggling against each other. In these ranked lineage–based societies, kinship, generation, and regionality were key elements of identity (Carmack 1973; Fox 1987; Hill and Monaghan 1987). In the sixteenth century, after European diseases decimated immunologically unprepared populations, the Spanish colonial administration further decentralized Mayan society by breaking up indigenous states, depriving elites of wider powers, and resettling their colonial subjects into small agrarian communities (reducciones). Repeated histories of fragmentation produced diverse, historically related Mayan languages, yet another central facet of identity. In practice, colonial Catholicism with its community-specific saint societies, and shamanism with its localized mountain shrines, heightened the intimacy of local identification (Cancian 1965; Carlsen 1997; B. Tedlock 1982; Watanabe 1992).

New World Spanish elites and their locally born descendants, the creoles, spoke of indigenous peoples as "indios," "indígenas," and "naturales." Mayas used these terms but also spoke in their own languages of "our people," used community-specific names for themselves, or, in a countervailing discourse, referred to themselves in the regionalized idiom of language groups as Kaqchikels, Quiches, Mams, and so on. The *municipio*, a countylike regionality with outlying settlements that ringed an administrative center, became a primary way of defining community. Hostility and envy were often projected onto neighboring communities through narratives of people who were able to transform themselves into other beings who brought sickness to other towns and their own. Regional rivalries were remembered in a historical perspective, including stories of tactical alliances some Mayan states made with the original Spanish invaders as leverage against other indigenous states. Within municipios, economic and bureaucratic structures—which generally ensured power differences between indigenous and Hispanic communities—were burlesqued at community festivals, critiqued in narratives of moral retribution, and resisted through the elaboration of parallel religious and jural institutions.[4]

Anthropologists have found many ways of narrating Guatemalan history and identity politics. *Antiracism narratives* speak of agrarian communities as centers of cultural resistance to colonial rule. According to this perspective, Mayan culture gained its colonial and postcolonial forms in oppositional discourse to Guatemalan racism, which has changed in character in response to economic transformations without losing its principle of ethnic hierarchy or its invidiousness over the last five hundred years (Cojtí Cuxil 1994, 1995; Curruchiche Gómez 1994; de Paz 1993; Esquit Choy and Ochoa 1995; Guzmán Böckler 1996; Lovell 1988).

Mayas have replied to domination and exploitation with an effective blend of Mayan-Catholic religions, strategies of separatism, and regional economic practices that have allowed some Mayas greater commercial autonomy (Smith 1993; Warren 1989). This perspective conventionally begins with the colonially imposed ethnic division of labor that forced Mayas into the role of impoverished agricultural laborers who, in order to make a living, worked on Spanish and Ladino plantations and, more recently, on commercial farms for export.

The point of this line of analysis is not that Mayas and nonindigenous Guatemalans, who currently call themselves Ladinos, are separate "races" but rather that social life is widely informed by a racializing ideology that naturalizes social hierarchy and equates political marginalization with inherent inferiority (Sam Colop 1991). From the sixteenth century onward, elites used this ideology to police their own marital alliances and to consolidate power across commerce, government, and the church (Casaús-Arzú 1992).

By contrast, *continuity narratives* focus on the persistence across centuries of pre-Columbian beliefs and practices that demonstrate the success Mayas have had in constituting a cultural world that is more than a reflection of colonial society (Carlsen 1997; Carmack 1973; Gossen 1984; B. Tedlock 1982; Vogt 1969; Watanabe 1992). Mayan languages, cosmology, beliefs in transforming selves, distinctive notions of "soul," shamanism, base-twenty mathematics, and distinctive calendrics are examples of generalized continuities over great periods of time despite tremendous changes in other aspects of culture (OKMA 1993). Rather than existing outside history, Mayas inhabit a distinctive stream of history, perpetuated through languages and beliefs that antedate the conquest. This view often argues against Mayan culture as a reaction to ethnic oppression.

Challenging both views, *hybridity and mestizaje narratives* deny that there is a specifically "indigenous" story to tell by pointing to the blend of cultures and of family lines that occurred during the colonial period. From this perspective, the ethnogenesis of Ladino as an intermediate category between *indio* and Spaniard is a story of indigenous acculturation (Friedlander 1975; Hale 1996; Lutz 1984; Morales 1998; Smith 1990; Wasserstrom 1983). Early in the colonial period, waves of cultural synthesis and physical mestizaje undermined the initial distinction between indigenous and nonindigenous peoples and thus erased the future legitimacy of political claims in terms of ethnicity. The process has only accelerated in the present. Initially, Ladinos were thought of as Spanish-speaking indios. It was only in the nineteenth century, when state policies encouraged Ladinos to resettle in indigenous towns as local officials, labor contractors, and liquor dealers, that a new consensus emerged that gave Ladinos a distinctive status as nonindigenous Guatemalans (Smith 1990).

Many analysts argue that using the language of discrete ethnic categories only hides the cross-ethnic character of class oppression for the rural poor and ignores the fact that Ladinos do not collectively oppress Mayas. It is a very few rich European and "white" families that have sought to stand outside the grammar of ethnic opposition and that control most of the country's wealth (Smith 1990). Therefore, the conventional ethnic polarization is an example of the lingering of conventional distinctions—Indian and Ladino—far past their historical moment of social relevance.

Cultural anthropologists who have focused on the production of cultural distinctiveness are increasingly criticized for narrating ethnic histories. In the contemporary world of nationalist conflict, the academic project of documenting the revitalization of ethnic difference is seen as actually contributing to polarized conflict in multiethnic states. In Guatemala, the misstep is said to involve a failure to document the countervailing process of cultural blurring and transculturation, the flow of individuals among multiple identities, and the transformation of the terms of identification outside the confines of polarized ethnicities. For many on the old left in Guatemala and some on the newer social movements' (or *populars'*) left, class remains the issue, and deconstructionist methods, the tool to make their case (Warren 1998).

Social analysts, including the present author, have tended to see these alternative formulations as being at war with one another. We have tended to teach each other's analyses not for their heterodox moments but for the ways in which they represent opposing schools of thought. By contrast, in this essay I hope to explore the possibility of an excluded middle for the analysis of identity politics—the coexistence of multiple politics and histories that are obscured by the antagonism of these anthropological constructions. The continuity, resistance, and hybridity narratives are each in their own way salient to anthropological understandings of the impetus and dilemmas of activism. Being Maya is not a singular identity for indigenous activists, ethnicity is not a separate domain but rather a product of all sorts of transnational culture flows, and the struggle for justice involves the creation of very different activist communities. As a result, antiracism activism becomes a form of political action that its practitioners perceive as a challenge to Guatemala's persistent yet diffuse racializing ideology and its everyday effects in social practice and institutional arrangements. That these challenges take place in very different arenas and that much activism is not seen as political by others are telling characteristics of this social history.

MAYAN CULTURE AND THE INDETERMINACY OF SOCIAL RELATIONS

There is a special signature to personhood in Mayan culture that shapes activism and its reception by wider publics. On one hand, the self is thought of as not fully knowable and potentially unstable. On the other hand, the world is saturated with corrosive envy *(envidia)*, the product of a zero-sum reality in which one person's gain inevitably becomes someone else's personal loss. This diffuse view of the nature of social relations continues to serve as a backdrop to community affairs. It leads to a special tolerance of multiple points of view yet poses challenges for leaders, who face skeptical publics and sharp resentment of individualized recognition and success.

Mayan responses to an ambiguous and unstable world have long emphasized collective leadership, consensus making, and the tolerance of different rationales for action in the face of the diversity of individual reasoning and intentions. Families have commonly turned to shaman-priests *(ajq'ij)* and ritual guides *(k'amöl b'ey)* as intermediaries to unmask hidden truths. Misfortunes cause individuals and communities to seek shamanic assistance to interpret and redress wrongs and to seek material blessings. Since the conquest, however, Christian missionaries have demonized shamans for engaging in "witchcraft" *(brujería)* and repeatedly forced them underground. By contrast, the ritual guides, who operate with highly stylized formality in community events, were integrated into Mayan Catholic public culture during the colonial period. Activism, leadership styles, and Mayan cultural resurgence have been influenced by these notions of personhood and social mediation and by the need to reply to the system of domination current in the country at any one historical moment.

KAY B. WARREN

THE OLDER GENERATIONS: TRADITIONALISM AND RELIGIOUS REBELLION

In 1993, from the living room of his house just outside San Andrés, Don Gustavo's harangue to me about his nephews Alfonso and No'j was spontaneous and intense:

> I've talked to those who head this movement. To really recover Mayan culture, we would have to return to the ways of our ancestors. To recover everything we would have to speak our indigenous language. Yet we are the guilty ones with our children. None of our children speaks our language. I'm not going to correct these people; they are very educated. But my view is: how are we going to reclaim our culture, how are our children going to recuperate it if we are the ones who teach our children modern things, new things? To recover this, we would have to go back to the kitchen and cook on the floor over the three stones, the *tenemastes*. But these intellectuals don't have stone hearths, they probably have something even better than my wood stove.
>
> At the great university and grand meetings of our indigenous people, the indigenous intellectual gives a talk on indigenous culture. But when he goes to give the talk, he should be wearing indigenous dress. Why doesn't he? To recapture our culture, he should wear indigenous dress. I tell you with pride this is what I wear. Some may say we look like clowns. But they should put on indigenous dress.
>
> Once, two of these great intellectuals argued. One said to the other, "If you are going to give these talks, you have to wear indigenous dress. No one will believe you, dressed as you are now."

Don Gustavo Ixim, the focus of this extended family biography, has struggled for five decades to organize the community of San Andrés within the scope of regional networks of groups belonging to the organization Catholic Action. Now in his seventies, he narrates his life as one of tireless leadership, community building, and political savvy in religious and civic affairs. His personal identification with and submission to the authority of the Catholic church and its teachings are fundamental to his life, as they have been to his older brother, Don Luis, who is also a catechist. There have been times of deep disillusionment in Don Gustavo's life. As a youth he struggled personally over his wife's inability to have more children after dangerous pregnancies and the birth of daughters early in the marriage. Then, and later in his life when he was caught up in the hard-drinking political culture of public office, Don Gustavo faced self-destructive bouts of alcoholism. With his health and credibility seriously threatened by drunkenness—he was killing himself, as everyone could see—he struggled back by quietly joining AA in a neighboring community. He presents his life story as a witness to the struggle against alcohol abuse and the constancy of religious faith that informs his ceaseless drive for institution building in the community.

In his youth, Don Gustavo's father migrated from the K'ichee' town of Totonicapán to San Andrés in the Department of Sololá and sought, with only partial success, to shed his image as an outsider in the endogamous community. To gain membership, he offered service in the Maya-run saint societies (cofradías), participated in other traditionalist activities, and "invented" the practice of bringing well-known marimbas to the town for the liminal dances at major festivals. In turn, his sons learned traditionalist beliefs and took advantage of the education available to peasant families—three years of local elementary school plus another two years of informal tutoring during which they learned Spanish. Their hopes of further education were dashed by a political coup that stripped rural youths of their scholarships. They married women from humble families in the wider municipio and worked as day laborers, agriculturalists, and brick makers.

The sons, however, decided on an unconventional path when they opted to join a new religious group organizing in the community. Catholic Action, part of a national movement to bring indigenous people into the fold of sacramental Catholicism, categorically opposed the gerontocracy of the traditionalist civil-religious hierarchy, welcomed all Catholics as equals before God, and encouraged youthful leadership. The sons' conversion was a stunning move because it meant not just turning their backs on their father's tactic for community membership but also challenging the delicate balance of ethnic relations in the town.

Community-focused traditionalism can be seen as an attempt to maintain moral space in a world dominated by the ethnic other, epitomized in this town by the Ladino landholder. After marriage, young Mayan men were conventionally drafted to join the civil-religious hierarchy, a uniquely town-focused Mayan organization, first in the lowest position in a saint society or as a messenger for town authorities. Over time, they worked their way to higher positions in the moral and civil administration of the community through voluntary—and sometimes not so voluntary—service that often entailed heavy expenditures to host community events. Participation gave a localized Mayan shape to generationality. Revered elders became the heads of saint societies and learned the role of the k'amöl b'ey, the ritual guide and archive of religious knowledge who spoke at rituals and marriage negotiations. They joined in the board of overseers, or *principales,* that oversaw the moral community, drafted new officials, and settled interpersonal disputes within the Mayan community (though not between Mayas and Ladinos). It seems that Ladinos understood the politics of traditionalism: that the saint societies and customary law were nonthreatening forms of separatism. In their minds, these practices accompanied submission to a division of labor that compelled Mayas to work as impoverished laborers for non-Mayas.

The "hidden transcripts" (Scott 1990) of traditionalism—liminal moments when social dramas and communal dances ridiculed and inverted local power structures, including plantation life, the authority of Mayan elders, and parents' authority over their children—were either accepted as entertainment at major religious festivals or never understood by the dominant ethnic group for what they were.[5] Significantly, when Catholic Action began to organize, local Ladinos threw their support to the traditionalists.[6]

In the narrow construction, Catholic Action was an attempt to counteract the religious authority of traditionalist Catholicism and shamanism and to reintegrate local congregations into the formal hierarchy of the Catholic church. Catechists—who were literate, bilingual, and specially trained lay leaders of the congregation—worked to convert townspeople away from the heterodox practices of the saint societies. Politically, Catholic Action was part of Archbishop Rossell y Arellana's program in the 1940s and 1950s to depoliticize impoverished indigenous populations, who, national elites feared, might find communism more attractive than grueling, poorly paid plantation labor.

During the revolutionary presidency of Jacobo Arbenz (1951–1954), Don Gustavo awakened politically when, as a young adult who had worked on local plantations, he was invited to join one of the newly constituted agrarian reform committees. The committee's mandate was to identify, for possible redistribution, plantations in the region that were not cultivating all their land. The group had barely gotten under way when a United States–bolstered counterrevolutionary force led by Carlos Castillo Armas successfully invaded Guatemala and took over the government in 1954. Although the redistributive policies that involved peasants in mainstream politics were quickly dismantled, a younger indigenous generation had experienced something novel— politics outside the scope and age structure of their communities. This early exposure appears to have had a catalytic impact on Don Gustavo's life, even as he turned to Catholic Action, the organization that conservative elites had chartered for young activists, and internalized the archbishop's hatred of the revolutionary period for its radical politics and anticlericalism.

In practice, local catechists such as Don Gustavo repoliticized the Catholic movement, using its universalist language to legitimate the struggle against ethnic discrimination, hateful stereotypes, and social hierarchies that marginalized indigenous people in community affairs. Catechists urged this worldly action to mirror their newly found religious universalism, and they organized the first community groups to promote free access to elementary schools and agrarian cooperative membership. At the time, these were courageous acts that responded to the poverty of Mayan congregations and challenged the status quo along two important fronts. Abolishing school fees meant that more Mayan parents could afford to send their children to school. Access to chemical fertilizer purchased with credit from the cooperative increased local yields so that fewer Mayas had to work seasonally on coastal plantations, often in dangerous conditions, for the pittance of fifty cents a day. U.S. development agencies encouraged these efforts and financially supported the cooperative movement as an antidote to leftist politics. Thus, with external support from various sources, the San Andrés catechists began the long process of undermining traditionalism and challenging the ethnic division of labor and politics in a town where 25 percent of the population was Ladino.

To differentiate their Christ-centric sense of Christianity from the worship of the saint societies, the catechists dispensed with the practice of elaborate processions of the saints and focused on study sessions and rosaries during the week and mass on Sundays. They rejected the social relations that structured the saint societies: the elaborate ascending scale of offices through which adult men moved during the course of their lives to gain moral authority and finally become community elders. Rather, Catholic Action offered leadership positions and continuing education on a wide variety of topics and created a generation of locally based cultural brokers in wider social and political affairs. Young men, and in some cases young women, could now speak out on morality, though their authority and frame of reference were rooted in contemporary institutionalized Catholicism rather than in the local community.

In an interesting way, however, Catholic Action came to reenact the older principle of gerontocracy: as the first catechists matured, they became elders and overseers of the movement, and youths were channeled into specialized groups and choirs. The life cycle of the founding catechists created a new social hierarchy, a large and very active congregation, and qualms among secular youths about this religious reply to traditionalism.

There have been other limits to Catholic Action's universalism. On the whole, wives play private supportive roles to their husbands' leadership. Don Gustavo's wife, Elena, who remains illiterate despite the group's stress on continuing education, keeps their busy homestead running. Few girls of her generation had access to much schooling, and those who came from outlying hamlets, as she did, often remained home to work. There was never an opportunity to catch up. Don Luis's wife, María, has always been an entrepreneur, adding important income to the family economy through her regional weaving business. Neither woman has the time or inclination to serve actively in the organization founded by their husbands.

Younger members of the Ixim family, including Alfonso, Don Luis's eldest son, chafed at the personal discipline required of leaders in Catholic Action. Rather, these youths decided to use their education, the right to which had been won by activist parents, to dispute the conventional ethnic division of labor. They were looking for something other than hard manual labor and subsistence farming to support their families. Some became development workers and teachers; others migrated to the capital and the coast for work. Activists who stayed in their home communities found pathways to local influence through community service and neighborhood improvement projects. They finished the project of tearing down traditionalism through a legal challenge of the unpaid service demanded by traditionalists for their organizations.

Throughout the highlands, elders like Don Gustavo narrated this change in stories of intergenerational betrayal. The classic story describes a father's visit to his son, who is pursuing studies in an urban high school. Seeing his father at the edge of the school yard—wearing his community's hand-spun white cotton shirt and pants covered by a black-and-white plaid wool apron—the youth tells his friends that he will be right back. He greets his father with news that all is well at school, makes plans for a visit home during the next vacation, and receives favorite food and praise from home. Returning to his schoolmates, the youth explains the encounter to them: how thoughtful it was that an old family servant came to bring presents and good wishes from his parents. The story, of course, is one of betrayal and denial. The youth, with his Ladino friends in the city, is trying to pass as a Ladino. To accomplish this, he must deny his father and, by extension, his family and community.

The catechist parents of educated youths, however, did not invent this worry. Rather, it is a transformation of an older intergenerational tension. The saint societies in their formal prayers, recited by the ritual guide, mourned the possibility that younger generations might ignore their elders on the path of life, "throwing them down" and dismissing them as models of moral action. Perhaps, said one prayer, the elders will be forced to ask God to punish the youths, to call for their time. Some Catholic Action parents fantasized that their children would learn martial arts and beat them up. Others affirmed the older fear that their children would pass as Ladinos outside San Andrés to get ahead on their own.

BACK TO THE FUTURE: AN EXPERIMENT IN REVITALIZATION

In San Andrés, the catechists felt that one way out of this double bind—whether to educate one's children or not—was to involve their children in efforts to reinvigorate Kaqchikel culture. After Catholic Action's earlier hostility toward *costumbre*, I was surprised to see Don Gustavo spearheading an effort to revive traditionalism in 1989. In the 1970s, Catholic Action had undercut traditionalism through direct competition, a tactic it used after its initial attempts at accommodation foundered. It deprived the saint societies of willing participants by demanding that converts stay away from processions, rituals, and community festivals. Its members denounced the heterodoxy and "impurity" of the civil-religious hierarchy, whose celebrations involved liminal drunkenness and sexual license at major celebrations such as Holy Week and the feast of the community's patron saint.

Catholic Action, with help from growing evangelical congregations, emerged triumphant. By the mid-1970s, the statues of the saints were cared for in private homes rather than in the brotherhood shrines, which had fallen into disuse. Respected principales no longer called everyone to serve the community for a year at a time in the saint societies, the community church, or the municipal offices. Ritual guides no longer choreographed the meetings and processions of the civil-religious hierarchy so that each wing of the organization was well represented and people found their rightful place in the elaborate social rankings. The poetic dialogues of prayer were no longer recited before ritual meals. Occasionally, a particularly devoted person would refurbish a shrine and take on public duties; at one point, several Ladinos assumed the task, then a highly religious Mayan woman. But the communal dimensions of the celebration withered.

What astounded me most in San Andrés in 1989 was the surprising resurrection of saint society rituals long after their apparent demise. Catholic Action decided to dramatize them as *actos culturales* to audiences of hundreds of Mayas who found themselves absolutely entranced by the productions, which were held to inaugurate the new social salon at the church. Moreover, Don Gustavo, who had done everything he could to undermine the legitimacy of the traditionalists, enthusiastically described his duties as the work of a k'amöl b'ey, a ritual guide.

In this experiment, Don Gustavo saw his role as that of rekindling memories to teach young people about their cultural identity. For the catechists, the rituals were no longer sacred ceremonies; rather, they were plays in which young people—always in male-female pairs dressed in newly acquired traditionalist outfits instead of their everyday Western clothing—played the parts of the ritual guide, the saint society head, his assistants, and their respective wives. As the catechists emphasized, the plays were held not in sacred space, not in the church's sanctuary, but rather in the new hall, which they anticipated would be the center of active youth programming for the congregation. The vignettes were perhaps an hour long altogether, in contrast to the three to five days of rituals and processions at the key junctures of the sacred calendar in the past.

With the blessing of several Catholic priests who watched the event, Don Gustavo and the other catechists organized a selective remembering of saint society rituals with the explicit goal of affirming what had now become problematical: the continuity of Mayan culture. This was "imperialist nostalgia" (Rosaldo 1990) from indigenous insiders, for clearly, in challenging costumbre and promoting nontraditional education, the activities of Catholic Action had eroded local commitments to these forms of identity and cultural distinctiveness. Nevertheless, for Catholic Action the authenticity of the skits rested in the immediacy of their connection to traditionalist rituals in San Andrés. Knowledgeable grandparents had been consulted, along with a retired ritual guide, so that the rituals would be just right. As one leader put it, "We are doing our own ethnography for these rituals."

The festival showcased young couples who marched in procession to the stage, reenacted the saint society's preparations for the titular feast of the town, and celebrated the harvest ceremonies including the storage of the crops and the hand-grinding of corn for tortilla dough, a process long-ago replaced by machines. Notably missing were the high points of traditionalist practices: the fraternal ritual meals during which the guides offered their dialogues, the worship at altars overflowing with saints who were periodically taken through the town in procession, the drunken nights of marimba music and dancing at the close of major celebrations, and the shaman-priests seeking family blessings. The selectivity of religious memory appeared to be driven by the compatibility of certain traditionalist activities with Catholic orthodoxy and the continuing unacceptability of other activities and icons.

What became compatible or incompatible for Catholic Action was the historical product of the interplay of the two religious organizations (Warren 1989). Thus, echoes of the older tensions between Catholic Action and the traditionalist saint societies resurfaced in the commemoration even as the event was explicitly about recapturing the ever-problematic youth.

The focus on the next generation was strategic, given the prevailing fear that youths who associated Mayan culture with agrarian poverty and marginalization would abandon their community. In response, catechists deliberately tried to update Mayan culture so it would be more attractive to current social needs. This meant acknowledging that young adults, especially those with high-school educations and nonagricultural aspirations as teachers and office workers, needed social recognition and a respected place in the community. They, not the elders, were the new organizers of and commentators on skits during the festival. Another anxiety close to the surface was that the Catholic church would lose the next generation to the evangelicals. The festival was designed to counterbalance the evangelicals' alleged lack of interest in maintaining Kaqchikel culture.

These concerns may well explain the focus on couples and the interest among catechists in reviving traditionalist marriage negotiation rituals. Historically, the *pedida,* which involved ritual guides as go-betweens for the families of the groom and bride in an endogamous community, called for a prolonged and stylized set of rituals to express heightened respect for parental authority. Narrative tension, one of the most enjoyable parts of the ritual in people's personal and historical accounts, was interjected as the bride's family feigned uninterest or coolly asked for more time to deliberate. The pedida was another focal point of Mayan traditionalism, although I did not understand its importance during my first fieldwork in 1970 because of my own bias—an uncritical reflection of the sentiments of my university department and the discipline at the time—against doing research on devalued "private" family issues or on women.[7]

Traditionalist marriage negotiations were part of a discovery procedure, another variant of unmasking in a culture where other selves are not fully knowable, to see whether the girl's parents opposed the union. Initial refusals on the part of her parents were expected; in the event of serious impediments, it is said that the girl's family would throw chiles on their cooking fire or bring hot water to the door to signal an unacceptable match. Rituals called for gift giving and a marriage ceremony, after which the couple lived together, often with the parents of the girl until the groom paid off his obligation. At that time, his family was expected to offer a house site near those of his father and brothers, where the family home would be constructed.

The emphasis in 1989 was on the use of the ritual to promote the continuity of congregations and Mayan identity, ensuring that young people could marry within the town into families that shared religious commitments. Another veiled concern might well have been the growing numbers of single mothers, something that is said not to have been a problem in the old days because marriages were arranged as soon as adolescents showed any sexual interest.

As much as everyone enjoyed the excitement of two days of reenactments and nightlife in a normally quiet, dusty town, the festival reenactments soon lost momentum and were abandoned by Catholic Action. Don Gustavo explained that the church hierarchy, despite its great consternation about evangelical conversions of young people, had decided not to sanction these practices. Another aspect of this decision was most likely the fact that youths active in the Pan-Mayan Movement, which was just picking up steam at that point, had a convergent project of revitalization, but one with very different religious goals including the revitalization of the authority of traditionalist shaman-priests *(ajq'ijab)*.

THE RESTLESSNESS OF THE NEXT GENERATION

Don Gustavo's nephew Alfonso, in his early fifties at the time of this writing, had experimented with ethnic "passing" when he worked in Guatemala City as a mechanic in the late 1960s. With six years of education, including studies outside the town in Quetzaltenango, he might easily have disappeared into urban life; he was literate, fluent in Spanish, and restless. When home in San Andrés, he refused to carry firewood with a tumpline across his forehead because, for him, it marked the submission of Mayas to degrading poverty. Alfonso had inherited his family's disdain for traditionalism and thirst for authority, but there was initially no employment outlet in the town for his energy. While he was at home for a quick visit in 1971, Alfonso and I struck up a friendship as 24-year-old age mates, and he joined my dissertation research team for six months. To his parents' delight, the work reconnected him with San Andrés and his family after an absence of three years. My fascination with local culture, however, had little impact on Alfonso, who demeaned traditionalism as archaic and shamanism as witchcraft. In his view, anthropological research helped him refine skills that he later put to use working for the national federation of agricultural cooperatives.

Alfonso narrates his life as an individual who successfully organized Mayan peasants into agrarian and housing cooperatives and gained a regional following through his knowledge of bureaucratic procedures, national law, Mayan culture, and the Kaqchikel and Spanish languages. His antiracism work was decidedly secular. During the day, he visited the agrarian communities in the region to establish new cooperatives. At night, his house always had visitors: illiterate farmers with a bureaucratic worry they could express only in Kaqchikel, someone who needed legal help in a dispute, schoolchildren with assignments on the history of the town.

As the only Maya operating out of the district office, Alfonso enjoyed regional influence; he became an avid participant in national organizations, advanced technical courses, and political meetings where local leaders were courted by national political figures who sought rural votes. His political base grew, as did his ties with politicians and party organizations; he yearned for political office. Alfonso had found his way in a system that cynically patronized Mayas; he was locally based but transregionally concerned. In the late 1970s he ran for a congressional seat and apparently won the election only to find that, in the turmoil of the counterinsurgency war, the election results had been nullified.

Guatemala's most recent counterinsurgency war, from 1978 through the mid-1980s, threw a spotlight on the vulnerability of Mayan activists. State surveillance was extreme, death squads and the military targeted local leaders as potential guerrilla sympathizers, and populations were terrorized as military outposts and clandestine cemeteries were established near rural towns. Catholic Action and the cooperative movement were now branded as communist by the army. Indigenous leaders were thought to be disloyal and dangerous because they were culturally different from the Ladino mainstream and because they were able to mobilize others.

During the worst offensive of the counterinsurgency war, in 1980–1983, an estimated 26,000 to 35,000 people were killed, 440 villages destroyed, and over a million people displaced from their homes as refugees (Ball, Kobrak, and Spirer 1998; CEH 1999; Manz 1988; Schirmer 1998). The 1999 Guatemalan truth commission estimated that the full 36 years of internal war resulted in 200,000 deaths. Its official review of the evidence shows that the army authored 93 percent of the violence, and the guerrillas, 3 percent; the remaining 4 percent is unattributable. It is estimated that 83 percent of the war fatalities were Mayas, and 17 percent, Ladinos (CEH 1999). In short, this was a genocidal war.

In the early 1980s, most leaders went underground, community organizations disbanded, and religious congregations kept low, nonpolitical profiles. Many Mayan leaders were killed, as were unaffiliated people. Some communities internalized the violence; that is, local feuds and envy caused people to denounce each other to the army or the guerrillas. The war sowed seeds of distrust in rural communities. People were picked up by the army or guerrillas, tortured, and disappeared. Were they alive or dead? It was unsafe to inquire. The social consequences of terror were described in family metaphors: the horror was that one could not even trust one's own family in the midst of uncertainty and violence. Other selves were unknowable; perhaps one's own relatives sympathized with the guerrillas or the army and were informing to one side or the other for money or perhaps because they had been threatened. At the apogee of the violence, it became too dangerous for leaders to function as advisors and unmaskers of other selves who might be in dangerous alliances. Both Gustavo and Alfonso were lucky to have survived the war. They ceased virtually all public activities, avoided unnecessary travel, and kept to themselves politically. San Andrés was deeply affected, and other Mayan leaders, among them two bilingual teachers, were killed. Luckily, the town escaped the massacres that decimated whole communities to the north.

As Guatemala emerged from the worst of the armed conflict in the mid-1980s, Alfonso's work in the cooperative movement slowly regained momentum. His many scrapbooks document continuing activism, his marriage to a Mayan schoolteacher, and the achievements of his children in school. Their house was a center of activity for the extended family and his public responsibilities. The rooms were comfortable and brimming with technology: a typewriter for late-night work in his office, a refrigerator in the storeroom, a propane stove in the kitchen (which had yet to displace the raised wood fire for cooking, however, because of the fear of explosions), and, in the family room–bedroom, a stereo for daytime music and a television for evening favorites like *MacGyver*, *Sábado Gigante*, Mexican cowboy movies, and the national news.

DIFFERENT PATHS TO PAN-MAYAN ACTIVISM

During the violence, new social forms were emerging at the margins of power, as can also be seen in this volume's case studies of Northern Ireland, Mexico, and Nepal.[8] Some Mayas were thinking in more explicit cultural terms of a wider social movement focused on the revitalization of Mayan culture. In the early 1970s, a nongovernmental organization called the Francisco Marroquín Linguistics Project brought together Mayan youths, who had been nominated by their communities throughout the highlands, to participate in linguistics courses to generate dialect surveys, dictionaries, and educational materials in Mayan languages. Other Mayas had battled their way into national universities and wrote theses critiquing racism and envisioning a Maya-specific politics (Cojtí Cuxil 1995; Otzoy 1988; Sam Colop 1983). A few received fellowships to study in Europe or the United States. By the late 1980s, these networks had created a host of research centers and the Pan-Mayan Movement, which now promotes national forums for indigenous rights (Cojtí Cuxil 1994, 1997; COMG 1995; Warren 1998). The movement has been spurred by activists in their forties and fifties, who participated in the nascent movement in their twenties, and is fueled by younger students, teachers, and development workers.

Alfonso's youngest brother, No'j, in his early thirties at the time of this writing, lived through the violence as a young teenager. Later he was offered a scholarship by a linguistics project, Oxlajuuj Keej Ajtz'iib Maya', and, with years of professional training, grew active in the Pan-Mayan Movement's efforts in language revitalization. With support from North American linguists and European funders, his group has published sophisticated linguistics research on major indigenous languages and general education materials on Mayan language and culture (OKMA 1993). Its antiracism work has taken the shape of creating a wider sense of a Mayan nation and responding to the *cultural* needs of rural communities, including education at all levels. The group speaks of urgent work against the flow of history and the mestizaje narrative (which they call *ladinización*) in an attempt to halt the process of assimilation and the loss of native speakers of Guatemala's 21 Mayan languages, four of which have between 360,000 and 1 million speakers (OKMA 1993).

No'j's historical generation is the first in San Andrés to aspire successfully to university education. In Guatemala City and in Quetzaltenango, Guatemala's second city, special part-time programs have been established for Mayan commuters, many of whom already have jobs and families to support. In the capital, Mayan linguistics programs at two universities have attracted activists who study in addition to their regular jobs and volunteer teaching. Like many other activists, No'j maintains strong ties with his home community. In the first years of their marriage, his young wife and their children have lived back in San Andrés, where the younger brothers of the family constructed homes. Despite urban work and ongoing university studies elsewhere, No'j's generation is striving to follow the Mayan preference for brothers to co-reside with their parents in a patrilocal configuration. As families grow past the size of the parental compound, older brothers move to nearby parcels if they can, and they maintain the extended family through frequent visits, joint meals, and child-care arrangements.

As a youngest son, No'j will inherit his parents' household and the responsibility of their care late in life. This practice has given No'j other ways in which to be Mayan. Like many urban activists in the movement, however, he has broken with the endogamy of the community and married a fellow activist from another region of the country whom he met at work. In his practice of cultural resurgence, No'j has the passion of a convert. He speaks only Kaqchikel in the family compound so that his children might begin their lives as monolingual Maya speakers. This self-conscious practice seeks to counter the shift to Spanish that occurred in many Kaqchikel Maya homes in the 1970s (Garzon et al. 1999). Moreover, No'j insists on speaking the Pan-Mayanist version of Kaqchikel, which strives toward regional standardization and avoids common Spanish loan words in order to signify the modern capacity and autonomy of the language. Strikingly, No'j's revitalization inverts the conventional generational authority of cultural transmission and substitutes standardized Mayan culture disseminated by Pan-Mayan research centers, such as his own, for local practices.

On the home front, No'j has been only partially successful. In a quiet way, his parents have proved to be unwilling to submit themselves to the discipline of revitalization, primarily because their family strategy has always been a bicultural one, in which it is important for children to master Spanish and Ladino practices in order to make their way in the world. During the week, while No'j works in the city, his mother and father subversively switch to Spanish in dealing with their grandchildren and daughter-in-law, who in any event speaks a different Mayan language and still finds Kaqchikel a challenge.

The hardest part of revitalization for the older generation has been the renunciation of Christianity by many Pan-Mayanists. No'j and his older brother Alfonso see Christianity, in all its incarnations, as colonialism (Pop Caal 1992).[9] No'j remains decidedly secular at this point in his life and rejects all religious authority, much as his older brother once did. Alfonso feels that Christianity would be better replaced by shamanism for family rituals and communal celebrations of the Mayan New Year. In a surprising move, he has become a shaman-priest (ajq'ij), training with other regional Mayan priests in ritual and calendrics and adopting the name Nimajay. For a while, he left office work—which had soured with dangerous interpersonal tensions—and dedicated himself to the revitalization of traditionalist councils of elders through COCADI, a national organization centered in Chimaltenango. His wife, a professional in her own right as one of the first generation of Mayan teachers in the San Andrés schools, has family and revitalization contacts that facilitated this new geographic connection. But Alfonso worried about giving up his local authority, feeling that in middle age a definitive move to build a new career from scratch might be too difficult. Moreover, forgoing the entitlements of patrilocality would deprive him of his familial power base in San Andrés. Thus, gender politics complicated the decision to relocate. Masculinity's entitlements—especially those defined by kinship, family residence, and communal authority—are locally grounded and quickly eroded by a change of venue. Alfonso felt that participation in nationally prominent organizations would compensate for a decline in authority in other spheres.

Alfonso has found deep personal satisfaction in performing family rituals for blessings and healing, promoting traditionalist authority in communal affairs, and participating in conferences where shaman-priests add seriousness of purpose and authenticity to the proceedings. Many of his old organizational talents have been transferred to this new interest. He is now an insider in a wing of the movement in which practical experience in community organizing, not university education, is important.

At times, tensions have emerged between the academic and shamanistic wings of the movement, though they are engaged in overlapping forms of transculturalism to promote Mayan culture. Both groups, for example, invited the late art historian Linda Schele to conduct workshops on Mayan glyphs and their translation. In 1993, she held meetings in San Andrés that brought catechists, teachers, shaman-priests, and other community leaders together. Regular minicourses for Mayan leaders have been held in Antigua and Chimaltenango.

The scholarly wing prizes the esoteric, practical knowledge that shamans have of ancient culture, religion, and calendrics. Many seek shamanic assistance and have the interlocking cycles of the Mayan calendar programmed on their laptops. Yet the young professionals, caught in a culture of bureaucratic credentialing as they seek funding for their projects, also have wondered how one knows whether a shaman-priest is deserving of his or her authority, given that they know of no formal body that regulates this status. (In fact, shamans now have their own federation, training programs, and investitures, though their activities are not always public.) At Pan-Mayan meetings of the scholarly wing, such as the 1994 national conference on Mayan educational policy, shaman-priests found themselves invited to officiate at rituals but having to protest to gain voice as educators with their own concerns for revitalization.

The older generation of the Ixim family is confounded by its children's participation in Pan-Mayanism. They see great irony in a movement that idealizes respect for elders yet in practice takes away their authority and moral voice. In his 1993 harangue, Don Gustavo bitterly outlined the contradictions he saw in the movement: its selective language of cultural recovery, embrace of modern technology, use of Spanish, and men's avoidance of indigenous dress that would mark them as ethnically distinctive and tied to rural communities. He used ironic language—"the great university," "the grand meetings," "the indigenous intellectual"—subversively to widen the distance between university and community affairs. In practice, the children of his family have eroded these separations. For his part, Don Gustavo is a respected local and regional intellectual who has organized hundreds of meetings, great and small, and has made a successful living with his hands. He has explored the feasibility of growing indigenous medicinal plants for a company that offers organic products to customers through catalogue sales. One wonders whether Don Gustavo used this ironic language to express his resentment of emerging class tensions and a youthful generation that has done little if any direct agricultural work but rather celebrates its achievements in other technologies. He has invented new narratives of betrayal—animated with propane stoves that everyone fears will blow up.

By contrast, his older brother and fellow catechist, Don Luis, speaks with equanimity of the cosmic Mayan life cycle in which an older generation dies so that new generations might be born (Carlson 1997). He sees the inevitable end of what his generation has been able to achieve through its efforts in the church, schools, commercial crop production, and local government. Given its historical circumstances, his generation has advanced the cause, especially from the days when indigenous people were expected to step off the sidewalk with hats in hand so Ladinos could pass unimpeded. Now the next generation will assume the struggle with different tactics, only to be replaced by still other generations.[10] It is interesting that Don Luis chooses the ancient Mayan language of cyclicity to express the blend of continuity and discontinuity involved in struggles on so many fronts to strengthen community. Both elders deeply value the dedication of their entire adult lives to faith in Christ and religious activism. No doubt they are pleased that still another of the family's sons has combined leadership in neighborhood improvement projects with religious devotion as a catechist organizing local choirs and offering religious instruction at a nearby Catholic girls' school. The idea that the God of their people and their children might be another divinity—the builder-modeler Tz'aqol B'itol of ancient Mayan mythistory[11]—is far beyond these elders' capacity for personal transformation.

GENERATIONAL CHANGE AND IDEOLOGICAL DIVERSITY IN PAN-MAYANISM

Much anthropological ink has been spilled over the Ladino-Maya opposition in Guatemala. Yet the preceding biographical accounts reveal additional sets of contestations and oppositions that shape and are shaped by participants' identities within the dynamics of Mayan identity: revitalization ideologies, kinship, religion, and gender.

In Mayan communities, the tensions provoked by changing political and economic circumstances have been experienced in a language of generational change. What has been striking in this family biography of San Andrés Mayan activists is the interweaving of generations, life-cycle dynamics, organizational genesis, and national politics. There has been an interplay of discontinuity and rejection of Mayan practices with continuity and revitalization. Each generation and subgeneration has found its own language for critiquing racism and discrimination and has been judged in some way as complicit by the next generation. Sherry Ortner's (1995) call for thick ethnographic description to examine subgroup politics as something beyond the overdetermined reflection of wider social hierarchies and her challenge to anthropologists to pursue the interplay of resistance and complicity in intergroup relations finds strong resonance in this analysis.

As we have found, there are important, specifically *intra*generational dynamics to this family grammar of identity and activism. In Mayan families, the eldest and youngest sons are important markers of generations. The eldest has important authority and becomes almost a father figure to the family. Even today, the eldest son *(nimalaxel)* is routinely consulted for personal advice by younger brothers and sisters. Alfonso's easy authority, articulateness, and activism was reinforced by his position as an eldest and by his experiences of organizational authority. The youngest *(ch'ip)*, who is expected to be indulged by his parents, inherits the family homestead and the responsibility of their care at the end of their lives. Thus, No'j—who might have drifted off to Guatemala City as his brother did for a while, or to the United States as other Mayas of his generation did—was called back to San Andrés by kinship obligations and by a Pan-Maya ideology that stressed the importance of regionalized language revitalization and ties to family and community. Ruralcentric kinship served as a crosscurrent to the urbanization of the Pan-Mayan Movement. For educated youths, the issue is how to balance rural responsibilities and urban job opportunities. One answer has been to structure jobs around weekly commutes to home communities. Urban groups working on Maya linguistics and nonformal educational projects have been surprised to discover large proportions of ch'ips among their professional staffs.

It would be a mistake to talk about Guatemalan politics as if they were separate from and external to family dynamics—a reinvention of the domestic-public split that feminist anthropology has so successfully critiqued (Bourque and Warren 1982). Clearly, in the Mayan case, the politics of generations—their specific experiences of economic migration, revolutionary government, civil war, and peace processes—have been part of a synergistic relation between community and national politics.

This analysis suggests that the ideological diversities of the Pan-Mayan Movement—especially the community development and shamanic groups versus the university-trained pan-community professionals—are not simply the by-products of community loyalties or differences in the educational opportunities of certain regional language groups. In addition, Mayan constructions of kinship (which structure family authority and cyclical generations) and the person (which place limits on power through the assertion of individual heterogeneity and skepticism of others, and through stress on intermediaries rather than dogmatic leaders) contribute to this diversity.

These findings also suggest that the structural tensions of Mayan kinship are being negotiated at least in some families through the diverse currents within Pan-Mayanism. Perhaps the specialization of members of the Ixim family in branches of Pan-Mayanism that value different talents mutes some of the envy that public success often brings. In promoting contrasting streams of the movement, Alfonso and No'j have made room for various kinds of protagonism that seek to reshape the social worlds inhabited by the nation's indigenous majority.

Clearly, elements of the antiracism, cultural continuity, and hybridity narratives are at work in this phenomenology. The present analysis suggests that antiracism narratives are incomplete to the extent that they focus on "the other"—the racist—without a full consideration of the dynamics and diversity of indigenous identity. As we have seen, the continuity narrative is not as linear as its language suggests. Rather, there is an interweaving of historically deep and tacit elements of Mayan culture with current debates about community and identity. This analysis also suggests a wider construction of mestizaje, one that considers the Pan-Mayan Movement's distrust of this language and, rather than biologizing the process of ethnic mixing or treating it as a fait accompli, traces the transnational cultural flows that at different moments have intensified Mayan identity.

This methodological approach, which focuses on the social history of interlocking individuals as protagonists in the structured worlds around them, has implications for the way we conceptualize the personal and the political, the interplay (rather than any mutually exclusive nature) of continuity and discontinuity, and the relation of individuals to social criticism. It may also shed light on Mayan creativity and on the Mayas' proclivity to generate a tremendous number of leaders only to find that others resist their constituted authority. Many have commented on the proliferation of Mayan organizations in the Pan-Mayan Movement—at each conference, new organizations and networks are launched to transcend the divisions of existing groups. With its focus on cultural rights and the condemnation of widespread bigotry and structural discrimination, the movement's agenda is a diverse one: the demand for increased Mayan representation in all major institutions, from the congress to the mass media, the rejection of the monocultural educational system, the officialization of indigenous languages in all public arenas, the recognition of customary law, the recognition of Mayan religion and religious sites on a par with other religions, and the involvement of Mayas in defining national "development" priorities (Cojtí Cuxil 1997; Esquit Choy and Ochoa 1995; Fischer and Brown 1996; Warren 1998).

Some anthropologists have pointed out that Mayas have not had the political or economic resources to build large formal organizations to press for their goals of a "multiethnic, culturally plural, and multilingual" state. This situation, however, appears to be changing with the involvement of European funders who have opened up new possibilities and generated demands for centralized indigenous organizations through their peace accord projects. Other observers have argued that the proliferation of grassroots organizations is a cultural tactic born of the uncertainties of Guatemalan politics, which brutally punished overt opposition during the civil war. This analysis suggests additional factors: the interplay of the social relations of generational change and the dilemmas of Mayan constructions of personhood and leadership as mediators of political struggle.

Notes

1. I am indebted to Dorothy Holland and Jean Lave for the challenging assignment and for insightful feedback that refined this line of analysis. My thanks also go to my co-participants in the 1995 SAR seminar for stimulating and thoroughly enjoyable exchanges on many of these issues. This essay appeared in a slightly different form in my book *Indigenous Movements and Their Critics* (1998).

2. Examples that come to mind are Scheper-Hughes 1992, D. Tedlock 1993, Behar 1993, and Castañeda 1996.

3. This Western frame of reference is hardly static, as Ariès's (1962) classic work demonstrated. We have also witnessed the politicization of certain generations (such as that of the rebellious 1960s) and the attempts of advertisers to identify or create new generational markets (the "baby boomers" and "generation X"), with varying amounts of success.

4. For example, in San Andrés, festival plays made fun of plantation life. These liminal events were historically updated with the burlesque of contemporary authority figures: at the end of the civil war, costumes included camouflage, and more recently in Chiapas, Mexico, costumes represented forestry officials (Nash 1995). Students have long produced urban variants of these social critiques, such as the Huelga de Dolores, which takes on national authority figures and has often been banned by thin-skinned governments. Oral narratives, such as the Lord of the Wilds (or *rajaw juyu*) genre, focused on moral retribution. All Ladinos and those Mayas who engaged in nontraditional work, women who slept across ethnic lines, and anyone who engaged in incest were punished for

misdeeds in a volcano hell that took the form of a plantation where the punishment was eternal work (Warren 1989).

5. In one key drama, enacted at Holy Week, a Ladino-like figure—Xutio, San Simón, or Judas, as he is alternatively called—takes on local men in rough mock battles through the town. Later he takes effigy form and is given candles and offerings by petitioners in a shrine at the jail. At the end of Holy Week, Xutio is hung high on the Calvario church's facade. After the resurrection, the figure is lowered, torn apart limb from limb, and burned behind the jail by townspeople. Clearly this figure has an ethnic dimension, and just as clearly, the polysemy of the symbolism is not exhausted by an ethnic reading. See Nash 1968 and Warren 1989 for analyses of this figure in different communities.

6. This was a common pattern in the highlands. See Falla 1978, Brintnall 1979, and Wilson 1995 for details on Catholic Action in other regions.

7. I remember making this decision quite strategically in 1970 as I cut off interviewees eager to discuss pedidas in favor of what I saw as more important public rituals and formal institutions. Feminist anthropology made the implications of this selectivity increasingly clear to me. See Bourque and Warren 1982.

8. For other comparative case studies, see Warren 1993.

9. Early in Pan-Mayanism, the saint societies were rejected as well. They were seen as another instance of Spanish colonialism, in contrast to the autochthonous character of shamanism. That the state offered financial incentives for saint society processions and rituals to spur tourism further stigmatized these organizations. More recently, with the goal of revitalizing councils of elders, there has been a reassessment of the contribution of the civil-religious hierarchy (see Raxche' Rodríguez Guaján 1989; Pop Caal 1992; Esquit Choy and Ochoa 1995).

10. Perhaps Don Luis saw the irony, too, in Alfonso's decision to mark his son's high-school graduation with both a Mayan ceremony and the traditional graduation mass favored by urban youths.

11. Dennis Tedlock (1983) put this innovative idea to great use in his analysis of Mayan hermeneutics.

4

From Women's Suffering to Women's Politics
Reimagining Women after Nepal's 1990 Pro-Democracy Movement

Dorothy Holland and Debra Skinner

Like the other chapters in this volume, ours began with the study of contentious practices in a particular time and place—a Hindu women's festival in a rural area of central Nepal. In the area we call Naudada,[1] women used the Tij festival as an opportunity to criticize Nepali laws and cultural practices that privileged men. During the years when political dissent was dangerous, the festival was also occasionally a place where subversive songs against the government were aired. In the theory guiding us, not every argument, fight, biting comment, or other form of contentious local practice is significant, only those that interrelate with long-term, translocal, enduring struggles. Critical commentary voiced at local Tij festivals has been important in, and shaped by, ongoing gender struggles and political conflicts in the district and the nation.

Here we follow remarkable changes in women's dissent during the late 1980s and early 1990s, a period that coincided with the growing expression of political unrest across the country. In 1990, protests and demonstrations by the Pro-Democracy (or People's) Movement led the king of Nepal to acquiesce in replacing the 30-year-old, repressive, single-party panchayat system of government with multiple parties and popular elections. Especially consequential for the Tij festival were the diminished controls on political expression. Under the new conditions, criticism of the government no longer endangered an author's freedom. In the festival of 1990, the women's groups composed and sang mostly *dukha* (hardship) songs, similar to those that one of us (Skinner) had earlier heard during the 1986 festival. In 1991, they composed and sang mostly songs of a different type—*raajniti* (political) songs. In addition, a Tij singing group composed entirely of schoolgirls and based on political party affiliation rather than on neighborhood and kinship ties appeared for the first time in Naudada. Earlier that year, a procession of women had marched through Naudada shouting for equal rights and for better treatment of wives and daughters. Also, a group of irate women had banded together to threaten a local man known to drink excessively and abuse his wife. The complaints of the marchers and of the women's posse were old themes from Tij songs, but the forms of contentious practice (the march and the threats) were new.

In examining such changes, social practice theory guides attention to two sets of dense relations: one between local contentious practices and enduring struggles, and the other between these practices and subjectivities. The focus in this chapter is on the latter set of relations, on "history in person." For the women in the area of our study, Tij songs and other practices related to the festival have special significance as media of both political action and self-understanding. Changes in the songs reverberated not only in the shaping of contentious behavior but also in the formulating of personal issues and concerns.

In the analysis of Tij songs that follows, we look closely at the articulation or orchestration of the parties to the struggles depicted in the songs. In particular, we draw upon "dialogism," a way of conceptualizing social and intimate life articulated by M. M. Bakhtin and his associates and adherents (e.g., Holquist 1990). Dialogism posits that human existence is continually constituted in dialogues carried out both in the social world and in inner speech. It pays attention to the relations among participants in the dialogues, and it assumes that the boundaries of identification can shift. Viewed through the lens provided by dialogism, Tij songs critically depict the adversaries who cause women pain and deny them resources. Relying upon Bakhtin's notions of authorship and orchestration, we explore the songs' positioning of self among their casts of characters.[2] This analysis of the songs helps in understanding the texture of contentiousness and the permeability of the boundaries between the participants, both before and after the Pro-Democracy Movement. Through improvisations that responded to the changing political climate, the makers of Tij songs contributed to a dramatic shift in their collective and intimate identities.

THE TIJ FESTIVAL

The Tij festival in some form is most likely several hundred years old, predating the migration of Nepal's Hindu population from northern India. Although recent anthropological research has attended to the festival's significance for gendered and other kinds of contention, in the earlier literature it was described and analyzed as part of a sequence of religious rituals referred to as the Tij–Rishi Panchami complex (Bennett 1983; Bouillier 1982; Goodman 1981).[3] These descriptions included the dancing and singing that occurs on the day of the festival, but they contextualized these activities within the religious observances—fasting, performing *pujaa* (worship), and ritual bathing —that, in addition to the feast on the night before Tij, take place over a four-day period. They interpreted this series of activities in light of Hindu religious texts, explaining that the rituals call for an emulation of the ideals of womanhood represented by the devotion of Parvati to her husband, Shiva, and of the acts of atonement performed by the wives of a group of Hindu holy men called the Rishi. By fasting on Tij Day, women act to ensure long lives for their husbands. By ritually bathing on the day of Rishi Panchami, they act to absolve themselves of sins associated with menstruation.

Lynn Bennett (1983:218–234), who presented the most complex of the earlier published analyses, described the Tij portion of Tij–Rishi Panchami as a time of license—a reversal of what is expected during the rest of the year, a deviation from the "Hindu ideal of womanly behavior" (p. 225). Women are supposed to be shy and modest, yet the dancing they do on Tij Day, representing Parvati's seduction of Shiva, is considered erotic and highly suggestive. Bennett interpreted the sexuality expressed at the festival as being licensed by the ascetic rituals that bracket the performance (i.e., the fasting before and during, and the ritual bathing after) and therefore regulate it. She argued that these rituals, done on behalf of husbands, could be viewed as controlling women's sexuality and reaffirming patrilineal principles (Bennett 1983:222–225). Bennett went on to suggest that the women who perform Tij–Rishi Panchami rituals "have accepted the restrictions placed on them by the dominant ascetic and patrilineal ideology of Hinduism" (1983:234).

At the time of our study, Naudada was some eight hours west by bus from the area close to Kathmandu where Bennett had done her research more than a decade earlier. Bennett and others had paid little attention to the songs that were being produced for the festival or to the groups that were authoring these songs. In Naudada these songs criticized the structural position of women in Naudada and recounted the dilemmas and deprivations that subordination caused in women's lives (see also Ahearn 1991; Enslin 1998; Holland and Skinner 1995a; Skinner and Holland 1998; Skinner, Holland, and Adhikari 1994). Thus, in Naudada, the Tij festival appeared to have a quite different relationship to history-in-person than it did in the earlier descriptions. It was one of the few forums in which women could publicly criticize Nepali society and its treatment of women. Moreover, judging from the energy and attention that women devoted to different segments of Tij–Rishi Panchami and from their talk about the different components,[4] the festival and its songs lay at the core of their engagement with the complex.

In our intensive ethnographic study of Tij, we were struck by the long-term significance of this event for its participants. Older theories in anthropology would have treated Tij as a ritual that managed contentiousness by annually siphoning off the frustration and irritation accrued by women as holders of inferior social positions. Our research suggested a different analysis. Echoing Bennett's analysis but focusing on the content of the songs, not on the singing and dancing, men both in Naudada and elsewhere in the country spoke to us of the festival as a time of license during which women were *allowed* to air their complaints. Especially in the years preceding 1991, Tij songs were constrained in public to the time of the festival. Singing the songs in public at any other time of year was said to be a sin *(paap)*. Nonetheless, women made private use of the songs year-round. Prompting our studies in 1990 and 1991, Skinner's 1985–1986 interviews and research with girls and boys in Naudada noted that the girls frequently used Tij songs and other folk songs to convey their senses of themselves (Skinner 1989, 1990). In our later research, we learned that women sang these songs to themselves year-round; the songs were cultural forms that they used continually to understand themselves as women (Holland and Skinner 1995a, 1995b).

We credit women's participation in the production of Tij songs and their reliance upon these songs for self-understanding with cultivating a collective critical consciousness, and we suspect that this consciousness has considerable historical depth. Even the oldest women we interviewed—those in their sixties and seventies and one 86-year-old—remembered critical Tij songs from their youth. Before the Pro-Democracy Movement, the public expression of this consciousness had been almost completely constrained to the time of the festival, but in the wake of the movement it provided a basis for new forms of contentious practice. In 1991, women formed a procession in Naudada and marched to the *tati*, a public center of the area, where they shouted demands for better treatment and equal rights. The practice of demonstrations, especially ones carried out by women, was new for the area, but the demands were not. They had been given social and subjective shape year after year at the time of the Tij festival.

After returning from Nepal in 1990, we heard news of political parties and feminist groups that convinced us of the validity of our analysis. These groups had begun writing and publishing Tij songs in small, cheap booklets sold in bookstalls. In 1990, we located five Tij songbooks published by such groups in the regional centers and bazaar towns along the highway. None was in use in Naudada, but a year later we found eight times as many songbooks in the bazaars, at least five of which showed up in Naudada. The songbooks prompted further investigations. We found that groups associated with the newly legal political parties, both in the regional centers and, to a lesser extent, in Kathmandu, were paying attention to the Tij festival.[5] They and feminist groups were involved in producing Tij songbooks. Political activists were seeing the festival, especially in rural areas of Nepal, as a place for instruction in communist and/or feminist perspectives. In 1991, we devoted time not only to locating songbooks and observing their use by individuals and groups in Naudada and elsewhere, as we had in 1990, but also to tracing the songbooks back to their producers. Our interviews with the authors of the songbooks, described in detail elsewhere (Holland and Skinner 1995a), left us with no doubt that the writers, many of whom had been involved with the Tij festival before becoming active in the political group sponsoring the songbooks, saw Tij as a vital connection to the hearts and minds of rural women. Appreciating their enduring significance as a medium of gendered conflict, political actors sought to use Tij songs as a resource for their struggle.

We turn now to describing the festival, partly in order to convey how a one-day event could be so important.

THE EMOTIONAL AND PRODUCTIVE SPACE OF THE TIJ FESTIVAL

The outward signs of the festivals we attended started weeks before the day of Tij. Women of the various Tij groups began collaboratively composing and rehearsing the songs they would sing on Tij Day. Adult women and girls not in school composed songs as they worked together in the fields. Schoolgirls worked on songs at school. Both groups joined together on a neighbor's porch at night to rework the songs and practice the singing and the dancing they would perform in public on the day of Tij. These night sessions provide a beginning point for describing the special time of Tij. They were important times when not only the content of the songs but also the emotional atmosphere of the festival began to take form.

The nighttime practice sessions were not always easy for us to get to. Less familiar with the terrain than our local friends traveling with us, we had to pick our way carefully as we followed the narrow trails and eroded paths made slick by the ending, but still significant, monsoon rains. In the darkness, we passed along the edges of fields where women had worked earlier in the day.[6] Scheduled according to the lunar calendar, the festival falls during the time of the year (sometime between mid-August and mid-September) when the rice plants in the irrigated fields must be weeded and the upland dry rice crop harvested.

Owing to the distance, our trips to the practice sessions sometimes took as long as 45 minutes. We had to travel along and across the set of interconnecting ridges that linked the hamlet where we lived to one of the other 30 clusters of houses, or *gaon*s (hamlets), of Naudada.[7] The Tij participants, in contrast, had only to walk the relatively short paths to the houses of their neighbors, almost always their relatives, who lived in their gaon. The Tij groups were made up of girls and young women—the core group composed of members aged 10 to 25— who all came from the same gaon.

In the ethnographic terminology used for Nepal, Naudada is a mixed-caste, predominantly Hindu area.[8] "Mixed caste" distinguishes it in the literature from those areas in Nepal where one of Nepal's many ethnic groups (e.g., Tamang, Gurung, Magar, Sherpa) predominates. "Hindu" signals the importance of caste and Hinduism in the everyday lives of the people of the area.[9] Each gaon through which we traveled was composed of extended families related to one another patrilineally. Owing to the practice of caste endogamy, these gaons were for the most part homogeneous by caste, and thus the Tij groups made up by the daughters of the gaons were homogeneous by caste as well.[10]

We were guests at the practice sessions, sitting in as the girls and young women, who were sisters or otherwise consanguineously related, went about their task. Playing off their practice of addressing one another as *didi* (older sister) or *bahini* (younger sister), we refer to these groups as the *didi-bahini* of the gaon. On the porches, small girls too young to participate stayed in the feeble light of kerosene lanterns, listening to the singing and watching the dancing. So did boys and a few men, though they hovered on the darkened periphery. Some of the older women who had married into the gaon years before participated in the singing and dancing, but the younger women carried on the major activity.

The young women who had recently married were especially important to these practice sessions. Because hamlets were composed of patrilineally linked males and exogamous practices required that people marry outside of any consanguineal relations within seven generations, and because of the still strong preference for marrying within one's *jaat* (caste), parents often married their daughters into families living long distances away. All the daughters of the gaon faced the prospect of one day being married to a man whom they were unlikely to know and whose house was potentially hours or even days away from their *maita*, the family home in which they had grown up. At the time of the Tij festival, recently married women and women who had only one or two young children were allowed to return to their maita from their *ghar,* or husband's home. This was the one opportunity when the young married women were definitely to be permitted to return to their maita. It was their opportunity for respite from work and for ears sympathetic to the situation they faced in their ghar. The returning women were greeted with strong emotion by their didi-bahini and felt relieved to be among friends who listened to their travails in their ghar. It was not unusual for one or more of their stories to become the topic of a Tij song the group composed that year.

At the practice sessions, the didi-bahini were reunited as a group in a setting that was, for women of Naudada, unusual—an informal, nighttime gathering. While preparing for the Tij festival, women had liberties not enjoyed the rest of the year. Ordinarily, they were not free to meet at night. Seemingly intent on having a good time, the women at the practice sessions joked, composed and practiced songs, and, as the day of Tij approached, danced—another activity, as Bennett pointed out, normally considered inappropriate for Hindu women. The jokes, dancing, and playful efforts to get us to dance created a festive, somewhat ribald atmosphere. The special emotional atmosphere of Tij grew from these practice sessions and, in no small part, from the poignancy of the reunion of the didi-bahini groups with their out-married sisters. Also discernible among the mix of feelings was an air of excitement about the songs that were being created. The women were concerned to create songs that their listeners would find interesting and that expressed a sense of competition, vying for the attention of the crowd with the songs of other groups that would be there on Tij Day.

The songs themselves, the ones that the groups were making up and practicing on those nights of the practice sessions, were affecting as well.[11] Many vividly depicted moving scenes in the lives of women, situations to which the women of Naudada were not strangers. The songs cast these situations as unfair. Consider the following lines from a song that attracted much attention from the crowd in 1990:[12]

> ### Song 1
> *Listen to the description of the drunken husband.*
> *Rising in the morning, he goes down to the hotel,*

Who will do the household chores?
The hotel girl has probably [already] made the tea [for the day].
The raksi *[distilled liquor] has finished all the money.*
The household wealth has all gone to the hironi *[a cinema*
role; here refers to the hotel girl].
The most fertile land is all finished because of his drinking
raksi.
Whatever money you have, it is not enough,
Two or even four bottles of raksi is not enough for you.
If I say, "Don't drink," he replies, "I'm not drinking your
father's [property]."
The most fertile land is gone and still he does not know [how
much he has spent].
The best land is gone because of the drunkard husband,
How will we spend our lives?

Both this song and the one to follow are examples of dukha (hardship, suffering) songs, a major type of Tij song that we explore in more detail later in the chapter. Whereas the preceding song criticizes the limited resources and rights of a wife caught in a bad marriage to a drunkard who wastes the family's money and land, the next one denounces the privileged treatment of the son over the daughter.

Song 2
[The daughter says:] I rose in the morning to pick flowers,
But did not pick them because they were covered by dew.
Parents just keep the daughters to do work at home,
But not even a small piece of courtyard [i.e., land] is given [to
daughters].
[The parents say:] The small piece of courtyard is needed to dry
the paddy,
Go, daughter, to your husband's house to get your property.
[The daughter says:] We have to go empty-handed [to our hus-
band's home],
The brothers fence in their property.
Brothers' clothes are so many that they rot away in a box,
But when they have to give us a single cloth, tears come to their eyes.

Tij songs described women's lives with passionate words and images and in ways that resonated with stories told to us and to others of actual life events. We heard young girls recounting how hard their older sisters cried as they were being carried away on the marriage litter to their husband's house. We witnessed a woman telling and, on several occasions, demonstrating how she, with her fifth child, still an infant, hid in a nearby field, fearing that the baby would cry and attract the attention of her enraged, drunken husband—a man who, regardless of what she had to say, gambled away the land upon which they depended. We listened to a son's story of his mother, who was literally displaced by a co-wife. She and her son were moved from the main part of their house to a small addition built on the side. She had to watch as her new co-wife enjoyed the husband's resources and affection that she once had—a deprivation, according to the young son, that led her nearly to madness for several years.

Tij songs not only publicized stories such as these but also interjected a strongly critical commentary into their telling. They contested the system of gender privilege instituted in Nepali law, carried out in social practice, and interpreted through religious texts and teachings. They decried women's limited rights to inherit land, their lesser access to education, and their constant vulnerability, under polygyny, to having to share their husband's resources and affections with a co-wife. At the time of our research, women could inherit land only under rare circumstances. Legally, the right of a husband to take a second wife was limited to certain situations (see Bennett 1979:63). For instance, a man was allowed to marry a second woman and bring her into the house as a co-wife when no child had yet been born to the first wife or remained alive after 10 years of marriage. Yet even in cases of women who were aware of their legal rights (and many were not) and who could have brought charges against a husband who had illegally married a co-wife, none, to our knowledge, ever brought charges. For one thing, they were dependent upon their husbands and their husbands' families for food and shelter. In practice, despite the rarity of permissible situations set out by the law, little stood in the way of a husband who wished to bring in another wife.

These were the sorts of concerns the Tij groups took in song to the festivals.

TIJ DAY

On the day of the festival, the Tij groups came together to the public tati, a flat space surrounded by a temple, several community buildings, and the steep hillsides characteristic of the area. Women came dressed in beautiful red and pink saris, and young girls in their best blouses and skirts, to sing and dance for the crowd that had gathered.

In 1991 especially, the tati was extremely crowded. At times there were as many as four groups of singers and dancers performing simultaneously, and 400 or so closely packed onlookers. It was hard to see. The spectators, both men and women, jostled and elbowed one another in order to glimpse the dancers over the many umbrellas held up against the hot sun. Some people sat on the broad steps leading up to the temple; others perched in trees. Children ran to and fro. At times, parts of the listening crowd surged to see a new group that had just come in or to hear a song that was attracting particular attention. As the day went on, excitement seemed to mount.

With the onlookers surrounding them, the women sat on mats laid out on the ground and sang their songs as one of their number danced. Each dancer arose in her turn, tied a bracelet of small bells on her ankle, and began the stylized dance associated with Tij. The dancer stamped her foot rhythmically, rotating herself in place, and made graceful, flowing gestures with her hands and arms. Accompanying the dancer, the group sang songs in loud voices.

The songs varied little in melody, rhythm, rhyme, or structure. All were composed of a number of rhyming couplets, and each line of the couplet was repeated twice before the singers moved on to the next line. The onlookers reacted to the songs and dancing. Sometimes they responded with words, evaluating the songs with friends. Sometimes they responded with their rapt attention and even tearful expressions, and sometimes with movement as they wandered away or rushed to hear another group.

The day on the tati ended, as it had the previous two times we had observed the festival, with the remaining groups being displaced at twilight by an activity associated with the Newar caste, one of those in the middle range of the caste hierarchy. First, the raucous horn announcing the *lakhe* (a masked dancer who represents an evil male ghost) could be heard in the distance coming closer and closer. Soon, the masked figure, scarves tied to his wrists, burst into the area and began his dance. In 1991, one of the Tij groups tried to keep the crowd's attention by putting up two dancers at the same time, but this novelty worked only briefly. Eventually, the group gave up and went away.

THE TURN TO RAAJNITI SONGS IN 1991

The Tij festival of 1991 differed from that of 1990 in ways other than the unusual attempt by a Tij group to continue singing despite the entrance of the lakhe.[13] The most significant change was the preponderance in 1991 of raajniti, or political, songs. In 1986, Skinner had heard only a few of these songs. Again in 1990, the songs were mostly dukha songs. The following example is a raajniti song that was composed for and sung at the 1991 Tij festival in Naudada. It is a sarcastic song about the Nepali Congress Party.[14]

> *Song 3*
>
> *Sisters of Nepal, we need Congress.*
> *We can say that rivers and countries are common [to India*
>   *and Nepal].*
> *You can cheat the people.*
> *If you want to be rich, you need Congress.*
> *Businessmen can sell goods at a high price,*
> *Therefore, Congress is needed in this Nepal.*
> *You can smuggle and murder.*
> *If you want a job, you need Congress.*
> *You can fire communist people from their jobs.*
> *Poor people who have nothing need Congress.*
> *You can rape the women freely,*
> *Therefore sisters, we need Congress.*
> *You can terrify, murder, and loot.*
> *Therefore all people need Congress.*
> *We faced up to any type of foes,*
> *Best wishes for Tij 2048.*

Questioning older women and men, we heard about raajniti songs remembered from more than 40 years earlier. Raajniti songs, like dukha songs, had been a recognized genre within the productive capacity of Tij groups for decades at least. The elimination of reprisals for criticism of the government and the lessening of danger, at least as people perceived the situation, came fully in 1991, and with their arrival, external constraints on the singing of raajniti songs were virtually abolished. In the festival of 1991, raajniti songs were the songs women wanted to sing.[15]

Told from the perspective of women, the raajniti songs, like the dukha songs before them, threw into relief inequitable relations between men and women and marked out the position of women in such a world. Nonetheless, despite their attention to the same issues as those raised in dukha songs, raajniti songs had a very different feel to them. In the context of Nepali history, the raajniti songs provided a basis for a shift in history in person. With the help of Bakhtin, we devote the remainder of the chapter to this shift and its consequences.

DIALOGISM AND THE SONGS OF TIJ

In Bakhtin's conception, selves are always in practice. They are always caught up in dialogic relations. Moreover, the dialogues are "authored" through cultural genres. They are figured in the words and acts of Tij songs or some other cultural genre. Out of the welter of senses of self potentially evoked by the activities and events of daily life, these genres foreground particular identities. Moreover, they cultivate a view of the world from a particular social position. Raajniti songs in 1991, for example, were written from the social position of *educated* women and offered a political perspective on women's issues.

Bakhtin (1981) suggested that selves are "orchestrations" of the words and voices of others. In this process of authoring, a self exists chiefly in indirect ways: in the manner in which others are positioned relative to one another and to self, in the commentary on others conveyed by the author's presentations of them, and in the relationship the author develops with her audience. Identities, in this view, are orchestrations authored in the terms and story lines of the cultural genres at hand and in the words and voices of socially known others.

As the reader has likely noticed from the songs reproduced earlier, dukha songs present self in dynamic constellations or orchestrations of figures from the domestic world, and raajniti songs, from the world of party politics and state officials. A closer look shows that the issues addressed in dukha songs and responses to them take place *within* the song world, the world depicted by the song; for raajniti songs, the potentiality of the dialogue is *between* the author or narrator and the audience addressed by the song. The contested borderland of subjectivity, the "live" versus "frozen" terrain of relations between self and others, in other words, lies in different realms for the two types of Tij songs.

Selves in a Dynamic Constellation of Others

The dukha songs that we recorded or were told about all had to do with domestic relations—with such things as unfair assignments of domestic work and the male bias in decision making about family and household resources, including particularly about which children would receive formal education. They also criticized the structural features that privileged males and circumscribed women's position in the household.

This world of domestic relations is populated in the songs by people identified according to their kin relationship to the internal narrator of the song. In several songs, for instance, the mother-in-law is the primary antagonist. We hear, in the following song (which is at least 80 years old), not just about the mother-in-law but about all of the adult kin in the woman's maita as well. The *gurau*, we were told, was a powerful shaman able to change his form, but the figure appears in this song as a symbol of the narrator's husband.

> *Song 4*
> *[Daughter:] In the dark month of Saun,*
> *Mother, open the door.*
> *[Mother:] You worthless daughter who ran away from your*
>   *home,*
> *I won't open the door.*
> *[Daughter:] With a bundle of wet, stinging nettles,*
> *The mother-in-law would beat me.*
> *The gurau has come from the other side [the next village].*
> *Mother, please open the door.*
> [The whole song is repeated, substituting different kin
> terms for mother and daughter in the line that follows.
> The daughter, in other words, pleads in turn with all the

relatives who would be found in her maita: her father,
her elder brother and his wife, her younger brother and
his wife.]
The gurau has reached here.
Please open the door.
[The singer, in this case, did not finish the song. She
explained that the mother finally opened the door, but
too late. When the daughter was halfway in and halfway
out of the door, the gurau snatched her.]

In this song and the next, the role of the narrator is submerged.
Instead, we hear the direct speech of a woman, here in the role first of
a daughter imploring her mother and then of a kinswoman seeking aid
from the other members of her kin group. We hear the voice of the
mother replying to the daughter, and later the voices of the other kin,
and then the daughter once more describing her plight and making a
plea. Substituted as they are for one another in the stanzas, and always
giving the same response, the woman's kin present a unified refusal to
shelter her from the injurious conditions of her husband's family's
home. The wife/daughter has nowhere to turn.

In Song 4, the "Gurau" song, the wife/daughter plays out a scene
that is often repeated in the dukha songs and learns the lesson that her
family of origin may well refuse to shelter her against the abuses she
faces in her husband's family. The next song depicts another potent
scene in a wife/daughter's life—the giving of the daughter to her
future in-laws. Again, a constellation of kin is arrayed against her, a set
of others who are unmoved by the woman/daughter who narrates the
song. Her subjective experience of the situation is of little moment to
them. Only her friends care.

Song 5
They [the guests] have come to ask for her hand in marriage,
*   but she didn't know.*
I say, what kinds of guests are these?
My parents call me [to meet the guests] saying they've come for
*   some work.*
Could it be that my parents' intention was to make me marry?
With these thoughts, I went to the forest.

The whole day, thoughts churned in my man [heart/mind].
Returning from the forest [I saw] grains drying [in the court-
    yard in preparation for a special occasion].
My brothers and sisters began to say we'll eat kasaaro *[sweet-*
    meat served at weddings].
Coming back from the forest, I did my daily work.
My friends began to tease me.
At four o'clock in the afternoon the wedding party came,
This removed my happy look.
My best friends began to gather around me,
They started to cry seeing my face.
At twelve noon, I was put in the palanquin.
They nearly dropped me in the Sisa River.
At six in the evening, we reached the husband's home.
To me, the whole world had become dark.
I gave birth to a son, Rajeshwor, and a daughter, Laksmi.
My friends are scattered east and west.
"You come from this side, friends, to the Damauli gate,
I'll come from this side to meet you."
The friends said, "We'll come," but they had to cross the Sisa
    River.
I remember my best friends and cried [because I couldn't cross
    the river].
When the Sisa River rises during the monsoon it seems as big as
    the Gandaki.
Friends, we've done all we can do; our lives are finished.

Here the powerful others of the song world—the young woman's parents and the wedding party that has come to fetch her—relentlessly play out their roles. Their generic actions are signaled simply by the mention of special foods and the bringing of the marriage litter on which they will transport her to her husband's family's home. We get no sense of any individuality or subjectivity on the part of those powerful others, and they "address," in Bakhtin's sense of "act toward," the woman in a way that seems totally oblivious to her feelings and reactions.

In this constellation of self and others, the daughter's friends provide a counterpoint to powerful others. They respond to the narrator's apprehension of the situation. They have empathy for her. They agree to what she asks. They eventually come to share her situation. She talks to them inclusively as "we." "We've done all we can do, our lives are finished."

In raajniti songs, the endemic conflicts or struggles for women are distributed over a very different social constellation. Lines from one of these raajniti songs clearly show this point.

> ### Song 6
> *Everywhere people say* bahudal *[the multiparty system] has come.*
> *Oh, brothers, tell us your advice.*
> *Bahudal came after discarding the panchayat [government system].*
> *In this time, let's do something.*
> *In Khaireni bazaar, a telephone booth,*
> *Everyone listens to the news.*
> *It's the month of Baisak 2048,*
> *All over the country, people here and there talk about the [past] election....*
> *After [Congress] won the election, dukha [problems] came to the people.*
> *Look everyone, see how expensive goods have become.*
> *[Soon] one* pathi *of rice will cost 50 rupees.*
> *Without food the suffering people will die.*
> *One liter of cooking oil costs 90 rupees....*
> *During the campaign, the [Congress] leaders visited all the villages,*
> *Congress ate by selling the flag [profited by selling Nepal's resources].*
> *Everybody cast a vote for Congress thinking they would have* sukha *[happiness],*
> *Now the people will survive by breaking stones [i.e., doing hard manual labor].*
> *Taking money, people cast [their vote] for the tree [the symbol for Congress],*
> *Now the poor will have dukha.*
> *Rich people will have the money,*
> *Poor people will not have money.*

The rich people are Congress mandale [i.e., the old panchayat
 people have become members of the Congress party].[16]
What the red flag of Congress has done so far!
Congress suppresses the people more these days.
All the poor people are left behind.
[Those] Congress asses are dominating [us].
Now the poor people have to tolerate it.
The industrialists started to weave malmal [high-quality
 clothes],
[And now] all the poor people can't buy it.
Not only this, they tried to eliminate our women [by selling them
 into prostitution in India],
The big mandales did this.
Hey, sisters, let's arise in every village,
Let's arise to destroy Congress....
The women are dominated.
The composition is done by man [heart/mind] and written by
 the pen.
Good-bye to our revolutionary friends.

The world of raajniti songs is populated not by mothers-in-law who demand too much work or husbands who threaten to bring in co-wives or fathers who send their daughters to unhappy marriages. Instead, it is populated by political parties that do nothing to improve women's rights, by former government officials and their mandale who sell women into prostitution, by "the people," who protest the favoring of rich people and industrialists, by women as an interest group that demands equal rights, and by India, which bad politicians allow to exploit Nepal.[17] Self is embedded in this world as a neglected, mistreated, gendered citizen who is rising up to deny the Congress party control of the government.

Shifting Boundaries

Tij songs serve as a medium, albeit a muted one, of social positioning. The songs identify self and others in a world of gender relations and evaluate distinct types of persons making claims about good and bad. In Bakhtin's conceptualization, however, discourses and the genres associated with them do more than position people. Dialogism directs us not only to the constellations of self-among-others that the songs portray but also to the openings discernible between and among them. The songs provide a dynamic potential for the boundaries between self and the characters in the song to shift over time through incorporation of the words and voices of others. Not only is it possible for the constellation of self and others to shift with the entry and exit of characters, but the self can also draw closer to, become more enmeshed with, or move away from particular others. One of the exciting aspects of dialogism for the issues raised during the School of American Research seminar is the subtle means it posits for identity reconfiguration in contentious situations.

Dialogism pays special attention to the variety of ways in which self-authoring incorporates the words and voices of others (Bakhtin 1981, 1990). Bakhtin grants importance to how the voices of the others that inhabit the self are depicted, arguing that the portrayals index the composition of the "I-for-myself" and the "other-in-me." In more fluid compositions, the voices of others are not simply copied but personalized through the author's commentary. Authoritative voices, by contrast, are taken into the self in encapsulated, insular form, producing a rigid boundary between the "I-for-myself" and the "other-in-me." In cases in which the distant others are less powerful, the self authors them as objects—in Holquist's (1990:34) words, "mere others" or, in the worst of cases, "mere things, lacking any subjectivity."

Bakhtin and Volosinov (Volosinov 1986 [1929]) scrutinized cultural texts such as Tij songs for what they called the "reported speech" of others. Reported speech is both a description of what someone said—that is, did linguistically—and the author's commentary on that person. In Bakhtin's writings, reported speech is an exemplary means by which dialogic others are related in *inner* speech and through which others become either increasingly personalized and drawn into the "I-for-myself" or increasingly distinct, distant, and crystallized as the "other-in-me." In *public* speech, the reported speech of others likewise is commented upon by the speaker's tone or gestures of disdain or respect and is identified either as (increasingly) separate from me/us or as (increasingly) part of me/us. Reported speech evokes associations with social power in any regard, but it also can carry the infusions given it by the speaker. Because the teller or author of reported speech is the source of both the description and the commentary, Bakhtin surmises that he, she, or it is the author of the orchestration of the multiple voices, of the relations between selves and others, that are contained in the text.[18]

To the extent that the forms for reporting another's speech reproduce it faithfully, Volosinov (1986 [1929]) wrote, the form follows a "linear style." This style contains no authorial commentary. The author's commentary does not infuse the reported speech and so maintains the strictest possible boundaries between the author's voice and the voice of the person or group whose speech is being reported. In linear style, truth telling—a direct reporting—is what is important. In "pictorial style," in contrast, the author's commentary on the other's behavior is indicated. If the genre allows a pictorial style, then the author's voice is insinuated through the depiction into the voice of the other. The boundaries between the self and the persons depicted are thus less distinct in this style. When even more enmeshed, the author has begun to personalize the words and the voice of the other, producing a hybrid, truly dialogic speaker.

What of the others who populate Tij songs? Do the groups authoring these songs report the voices of husbands and mothers-in-law solely with an eye to faithful representation and so maintain a rigid boundary between the "I-for-myself" and the "other-in-me"? Or is there fluidity between the author and these others? Is there rigidity in the relation of the authoring (self) to the other or, to the contrary, more open-endedness?

Closely allied to the question of how speech is reported and acts depicted is the dimension of subjectivity. What sort of subjectivity does the author assign the characters, including the narrator? Do the accounts of other characters convey some sort of subjectivity on a par with the author's, or do these remain simply generic, formulaic characters? By definition, the more "monologic" an account, the more dominant the author's voice and the less subjectivity allowed the characters she is authoring. At the extreme, characters are fixed and frozen, formulaic, uttering and doing nothing at odds with their stereotypic characterizations. Or, in another form of monologue, they are simply the pliable objects of the author, lacking any integrity of their own.

Such characters yield little to the possibility of a changing configuration of self to other. Frozen characters bespeak frozen relations. The author may regard the speech of another as authoritative—owing to office (e.g., the speech of the Pope) or to genre (e.g., the speech of generic figures of folktales)—and therefore beyond authorial commentary and evaluation. In such cases, relations between the self and others are arrested, in a sense, or, in a translation of the words of Vygotsky (1960:137), "fossilized." The relations are crystallized, with no movement or opening for movement.

Characters who have their own subjectivity, on the other hand, have an open-endedness about them that approaches that of the author's subjectivity. They have, in a sense, a life of their own. They are open and unfinished, as the author is, and the relationship between them remains open and fluid. We might expect opponents in struggle to produce fixed orchestrations with rigid boundaries between themselves and their enemies. On the face of it, we might expect only monologues about those with whom one is in conflict. In the case of contentious practices at the Tij festival, some boundaries are closed, but others are not.

Reported Speech in Tij Songs

At first glance, Tij songs might seem a limited genre for expressing the complex and potentially shifting textures of dialogic relations. Bakhtin differentiated cultural forms according to their potential for representing hybridized voices and selves in a fluid way. Poetry, for example, in his view (Bakhtin 1981), tended to be more monologic than the novel. Because of its form, it could not help presenting characters wholly dominated by the author's intentions, and while those characters could change, the changes could be only external, subject to alterations in the author's life and world. Change in the novel, however, takes on a kind of internal sense arising from the open-endedness, the quasi-subjectivity, granted to characters and their interactions.

Tij songs have aspects that make them likely to be more monologic than novels. They are short. Those we heard and recorded in our research area were bound to a particular rhyme structure, intonation pattern, and melody, and in fact those structures remained constant (Skinner, Holland, and Adhikari 1994). Lyrics were the only variable, the only means by which others could be differentially described and commented upon.[19] Despite the fact that the song form, as compared with the form of the novel, for example, limits the possibilities for authoring the self and its relations to others, we found a suggestive dialogic texture.

In the dukha songs we have presented as examples, relations between selves and others appear rather rigid. The verbal and other actions of the husband, the mother-in-law, the parents, and other kin are generic. Contentious dialogue between the women and those who mistreat them appears to be arrested, paralyzed, or fossilized, at least for the time being. In the examples given so far, the boundaries between self as daughter, or self as daughter-in-law, and the constellation of kin to whom the narrator is related are fixed. The speaker's fluidity lies in her relationship to her friends.

Indicative of the generic feel of the others with whom the narrators struggled was their anonymity. In the dukha songs, no one gave the names of abusive husbands or parents who shortchanged the daughter on her inheritance. Some listeners, undoubtedly, inferred connections between the identity of the woman whose story it was and the likely subjects of her story, but thanks in part to the collaborative authoring of the songs, there was always doubt. Although there were women identified as *sipalu* (expert) in composing Tij songs, and people sometimes guessed whose story was being told, the women never accused anyone in particular, and no one ever had to answer to the accusation. Instead, the songs gave abusive husbands and fathers little individuality. By contrast, in the raajniti, or political, song, the Nepali Congress Party, specific politicians, and the former government were directly named as mistreating women.

There are cases, in both the older and the newer dukha songs, in which the particular person in the kin role is evoked and in which the otherwise generic mother or husband takes on more specific characteristics—some individuality. Husbands are the most likely to be differentiated. There are alcoholic husbands, for example, and husbands who think the wife is not good enough. The following example is an older Tij song about a husband criticizing his dark-skinned wife.

Song 7
[Wife:] People say that Tij has brought happiness.

Give me a sirphula *[a golden hairpiece to wear during Tij].*
[Husband:] Woman, you are too dark,
A sirphula would not suit you.
[Wife:] The Vedic script is black,
So don't read the book [since it too is black].
[Husband:] Woman, you have spoken such things?
I will have a second marriage.
[Wife:] If you have a second marriage,
You won't get such a woman as us [black-skinned women].
You may get a beautiful and skillful woman,
But you won't get a woman as skilled as us.

The depiction of the drunken husband in Song 1, a newer song, is an even better example than Song 7 of a "pictorial" style. Not only does the narrator in Song 1 sometimes take on the direct role of a commentator, asking questions rhetorically such as "Who will do the household chores?" but she also conveys her evaluation of the husband by referring sarcastically to the barmaid in the hotel, with whom he flirts, as a hironi, a cinema role played by a beautiful young heroine.

Still, despite the differentiation of the husbands according to non-generic characteristics in the two songs, the sense of both husbands' actions falls back upon their structural position as the male of the marriage. In the song about the dark-skinned wife, the man refuses the woman's request for jewelry to wear to the Tij festival and instead threatens her with a co-wife or abandonment. Either eventuality, but especially the latter, would seriously endanger the woman's survival, for she lacks any other means of support. The drunken husband likewise retorts from the basis of his privilege as a husband, "I'm not drinking your father's [property]." He says, in other words, "You can say nothing to me about what I do with the land." Thus, the dukha songs range from those in which the woman is in tension with a set of fixed structural positions to those in which the woman is in tension with a husband whose partial individuality is still, in the final analysis, reduced to, or addressed in, his more privileged structural position.

Reported speech in raajniti songs is more curtailed. The others of raajniti songs, the *panchas* (the officials of the opposing political party, the rich people), are generic objects of critical commentary and calls to action. They are presented in a fixed manner. Stock atrocities are attributed to them, and they are assigned little subjectivity. Many of the songs, on first hearing, strike us in fact as straightforward propaganda.[20] The others of the political world depicted in the song text are not the others with whom the authors are fluidly engaged. Instead, the fluid engagement, as we recount in the following section, is with the imagined audience for the songs.

Boundaries with Other Women

Bakhtin brings out another aspect of verbal art that is pertinent here, the relationship between the author proper and the narrator of the tales that are told. This relationship and that between the author and her imagined listeners are additional points where fluidity in the constellation of self and other is possible.

In Tij songs, especially dukha songs, the author proper rarely distinguishes herself from the narrator she creates in song. The author is fully identified with the narrator; they speak from the same position or perspective, usually that of a wife or daughter, and remain within the inside context depicted in the song. Only infrequently does the author comment on the narrator or address remarks to the imagined audience of the narrator's story.[21] It is highly unusual for the author of a dukha song to speak directly to her audience, as she does in the next song (through line 14). In most of the dukha songs we heard, including those discussed earlier, the narrator stays in this position of overt commentator only briefly, if she adopts the position at all. Then she steps "down" into the role of the situated actor, reporting her feelings and actions live from the scene, so to speak. The narrator of the next song waits until the fifteenth line to take this step.

> *Song 8*
>
> *Who embroidered my handkerchief?*
> *In this song, [I'm going to] sing about the uneducated boy.*
> *The boy of Kaliyug is very much a nakkala [i.e., dresses up and acts like a movie "hero"].*
> *He doesn't have a cap on his head, but he allows his hair to grow long.*
> *After combing his hair, he puts the comb in his pocket.*

> *The boys of today are always found in* rodi *[places where boys*
> *and girls gather to sing, an institution associated with*
> *Gurungs of Nepal].*
> *After going to the rodi, he pours and drinks raksi continuously.*
> *If he sees a girl, he acts like a nakkala.*
> *If he sees a girl, he calls her with his eyes.*
> *The housewife starts to shout.*
> *He orders his wife to work a lot.*
> *He sends letters to the village girls.*
> *The husband's letter came half-filled with songs.*
> *The wife started to weep after seeing the letter [the husband*
> *mistakenly put the letter to his girlfriend in the wrong*
> *envelope].*
> *[Wife:] You bring a co-wife; we will throw cow dung together*
> *[a satirical line that the co-wife will be a help to her].*
> *One head and two* namlos; *there is no difference.*[22]
> *If wives get along, both will shout from two sides [to the*
> *husband].*
> *Then the husband will realize when he loses consciousness.*

In dukha songs, the authors are fully identified not only with the narrators but also with their imagined audience. In raajniti songs, in contrast, the authors and narrators address their audience directly, speaking as gendered, political actors—a position and perspective distinctive from those of the dukha songs—and their identification with their audience is ambivalent.

The position that the narrator takes in the following song is common to raajniti songs. She is in the overt role of a knowledgeable commentator who informs those listening about the patterns of historical events and the meaning of present circumstances.

Song 9

The panchas ate the flesh and even the blood [of the people],
At last we brought bahudal *[the multiparty system].*
In the time of the panchayat, women were left behind [i.e., fell
behind].
Brothers and sisters, listen to what they had done.

When a daughter was born and reached the age of seven,
They used to force her to marry.
But now the age of seven is the appropriate time for daughters
*   to go to school.*
Daughters had to go to their husbands' homes, weeping.
Sons and grandsons go to school and daughters are at their ghar.
She was seven when she was married and sent to her ghar.
This is the government's order, and all the people don't have knowledge.
Daughters are not allowed to study [and are ignorant, innocent].
There were a few women who were courageous [and came forward].
If they move forward, people say they have loose character.
If women say something in a men's gathering,
"Your daughter will now elope."
Villagers say these things to the parents.
Parents scold the daughter.
Government, give us democracy.
The panchas were trying to finish off the women.
When the daughter is grown up, she is sent to her husband's home.
There is no benefit in educating the daughter.
You quickly give your daughter to a poor house,
But you educate your sons and grandsons as much as you can.
This type of regime by panchas cannot be long-lasting,
Women will no longer tolerate what has gone on in the past.
Women came forward saying they would no longer tolerate it,
We had fought for democracy.
Rise up, sisters, now there is no fear,
Clapping cannot be done by a single hand [i.e., the country
*   cannot be developed only by men].*
You [the panchayat government] have given trouble to women
*   for thirty years,*
You had sold unmarried daughters for raksi [distilled alcohol].
You had even sold seven-year-old girls.
With this money, you filled your bellies with raksi and chicken.
They [the panchas] had meetings just to get money.
What could be expected from the panchayat regime, which used
*   to take bribes?*
Great plans had been passed by the government.

The village panchas had drunk raksi [there was corruption in
   the planning].
School and road funds were eaten by the panchas.
Now that the panchas are gone, it is good.
So many women died in the People's Movement.
Women, you have become martyrs; we respect you.

The author summarizes, explains, and evaluates those actions of the
politically powerful that affect women and other oppressed people past
and present. She tells of women's resistance and encourages the audience to do more of the same.

In the case of dukha songs, the author(s) worked to affect, to
speak to, other women like themselves.[23] Only secondarily did they
seek to reach the fathers, husbands, elder brothers, and mothers-in-
law listening to them sing on the day of Tij. The didi-bahini groups
that composed the songs wanted to be popular on the day of Tij; they
wanted to attract as many listeners as possible. Nonetheless, they composed primarily for women like themselves, and so, for themselves. In
Song 5, about the experience of being suddenly carried away without
warning to a marriage and the husband's home, the narrator is telling
the story for the didi-bahini of the gaon. This intended audience was
one that did not have to be lectured on the situation of women or per-
suaded of the emotional difficulties it wrought. Tension did not exist
between audience and author; it subsisted between the narrator and
the array of kin she faced as a woman. The author-narrator depicted a
self embedded in a dynamic constellation of others generically constructed by their structural relationship to herself. As the author-narrator in Song 5 becomes more aware of her impending marriage, for
example, she comes to stand apart in sorrow from her self embedded
in a constellation of kin, and she is comforted only by the friends
among her didi-bahini.

The authors of raajniti songs, on the other hand, address an audience as though its members might need to be enlightened. When we
spoke with the individuals and groups responsible for the songbooks
that began to circulate in the early 1990s, we were told explicitly that
the songbooks' purpose was to reach women who were "unaware" and
"politically unconscious." We learned that women were differentiated

according to their political "awareness" and "consciousness," an awareness that was associated with exposure to schooling. Composers and producers of the songbooks positioned themselves, in both the prefaces to the songbooks being circulated around the time of the festival and in their overt, stated purposes for the songbooks, as enlightened helpers of women who "are in darkness." A song called "All Nepal Women's Association under the Red Flag," which was sung in Naudada and is reproduced below, addressed uneducated women initially with the line, "Mothers and sisters who are in darkness."

People had the conviction—based clearly upon Nepal's history of repressive government, a history peculiarly devoted to the denial of formal education—that those without sufficient schooling lacked knowledge of their own oppression by the ruling elite. Literacy statistics indicated, and people firmly believed, that women had enjoyed even less schooling than men, and so they were, in the minds of others, likely to be "politically unconscious."[24]

"All Nepal Women's Association under the Red Flag" shows the dialogic focus of raajniti songs. The dynamic source of development in the songs could be characterized as lying between the author and her listeners. The engaging dialogue is between the authors, educated women, and the listeners, uneducated women.[25] In the brackets underneath the lines, we note the shift in the author-narrator's position in relation to the audience.

> **Song 10: All Nepal Women's Association under the Red Flag.**[26]
> *Mothers and sisters who are in darkness.*
> [The author-narrator is distinct from the mothers and
> sisters she addresses, "who are in darkness."]
> *You get up, now it is morning [i.e., time to start the revolu-*
> *tion]. The monarchy made us slaves.*
> [Author-narrator identifies with her audience. Their
> pasts were shared pasts.]
> *Before the People's Revolution, Nepal's divine right king ruled.*
> *We become one to break this monarchy.*
> *Who can say that women are men's puppets?*
> *Our problems become like flames [i.e., they start to burn].*
> *Our life has been spent in doing household work.*

We are the slaves of this monarchy.

The women of other countries have done so much development.

We are backward only because we are dominated.

[Because of this shared background, all of us women in
    Nepal are backward in comparison with women else-
    where in the world.]

*So many women could not get justice and their lives were
    spoiled.*

[Author-narrator reports on atrocities against other
    women:]

Namita and Sunita were killed in Pokhara.

The women were compelled to sell their bodies.

The mandale sold the women in India.

Now we cannot tolerate this because our village women are sold.

[Speaking to the audience as distinct, but using an
    inclusive pronoun:]

We women who want justice, let's be united.

Those are all friends who want to see men and women as equal.

Let's recognize which party is our enemy.

Women, let's understand this much.

We should bring democracy by uniting.

By supporting the struggle of men.

By staying under the red flag of Akhil.

Let's be active and take part in this struggle.

The nursing child was orphaned.

Some friends were dead; there is no way to see them.

You don't have to deceive by saying white is black.

[Now addressing a hated government:]

The terrorist monarch now has no power.

[Returns to the role of an overt commentator and analyst:]

*Though the two wheels of the chariot [i.e., men and women] are
    the same, women are different.*

If one of the wheels cracks, the chariot will fall down.

It is a little hard to understand the truth.

We should take the side of truth.

[Referent for "we" here could include a larger group
    than just women.]

> *Give women rights equal to men.*
> *Remove the inequality between women and men.*
> *You don't deceive us by showing us books [i.e., equality may be*
>   *in the books, but it is not in practice].*
> [Addressing those who oppress women again and draw-
>   ing all women into the "us"].
> *We don't need the individual selfishness [i.e., we don't want*
>   *more rights than men].*
> *If we say women's rights are a small thing, the opportunists*
>   *will leave us on the way [i.e., we will be left behind].*
> *Powerful persons of the country, you listen to our problems.*
> *Now this song is finished. Good-bye.*

The author-narrator of the preceding song takes an equivocal position toward her audience. In the beginning lines, she is shown separate
from, different from, unlike those women she addresses. But as the
song continues (lines 4 through 10), the author-narrator admits to a
shared past, and by line 11 she concludes that this shared past has left
all women in Nepal, not just the currently "unenlightened" mothers
and sisters addressed by the song, backward. The author-narrator then
moves away from identification with her audience and tries to persuade
her listeners to join the political movement and party that she believes
will best help them. She provides an analysis, an evaluation, and a call
to action. Meanwhile, the perpetrators—the monarchy, those who
would say that women are men's puppets, mandale, those who give mis-
information to persuade people that black is white—are others portrayed in the song as frozen and fixed. The movement in the song and
the points of tension occur not between those others and the author-
narrator but between enlightened, educated women (in the person of
the author-narrator) and uneducated, unenlightened women. And the
latter do not stay fixed. Instead, the boundary between the enlightened
and the unenlightened moves, becoming more and less encompassing
as the song goes on.

THE TIJ FESTIVAL AS A SPACE OF AUTHORING

Shifting boundaries and unresolved tensions characterize the
space in which identities are authored. In the case of the Tij festival, the

potential of the song genre, the legacy of an enduring struggle with the state over access to schools, and the circumstances of the Pro-Democracy Movement combined to make boundaries out of emerging differences.

We have so far presented Tij songs and practices as though they were solely the media and associated activities of struggles taking place over the position of women in Naudada. But the Tij festival was clearly an event that many sought to appropriate for other ends.[27] Equally important were the additional, discernible (though mostly unremarked), tension-filled layers of difference and heterogeneity within festival practices.

Women who participated in the Tij practice sessions and on the margins of the festival were also identifiable in terms of education, political party, caste, and even wealth. Besides the gender struggles and the emerging divide of education, we observed tussles and tensions that could have been related to caste or ethnicity. Tij was associated with the two "highest" castes, Bahun and Chetri. In a sense, they owned the festival. Nonetheless, Newars, a caste in the middle range, and Damai, considered "untouchable," composed Tij songs. The former were uneasy about performing their songs in the public space on the day of Tij, and the latter were unwilling even to attempt it.[28] Although caste-related tensions were more inchoate than those related to gender struggles, they were part of the range of contentious practices important at the festival. Together with other possible gendered identities at the festival, caste constituted an additional basis in the name of which a woman might act.

The songs, we argue, were not only the center of people's attention at the festival but were also significant in singling out the identities to which participants attended. The songs "developed" gender at the expense, some might say, of other possible struggles that threatened to emerge at the time of Tij. The songs, too, were significant in the emergence of education as a divide among women.

Especially following the Pro-Democracy Movement, Tij groups began noticeably to fracture and reconfigure according to women's experience of formal schooling and party affiliation. In 1991, Tij groups in the regional centers, such as Gorkha, Pokhara, and Narayangarth (Holland and Skinner 1995a), split into those that sang mostly dukha songs and those that sang mostly raajniti songs. The latter were in turn divided by political party. In Naudada, the fractures were not carried to such extremes. There, each group, save one, sang both types of songs and was formed from the didi-bahini of different gaons, not by preference for Congress or another political party. However, the Naudada women were effectively split within their groups. Girls and young women who had gone or were going to school and who identified themselves as educated contributed most to the raajniti songs. The dukha songs tended to be more the passion of women who had little or no schooling and were considered to be uneducated.

In 1991, there were a number of improvisational moves into new spaces and times from which Tij activities had previously been barred. Schoolgirls showed us Tij songs, for example, that they had written down and circulated several months before the date of Tij. In prior years, Tij songs were limited in their public circulation to the several weeks preceding and encompassing the festival. Singing Tij songs in public outside the time of the festival and the practice sessions leading up to it, women had told us in former years, was forbidden. But the most remarkable shift in 1991 was the one we have emphasized: the turn of the songs to party politics and criticism of the government.

That shift ushered in a new emphasis on political antagonists to women's struggles for equal treatment and, in doing so, inadvertently opened up other lines of struggle and division between the women themselves. Late in the afternoon on Tij Day, 1991, a new group appeared in the tati at Naudada, a group of schoolgirls who sang only raajniti songs and only those that praised the Congress party. This was a group united not by relations of kinship but by the affiliation of their respective gaons with the Nepali Congress Party. Furthermore, the girls all wore student garb, the blouses and skirts that they wore to school; none wore a sari, the traditional type of women's clothing that predominated in the other groups, even those that included students. By dress and other indicators, the schoolgirls were emphasizing their identities as educated women. In addition to the inchoate struggles around caste and the more noticed struggles of partisan politics was an emerging, troublesome split related to education.

Socially identified types or groups of people are deeply entangled, from a dialogical standpoint, with the production and "ownership" of particular genres, spaces, and positions. We have already indicated that Tij songs and their public performance were associated with, or "owned by," Bahun and Chetri women. Even more importantly, raajniti Tij songs were "owned by" educated women. Whereas any woman who had experienced life as a daughter or daughter-in-law in Naudada had the knowledge to compose dukha songs, only those who were literate and had studied several years in school were considered competent to compose raajniti songs. These epistemological expectations gave a special value to "educated" women, one that corresponded to a general value granted to formal education and one that affected women's feelings about their value as marriage partners and as contributors to the Nepali nation (Skinner and Holland 1996, 1998).

Dukha songs, their composers say, come from experiential knowledge gained, in no small part, through emotional response. Thoughts and feelings are stored in the *man* (the heart/mind located in the chest [see McHugh 1989; Skinner 1990]) and provide the inspiration for dukha songs. Raajniti songs, on the other hand, are more a matter of fact. They fall within a more general type of Tij song called *ghatana* (incident) songs, which report events and conditions. Ghatana songs are about incidents, happenings uniquely of a moment, such as an accident, murder, suicide, or political event. Any woman who knows what being a daughter, a daughter-in-law, or a wife is like can draw upon the feelings and thoughts in her *man* to make up a dukha song. To compose a raajniti or ghatana song, on the other hand, one needs either to have witnessed an event or consulted someone who did. Legitimate sources of print or broadcast news are acceptable as well. Members of Tij groups might also ask their brothers to write about an incident for them or take material from printed Tij songbooks to create the songs they claimed as their own (see Holland and Skinner 1995a; Skinner, Holland, and Adhikari 1994). Thus, the narrator of a dukha song evokes common knowledge and wisdom, the sense and feeling that come from being a participant in domestic relations. The narrator of a raajniti song communicates a description and evaluation of what has transpired in the public world of government and political action.

We have discussed in previous publications the split that has emerged in Naudada and more broadly between educated and uneducated women (Holland and Skinner 1995a; Skinner and Holland 1996,

1998). Uneducated women were sensitive to this division, which, we pointed out, is evident both in women's statements to us and in many of the dukha songs. They indicated in speech and song their awareness that they were considered, and sometimes felt, inferior and of lesser social value. Raajniti songs, we have argued here, both promoted this evaluation and yet at the same time depicted the insubstantiality and the permeability of the subjective boundary that separated the two kinds of women. The emergence of these fractures among women according to education flowed as a long-term consequence of the historical struggle for access to education in Nepal and of the different epistemologies peculiar to the two types of Tij songs.

CONCLUSION

Gender relations in Naudada in the late 1980s and early 1990s—the Naudada we know—could be characterized as a thoroughgoing system of male privilege. The relations were deeply rooted and historically institutionalized, pervasively bound in the country's laws and in widespread social practices and cultural understandings. Gender relations were nonetheless far from static, fixed, frozen, or accepted without tension. The Tij festival was an important place for local contentious practice over gender positions and the reimagining of gender relations and feminine identities. While home to a number of incipient struggles over differentiation by caste and, especially after 1990, by political party, the central practices of the festival and the songs produced through those practices put flesh primarily not to caste identities or even to party identities but to identifying women as due for relief from a world of gender relations in which they suffered.

A close analysis of the Tij songs, inspired by the work of Bakhtin and his associates, gives us a sense of the important subjective tools, if not the subjective sense, that women have available to them for understanding the social and material conditions in which and against which they have been formed. Analysis of those songs destroys any simplistic idea one might have of Naudada's ongoing gendered struggles. They explode any one-dimensional view of a static struggle dictated solely by the weight of external forces, any conception of women as simply *resisting* male privilege and reproducing gendered identities that align them the same way from one generation to the next. Whether we consider the dukha songs that predominated before the Pro-Democracy Movement or the raajniti songs that predominated after the movement in 1991, we see that the struggle is distributed, so to speak, over a set of others. They are set within figured worlds (Holland et al. 1998) that contain multiple others. In the case of dukha songs, the figured world is that of the household and domestic relations, populated by fathers, husbands, mothers-in-law, husbands' older brothers, husbands' older brothers' wives, and so on—all others set vis-à-vis the didi-bahini, the narrators-authors. In the raajniti songs to which the groups turned in 1991, the situation is yet again more complex. The self or selves are distributed not only over the public world of political others—such as the panchas, politicians, specific political parties, and the king—but also, and more importantly, over the shifting relation of educated to uneducated women. The self of raajniti songs is sometimes and ambivalently other.

The close analysis of the songs not only suggests that the self-in-struggle is caught up in a field of interrelated others but also directs attention to the point of development—the active, living point of the dialogic relations between self and other. For dukha songs, the point lies at the emotional intersection between the woman and others in similar structural positions in the domestic world. For raajniti songs, the point lies not within the textual world created by the song but in the world presumed by the text's performance, at the intersection between women who seem to have been consigned to the past—the uneducated women—and the women of the future, those who are "educated" and no longer "backward."[29]

How quickly the struggle had been reimagined; how quickly the women who had been educated were singled out against those who were uneducated. The generativity of the Tij genre, the easy improvisation of raajniti songs, a simple variant on ghatana songs, enabled the quick turn, the rapid reconfiguring of gendered struggles. Practices of collaboration and epistemology provided a ready elaboration of the value of literacy and of access to books and news of political events and political stances, and thus created a boundary drawn between the women.

Analysis of the raajniti songs reveals another, less obvious point in the actions of the women in Naudada. The author-narrators of the raajniti songs sang from the perspective of educated women trying to convince their illiterate sisters to become politically "conscious." Yet in the songs, they sometimes slid across the divide that supposedly separated them from the uneducated and admitted that the boundary between them was permeable—that, in comparison with the women of other countries and perhaps with better educated women in Nepal, they, too, were "uneducated." The line or boundary of demarcation, in other words, ran through as well as between persons. Moreover, we note the possibility that the "educated" girls and young women will come increasingly to rely on songbooks produced outside the area and so will forget the collaborative practices that have been significant in creating the emotional atmosphere of Tij and in constituting the groups as social actors. This forgetting would surely weaken local Tij groups' ownership of the festival and its signature genre, the songs. As Tij opens onto a broader political world through the songs that compose it, it may lose its importance as an event where women build, against the odds and currents of daily life, a place and sense of their significance and solidarity as women.

Notes

We are thankful to all of the participants in the advanced seminar for their input and especially to Jean Lave and Kay Warren, who took the most time with the manuscript. Another rowdy bunch who commented helpfully on the paper were the fellows of the UNC-CH Institute for Arts and Humanities faculty seminar in the spring of 1995. A fellowship from the institute to Holland provided time to work on the paper. The National Science Foundation funded the 1991 research in Nepal. Special thanks also go to William Lachicotte for his insightful comments on the paper.

1. Naudada is a pseudonym, as are personal names.

2. A note of caution: "Self" should not be taken in this chapter as referring to the Western idea of an isolated, coherent, unified subject. Bakhtin's conception is far too social and cultural to be confused with such a notion. Moreover, any person or group is likely to have multiple selves, and the "self" of a person is difficult to distinguish from the self of a group.

3. Bennett related Tij to Rishi Panchami explicitly; the others, implicitly. Bista (1969), in contrast, explicitly stated that Tij and Rishi Panchami were not related.

4. Knowledge of Brahmanical teachings associated with the rituals appeared to be limited among the women and even among some of the priests. At least, there was some disagreement among the latter.

5. We had research assistants in Narayangarth and Kathmandu at the time of the 1991 Tij festival. We learned about the festivals in Pokhara and Gorkha through interviews.

6. The daily activities of Naudadans, especially the women, revolved around agricultural and domestic work. Most families subsisted by farming, although some of the Bahun and Chetri families held enough land that they could sell their produce. A few men held salaried or wage jobs located in or near Naudada, and some worked outside the area, coming home weekly or even less often.

7. The area we concentrated on within Naudada consisted of a grouping of 10 gaons, or hamlets, that were near the headquarters of the local governmental administrative unit of Naudada. (This local unit, formerly called a panchayat, became designated as a "Village Development Committee" [gaon bikaas samiti] after the 1990 Pro-Democracy Movement.) Oriented to many of the same government offices and public spaces, these 10 gaons of Naudada were further joined together by concentrated individual interactions, relationships, rivalries, and comings and goings.

8. In local talk and practice, the people of Naudada divided themselves into several caste/ethnic groups: Bahun and Chetri, upper-caste groups who together constituted a slight majority of the population; Newar and Magar, ethnic groups fitted into the middle of the caste hierarchy; and lower-caste groups including Damai, Sunar, Kami, and Sarki. The complexities of these ethnic/caste groupings were made plain to us daily. The groupings varied in significance and in their implications for the day-to-day lives of Naudadans from one context to the next (e.g., from home to tea shop to school). They were variously reflected upon in some situations and seemingly taken for granted in others. As for the crafts and services conventionally associated with the lower-caste groups (e.g., Sunar, goldsmithing; Sarki, leather working; Damai, tailoring and providing music), it appeared that only a minority of the members were relying on their craft for the majority of their subsistence. Nonetheless, most lower-caste families, especially among the Damai, still had upper-caste families who were their *bista* (patrons). They supplied their services as tailors and musicians, in the case of Damai, to particular Bahun or Chetri families in return for a portion of the upper-caste families' harvests.

9. Scholarship on representations of India and its history through "caste,"

"Hindu," "village," and other terminology has proceeded apace (see, for example, Dirks 1992). For example, the term "Hindu" often refers to a narrower but still complex category, "Brahmanical." Much ethnographic work remains to be done on the ways in which Brahmanical practices and ideology are produced (as undertaken by Barth [1991] for Bali, for example) and politically maintained. As Dirks (1992) pointed out, terms such as "Hindu" may in some cases replace "politics" with "religion." Meanwhile, the comparable subjection of representations of Nepal to historicization and critical analysis is more recent (Benjamin 1989; Pigg 1992). For example, Holmberg (1989) felt it necessary to caution against the assumption that groups reified in documents such as the Muluki Ain, the general civil and criminal code of Nepal that was first formulated in the mid-nineteenth century, had a consolidated ethnic identity prior to the nineteenth century.

10. Tij is described in the literature (Bennett 1983; Bista 1969; Bouillier 1982) as an activity of Bahun and Chetri women. As we describe it in this chapter, the picture for Naudada is more complex (Holland and Skinner 1995a:286; Skinner, Holland, and Adhikari 1994). Ahearn (1991) also reported research near Tansen that depicts the ways Magar women practice Tij.

11. For descriptions of the collaboration processes, see Skinner, Holland, and Adhikari 1994 and Holland and Skinner 1995b.

12. We collected verses from and/or information about roughly 1,000 songs. Samples of the songs, including this one, are translated into English and transliterated in romanized Nepali in Skinner, Holland, and Adhikari 1994.

13. There is insufficient space in this chapter to do justice to many of the events of the 1991 festival. See Holland and Skinner 1995a for a fuller account and analysis.

14. Notice that the Nepali Congress Party is being cast in this song as a political party that not only fails to help women but actually worsens their position. Some party activists considered the representation of the party by Tij songs significant. The communist party groups were much more active in producing Tij songbooks than were Congress groups. Of the 41 songbooks that we found in 1991, 30 were associated with one of the communist parties. Seven were pro-Congress. When we traced the pro-Congress books back to their authors, the producers explained that they felt the need to counter the pro-communist, anti-Congress books.

15. See Holland and Skinner 1995a and Skinner, Holland, and Adhikari 1994 for further discussion of the relationship of national political events to the content of the songs.

16. *Mandale* was a term for unscrupulous characters assumed to be henchmen of those in power during the panchayat era.

17. In Bakhtin's terms, raajniti and dukha songs have different *chronotopes*. This notion, almost literally (though by inversion) translated as "spacetimes," is one of the definitive features of genres, perhaps the principal feature. A chronotope establishes the kinds of landscapes and modes of temporality that are possible for all human activity portrayed within the genre. It is, in this sense, the universal setting of all possible generic narratives, the genre's world. Chronotope is similar to the concept of "figured world," which we discuss elsewhere (Holland et al. 1998).

18. An edited volume by Hill and Irvine (1993) substantially increased the amount of attention to "reported speech" published by anthropologists and anthropological linguists. Among others in that volume, Besnier (1992:161–163) summarized linguists', philosophers', and literary critics' and anthropologists' exploration of the phenomenon of reported speech. He then proceeded to a study of his own, regarding ways in which Nukulaelae Islanders manage, through the ways they report speech, to convey affective commentary about others as, at the same time, they skirt responsibility for the commentary. Here we are considering reported speech to provide a perspective on identity within a dynamic constellation of self and others. As described in chapter 1, Roger Lancaster has usefully extended Bakhtin's approach from language to behavior. See also Holland et al. 1998, especially the chapter entitled "Authoring Selves."

19. In order to appreciate the constraints of different limitations, one might compare the types of reported speech in Tij songs with those that Besnier (1992) described for speech on Nukulaelae in the South Pacific. People on Nukulaelae favored a certain way of describing the actions of others. They described their speech. Everyone's talk was riddled with the reported speech of others. Nonetheless, Besnier found the forms of reported speech on Nukulaelae to be quite limited and in the form of what Volosinov referred to as "linear style" (Besnier 1992:168). Shunning direct evaluative descriptions of others, the people of Nukulaelae strove for truthful accounts of the content of the speech of others. It was only through the limited means of prosodic features that evaluations could be conveyed. In Tij songs, in contrast, because of the constraints on intonation, prosodic features were rendered inoperative. Instead, in Tij songs the words describing the reported speech carried the commentary.

20. We did hear in raajniti songs a few interesting variations from the stock attributions of atrocities to political opponents. Song 3, for example, presents an argument for the Nepali Congress Party that is totally facetious. Another song

gives a pictorial presentation of drunks in Naudada, blaming their condition in part on the Congress party.

21. Song 5, which asks "What sort of guests are these?" is an unusual dukha song in that, at least for a very brief segment, the author and the narrator are distinct. In the beginning line, the author knows that the guests have come for the woman/daughter's wedding, but the woman who is the narrator does not.

22. A *namlo* is a rope with a band that is placed on the head for carrying loads on the back. This line means: One husband and two wives; he'll have to bear two loads, and he will have problems.

23. Again, it is important to remember that the songs were composed in overt collaboration (see Holland and Skinner 1995b; Skinner, Holland, and Adhikari 1994).

24. This discourse of "awareness" weighs most heavily upon the older generations of women, who by and large had no chance to go to school.

25. There were two main women's organizations associated with political parties in 1991. The Akhil [All] Nepal Women's Association was pro-communist, and the Nepal Women's Association, pro-Congress. Some of the Akhil groups we talked to organized the publication of Tij songbooks along with other organizing activities such as political classes on women's problems. Of the seven pro-Congress Tij songbooks, three were approved by the local Congress women's organization as a sort of courtesy but were not initiated by the organization. Of the remaining four, two had only one song and the other two were written by the same person.

26. This song and its title came from one of the songbooks that was circulated in the 1991 season.

27. In other parts of the district, for example, government officials tried to use the Tij festival as a place to distribute information about family planning. In an area not too far from Naudada, local leaders came up with the idea of a song competition between different locales. Straightforward commodification of the festival had occurred to still others: the songs sung on Tij Day were tape-recorded and offered for sale. We have already seen that the political parties were competing for recommendation in Tij songs. Some of the prefaces to the songbooks even contested the analyses of women's inequality in dukha songs, arguing instead for a Marxist analysis. Readers interested in this dimension should see Holland and Skinner 1995a.

28. In an incident already described, we saw an improvised effort on the part of one of the Tij groups in 1991 to keep the lakhe from displacing the Tij

groups from the tati. While the statements of the women who tried to keep the crowd's attention suggested that the unnamed struggle had to do with gender, it is conceivable that it was also related to caste. Tij was associated with castes different from that of the lakhe.

29. A significant number of the women we spoke with in Nepal were involved in political and feminist groups concerned to find a better bridge between themselves and women cast as "uneducated." Despite what the songbook prefaces might suggest, these women had little interest in instructing uneducated women about the shortcomings of their analyses. Instead, to build a bridge, some had returned to dukha songs. They had already included, or spoke of plans to include, dukha songs in their publications, in order both to reach out to "uneducated" women and to remind themselves that they, the educated women, were not yet immune to the effects of the same tense relations addressed in the dukha songs, relations between women as daughters and wives and the others of their household. The two forms of song themselves had become indexes of the divisions between women, and their arrangement or orchestration had, for these activist women, become a way of working through that division.

Part Two

Practices of Identity in Enduring Struggles

5

Placing the Politics of Black Class Formation

Steven Gregory

> We are still in the process of experimenting with a new form
> of politics where the constitution of identities, the winning
> of identification, is itself part of the struggle, not something
> preliminary to that struggle.
>   —*Stuart Hall, "Discussion,"* Black Popular Culture

Arthur Hayes was weeding a triangle-shaped lot across the street
from his house in East Elmhurst, Queens, when I arrived. He shook the
soil from a huge clump of weeds and topped off the last of three Hefty
trash bags. "I decided to make a garden in this lot twenty years ago," he
declared, wiping the sweat from his forehead and smiling. "That was
after a neighbor almost ran over a drunk who was sleeping in here with
all the weeds." He pulled off his canvas work gloves and then raised
them to shoulder level to show me how high the overgrowth had been.

A tall, large-framed man, Hayes was president of the East
Elmhurst–Corona Civic Association, the most powerful black homeowner association in the area. Founded in 1952, when East Elmhurst
and nearby Corona were experiencing the brunt of postwar urban
decline, the civic association emerged in the wake of the civil rights
period as the neighborhood's most influential civic group, eclipsing
the NAACP, churches, and other community institutions in its capacity
to muster and sustain a sizable, largely homeowning constituency.

In recent months, members of the association had complained
about receiving parking tickets on blocks where the "No Parking" signs

were missing or unreadable. To address this problem, Hayes had decided to conduct a block-by-block "inspection" of the area to assess the condition of its signs. The completed survey would be presented to a New York City Traffic Department representative at the next civic association meeting.

Born in Louisiana, Hayes grew up in a small oil town in Texas. In the 1930s, like many other African Americans, he migrated to Harlem and, after serving in the war, found work as a seaman on a passenger ship. In the mid-1950s, Hayes and his family bought a home in middle-income East Elmhurst with a Veterans Administration–insured mortgage.

"Was mostly Italian and Irish and some Germans too when we first got here," Hayes told me, waving his hand at the houses surrounding his detached home and landscaped yard. "They were all pretty nice but they were leaving. At the time, they were going out to Long Island–Levittown and places like that. See, we used to have the G.I. Bill back then."

We began the tour on Astoria Boulevard and Ninety-third Street, which marked East Elmhurst's border with predominantly white and Latino Jackson Heights to the west. I checked the readability of each sign, and Hayes noted the location and condition of each on a clipboard. Many of the signs had been worn by wind and acid rain, leaving only a bleached white surface with traces of pink lettering.

Between signs, Hayes told stories about his experiences growing up in the South, underscoring the race pride that his family had instilled in him. As we zigzagged our way south into low-income Corona, he pointed out important places in the community's past. When we reached the Refuge Church on tree-lined Thirty-fourth Avenue, Hayes told me that the site had been an early home of the First Baptist Church.

"See, the church has always been a sanctuary for blacks," he said. "It was the only place where we could be complete men for a few hours a day." To stress this point, Hayes explained that most of Corona's Baptist congregations had been organized by small groups of people who mortgaged their homes to finance their churches. He then called my attention to a vacant lot next to the church that was being used as a dump for car tires. The narrow lot was littered with a motley assortment of bald tires. A pink refrigerator door, its corners eaten away by rust, rested awkwardly against a jagged chunk of brick and mortar.

Hayes told me that he had been monitoring the situation for some time and believed that tire repair shops operating illegally in residentially zoned buildings were dumping their tires in the lot. He made a note on his clipboard.

When we reached the Congregational Church farther along Thirty-fourth Avenue, Hayes returned to the topic of the black church, speaking about the role of its former pastor in the struggles of the civil rights period. "Sherard was a strong leader in this community. You see, ministers can say things that other people can't because they wear the collar." He pointed to his neck and smiled. "Our problem has always been unity," he continued. "A lot of people up in East Elmhurst look down on people in Corona even though their churches are still here." As we turned onto One Hundred Third Street and headed back toward East Elmhurst, Hayes discussed the leadership potential of the community's ministers, assessing the ability of each to bring together various segments of the community.

For the remainder of the inspection, Hayes continued his commentary, reading the signs of the present against the multilayered histories of place. For Hayes and other activists, an illegal dump or effaced parking sign was not simply an eyesore, a mere violation of the spatial economy of the present. Rather, embedded in the recollected meanings of place, such threats to the built environment were also assaults on the collective memory of the past, which formed the bedrock of the community's identity and political culture.

Michel de Certeau (1984:108), writing of these invisible identities of place, observed:

> It is striking here that the places people live are like the presences of diverse absences. What can be seen designates what is no longer there: "you see, here there used to be...," but it can no longer be seen. Demonstratives indicate the invisible identities of the visible: it is the very definition of a place, in fact, that it is composed by these series of displacements and effects among the fragmented strata that form it and that it plays on these moving layers.

Arthur Hayes's inspection, like other everyday negotiations of the neighborhood landscape, was thus an act of recapitulation: a looking into, recovery, and rethinking of the multiple meanings of place and of the identities of its inhabitants. For in reading the signs of neighborhood—the sites of struggle, sacrifice, achievement, and defeat—Hayes was also constructing community identity: a "we" who mortgaged our homes to build our churches, a we who fought for civil rights, and a we who are divided along the lines of class.

I begin with this reading of the signs of community not only to highlight the heterogeneity of African-American identity but also to stress that this diversity is produced and negotiated in the everyday lives of people and in urban landscapes that are shot through with power, history, and meaning.

This chapter examines the formation of African-American class identities within the context of community-based struggles over the built environment. In these contests, conflicting claims to identity, to public memory, and to the "moving layers" of spatial meanings, as de Certeau put it, are exercised and disputed across a complex political field where the quality-of-life concerns of residents frequently clash with the space development strategies of public and private-sector elites.

By unpacking the *politics* of identity underpinning these protracted struggles over the built environment, I want not only to shed light on the social processes that constitute people as political agents—subjects who recognize and act upon specific historically constructed commitments—but also to suggest that possibilities for emancipatory political action rest precisely on our ability to conceptualize and intervene in the everyday politics of "moving people."

THE QUESTION OF BLACK CLASS IDENTITIES

Recent discussions of the changing significance of race and class for African Americans have, on the whole, failed to capture the complex manner in which neighborhood activists such as Arthur Hayes conceptualize and negotiate these categories in their everyday lives and politics. Simplistic accounts of black class structure, driven by binary and androcentric models of black identity that contrast "middle class" with "underclass," "old heads" with rowdy teenagers, and "respectable" men with those who are not, are called into service to map the moral frontiers of the black "ghetto" and explain the "tangle of pathology" of the poor (Wilson 1987:21).

Mitchell Duneier (1993:109), explaining why black working-class men are regular patrons of a Greek-owned cafeteria on the outskirts of Chicago's black community, observed:

> Many of the black regulars no longer feel sufficiently comfortable in the ghetto to engage in the type of interaction that once predominated there. They feel an intense desire to rise above what they sometimes term the "negativity" of the streets, the moral isolation inherent in ghetto life. When they speak of the desire to escape from the lower depths in which they find themselves submerged, they mean they want to make contact with a world that is appropriate to their own sense of moral worth, one that represents the greater order.

Here, as in similar accounts of the "bifurcation" of the African-American class structure, the concept of class, loosely defined by some researchers as income-earning capacity, is deployed to plot the imagined frontiers between the morally isolated inner city and the "greater order" of mainstream society. This tendency to conceptualize African-American class positions as transparent and fundamentally *moral* reflexes of occupational status not only obscures the complex determinacy of black class identities but also depoliticizes the concept of class by treating class as a static category unmediated by relations of power and processes of political struggle.

Classes are neither given by occupational status nor, as in dogmatic Marxist perspectives, *necessarily* determined by the positioning of agents within the social relations of production. Rather, class identities and their constituent social meanings are formed and re-formed through political and cultural practices that occur at multiple sites in community life. "Historical subjects," Stanley Aronowitz wrote, "are *themselves* an effect of struggles about class formation whose discontinuity is determined by phases of capitalist development which are in turn the outcome of the relatively autonomous economic, political, and ideological relations within the totality of social relations" (1990:106). Although the relative autonomy of these relations in any given social formation remains an open question, this practice-oriented approach rejects a priori (and apolitical) conceptions of class and insists that class identities are effects of political struggles over class formation rather than unmediated reflections of that process.

Turning now to my ethnographic research in East Elmhurst, Queens, I examine the formation of black class identities through the cultural politics of grass-roots activism. I emphasize the role played by neighborhood-based institutions and social practices in shaping African-American class identities. In contrast to static and binary models of the African-American class structure, I underscore the heterogeneity and fluidity of black class identities and of the ideologies that call them into being. Class dispositions are exercised, contested, and reworked at a variety of sites in neighborhood life. In these settings, ranging from church services and block club meetings to annual dances sponsored by community groups, attitudes about class are publicly articulated in relation to multiple and often opposing interpretations of community needs and political interests.

I also stress the role of the state in configuring the political and discursive terrain upon which African Americans confront these issues of community need, interest, and identity. Though class identities are composite, unstable, and constituted along multiple axes of difference, they acquire coherence and durability within the context of specific arrangements of power. Accordingly, I demonstrate how the state, during the course of winning support for urban development projects, incites the articulation of class attitudes and subject positions by exercising control over the public sphere of neighborhood activism—that is, the "structured setting[s] where cultural and ideological contest or negotiation among a variety of publics take place" (Eley 1992:306).

MOVING PEOPLE: NEIGHBORHOOD ACTIVISM AND THE POLITICS OF IDENTITY

On March 2, 1994, a Continental jet skidded off runway 13-31 at LaGuardia Airport in Queens, dipping its massive, cone-shaped head into Flushing Bay. Although there were no injuries, the incident followed a U.S. Air accident two years earlier that resulted in the deaths of 27 people. The March mishap increased political pressure to expedite plans to construct a runway safety overrun on land reclaimed from Flushing Bay. The safety overrun, airport officials maintained, would provide a margin of safety for aircraft overshooting the runway as well as work space for emergency vehicles and equipment.

LaGuardia Airport, operated by the Port Authority of New York and New Jersey (PANYNJ), has been an ongoing target of activism for the predominantly middle-income, African-American community of East Elmhurst. Civic and block associations have repeatedly fought with the port authority over airport expansion, noise pollution, and, most recently, the authority's plan to build a high-tech, elevated rail system, or "people mover," linking Manhattan's central business district to the two Queens airports, LaGuardia and JFK. For residents of East Elmhurst, airport development has meant the colonization of their community and the deterioration of its quality of life. "The Port Authority and the city," City Councilwoman Helen Marshall told a newspaper in April 1994, "are more concerned about a land grab than they are about [airport] safety" (*Newsday*, 8 April 1994, p. 32).

Created by a treaty between New York and New Jersey in 1921, the port authority is a leading public instrument of regional planning with authority over transportation and commerce-related facilities in the bistate region. Self-supporting and directed by 12 appointed commissioners, the port authority is relatively immune to political pressures and controls (Danielson and Doig 1982). This lack of accountability makes the port authority a formidable, if not indomitable, adversary for community activists and local officials. "After years of working with the port authority," an East Elmhurst activist remarked, "I've seen their arrogant attitude with regard to community needs and their refusal to accept anything except the plan that *they've* offered." For residents of East Elmhurst, the port authority embodies power that is not only elusive and unaccountable but also perceived to be in the service of urban development policies promoting the "outside" economic interests of Manhattan-based elites.

Opposition to the safety overrun drew on a complex set of issues, concerns, and anxieties embedded in the social history of East Elmhurst. Residents argued that the runway overrun would restrict the circulation of water in Flushing Bay, aggravating water pollution problems and degrading the quality of life of black homeowners in the bay area, or "North Shore." For this reason, activists insisted that the overrun be built on piles or stilts rather than on landfill.

The North Shore, which includes Ditmars Boulevard, an affluent black residential strip, has been a potent symbol of black upward mobility throughout the community's history. For African Americans, residence on the shore signaled elite status, evoking images of littoral leisure and opulence tied to the North Shore's status as a residential enclave for the professional and powerful early in the twentieth century. For contemporary residents, Ditmars Boulevard and the North Shore represent the delicate frontier of black middle-class progress; it is a place in which the "past sleeps" (de Certeau 1984:108).

This landscape of progress has been threatened since the early days of black settlement in the area after the Second World War. The building of LaGuardia Airport and the Grand Central Parkway (which skirts Flushing Bay) during the 1930s undermined the social capital of the North Shore just as African Americans were making inroads into once racially segregated East Elmhurst. Subsequent development activities at LaGuardia Airport have continued to threaten the quality of life of black homeowners, inflaming memories of the past and anxieties about the future.

In April 1993, Community Board 3, representing East Elmhurst and adjacent neighborhoods, held a public hearing to review the port authority's proposal for the safety overrun. New York City's community boards are local, government-sponsored advisory boards that, composed of local residents, exercise limited authority over decisions concerning land use, zoning, and municipal service delivery. Though African Americans constituted a minority on Community Board 3, its Aviation Subcommittee, charged with monitoring airport-related problems, was composed almost exclusively of East Elmhurst residents.

By a vote of 31 to 1, the community board rejected the plan for the runway overrun, noting that the port authority had "failed to give the Board rational alternatives to a landfill safety overrun." Since community boards have only advisory power, Board 3's vote failed to veto or amend the project. The port authority's proposal for the runway overrun was recommended for approval with unusual dispatch by the City Planning Commission one week later, and on June 14 it was approved by the City Council.

Activists in East Elmhurst were outraged, not because they were opposed to the safety overrun per se, but rather because they felt that their concerns had been ignored during the land use review procedure. Their inability to shape the outcome of the project underscored the ineffectiveness of formal mechanisms of political participation, particularly when local activists are confronted with regional development programs supported by powerful and often unaccountable institutional elites.

The experience of the runway safety overrun provides a context for examining the response of neighborhood activists to a second port authority project, one that they would confront only days after the City Council approved the overrun plan. As an African-American member of Community Board 3 put it, expressing her frustration, "You know, it's like you don't get hit by one car, you get hit by four because they're following right behind each other!"

The second car was the port authority's proposal to build an elevated light rail system linking Manhattan's central business district to the two Queens airports. The light rail project, called the Automated Guideway Transit system, or AGT, was strongly supported by the Queens borough president who, like port authority officials, viewed improved airport access as key to bolstering the city's competitiveness in the global economy.

In organizing against the AGT, however, neighborhood activists would adopt a very different strategy. Rather than mobilize themselves through existing institutions, such as the community board or the offices of elected representatives, activists would struggle to constitute alternative arenas for political participation and alternative allegiances: political spaces and alliances that would transgress fixed definitions of "community" and disrupt static, place-bound identities tied to constructions of race, class, and neighborhood differences.

By contrast, the port authority's strategy and procedures for winning public approval of the AGT would buttress bureaucratically defined constructions of community and narrow, place-bound formulations of political interests. Through practices of "community outreach" in disseminating information about the AGT, soliciting and managing public comment, and negotiating with local activists, port authority officials would incite and invigorate constructions of subjectivity that stressed the property-based, quality-of-life concerns of African-American homeowners over broader or "structural" issues of environmental justice. By examining these practices and the resistances offered to them, I emphasize the contested quality of class identities and illuminate the mechanisms through which the exercise of power constructs political subjects, enabling and disabling possibilities for action.

LA DÉTENTE

Residents of East Elmhurst had become increasingly alarmed about the people mover as details of the port authority's plan became public knowledge during the summer of 1994. In the plan, the AGT would originate at a central terminal at Fifty-ninth Street in midtown Manhattan, cross the Fifty-ninth Street Bridge into Queens, and continue "in an elevated condition" (as officials put it) east to LaGuardia Airport. For the East Elmhurst section of its route, the elevated tracks would follow the Grand Central Parkway along the shore of Flushing Bay.

At block and civic association meetings in East Elmhurst, African-American residents expressed a wide range of concerns. Many felt that the construction and operation of the people mover would degrade the quality of life of residents living along its proposed route, adding to the airport's noise pollution problem and lowering property values. Moreover, activists felt that the siting of the elevated AGT along the North Shore undermined the community's long-standing struggle to clean up Flushing Bay and develop a public park and promenade along its shore. Finally, residents were outraged by the fact that access to the people mover would be restricted to airport passengers.

This restriction, a particular bone of contention among Queens residents, was the result of the mechanism that would be used to finance the project. The estimated $3.5 billion cost of the AGT system would be financed by a Passenger Facility Charge or tax (PFC). Under this federally authorized program, the port authority is empowered by the Federal Aviation Administration (FAA) to collect a PFC tax on airline tickets to finance improvements in airport facilities, such as the renovation or expansion of terminals. However, FAA regulations governing the program stipulate that PFC funds must benefit only airport passengers. By proposing to finance the AGT with PFC funds, the port authority was "dedicating" the system to airport passengers. Although non-airport travelers would not be excluded from riding the system, they would pay fares well beyond those of the public transit system and as high as ten dollars. From the standpoint of residents of East Elmhurst and neighboring areas, they were being asked to bear the environmental hardships of a transportation system that they would be unable to use.

On June 16, 1994, a community meeting was held at La Détente Restaurant in East Elmhurst in the face of growing alarm over the port authority's airport initiatives. The meeting was organized by Joyce Cumberbatch, a retired deputy superintendent of schools and member of the 96th/97th Street Block Association. With a constituency of about 40 African-American households, the 96th/97th Street Block Association had come to be known as the "pit bulls" for its members' aggressive mobilizing activities around airport-related problems.

In 1988, for example, the association challenged the plans of a hotel owner in the airport area to operate his facility as a shelter for the homeless. Though their opposition to the conversion of the Travelers Inn, incited by a rash of burglaries, focused initially on the presence of "undesirables" in the quiet neighborhood, Cumberbatch and others succeeded in forging a new consensus among residents that directed attention to conditions at the hotel for the homeless. Cumberbatch recalled:

> We forced [the owners] to put a cap on the number of people they could have at the hotel. And we said, "Okay, if you're going to have them there, you've got to treat them like human beings. You have to give them refrigerators, you have to make sure that the children are taken care of, and that their education is not disturbed." We put those criteria in because we felt that it wasn't fair to say, "We don't want it." Because who are we to judge? After all, we could be in their situation one day.

Born in Jamaica, West Indies, Cumberbatch moved to East Elmhurst in 1958 from Harlem, where she had attended Harlem Hospital's school of nursing. "When I came here, East Elmhurst was like an oasis," she told me in her living room as jet engines roared overhead. "But the airport has changed all that." Prior to working with her block association, Cumberbatch had been active in school politics in Brooklyn and in south Queens. After retiring from her job and assuming responsibility for the care of her 98-year-old mother, Cumberbatch directed her energies to community issues in East Elmhurst. "This area has been very good to me. So I said to myself, 'The only way I can pay back what I've received is to get involved with the AGT issue.'"

As controversy over the port authority's plans to build the safety overrun and AGT system escalated during the summer, Cumberbatch began discussing the airport problems with her neighbors. She also began to investigate reports from residents of elevated cancer rates in areas adjacent to the airport. In May, the president of the 96th/97th Street Block Association suggested to Cumberbatch that she convene a block association subcommittee in her home to address airport-related problems.

The subcommittee's purpose, she later told me, was not only to build a consensus of opinion among residents on the port authority's development plans but also to develop a position that would frame opposition to the AGT as an issue of environmental justice, rather than as a reactive, "not-in-my-backyard" response to urban development.

> I heard this same rhetoric over and over again: "We don't need this, we don't want this." But nothing to support why [the AGT] shouldn't be. I thought that we needed some hard evidence of why it should not be, rather than simply taking an emotional stand. I felt that the port authority would listen to that more careful than neighborhoods just saying "not in my backyard," as an emotional issue. Because that's how the port authority would interpret it, although it's more than that. If we just say, "Hey, it's our neighborhood, we don't want this," it becomes a NIMBY thing—that communities don't want anything new in their neighborhood. And that's not true. It's true in one sense, but it's also the hazard that it's going to bring into the area. It's the change in lifestyle that we're against.

Key to the strategy pursued by Cumberbatch and the newly formed block association subcommittee were the goals of technical empowerment and coalition building. Familiarity with the "hard evidence" of urban development and its environmental effects, the subcommittee believed, would be crucial to comprehending the port authority's plan and to formulating, as Cumberbatch put it, a "proactive" position rooted in a critical analysis of its complex technical features and environmental implications. On the recommendation of her daughter, a program officer with the Joyce Mertz-Gilmore Foundation, Cumberbatch contacted the New York Public Interest Research Group (NYPIRG), a not-for-profit public watchdog and advocacy group, and the New York State Environmental Justice Alliance, a coalition of environmental justice organizations.

The block association's outreach to organizations that were addressing environmental and transportation questions not only in the context of the regional political economy but also as issues of environmental justice provided activists with the resources to rearticulate "backyard" interests in the technical and systems-focused discourse of urban planning. It also enabled them to recast their local concerns as a question of regional fairness—that is, an issue of the disproportionate environmental burden that minority and working-class areas bear in urban development practices (Bullard 1990, 1993).

Stressing the empowering quality of this regional overview and technical competence, Cumberbatch recalled: "I know that the port authority wasn't happy with us having those people in, our technical assistance. Because it escalated the issue. You know it gave it a new dimension which I don't think they were really expecting us to have. [The port authority] thought that it was gonna be the same old N-I-M-B-Y."

The subcommittee also stressed coalition building. Both the runway safety overrun and the AGT would affect a number of communities in Queens. In the case of the latter, the AGT's proposed path, or "alignment," would affect areas of northern and southern Queens, as well as Manhattan's Upper East Side, where the central terminal was to be located. Although the port authority's Airport Access Program (the unit coordinating community outreach activities) had contacted some elected officials and community boards and held "scoping" hearings in certain neighborhoods, many felt that these processes had been inadequately publicized and had funneled information and public deliberation into official, bureaucratic enclaves that hindered community mobilization and coalition building.

Prior to the June 16 meeting at La Détente Restaurant, Cumberbatch and her subcommittee began networking with activists from other neighborhoods that would be affected by the port authority's plans. A friend in Jamaica, Queens, gave her the names of two women who led civic groups in predominantly black southern Queens. Cumberbatch and members of her subcommittee visited these groups to provide them with information about the AGT. "They had been kept in the dark by their community board," she later said, adding that the board had declined to meet with PANYNJ's Airport Access team. Again working through informal channels, Cumberbatch contacted Rose Marie Poveromo, president of the United Community Civic Associations of Astoria, through a visiting nurse who was attending her mother. "I knew she was from Astoria so I asked her who I should contact there. That's how I found Marie."

Poveromo, along with community activists from southern Queens and nearby Jackson Heights, attended the public meeting at La Détente. They were joined by Lou Blain, an activist with NYPIRG, Michelle Depasse, the executive director of the New York State Environmental Justice Alliance, and George Haikalis, an independent public transportation advocate, all of whom were to give presentations on the port authority's projects.

Cumberbatch opened the meeting, emphasizing the importance of being informed about technical matters pertaining to the two projects. Some residents nodded their heads in agreement. Others scrutinized the plans for the safety overrun, mulling over technical drawings and debating the meaning of engineering terms such as "turbidity curtain" and "rip rap."

"If you look at the data they gave us," Cumberbatch continued, "and the timetable, they're starting to make inroads now. So rather than wait until they have done their planning, and their planning hasn't included us, it is very important that we be in on it and be educated consumers so that we'll know exactly what they're planning to do in our community. And it's also important that the port authority take us *all* into consideration. And that means Long Island City, Astoria, Jackson Heights, East Elmhurst, Corona, and going down to Jamaica."

The themes of empowerment through access to information and coalition building across neighborhood lines remained focal points of discussion and debate during the two-hour meeting. On the one hand, the complexity and scale of the proposed AGT system challenged residents not only to decipher and appraise the multitude of technical, engineering decisions underwriting the project (for example, the port authority's decision to build an elevated and automated, or "pilotless," system) but also to consider the AGT's systemic impact on the economy and environment.

On the other hand, opposition to the port authority's regional development strategy and ideology of "global competitiveness" required activists to recognize their political identities, interests, and allegiances in ways that overstepped, if not undermined, the frontiers of neighborhood-based politics. Place-based identities, bound by administrative designations of "community" and by localized constructions of racial and ethnic identity, provide ineffective subject positions from which to formulate needs, interests, and strategies in relation to regional political and economic processes (Harvey 1989).

Following Cumberbatch's introduction, Lou Blain, the water pollution expert with NYPIRG, gave a presentation on conditions in Flushing Bay. He stressed the importance of viewing local quality-of-life issues within a regional framework and encouraged residents to consider the impact of the runway 13-31 overrun within the wider context of Flushing Bay's pollution problem.

Cumberbatch introduced the next speaker, George Haikalis, the independent transportation consultant and advocate of rail transportation. "Good," a woman blurted. "Where the hell were you when we were fightin' them about the overrun?"

The audience listened attentively as Haikalis described the port authority's AGT plan in detail. He and other critics of the AGT were opposed to the building of a discrete, high-tech airport access system that would be incompatible with the city's mass transit infrastructure. Instead, Haikalis contended, an airport access system should make use of and, where necessary, extend existing subway lines and roadbeds. This, he argued, would make the airport access system available to users traveling to and from a wider range of locations. The proposed system would not only provide relatively few transfer points between existing subway lines and the AGT but also restrict ridership to airport passengers and employees.

When Haikalis finished, an elderly woman from East Elmhurst called out, "I'm not gonna take no train to the airport. The people who are going to benefit are the people from Manhattan." A chorus of grumbles echoed her sentiment. Many felt that the port authority was again running roughshod over the neighborhood, privileging the needs of Manhattan residents over the quality-of-life concerns of the "outer boroughs."

Barbara Coleman, an African-American member of Community Board 3, asked, "What can we do to change this? It's impossible to get them to change their minds. They don't live in East Elmhurst. They don't see, out their window, a thirty-foot train. This is ridiculous. And I want from you some ideas to get them to change their minds." Haikalis responded by stressing the importance of coalition building.

Rose Marie Poveromo (RP in the following dialogue), president of the predominantly white United Community Civic Associations of Astoria, had been listening attentively to the remarks of Coleman and the others from East Elmhurst. She raised her hand to speak. "The Airport Access people have contacted us in Astoria," she began. "And my membership is *not* happy with it."

"That's right," exclaimed Barbara Coleman (BC), sitting behind her. Poveromo had been invited to the meeting by Joyce Cumberbatch and had never met any of the black activists at the meeting. During the course of Poveromo's comments, Coleman and others from Corona–East Elmhurst punctuated her statements with declarations of support. Encouraged, Poveromo stood and continued.

> **RP:** So...um, we're not unique. I think all of us together have indicated, not only to the port authority but also to the mayor and his very inept Department of City Planning...
>
> **BC [SPEAKING SIMULTANEOUSLY]:** Yes!
>
> **RP:**...that we in Queens County have *had* it!
>
> **BC:** That's right!
>
> **RP:** We are *sick* and tired of being dumped on.
>
> **BC [SPEAKING SIMULTANEOUSLY]:** and tired
>
> **RP:** The airport access, the monorail, right where we—They can give it any fancy name they want. The people of Queens County will *not* benefit from the air—from the monorail. It will not be for our use unless we travel from Manhattan to the airport every *day* and...go on a plane. We as residents of Queens County who

are going to have to live with this...*monster* twenty feet up in the air—And all the pylons and the graffiti and the dirt up underneath these...ah...this so-called high railing, we will not be able to use this access train. It will only be for the use of an airline traveler or personnel at the airports. This is a disgrace. The City of New York—The system is down. It's not only down with the port authority. It's down with every system. The left hand doesn't know what the right hand is doing. Foster care, child welfare, the City of New York, Department of City Planning, the mayor's office, the governor's office, the state—This system is *down*. And unless we all band together, all of us, community boards, civic associations...

BC [SPEAKING SIMULTANEOUSLY]: That's right!

RP:...block associations, all of us, we will not accomplish anything in Queens County. We all must stand together, fight together, be vocal and militant in order for these people who we put in office, ah...understand we will not reelect them unless they come back and *do what we want*. We're payin' the goddamn taxes here.

When the applause died down, Haikalis responded nodding his head in sympathy.

HAIKALIS: Well I—I just wanted to say one thing about—I live in Manhattan. But basically, people who live in Nassau and Suffolk Counties and work in Manhattan take the Long Island Railroad through Queens during rush hour. And if those people were to drive through Queens it would be a mess. I think you have to look at this from a systems point of view. We do need a way for people to get to—

RP: Yeah, but you misunderstand—Excuse me sir, with all due respect. The people—who live in Nassau and Suffolk County—unless they're going to the airport and getting on a plane, will not be able to use the monorail...

BC [SPEAKING SIMULTANEOUSLY]: Thank you!

RP: If they're working in Manhattan they cannot use the monorail.

If they're working in Queens County, they cannot use the monorail...

BC [SPEAKING SIMULTANEOUSLY]: Thank you!

RP: If we residents live here, we cannot use the monorail.

BC [SPEAKING SIMULTANEOUSLY]: We can't use the monorail!

RP: We're gonna get dumped on, have this goddamn thing twenty feet up in the air, have to look at it every goddamn day, but we're not gonna be able to use it.

BC: Right!

Haikalis *had* misunderstood. Poveromo's comments were not to be read as a reactive, NIMBY response to change, pitting the interests of local communities against the greater good of the region. In fact, Poveromo, Cumberbatch, and others *were* "thinking globally" and raising important questions about the fairness or evenness of regional development policies, procedures, and their legitimating discourses. As Joyce Cumberbatch later put it, "My community is New York City. It's Corona, Astoria, Manhattan, and everywhere else."

Following Haikalis's presentation, residents asked a barrage of questions about particular design features of the proposed AGT system. One East Elmhurst woman asked about luggage space on the trains. She had heard that AGT trains would have space only for light, carry-on bags, which she felt was evidence that the system was being developed exclusively for elite business travelers. Another woman challenged the claim that airport employees would have access to the system: "No matter where you get on you have to have a plane ticket." An elderly man asked what effect train vibration would have on homes.

As more people spoke, providing new information and new grounds for opposing the AGT, the audience became increasingly animated. Hamlett Wallace, the African-American chair of Community Board 3's Aviation Subcommittee, declared that the port authority had come to the board and made "a fictitious representation to us, playing on people's intelligence—the works." He continued: "One group gets one bit of information, which is not correct or only half-baked. Another gets another bit of information. The port authority is hoping that these people will not come together and that they won't understand what the other person's doing, which is their method of approach. All of us have to get together. This way we can make an impact. Otherwise we're not gonna get anywhere."

A roar of applause rose from the audience, along with shouts of "That's right!" Joyce Cumberbatch stepped forward, waving a notepad in the air. "This was our purpose, to get us together so that we could communicate and be in alignment with each other. Because if we're not, they're gonna shoot us all down. And it's so important. Each one of you represents about thirty other people, so this is *great*, this is a good working group. So now, what we have to do is plan, and plan very precisely what our next moves will be."

Cumberbatch's comments led to a flurry of conversations across the room. Poveromo announced that her group, the United Community Civic Associations of Astoria, would hold a public meeting in September that would bring community boards and civic associations in northern Queens together to discuss common concerns. She reiterated the charge made earlier that the port authority was carrying out a strategy of "divide and conquer" to contain and fragment community opposition to the project:

> What the port authority has done, and they are notorious for this, is to go to you and speak to you, go to me and speak to my association. What they're doing, is divide and conquer. They're very smart. They're calling it Airport Access and reaching out to the community. But what they should have done, and what they should do now, is call one huge meeting at LaGuardia and involve us all, and bring us all together, and tell one story. They haven't done that.

Like the speakers before her, Poveromo stressed the link between coalition building and the widening of the public sphere of community activism. The port authority's practices of "divide and conquer" served to limit and fragment community participation and opposition and to regulate and restrict access to information—information concerning not only the wider, systemic impact of the AGT project but also, as Wallace pointed out, about "what the other person's doing." In this way, PANYNJ's airport access strategy buttressed place-bound constructions of identity, interests, and needs by channeling access to information and citizen participation through existing bureaucratic procedures and political formations.

By contrast, activist appeals to "get together," to "be in alignment with each other" (a telling appropriation of the port authority's technical jargon), and to confront the port authority in "one huge meeting" articulated the need to transgress these static, bureaucratic frontiers and constitute a broader and more heterogeneous political space.

Barbara Coleman, raising her voice against the escalating din, turned to Poveromo and told her that community groups from Jamaica to the south should also be invited to the public forum in Astoria planned for mid-September. Poveromo turned around in her chair to reply. "Yes, and what we need from you is names and addresses of those organizations that we don't know how to reach out to."

Joyce Cumberbatch gestured to the representatives from Jamaica, reiterating the invitation to attend the Astoria meeting and participate in the coalition. One of the three women attending the meeting from Jamaica stood to respond. The audience became quiet.

> I'm the former president of the United Neighborhood Association and this...ah...has been rich and very informative. We were not aware of the impact that this kind of thing would have on our community. And now that I've been made aware tonight of all the things that are going on, I certainly will be bringing it up with my community people. Also, with our community board. Community Board 12 represents us and I don't really know where they stand at this point.

Her testimony provoked a new round of applause and animated cross-talking. Civic activists from Jamaica and other neighborhoods in southern Queens were seldom, if ever, seen and heard at community meetings in the north. "The Airport Access people should go to Jamaica," Barbara Coleman declared, as the meeting drew to a close. She tightened her brow and jabbed her index finger into the air. "And let's see what they think!"

"MORE BOUNCE FOR THE OUNCE"

On June 28, almost two weeks after the public meeting at La

Détente, the port authority's Airport Access team met at LaGuardia Airport with Community Board 3's Aviation Subcommittee, composed largely of African-American activists from East Elmhurst. At earlier meetings with the port authority, the subcommittee had raised concerns about the AGT's impact on the North Shore. Members of the subcommittee, which included Barbara Coleman, Hamlett Wallace, and Arthur Hayes, president of the East Elmhurst–Corona Civic Association, had argued that the elevated AGT would obstruct residents' "view corridors" of Flushing Bay. To meet these objections, the port authority had developed a number of alternative alignments for the AGT that were to be presented at the meeting by port authority consultants.

However, the meeting at La Détente had changed the playing field, widening the scope of neighborhood concerns about the AGT and involving new players in the process. On the one hand, the La Détente meeting had provided a public forum where residents were informed about regional environmental and transportation issues, as well as planning alternatives. Important questions had been raised about the overall design and impact of the AGT and, in particular, its preferential accommodation of Manhattan-based business travelers at the expense of Queens residents. This widening of debate and proliferation of contested issues stretched neighborhood concerns beyond that of the blocked "view corridors" of homeowners, which had been a central theme in earlier negotiations with the port authority.

On the other hand, the La Détente meeting had given East Elmhurst activists the opportunity to network with activists in other areas and, in the process, to collectively rearticulate place-bound, local identities and interests in transneighborhood terms. To the surprise, if not the chagrin, of PANYNJ officials, Community Board 3's meeting with its Airport Access team was also attended by white activists from Astoria (Community Board 1) and by the transportation and environmental advocates who had given presentations at La Détente.

As we shall see, PANYNJ's response to this widening of representation and debate was to funnel deliberation about the AGT system into enclaved areas of technical expertise and problem solving that, as Nancy Fraser has observed in a related context, "shield such matters from widely disseminated conflicts of interpretation" (1989:168).

Activists filed into the small meeting room set back from the art deco lobby of LaGuardia's Marine Air Terminal, once home to Pan American Airlines' clipper service. A team of port authority officials and consultants greeted people as they arrived. An employee served refreshments. The conference table in the middle of the room could not seat the unexpectedly large group of 25. Extra chairs were brought into the room for Rose Marie Poveromo and the others from Astoria, as well as for Joyce Cumberbatch and members of the 96th/97th Street Block Association. George Haikalis and representatives from the New York State Environmental Justice Alliance and NYPIRG sat on a leather sofa against the wall.

An outreach specialist with PANYNJ's Airport Access Program opened the meeting, stressing the evolution and durability of the port authority's negotiations with "the community." The outreach specialist's narrative of an orderly, step-by-step progress toward problem resolution would be invoked by PANYNJ officials on other occasions to keep the discussion on track:

> Needless to say, the community worked very closely with the Airport Access, and the Airport Access with the community, to come to some agreement. I can tell you it's a very arduous past, because we went back to the drawing board time and time again. It wasn't something that could happen overnight and it wasn't something that could be done in one short meeting or with one design. We turned out developing many, many designs that we presented to this committee. And at the last meeting we presented several options to the committee. One of the options was very acceptable to the committee. We went back and, as a result, that particular option is something that's going to be discussed tonight and I think the committee will find very suitable.

Then, as if to give public authority to this seamless narrative of dialogue and compromise, the official held up a newspaper article that had been published three days earlier. "And certainly," she began, "you're all familiar with the article that was in the paper." Everyone stared quizzically at the piece of paper dangling from her outstretched hand.

She continued. "If not, I did bring copies just in case some of you did not see it. It was in Saturday's *Newsday* talking about how the Airport Access has worked in the community, exactly what the plan is, how the concession has been made, how the alignment has changed somewhat to keep most of that community and the vision [i.e., view corridor] intact."

The article, entitled "East Elmhurst Gets Way on Airport Rail," reported that the port authority had agreed to construct the East Elmhurst section of the AGT below ground level in order to preserve homeowners' views of Flushing Bay. To the surprise of activists at the meeting, it continued: "The move, cheered by East Elmhurst residents and politicians, is expected to add $10 million to the planned $2.6 billion rail project." Queens borough president Claire Shulman was cited as crediting port authority officials with "responding to community concerns." Congressman Thomas Manton added that the agreement "represents some progress to satisfy the community so [the port authority] can get along with the bigger picture of linking the two airports" (*Newsday*, 27 June 1994, p. 28). In short, the article announced the community's acceptance of the compromise proposal three days before it had been presented to the community.

While residents were ruminating over the *Newsday* article, the official introduced Peter, a port authority consultant who would describe the new, below-ground alignment. Aided by aerial photographs mapping the various AGT routes in myriad colors and by a variety of technical drawings, Peter explained the strengths and weaknesses of the routes that had been considered and explained the port authority's compromise plan.

In response to the concerns of Community Board 3 and its constituents in East Elmhurst, the port authority had agreed to construct the East Elmhurst section of the people mover below ground level. Peter explained that the AGT would be "in an elevated condition" from the Queensboro Bridge to LaGuardia Airport. After leaving the airport, it would drop below ground level as it passed along the shore of Flushing Bay and then rise once more as it veered south toward Kennedy Airport.

"Excuse me," Rose Marie Poveromo blurted, waving her hand in the direction of the satellite photograph. "For those of us who are uneducated here, ah, what streets are we talking about? I mean you're showing me drawings but you're not mentioning street names." Faltering at first, the PANYNJ consultant gave names to the anonymous streets in the aerial photograph, pointing out where the AGT would meet the Grand Central Parkway in Astoria, skirt along the parkway to LaGuardia, and, on leaving the airport, drop below ground level as it passed through East Elmhurst. Poveromo shook her head defiantly and exchanged censuring glances with Joan DaCorta, president of the Astoria Heights Homeowners and Tenants Association. A flurry of questions followed.

Pat Beckles, a civil engineer and president of East Elmhurst's powerful Ditmars Boulevard Block Association, asked the consultant how the revised "below grade" alignment of the AGT would affect the view of the bay for homeowners living on Ditmars Boulevard. The PANYNJ consultant responded by displaying a series of drawings on large poster boards depicting the AGT's new "depressed" alignment in relation to the homes on Ditmars Boulevard overlooking the bay.

In the illustration, the AGT tracks were enclosed in a tube, partially depressed below ground level. The top of the tube, which protruded about six feet above ground, was capped by a concrete ceiling. The ground next to the tunnel had been built up, forming a landscaped slope or berm from the tunnel's roof to the park land fronting on Flushing Bay. Dotted sight lines in the drawing traced unobstructed "visual corridors" from the homes on Ditmars Boulevard, over the depressed tunnel, and down to Flushing Bay. The consultant passed the awkward poster boards around the room for people to examine.

Poveromo waved her hand to speak. "I don't understand," she began, raising her voice precipitously. "If you could accommodate one community so that they would have a view of the bay, why weren't you able to bury the entire thing so that every community would be accommodated?"

The PANYNJ consultant replied that it would be too expensive, citing the $10 million in added costs that would be incurred by the East Elmhurst depression. But before he could elaborate on the technical details, Poveromo interrupted again: "But you have to understand where the working people from Queens County are coming from. They're not gonna benefit from this. The only people that are gonna benefit from this are the airline travelers and the people who work at the airports. But those of us who live in these communities are going to be impacted adversely by this monorail, or whatever you want to call it."

Invoking "the working people of Queens County," Poveromo directed attention to the broader, regional implications of the AGT plan and, in particular, to issues of fairness in urban development planning. Her comments provoked disgruntled remarks from residents and a new round of site-specific questions about the elevated route of the AGT system through Astoria, Jackson Heights, and East Elmhurst.

Helen Sears, chairing the meeting for the port authority, held up her hands to quiet the audience. "If we are going to accomplish anything here tonight, we will have to agree on some ground rules." The port authority consultant, still holding the drawing of the visual corridors, informed the gathering that many of the issues now being raised had already been addressed at previous meetings of the committee. "It would probably take me only a few minutes," he added, "to address what we have discussed in past meetings. Now why don't I do that?"

The audience, only half of whom had attended the earlier meetings of the committee, resisted the consultant's appeal to a narrative of negotiated, step-by-step progress to the present. Joyce Cumberbatch asked what impact the revised AGT alignment would have on the yet-to-be-built park and promenade along the shore of Flushing Bay that had been promised by the borough president of Queens.

Again trying to get the discussion back on track, Sears intervened: "Well that's why we've got to finish this first, to address [the questions] that the committee has already raised and then we can go on from there."

The activists settled down, and the consultant continued his presentation. Focusing on the East Elmhurst portion of the AGT alignment, Peter explained how the landscaped slope abutting the AGT tube would serve as a "visual and acoustic wall" shielding the promised park and promenade from the sights and sounds of the eight-lane Grand Central Parkway, only yards away. He then uncovered a large poster board depicting the portion of the AGT route that would skirt Flushing Bay between the expressway and park land. The board displayed a photo blowup of the area. An illustration showing the depressed AGT alignment, the landscaped berm, and the yet-to-be-built promenade had been airbrushed on the photograph.

"This is a view," he began haltingly, holding up the large board. "If you were in a park, and the park were built and, ah, and the, ah…" Caught between the real and the imaginary, the consultant groped for an appropriate tense to describe the image.

> I think that one should imagine a promenade there. I think you can see here—This, by the way, is a mechanically drawn, very accurate perspective, using all the dimensions, and plans, and profiles that are there. It's a very accurate representation, because we don't want to fool ourselves, and we don't want to fool you. If you build this, you're gonna have a screen for the Grand Central Parkway. I think that this shows clearly that you're going to have a visual screen. And if you have a visual screen, you've got a noise screen. And the park itself is some-thing that's going to come along when the promenade is designed. Basically what you're going to have is a landscaped backdrop for the project. And the beauty of the berm is—For instance, if you look at the grass along there now, it's sort of wimpy looking. But if you tilt that up towards you [i.e., by con-structing the berm], all of a sudden, you're presented with much more green. And you get much more bounce for the ounce out of the landscaping.

While residents were puzzling over the photo-illustration, a port authority official added: "I think the point is, really…A number of peo-ple have raised the question, what does [the AGT] do for Queens in general? I think it provides a nice space that all the people of Queens can enjoy. It provides the opportunity—"

Before he could finish, the consultant interrupted, "It is a set-up for the promenade that the promenade does not now have. It's a set-up. And it gives you insulation from the parkway."

A setup indeed. Residents were being asked to regard the de-pressed AGT alignment as a visual and noise screen for a park and promenade that did not yet exist. Cumberbatch asked the consultant whether the port authority would uphold a commitment to landscap-ing the park and promenade. City Councilwoman Marshall intervened, explaining that funding for the future park and promenade had been committed by another source. The New York City Department of

Environmental Protection (DEP) would fund the park and promenade as mitigation for locating a sewage storage facility in nearby Flushing Meadows–Corona Park. The port authority, Peter added, would land-scape only the berm. "It was gravy," he declared.

Marshall's comments were quickly followed by a flurry of critical comments by activists from Astoria: they wanted their end of the AGT "buried" too. Fuming, Poveromo raised her hand to speak:

> Excuse me, sir, may I just indicate along with Joan DaCorta—
> We do live in Community Board 1, we are also members of
> Community Board 1, and we are also civic activists in the com-
> munity. And I would just like to indicate to you that we will not
> go with an elevated structure. And, certainly, what you have
> managed to do here is be divisive: divide one community
> against another, which is very, very bad. Because Queens
> County will suffer no matter what plans you come up with here.
> This will not benefit the working people of Queens County. As I
> said at the very outset, it will benefit the airline traveler, the
> tourist, and the people who work at the airports. We, down the
> line, will not benefit from this thing.

The debate between the Astoria activists and port authority offi-cials continued. After 15 minutes, Barbara Coleman intervened, recall-ing the meeting that had been held two weeks earlier at La Détente:

> We had a meeting and a consortium of Queens people, not only
> from Community Board 3, which may have been the loudest,
> but also from Community Board 1, and I do feel that their con-
> cerns are perfectly acceptable. Go back and come up with a bet-
> ter AGT. Because although what you're telling the East
> Elmhurst area would appear to meet the needs of most of the
> people in East Elmhurst, we are concerned about people in
> other communities. And I don't like the idea of you putting one
> against the other. Besides, you're going to catch hell from
> Community Board 12 when you get into Jamaica.

Coleman went on to question the need for a link between LaGuardia and JFK and asked why the AGT planners had not made use of existing rail lines and rights-of-way—points that had been stressed by the transportation advocates who had spoken at the La Détente meeting.

Trying again to keep the discussion focused on the plan for the East Elmhurst depression, Sears proposed that Community Board 1 form its own aviation committee, which would then meet with port authority officials to address the specific questions and concerns of Astoria residents. Grudgingly, the activists from Astoria and East Elmhurst consented.

Sears continued: "Now maybe we should go back to what was shown to you earlier, which was the depression in East Elmhurst and the promenade. Can we have a comment from the chair of the committee on exactly what your sentiments are about what was presented tonight?"

Hamlett Wallace, chairman of Community Board 3's Aviation Committee, stood to address the gathering:

> At this particular time, I'm pleased with the result. Hopefully this will be carried out. I think that this is a positive effort on the part of the port authority. As everybody knows realistically this AGT doesn't do anything for us. We want the port authority to be sensitive to our needs across the board. As far as this committee is concerned, we are pleased with the semisubmerged effort along with the beautification of our promenade. And I think that it will be an enhancement.

A grumble of discontent spread throughout the room. Joyce Cumberbatch cut her eyes to the members of her block association and raised her eyebrows in alarm. Poveromo and DaCorta stood and noisily collected their things. Arthur Hayes, president of the East Elmhurst–Corona Civic Association, addressed Ed O'Sullivan, director of the port authority's Airport Access Program.

"Just one question," Hayes began quietly, holding up a photocopy of the *Newsday* article foretelling the agreement that had just been reached. "Why was this information released to the press *before* we had an opportunity to meet?" The group settled back into their chairs and awaited O'Sullivan's response.

"We had prepared a press release," O'Sullivan replied, "in anticipation of your accepting this. We did not release it. However, an elected official, the press officer of an elected official…Somebody jumped the gun and released it on Friday. It was not the port authority. We had no intention whatsoever because all we would do by that is alienate people. So we did not release it."

People in the room snarled when O'Sullivan declined to reveal the identity of the political official involved. "Let me ask another question," Hayes continued. "I suspect that, since some time ago, you were meeting with elected officials prior to coming to this committee. Now we come here to discuss a point and you've already agreed on this thing. I think that it should be fair, that any information you discuss with elected officials should be supplied to the chairman of our committee so that we're aware of what's going on behind the scenes. Because we came here in good faith and made these recommendations and I think that we should be aware of everything."

Although Poveromo and the other activists from Astoria left the meeting pledging continued resistance, an uneasy settlement had been reached with East Elmhurst: an agreement whose conditions of possibility relied on the construction of neighborhood needs, identities, and interests in fragmented and place-bound terms.

The port authority's practices of community outreach and negotiation privileged and indeed reinforced local, place-bound constructions of neighborhood identity and interests. They did so by shielding broader questions about the AGT from deliberation and debate and by responding assertively to statements of need and interest that were formulated in narrow and depoliticized terms.

This governing of deliberation undermined the earlier attempts of activists to articulate claims of shared interests across neighborhood boundaries. When, for example, activists pointed out that the concerns of Astoria and other neighborhoods were not being addressed through the East Elmhurst compromise, thereby questioning the AGT's regional appropriateness and impact, PANYNJ officials recommended that Astoria's issues be addressed by its own community board.

If the port authority's outreach practices hindered coalition building, they also incited activists to experience, represent, and pursue wider and potentially generalizable issues and struggles within the context of the proximate environment—that is, as a defense of the rights of homeowners to enjoy their property. The more general question of whether or not the AGT was an equitable and reasonable solution to the airport access problem—and, by extension, to the city's economic problems—was contained. It was framed as an issue of preserving the "view corridors" of middle-class homeowners and of providing a landscaped "setup" for the yet-to-be-built Flushing Bay park and promenade.

Barbara Coleman, explaining later why she had not argued more forcefully against the East Elmhurst compromise, gave voice to the resulting paradox:

> The idea of putting the train in a trench is fantastic. Of course the community doesn't want the train. I didn't speak out, simply because there wasn't anything to say at that time. We don't want it, and I personally feel that it would be a waste of money. But they gave us the trench, and so in deference to them giving us that, I didn't say anything. What would I have said? I would have said, "We need a train like I need a hole in my toe."

CONCLUSION

Why *do* people defer to power—to what they don't want? Why do social groups frequently fail to articulate and act on common interests across differences? And why, when confronted with the systemic imperatives of power, do the participants in urban social movements often fall back on place-bound or NIMBY-like formulations of identity and interests?

East Elmhurst's struggle with the port authority suggests that this defensive response, this appeal to view corridors and property values, in the last instance was neither an unmediated expression of a transparent black, middle-class political identity nor simply the result of the difficulty experienced by activists of thinking globally from the grass roots (cf. Castells 1989). During the course of the struggle, activists articulated a complex range of opinions or subject positions regarding the AGT, sometimes emphasizing the structural inequities of the PANYNJ proposal as an issue of environmental justice shaped by power differentials and at other times falling back on local or "backyard" claims to individual property rights and the quality-of-life prerogatives of homeowners.

What *moved* East Elmhurst's activists to compromise, to accede to the fantastic idea of the "trench," was an ensemble of practices that, though contested, served to constrict possibilities for recognizing and articulating collective commitments to wider-based struggles for economic and political justice. These practices ranged from the port authority's divisive outreach practices, its policing of debate, and its discourse of techno-possibility to the outright manipulation of the mass media. They governed the political arena of neighborhood activism, enabling the formation of certain collective subject positions and allegiances while disabling others.

Barbara Coleman's comment, "I didn't speak out, simply because there wasn't anything to say at that time," conveys the sense not that there was nothing to be said but rather that what could be said *at that time* would not have mustered the efficacy or "illocutionary force" (Bourdieu 1991:100) needed to realign the people mover's opponents in support of a shared critique of its systemic impact. "What would I have said?" Coleman asked rhetorically. "We need the train like I need a hole in my toe?"

Coleman's reading of the situational constraints brought to bear on the politically sayable by the port authority's practices of governing public debate and deliberation underscores not only the malleability of political subjectivity but also the extent to which the latter endures as a "constantly re-created unity depending on the whole relation of forces in a society at a given moment" (Laclau and Mouffe 1982:100).

Activists from East Elmhurst and surrounding communities accurately perceived that PANYNJ officials were being divisive—conducting a war of position within these relations of force to recast opposition along the bureaucratically defined frontiers of local community and on the optical field of what Mike Davis has called "homestead exclusivism" (1990:159). And on this field, the port authority's appeal to residents to imagine a landscaped promenade and unobstructed view corridor of the North Shore enabled, if only provisionally, a formulation of community concerns that stressed their identity as black "middle-class homeowners" committed to a particular quality of life and experience of urban space.

In stressing the port authority's role in inciting these situationally bound class dispositions, I do not minimize their heterogeneity or the degree to which they are contested and reshaped in everyday practice.

To be sure, the meeting at La Détente Restaurant demonstrated that activists constituted themselves in a variety of ways and in relation to myriad readings of the interrelation of space, identity, and power: as working people of Queens County (versus Manhattan-based corporate elites), as subjects of "inept" and unjust structures of urban governance, and as members of a transneighborhood alliance mobilized to oppose a discourse and strategy of "global competitiveness."

In fact, many activists remained opposed to the project and were critical of the arguments made by PANYNJ officials and Borough President Shulman supporting the view that the AGT system was key to promoting the region's global competitiveness and to stimulating job growth in Queens. Barbara Coleman reflected: "I don't know how many businesses would be coming into Queens even under the best of circumstances. Whether businesses need access to the airport through a train system, I don't know. I listen to [Borough President] Claire Shulman and she says she's interested in businesses and the new jobs, and so on. Maybe her foresight is better than mine, but I don't see that many new jobs coming in as a result [of the AGT]. But that's the story they always tell to get what they want."

Rather, I argue that the formation of class dispositions and collective identities is an effect of political struggles that, waged at multiple sites in the public sphere, implicate a plurality of power relations and determinations. East Elmhurst's acceptance of the compromise plan was less the result of an activation of interests grounded in an a priori, "ready-made" black middle-class identity than that of a struggle over the social and political meanings of space, the definition of "community," and the interpretation of the city's economic development needs. Indeed, it was precisely the port authority's capacity to both organize and govern the public sphere of neighborhood activism that enabled PANYNJ officials to incite the formation of a middle-class homeowner stance and undermine possibilities for constructing alternative alignments of interest.

EPILOGUE

On October 20, 1994, port authority officials met with Community Board 3 to announce that the plan for the East Elmhurst "trench" and landscaped berm had been scrapped. As activists feared, port authority officials had failed to coordinate their planning of the AGT's East Elmhurst alignment with the Parks Department, the city agency charged with building the Flushing Bay park and promenade. Consequently, port authority officials informed the community board, it had been discovered after the East Elmhurst agreement had been reached that the North Shore was too narrow to accommodate both the AGT and the future park and promenade.

Corona–East Elmhurst's struggle against the port authority did not end in defeat. On June 1, 1995, George Marlin, PANYNJ's executive director, announced that the proposed 22-mile AGT plan was "dead" (*New York Times*, 1 June 1995, p. A1). Marlin, appointed by newly elected governor George Pataki, cited soaring cost estimates for the AGT as a prime reason for scrapping the original plan. Port authority officials feared that the AGT's cost, now estimated at $5 billion, could not be raised from the PFC ticket surcharge as first claimed and would require massive public subsidization.

One year later, the port authority's board of directors approved a new, smaller-scale plan for an elevated light-rail airport access system that would bypass LaGuardia Airport. Under the $1 billion plan, an 8.4-mile rail link would be built between Kennedy Airport and the Long Island Railroad's Jamaica Station in Queens (*New York Times*, 11 May 1996, p. 24). In this proposal, LaGuardia Airport would be served by a high-speed ferry system departing from Manhattan's East Side, which would be developed through a separate project (FAA/NYSDOT 1996). "It is a first step," George Marlin told *Newsday*. "There is minimal community opposition. The money is available. The technology is available....We have to focus in getting it off the drawing boards" [*sic*] (*Newsday*, 14 May 1996, p. A5).

Note

I would like to thank the other participants in the 1994 School of American Research advanced seminar "History in Person" for their very helpful comments on an earlier draft of this paper.

6

"Tekin' the Piss"

Paul Willis

> For the first six months they took the piss out of me. For the
> next eleven years I took the piss out of them.
> —*Worker in a foundry in the English industrial midlands, 1979*

As Begoña Aretxaga observed during discussion of my paper at the
SAR seminar, between the transgression and reproduction of a social
system undoubtedly lies the historical space for a theorized and
grounded sense of human experience. This is also to say that systems
reproduce themselves not mechanically but at least in part through
"self-directed" cultural forms, fulfilling themselves in a way that also fulfills some general system needs. This view differs from an account of
experience as arising from some kind of transhistorical human essence,
on one side, and from arguments that see it as arising from the determinations of economy or "discourse," on the other. Here is a historical
and dialectical space in which *specific* kinds of agency in determinate
conditions produce "creative" and challenging responses that nevertheless act finally to "re-create" aspects of what has been opposed. What
"fills up" this space between transgression and reproduction, and how
it does so, is truly the focus and material of "history in person."

One such "filling up" is the focus of this chapter: the "piss take"—
particularly in its fool's errand or "put-on" version—that is visited
so often upon young male manual workers during their "cultural

apprenticeship" after arriving "on the shop floor." My ethnographic example is specific to the factory culture of the English midlands during a particular historical period, and it is drawn from a class formation that has since been "rearranged" by devastating economic change, shifting and tightening labor regimes, and different varieties of gendered, racial patterns of worker response. Nevertheless, I would argue that we are dealing here with certain "long-term" cultural categories. They contain forms of knowing and belonging that, mutatis mutandis, persist through population shifts and diasporas and through different historical conjunctions. They provide the bedrock for the continuing currency and reproduction of a whole genre of "urban myths." These stories, myths, and practices pertain to structural aspects of capitalist formation per se, in particular to a grounds for inevitable, though variable, human response to the mental-manual division of labor, to the deepening real subsumption of labor to capital, and to claims by the managers of capital to control what we must now call "truth regimes" behind the "Entry Forbidden" signs at the point of production.

The "piss take" is a widespread form, especially in exaggerated male cultures; it is notable, for instance, in bar, sport, and criminal cultures. My arguments later in this chapter about relations of the symbolic to the "real" as brokered through the exercise of power, and about the specificity of certain kinds of "knowing" related to a variable sense of the (labor) powers of the self, have pertinence to all these sites. I would argue, though, that the major and connecting site for a certain kind of "rough" male humor continues to be the shop floor.

Other common informal names for the piss take include "taking the mickey," "ribbing," "pulling your leg," and "taking it out of you." It is elusive to definition and is reduced by it, but the piss take hinges most basically on a form of irony, on a "doubling" of reality, or being in two places at once. The *Oxford English Dictionary* classifies "to take the piss" as "coarse British slang" meaning to "mock" or "parody." This is close but misses the element of the real or assumed incomprehension of the victim about the meaning of what is said or unfolds. If you like, the piss take is "po-faced" (solemn or humorless) mockery. It involves a double reality or definition, only one of which the target is aware of, or is deemed to be aware of.

This real or assumed innocence of the victim is particularly characteristic of a specific form of the piss take visited upon young manual workers: the put-on, or fool's errand. The OED classifies "put-on" as a colloquialism meaning a deception or hoax. It is an irony played out with a physical dimension involving the real disposition of bodies, as in a practical joke, resulting in somebody's being in the "wrong place" or undertaking a useless activity without being aware of its redundancy— to use another colloquialism, the victim becomes involved in a wild goose chase. These practices are worked up sometimes into the particular rituals of "apprenticeship traditions" in the traditional elite craft occupations, but my focus in this chapter is on the more general form.

I present some examples of the piss take and the put-on in the form of a long, continuous extract from an interview with a single worker, whom I call Percy. I then examine these forms and analyze them both for their internal terms and mechanisms and for their "nonaccidental" connection and relation to some fundamental features of capitalist work regimes. The extract has an added methodological-theoretical feature of interest, for it shows the way in which I am developing my own analysis of the piss take "on the hoof" during the interview and also trying it out, for validity, on my respondent. He resists important aspects of my interpretation, as well as the language within which it is presented. I attempt to explain this reflexively within the terms of my analysis, also facing and admitting some of the irreducible difficulties of an interpretive approach, which Percy's responses so unambiguously raise.

This chapter presents some taped field data for the first time. It is drawn from the participant observation research I did subsequent to that reported in *Learning to Labour* (Willis 1977). In the more recent research, I revisited some of "the lads" at work and "clocked on," working alongside them and other workers for a period of days or weeks. This proved to be an effective approach for seeing what happened to the lads, and it also provided an excellent route—sponsored by the lads' familiarity with me—into adult shop-floor culture.

One such field assignment in 1979 took me to what I will call "Midlands Foundries." This was a mid-sized (250 workers or so) old factory in a declining, "scruffy" urban area producing engine castings. The technology was traditional, with sweating bodies moving around glowing blast furnaces like figures in a miniature Dante's inferno. Joey (the very lively and intelligent one from *Learning to Labour*) was working in a "site gang," mercifully outside the foundry, keeping the factory premises tidy and in reasonable repair, providing internal transport around the plant, and, most importantly, making and repairing wooden pallets, which apparently were in inexhaustible demand as platforms for handling, storing, and transporting castings. For two weeks I worked in the site gang, which was usually composed of ten workers. I perfected how to drive a nail in hard and fast. In and out of the pallet shed and often joining us in a small site hut for breaks and lunch was a stocky, animated, rather short man I call Percy. Percy had done most things around foundries and was currently the site lorry driver, moving materials and castings around internally. He was nearing retirement and was a well known and liked figure around the plant, always ready with a combative word or a pungent one-liner. When my workmates saw him approach the hut during break times there were nudges and comments: "Aye, aye, here comes Percy." He was a "good bloke" and "one of us" and right at the heart of a distinctive, masculine, rough-and-ready shop-floor culture.

I asked Percy if I could interview him at his home on tape about his views on shop-floor life in general but also specifically about the language used there and, in particular, something that had come to intrigue me—a distinctive form of heavy humor absolutely characteristic of the shop-floor relations I had observed at this and many other plants. On especially male shop floors, an absolutely central ingredient of the living culture was the piss take. This was often directed at young workers, specifically in the form of the put-on, but could claim anyone as victim. The piss take merged into other kinds of humor: "wind-ups," jokes, ribbing, kidding, "taking the mickey," extended practical jokes, and other sustained attempts to maliciously mislead. The piss take was no interval in another kind of text but, in its own right, a whole continuous modality of shop-floor relations. Sometimes it was difficult to believe the manifest content of a single word being exchanged.

The extended extract that follows is drawn from a long interview I conducted with Percy at his home. It illustrates the piss-take form without any need for commentary from me. It is also an example of a type of research relationship in which a naturalistic, "do not disturb the field" approach is supplanted by an interventionist one in which emerging ideas are actively tested out on "informants."[1] I am trying out on Percy an idea, a mentalistic reduction, and his resistance to it is interesting in terms of a fuller understanding not only of the piss take but also of how a certain kind of embedded meaningfulness operates. It interesting, too, as an illustration of the difficulties and dangers, as well as the opportunities, of "translating" this meaning into analytic categories.

THE PISS TAKE

PW: Jokes are there [i.e., on the shop floor] all the time, fifty percent of the time people aren't being serious, do you know what I mean?

PERCY: Oh I know what you mean, I know what you'm on about, I'll perhaps go in the mornin' and I'll say, "I'll get Harry goin' here, I'll get Harry goin'." Well the chaps know you see. Now there's Sam now. Now I take it out of Brian in the morning, "What's upset 'im?" or Sam, I say, "Sam, look at this bloody tea here, you don't call this bloody tea, do you, it ain't fit for a bloody pig to drink," and he'll say, "Oh, I've done me best ain't I," and others'll chip in, say, "Oh Sam, it's a poor drink o' tea," and Sam tek it serious see. (...) 'Cos you can try it on, talkin' to 'im [Sam] see.[2]

We were over there, one day now. Sam come in the hut, you weren't there, and there was like some bags come in, and you know what crisps [potato chips] are, well these looked exactly like crisps in a bag, and they was different colours, they was red, green, purple, white in this bag like, they was like pretty crisps, like dyed crisps, like in a bag. They looked lovely, and Sam had got these in his hand like that, and he was goin' [inspecting them]...he waited for me like he did. I said, "Blimey Sam, them are new, I ain't seen them before, where have you had them from?" He said, "Up the canteen." I said, "Let's try a couple, Sam, put 'em in my mouth" [spitting noise]. "Bleedin' shit," I said to him, like that, and they'd been plastic, they'd come out of a job, of a cushion or something like that, a plastic cushion had been packed with it. He'd put them in my mouth, looked like real crisps, I spat them out. (...)

Well, he had me on that.

So up there the one day we had, we don't do it now because
people was missin' their turns, whoever's birthday it was, there
must have been about ten on us in a gang at one time, and
twelve with the gaffers, and whoever's birthday it was used to go
and buy us all a cake each. Well it was costin' me a pound,
twenty-five bob to buy a cake each…and it come this week, it was
my turn, and so I went and bought these cakes, and you might
have had the same yourself, they're like a pie and they got all
that white cream on top. I brought two or three of them back.
Well, Sammy wasn't there…mind you, it weren't my idea, and if
I'd have thought of it I'd have done exactly the same as they
done…but it was Roy, the van driver, you know. "Let's have a bit
of fun with Sam," he says, so he got these cakes out, and these
crisps again out on his bag, and he put one of each colour
round, put them round, and the way he put them in they looked
like half slices of orange or fruit that was sticking in the top see,
he dug them in like in the cream, and put them round this cake.
I dayn't see what happened in the canteen, because I was in the
office with Preece. They had a cake apiece, and they went to the
canteen about four o'clock, and they all had a cake each, and
they said "Here's yours, Sam," and they gid it Sam, and he says,
"Oh, that's a posh one ain't it?" and he got, put it in, and he
went "Owwwww."…Of course they laughed their eyes out. (…)

I was sat in the office talking to Preece, and all of a sudden
the door opened, like that, and he [Sam] says, "You, you can
have this *back*," all of the cream splashed down his face, like.
And I says, "What the bloody hell's the matter, Sam?" He says,
"You done that." I said, "Sam, I don't know what you're talkin'
about, I ain't done it." Well, I hadn't done it, but I would have
done it, if I'd have thought about it. (…)

Eddy give the game away, I think it was Eddy that done it, I
think it was Eddy, 'cos Eddy was here at the time, and he busted
out laughin' when he was chewin' it." He said, "I know who's
done this," he says. "Bloody Percy's done this." (…)

He come down, "You can have this back," he says, and the
cream came off the top of the cake, and it smacked me straight

in the face, and I said, "Well I ain't done it, Sam, I tell you truly, honestly I ain't done it."

PW: And were you annoyed because it was completely fresh to you?

Percy: No, I warn't annoyed, I took it. As soon as Sam come in and threw it at me, straight away, it hit me like that, smack, "They've had Sam on." Soon as he come in like that and throwed it at me I know what had happened, well I laughed me bloody eye out. (...)

Well it's fun amongst yourselves, it's dry fun, you know what I mean, like, er...you got maybe like a subject like what you're very strong on, and you might say, well say for a bit of fun now, "A thing's black," you know, and, er...I'll say, "It's white." And we have a good argument right, and then the argument's finally finished, and then maybe two or three days later, we'm in the shed and you'll come in the yard and come in to have a cup of tea, like, come with us up the yard like that. I'll say, "He's a comin' again, let's get him goin' again today," and then you'll come in and I'll say, "It's like what was on about the other day, that being black and that being white." You'll say, "It is bloody black." "No, you can't convince me," and this and that. "It's bloody black." "No it ain't, it's bloody white." And you go on like that and then all of a sudden it'll dawn on you, "Oh, they'm at it again, they'm takin' the piss," you see. And they just get you goin' like that, and it ain't like vicious argument, you know what I mean.

PW: It's not meant to damage the friendship?

Percy: No, because you'll get a bloke on all the while and keep him arguin' all the while, and all of a sudden he'll say, "Ain't I a bloody fool, he's takin' the piss out of me." (...)

PW: It's a very obvious thing on the shop floor.... Is it a masculine thing? Would you use that piss-taking way ever with a woman—your wife or a daughter? Is it tied up with being a bit tough in a way?

Percy: It's accordin' to how the situation arises you know. I'm just tryin' to think of a subject where I could treat the women like that.

I could perhaps go down the club [i.e., the Working Men's Club] you know, and there's perhaps a woman and one of your mates come in, and he comes down and there's no room and he has to sit by this woman you know, he perhaps has to sit by her, and you know who her is, you know what sort of a woman her is, she might be a bit touchy like that, and you say, "Hey Alf, don't sit by her, her'll be taking advantage on yer," this and that you know. "What the hell do you mean, 'take advantage'?" "Well that's why we don't sit by you." And get her goin' like that you see. And he'll turn round to her and say, "Tek no notice, they're only pullin' your bleedin' leg." And so they pass it off. Anybody, if the situation arises, and if ever it arises, like, er…wherever it is, there's always somebody amongst you that'll take advantage on it…you know and get on with it. That's how you'm brought up on the shop floor really, as you'm always put on, the piss took out on yer and played up until you learn about them things. You learn after a bit.

PW: But it still goes on because you use it at the social club over somebody else, and you'll have a go with the chap that you know has got strong views, and you might be got going tomorrow, in a way they've found out which you haven't realized yet.

PERCY: Oh well, go down there, and my mates come in like that, and maybe his missus come in, her's got to sit by me and I'll say, "Hey, you got to behave yourself tonight, no messin' about like you did last week," and things like that, you know. And you'd come in like that, and maybe I'd walk in and you'd…bring your wife in…then maybe a month later, you'd perhaps come in the club perhaps several time during the next month without your wife. Then maybe, say a month later, you brought the wife in again. I'd say, "That's your wife, ain't it?" "Ay." "Well who was that one you was with last week?" And that's how you pass somethin' like that. Did you ever have that said to you?

PW: Oh yes. What's interesting is that I think it comes from the shop floor. (…)

PERCY: There's various ways. There's a thousand and one ways what you can tek it out of someone of the shop floor. (…)

PW: How important is it all [joking], I suppose is what's in my mind? How more livable does it make the day?

PERCY: Well actually it does help to pass the day, it livens the day up really. We tell each other a joke, or we tek the piss out of each other, like on a joke, you know what I mean, and it livens the day up.

Well, if you go round the place, like there's blokes like in the shop, say Harry and John. Now Harry's the one, Harry'll keep droppin', passin'…smutty little remarks out you know. When you work with Harry, you get a bit of enjoyment out of it, now if you was to work with Eddy and the other John, 'im who's always reading the Bible.

PW: I've noticed that, he's a Jehovah's Witness?

PERCY: He's a Jehovah's Witness, ah. If you was to work with Eddy and 'im, and you always worked with 'em, you'd be miserable, because they wouldn't hardly speak, you know what I mean. They would be doin' the job, and they wouldn't be talkin', just carryin' on, you know the day gets monotonous. Where if I was with Eddie, regular, I'd say to 'em, "God blimey, you might as well work in a morgue, as come and work with you bloody two."

And all of a sudden you'd get Johnny going, "pwwwwww." You know he keeps doing that bloody habit, he gets on your nerves he does, Johnny. It's only a bloody habit, and he never swears, he's got that book stuck in front of him all day long. (…)

PW: But just how important is that [joking]—you'd still rather not be there?

PERCY: It's a big importance at work that is. Say you were doing a job up the pallet shed now, the job it ain't interestin', doin' a job up at the pallet, it ain't interestin' at all. Well you can be doin' a job like a man playin' a piano. I could be playin' the piano and talkin' to you all the while I'm playin' it, and it don't affect me, it don't affect the piano playin'. Same as like Harry or them that work in the pallet shed, they can be repairin' pallets and still be passin' a joke and talkin' to you at the same time and it don't interfere with the work, and listenin' like to the patter of talk, you know, jokes and things like, time's a goin' by, and you're still doin' the work, and its more enjoyable, you know what I mean? You mek your own lot, your own job, like in the works, you know what I mean?

PW: Well, that's right at the heart of what interests me, you know, especially as the young worker sees that. I mean you'd still rather not be there, wouldn't you? You'd rather not be doing the work?

PERCY: Well everybody would, wouldn't they really? But I tell you summat else, I dunno whether they'll tell yer the same, but, say your week or your fortnight's holiday, I get bored at home and I seem to be more contented like at work like, than you are at home. Well I mean, when you'm at home you get into a routine, you go out and have a drink and you come back and sit in the house, and livin' together like, like say you and the wife, you've got nothing to talk about, but when you get to work, there's always summat to talk about, you know what I mean?...er, Like, "Have you done that job down the road?" Or, "About time they started to burn the stuff up the yard, lads." Little comments like that, summat to talk about all the while. If you're in the house, or say with your wife...how often do you speak to the wife when you'm in the house, really? I mean you ain't a chattin' all the while to her, are you? You're maybe readin' a book or summat in the house, am I right there?

PW: Yes.

PERCY: You do a lot more readin', or summat like that, rather than talk to the wife, like, if you're readin' a book and then the wife gets talkin' to you, like that, and you'm readin' a book. (...)

PW: I sometimes get the impression that blokes are quite glad to get to work.

PERCY: I am at times, yes, I admit really, more times than not, like that.... The biggest bugbear, say for a young chap startin' work straight from school or say comin' from college and say startin' work, is, er...the gettin' up in the mornin', because, it's hard to get up in the mornin', any mornin', 'cos I can always turn over and sleep an extra hour. (…)

I can get up in the mornin', but many's the bloody mornin'
I could 'ave rolled over and rested in bed longer, you know what
I mean. That's the biggest part of a young chap startin' work,
when he goes to school, he's got to be at school for nine o'clock,
ain't he? Well look at Joey, now, when he comes to our place
now, he's got to get up in the mornin', got to be in for half past
seven, he's got to get up at say for half past six, quarter to seven
every morning. Well that gets hard for 'im, because he don't get
in till late at night, he's off all hours, he don't come in till after
midnight half the time, Joey, and he's tired next mornin', and
therefore it's bloody hard work for 'im gettin' up in the
mornin'. That's the hardest part of the day's work really I think.

PW: Well, I notice it myself frankly when I go in. I mean to get
up that bit earlier, makes a big difference. But in your own case,
still…I mean, once you've got up and you're in, do you actually
feel it's nice to be with the blokes?

PERCY: How can I put this now…? You get up in the mornin',
you're maybe feelin' miserable. "Oh, I don't feel like bloody
work today." Well you go to work, and you see your mates in the
place like, and they say, "Oh, look at his face," you know, like
that, and I says, "It's all right," and they say, "Smile." "What's the
bloody hell to smile about," you know, anything like that, "Well,
you're with us now ain't you?"

Well it's like talk like that amongst your friends what meks
the day, you know what I mean. I'm goin' to work in the mornin'
you see, and, er…I'll go up to the garage in the mornin', I'll go
up the garage to pick the wagon up, and then I go like where
you clock in, like, there's like a bit of a room there, there's
always three or four blokes in there, "Good mornin'." "Good
mornin'." Some'll turn and say, "Bollocks," or whatever…and,
you know, you pass the day, and you stop talkin' to them for a
bit. "Oh well, I'll go and get the wagon down, go down, see the
lads now."

When you go down, straightaway you make for the hut, you
see, when you get down there, and when you go in there, you

don't know what to expect, what greetin', no good sayin' you know, even I don't. You don't know what greetin' you're going to expect, what greetin' you're goin' on. When you go in there and there ain't no greetin' for you, you mek your own greetin', you know what I mean?

PW: Well, I noticed it, because I was there. So even if you feel miserable, and you prefer to stop in bed at home, by the time the day actually starts....

PERCY: By the time you got up, now say tomorrow mornin', say, "Oh I feel bloody lousy, I ain't goin' today, stop in the house." Well perhaps I'll lie in bed another hour then...and yet if you lie in bed another hour, you don't want to lie in bed, I don't want to lie in bed like another hour when I'm here [i.e., at home], see, I want to get up.

If I come down here [i.e., the living room], the missus sees me, her starts to bloody moan, "What you got up for, gettin' in my road. Why don't you go to work," like that. Well after I've been here about an hour I say, "What the devil have I had the day off for, what am I here for, what have I had the day off for?"

You feel like, you get depressed, because actually when I'm at home, really, there's nothin' to occupy your mind, not summat to occupy my mind as regards that, which means that I'd sooner be at work alongside my pals than sittin' mopin' in the bloody house, do you know what I mean?

PW: And when you say "occupy your mind," when you get to work, it's difficult to know what occupies your mind, the job to be done, or being with your mates, and having a chat and a laugh and a gossip and seeing what's happening.

PERCY: Well it is yes, there is things like that, you know what I mean. There's, now when I'm on a job, now, I don't know what is, but, er, if I go on a job, I want to get it done and get back in the yard and get with the blokes, you know, I don't know what it is, but I like to get the job done, and get back with the blokes in the yard, maybe in the pallet shed and have a talk, you know what I mean.

There's umpteen subjects you pass, you know...maybe John is in there, and he's doin' like, he's knockin' nails in and he's goin', "pwwwwww," you know, and I'll go down and I'll go, "pwwwwww," tek it out on 'im, and there's little things...it's what they say, there's a song, isn't there? "Little things mean a lot," well there is that at work like, you seem to get more of a variety of talk and enjoyment at work than what you do at home, you know what I mean? (...)

Now we go down and fetch the pallets in, shift the scrap and things like that, and you got the blokes, 'cos when I'm with the blokes, I'm gettin' too old now for bendin' down throwin' scrap, but the blokes know, and they'm a workin', and I'll perhaps be tekin' the piss out of 'em, or tellin' 'em jokes while they'm a workin'. Well, I'm makin' my own life easier you can say, the times a goin' a bit, it meks the time go a bit quicker, you know what I mean, and them blokes, it's making them happier, you know what I mean? But if you get say, er...two blokes like Eddy and Johnny in the pallet shed, they'm just a hammerin' away all day long, they'm workin', perhaps workin' for what they feel like hours, say them start at say half past seven, feels they've been goin' a long time, look at the clock, "Cor blimey, it's only nine o'clock," like that, think that he's been workin' for hours, there's no pleasure in the job at all.

PW: So the pleasure in the job is partly the variety, but it's also you telling a joke. And it's that combination that interests me.

PERCY: It's a combination, but it's a combination of, er...like a runnin' commentary like on different things while you'm doin' a job. The job's borin', but you're doin' the job and listenin' the same time, and you ain't doin' a job, you know what I mean? Not in your own minds, you ain't doin' a job, you'm listenin', but you're doin' the job at the same time, do you know what I mean? The job's no longer overborin'. (...)

PW: To get back to the work situation, you said it [joking and taking the piss] was to make time go faster, why is it important to make time go faster?

Percy: Well, time, you know what they say, there's a song about that as well—"Time goes by so slowly" [singing]. Ever heard that song? Well that's how it is at work, if the job's uninterestin' the time does drag by you know, it meks such a long day, there's no interest in the job and it makes it a long day, but if you keep, like, passin' a commentary like...now and again...there might be two or three I'd talk to and joke, might spend a quarter of an hour or twenty minutes like that, but all the while, like especially if Brian or I am there, they'm hangin' on and hangin' on, "What's he going to say next," and they haven't got their minds on the job, they're got their minds on what I'm going to say next, and I'll perhaps think like that, "It's about time them bloody pair told me a joke." I've got the same thing on my mind. And all of a sudden, I'll say, "Have you heard this one," and they're all ears again, you see, they'm a still workin' doin' the job. It makes it more interestin' like, the work, you know what I mean. It's the talk at work that makes the time more interestin', do you know what I mean?

PW: If you told the same joke at night, though, in the pub, would it be to make the time go faster?

PERCY: Oh no, it would be to make people laugh. (...)

PW: What is the difference between the attitude of the shop floor and what you say, Eddy is the gaffers man. Just sketch to me the difference.

PERCY: Well, Eddy now...the difference between Eddy now...and say, er, Chris and Eddy, now Chris is perhaps in the office window, and lookin' through the window, and he'll see me, and say I'm goin' for my dinner, I might bugger off twenty to one, it's as good as one o'clock, I'll go about twenty to one. Chris'll turn round and talk to Preece [the site gang manager] and distract him from the window from me goin', he'd distract him. Now if Eddy was in the window, Eddy'd be lookin' out like that and he'd turn round, nobody else in the office, only 'im and Preece, he'd say, "Oh, Percy's off for his dinner." He'd tell Preece, you see what I mean? He'd pass the information on to

Preece that I was off for my dinner, that's his attitude see, he get's hisself into the gaffer's books, lettin' the gaffer know what's going on. Whereas if it were Chris that was in there, Chris would more or less distract the gaffer's attention from me goin', and the gaffer wouldn't think no more of it. If Preece was sat down and couldn't see me goin' out, Eddy'd say, "Oh, Percy's off for his dinner, bloody early ain't it," like that, you know what I mean. That's the sort of bloke that Eddy is, like that, he wouldn't back the men up, you know what I mean? (…)

If you see Joey again you ask him about that. Joey don't like Eddy as regards that, but he gets on with the other blokes all right, but Eddy gets on his nerves, do you know what I mean? If he's [Eddy's] a comin', they'll say oh this and that, but if Percy's a comin' or John, or Harry's comin', "Harry's comin', Harry's comin'," and they tek no more notice, see, but if Eddy's comin' they say, "Mind what you'm a sayin', he's here," you know what I mean. They wouldn't let Eddy hear anything, if they were saying anything disgruntled or anything like that. They wouldn't let Eddy hear.

PW: But is that shop-floor way then to some extent trying to resist authority? Not let Preece know what's happening?

PERCY: Yes. 'Cos if they'm doin' anythin' what they shouldn't do, they don't want the gaffer knowin' about that, do it on the quiet.

Like me now, I bring timber home or you bring a pocketful of nails home, summat like that, well you do it without the gaffer's knowledge. There's little things like that what goes on you see. Well if Eddy seen you, if Eddy seen me puttin' a few nails in my pocket…that's Eddy's way, now it's true, I can prove this. I say I've got a handful of nails to put in my pocket, and I say, "I need them for the shed up home," like that, "Oh all right, tek em 'ome in your pocket, you'm all right." Eddy'd go in the office later on and he'll say, "Oh, Percy's had a pocket of nails, he says he wants them for his house." He'd go and tell the gaffer, you know what I mean. Whereas if it was Chris or anybody like that or John or Joey or anybody seen me do it, they wouldn't go into the office and say, "Oh, Percy's had a few nails." It wouldn't enter their minds to tell the gaffer, but Eddy would, it's what they call…how could you put it now, like at school you get like a bloke who tells tales at the school, what do they call him?

PW: A tell-tale.

PERCY: Well a tell-tale, or he's a prat goin' to tell the gaffer, (…) that's the sort of bloke Eddy is. That's no kidding, I've said it to his face, I've been in the office and Eddy's been there, and I've been talkin' about one thing, you know, like that with the gaffer, and Eddy's agreed with everythin' the gaffer's said. I say, "Eddy," I says, "You may as well shut your bloody mouth," I says, "or I may as well shut mine, one of the two of us has got to shut up," I says, "because no matter what I say to the gaffer, you agree with him, so therefore it's two against me every time. If I say that bloody thing's black there, you'll say it's bloody white, you'll try and convince me it's bloody white, but you wouldn't convince me, Ed," I says. "There's two of you 'ere," I said, "No matter what you say or what the gaffer says," I tell 'em straight, I tell 'im [the gaffer] an' all, "You're wrong, that's bloody black, you can't make it white, I make it black, you can't make it white. No matter what you say, I'm convinced that's black, and you can't change my mind about it." And they've been on different subjects like that, and all the while they'm definitely right, I say, "All right you am right," I says, "I'm not goin' to argue no more," I says, "You think you'm right," I says, "You think you'm right, but I know I'm right, so let's forget all about it," and that's how it goes, like that. They wouldn't convince me. If I think I was in the right the bloody king wouldn't convince me, and I should still say I was right. (…)

PW: Why would you do it [take the piss], say to a young bloke (…) coming into the pallet shed. Would you be testing me in a way? Would you want to see how I replied?

PERCY: No actually, we're what they call breakin' 'im in, or bringin' 'im in on to the shop floor, do you know what I mean. You do them things and you say them things and it sort of breaks them in.

PW: Say a bit more about that, because I don't really know what you mean.

Percy: Well, you perhaps get a chap come in there like that and you [the new man] might come in there you might make a balls-up say of a pallet like, mek a mess on it, like that. And you'd be, "Oh...." You'd been in, started. We'd say, "You med a mess o' that," to frighten you, see, in case the gaffer come and, p'haps, try and cover up...."I shall say it's you...God blimey, don't make any more of 'em, they're bloody expensive, you know, if the gaffer sees that job it'll be the ruddy sack." You'll say, "You wouldn't will you?" and I'll say, "Well hide it so the gaffer won't see it, hide it." Like that. And the blokes'll be there and'll say, "Put it over there, we'll get the wood off, we'll do it again ourselves after." You'll pass it off like that, and perhaps I'll go outside, like on a job, and the blokes will turn round and tell 'im, "He's just tekin' the piss out o' you, can't you see it?" That's how you break 'em in. They'd tell you after I'd gone. What I'd said, like it was said more like a joke, like tekin' the piss out on you, and you'd fetch the pallet back, they'll say, "Oh put it in, that's all right that one is." You wouldn't tek no more notice. And it's to sort of break a bloke in.

PW: To break him in to what? To ignore managers perhaps?

Percy: To break 'im in, like to shop-floor attitude, you know what I mean? (...)

I learnt the hard way in the factory when I was younger. You all learn the hard way really. (...) There was one thing I'll always remember, well, two or three things....We used to have some... pullin' nails out of packing cases, down Phillips's. When I worked down there I was only a young lad, workin' for the first time.... "You gotta make that packing case up, pop down and see that fitter down there and ask him for the sky hooks." Well, I didn't know what the bloody sky hooks were, but I went down and I says, "Are you so and so?" he says, "Are." "Joe sent me here, wants the sky hooks." "Oh, are, the sky hooks, he's got 'em over there." I goes over there, "Er, got the sky hooks?" "We have had 'em," he says. "Where have they gone to now?" He says. "Oh, in the office, there, the gaffer's fetched 'em back in the office, go and ask him for 'em." And you'd go in the office, "Er...Joe's sent me down for the sky hooks, he says you got 'em here." "*Sky hooks! Out this bloody office, up the stairs,*" like that. And I fled. Of course...nasty like that, up the bloody stairs, they says, "You bloody fool, there's no such thing as sky hooks." That's how it goes off, you see. Right? They tek it out on yer when you first start to work. (...)

"Go and ask him for a left-handed screwdriver or a left-handed spanner"...summat like that, things like that, little things like that what you don't know nothin' at all about when you first start. You think, "Well, I've never heard of a left-handed spanner." "Oh aye, just the job." Go down and they make yer look a prat, you see. But when you're there a bit, you get used to them sayings, then you muck in with 'em then. (...)

No matter how cocky a kid is at school, how cocky he is at school, when he gets in a factory amongst the men he's subdued, and they'll do everythin' to him, they'll get 'im up to all the tricks, y'know, tell 'im to do all things, all these things, like silly ruddy things, and he'll do them and he'll...in the finish, he'll finally realize you know...as, er'm, they'm tekin' the piss out on 'im, and the next bloody time they say anythin' to im, he'll say, "Well," like if it was me, I'd say, "Oh, well I don't know where they are, you go and fetch 'em yourself," or, "Go to so and so yourself because I don't know anythin' about that," or, "I'll come with you and you show me what they are." They're knackered then, you see what I mean, as they've got to show you or they've got to fetch it theirselves, and that's when it starts to work off and they'll perhaps leave you alone for a bit and they'll perhaps go on to somebody else, and you'll listen, and you'll think to yourself, "Oh, he's a tekin' the piss out of 'im." And that's how you're gradually worked in on the shop floor, you know what I mean? There's that many things said and there's piss took out in so many different ways, and remarks passed, that it don't take long to pick the shop-floor way up, you know. It's surprisin' how it come on to you.

PW: I'm interested in that way, I mean is that way a good way, do you think it's a good way?

PERCY: Yes, because you get a chap from school say, come
straight from school, and, er…he may be a scholar at school,
summat like that, and he's a quiet sort of chap. Well, he'll go
into a factory and there's a good many people in the factory as
'ud put on 'im, you know what I mean, "Do us this," you know,
"Go and fetch us this," "Do this for us," and all this and that,
until he got used to 'em. They put on to 'em until he got used to
'em, and after he's been there for a bit, he thinks to hisself, you
start to think for yourself, you'll learn the hard way like that.

You'll perhaps say, "Go and fetch the barrel of sand up in the
furnace, go and fetch a new barrel of sand up." Well it ain't this
young kid's job and he don't say anything, so he goes and
fetches you the barrel of sand. A bit later you say, "Oh, I've run
out of cores, pop down there and get me a barre'ful of cores,
will yer," and he'll get the kid to go down and a get a barrow o'
cores, he'll go on like this a certain time, and the kid'll get used
to it. And he'd say, "I'm a doin' all his bloody work instead of
doin' me own work, I'm doin' his work an' all," and in the finish
it'll come on to him, and he'll say, "Go and fetch it your bloody
self, I'm fed up with runnin' about for you," and that's how they
work theirself in the floor you see. You get these things what
they say to try you out, but when you get to the floor you're
broke in, a kid from school is broke in, and really it's an 'ard way
to break 'em in, but they get these things put on 'em, or they
have the piss took out on 'em, or they maybe…there's a bloke
there puttin' on 'em, like to help him out with his work this and
that, and they're puttin' on to 'em but after a bit it dawns on
'em all, as they finally realize they 'ave 'ad it put on, and they'll
cut it out, they won't do it.

PW: How does the humour and the piss-taking connect with that,
though? I mean is it half pretending to push the lad, you're letting
him know that it is a joke, whereas if it was for real it would be…

PERCY: Sometimes, no, like it might be me and you, and I might
be an idle bugger see, and I don't want to do it, and I ask you
like to fetch me a barrow of sand or a barrow of core, summat
like that. Well I mean it, I ain't takin' the piss, 'cos I want you
to fetch it, you see, I don't want to fetch it, so I'm makin' 'im

fetch them. I say, "He don't know, mek 'im fetch 'em," summat like that. Well you ain't tekin' the piss then, and after a few times it'll suddenly dawn on the kid as he's doin' my work…and he'll turn round and he'll say, "No, fetch it yourself." That's how it's worked out actually…see, you are hardened, in any place you go to you're hardened in the hard way.

PW: This is exactly what I want to understand about what young kids come into, but I still can't personally quite understand it, you're hardened to just doing what's your job, without letting anybody put on you—is that what "hardened" means—what does "hardened" mean?

PERCY: Well it's…er, like say…now say I got a kid out of school, and I'm mekin' 'im do them jobs, well after a bit you'd get browned off of me tellin' you to do them things when you found out it weren't your job, and you know a bloke says and you find out then, perhaps two or three needed to tell you. It all works out the same way, you tell 'im, you ain't supposed to work for 'im, that's his bloody job, he's havin' you bloody on, he's makin' you fetch his bloody work for 'im, mek 'im fetch it his bloody self. Next time you wouldn't be there. Or maybe he'd say, "Go and fetch me a barrow of sand," you'd very likely walk away and take the barrow with you, park the barrow by the sand then bugger off. Then you'd walk back, and he'd say, "Where's my sand," and you'd say, "Oh God blimey, I've left the barrow up there, I've got to go on another job now, I've been took off, I've got to go another job," and the bloke says, "What sort of job you got to go on?" "Oh, the gaffer's sent me down, I've got to go down with some boxes," or summat. You can always find some excuse and the bloke's got to fetch his own. You do that two or three times, and the bloke won't 'ave you on no more, see what I mean?

PW: How does that connect with piss-taking and humour?

PERCY: Well, it ain't tekin' the piss really.

PW: But if that's hardening a bloke to the job, yet exactly the same thing you said went on when you're taking the piss out of the kid. (…). You said hardening in that way as well.

PERCY: It all goes the same way.

PW: I mean, is it the same thing? One's humour and the other could come to blows. A big lad might say "I ain't going to do that." Thump.

PERCY: No, they don't do that, no.

PW: Yet the humour seems to be a way of making the same point, but it's a joke. Do you see what I'm saying. Go back to the [sky hook] example, when you said "It's hardening him up" or "It's breaking him in to the shop floor."

PERCY: Well a young lad, a young lad wouldn't think of...even a hardened bugger at school, he wouldn't think of, er...er...say because if he was in the pallet shed workin' with the men, he wouldn't have, like, the nerve or the initiative to turn round like that and thump a man, you know what I mean? He could mek a complaint, he could go to the gaffer or someone there and say, er..."What's he keep tekin' it out on me for," like that you know. (...) You'll say, "You'll get used to 'im," you'll say, "He's always the same, you'll get used to 'im, it's just his way, you'll get used to 'im, just ignore 'im, like that. Things like that, several things like that, hardens you into the shop floor. It hardens his, er...more so like hardens his, er...his mind and, er...how can I put it...er, hardens his heart, you can say, it hardens his mind and hardens his heart, it like makes 'im more...like I say, hardened, meks 'im more hardened in the job, you know what I mean. He'll say, "Well I ain't got to do this and that, and it's nothing to do with 'im what I do," and it gradually dawns on yer, you can't really put it into words but whatever you do like that, and they tek it out on yer, it'll suddenly dawn on you, like me with the sky hooks down there. Well I never knew what they was, I never know they was tekin' the piss out of me until I finally got in the office, like the foreman he told me like, he told me, "You silly sod, there's no sky hooks." Then it suddenly dawned on me then as they'd been havin' me on, and then next time you'll say, "I'll watch him next time," and he'll say, "Go and fetch me a left-handed screwdriver," and you'll say, "Well there ain't one, I've never heard of one." "Well you'll get it down there." You'll turn round and say, "Well you go and ask 'im for it," and see what he tells you, and they'll forget it then, see what I mean?

PW: It's actually not occurred to me before, in a way, that putting on a bloke as a joke is, in a way, similar to putting on him to make him do more work, you're trying to get him to do something that's silly or that he needn't.

PERCY: You don't put on a bloke like…

PW: To get him doing your work which he needn't do, whereas the joke's the same kind of point, you're trying to make him do something that he wouldn't do if he hadn't fallen for the joke.

PERCY: Well, they don't do it like that really, like they wouldn't say, like say he was workin' for us two and I was the bad 'un, I wouldn't say, "Go and fetch me a barrow of sand," and then I don't want it, you know, take it back like that. I wouldn't make him do work like that.

PW: Well, it's work that the kid needn't have done in the normal course.

PERCY: No, but you wouldn't send the kid for summat that he didn't want, you know fetch his sand and things like that. Ah, but the sky hooks and things like that, that's a joke, that was a joke, then, like when they sent me for it, the bloke who sent me for it, he was havin' me on.

PW: But where does the joke come from? I mean, isn't it a bit the same as sending the kid for a bucket of sand? I mean one's a joke and one's serious, but they're both getting the kid to do something that he shouldn't have done.

PERCY: No, but, actually fetchin' the sky hooks and summat like that (…) it don't go with one man, the bloke who's sendin' you, who's havin' you on, and to let 'em know he's havin' you on, "Go and ask him down there, and he'll tell you." Well, he'll go down and the kid can go round the shop, you see, and they're all laughin' their bloody eyes out you see, then it suddenly dawns on the kid see, "They're havin' me on here."

PW: And the sky hook—is the funny bit with another worker, or when he gets to the foreman or manager?

PERCY: Well, when he gets to the foreman, it'll finally dawn on 'im because the gaffer will tell 'im, as they'm havin' 'im on.

PW: And is that the funny bit?

PERCY: That's the funny bit you see, like breakin' 'im in, like I say it's hardenin' 'im to the shop floor.

PW: Well, what's he learned from asking a silly question of the foreman?

PERCY: Well he ain't asked a silly question really, he's only asked for what he's been sent for, and the gaffer knows as the prat is the first one who's sent 'im down for it, and he'll say, "Oh so and so's sent me," and he'll say, "Tell him to get on with his bleedin' job," like that, "He's only havin' you on." Then of course you realize then as they've been havin' your leg on, and the blokes are laughin' at you in the shop, and when you've just left school and you go in the shop you'll start to laugh yourself, you know, and you'll agree with 'em, and you'll say, "You won't catch me no more." The next time he might say after a couple of hours, "Oh I've got a job here, go and ask 'im for a left-handed screwdriver," if you're sensible…but, anyone who's backward, they would do it again. They wouldn't continually take the piss out of 'em, because that would be bullyin' then, they wouldn't do it, like, on a shop floor.

PW: They'd stop at a certain point. But would they stop short of bullying? Cruelty?

PERCY: Oh God blimey, are, no, every kid as goes in the factory or anywhere he goes, they always tek it out on yer, every bloody where, they tek it out on yer. If you was to go on the shop floor, like straight away, when you was a young kid no matter where you went to, if you went to the Austin, the Leyland, the Rover. Wherever you went to, you can bet you'd have it took out on yer when you went there, because they always put you with someone to work with you know.

When you go in the factory, like no matter what place you go to when you first come from school, they'll say, "Well, go and work with 'im, he'll show you what the job is." You might be with 'im for a week, and if the chap's like a bit of a lad, he'll start havin' 'im on with these things, you see, "Go and ask him, I want so and so." Then you'll go down to him and he'll say, "Oh I ain't got them, he's got them over there." And they'll send you all round in the finish, and it'll suddenly dawn on you, even a kid, it dawned on me when I was down there, as they was havin' me on. And it comes to you.

PW: That is fascinating.

PERCY: It learns you the factory, how they go on in the factory you see.

PW: The way it goes on, where does that come from, is it about stopping people taking advantage of you?

PERCY: No it's life really that is, it's always been on the shop floor.

PW: It's a different way in a university or in an office or in a school. (…)

PERCY: Well, when you was at college (…) When you were a fag [English usage: someone who performs menial tasks for older boys in school] then, or summat like that, what they call fags don't they…

PW: Sometimes, but other people might take a newcomer and show him exactly what to do, and say, "These are the problems, this is how you deal with it." They wouldn't teach him in that way, which some people would say is a hard way.

PERCY: But in the college they wouldn't tek the piss out of them would they?

PW: They would but nothing like that. Not so continuous. It would stop sooner, and they'd say, well actually this is how it works, do this that and the other and you'll be okay. Whereas on the shop floor I think it takes much longer than that. That's what interests me, when a young chap comes to work, why not say to him, "This is the way to get on, this is the way to survive." Why is it a better way to do it by taking the piss out of him?

PERCY: Well they do, they do. If I was like workin' in a factory, like that, and say you was a young kid just left school and they put you to work with me, and I was doin' a job, I should, er, you know, weigh yer up, like that, and say you'd ask what the job was, and I might be puttin' screws into summat, or maybe tightenin' them up or takin' summat off or puttin' summat on. "Well what's that for?" I'd explain to you what it was, you know, and you'd learn like that, and maybe if in the meantime, I was a bit of a lad you know, and I'd got to know you for a bit, maybe three or four hours, and I'd think, "It's time we had a bit of fun with 'im." You'll do that, but after about a week or a fortnight it dies off, they get browned off. Maybe after a bit you've learnt that job and they go and put you with another bloke like that, and he'd maybe ask you a question like, "Go and fetch summat" again, and off you'd have to go again, and you'd go to the first bloke and you'd say, "He's sent me down for a back-ended pair of pli-ers," and the bloke'll say, "I ain't got 'em, they're over there." You'll say, "Oh I'm here again," and you'll go back then, and you'll say, "Go and fetch them yourself," something like that. After a bit you'll catch on to it.

PRELIMINARY ANALYSIS

The basic question or puzzle for me, then as now, in interpreting this long exchange is *why* the piss take and put-on are so prevalent in shop-floor culture as described and inhabited by Percy. In particular, do their omnipresence and durability cast any light on cultural aspects of capital-labor relations at their *most crucial* site? My basic "simple" answers are straightforward, and I am working them out and trying some of them out on Percy as I near the end of the interview. I am actually learning quite a lot here, or a lot is coming together that I had previously puzzled about, and I am trying to share it with Percy. In terms of the concerns of this book, my interpretation is grappling with aspects of the structural-historical formation of persons in a specific site. But Percy will have none of my specific interpretation. Faced with my reductive interpretation, he just tells the story again. The whole tale is the irreducible meaning for him, not any moral, homology, or connection to be drawn from it. It may be that my interpretation is wrong, but Percy is against all interpretation and does not see that there are any puzzles to be explained. He is simply trying to tell the tale about how you get "hardened" to the shop floor, and I keep interrupting him, showing a persistent obtuseness.

This is important and underlines a universal problem in interpretive approaches in the social sciences—what if "subjects" disagree with what you claim is the deep foundation and basis for the meanings, functions, and significance of their actions? Of course if they were to agree, in some ways it would be a bigger problem; if the truth were so simply written on the face of things, what would be the need of social science? But Percy's response in this case certainly indicates the need for more complex answers to my puzzle, answers that embrace more fully the properly active "in person" part of our formations in this book, facing, unambiguously, the difficulties of combining the two halves of our equation.

Here are my simple answers. No beating about the bush!

First, the piss take and the put-on are about learning the variable relation between the "real" (a better term might be the "material") and the "symbolic" at a particular site and about how they combine, variably, to produce real processes or the "reality" of that site. In this case the "real" is constituted by the physical elements, physical processes, and physical relations of production, not least the physical application of labor power through tools to the transformation of raw materials to produce useful products. The "symbolic" is constituted by *how* these things are defined, understood, and inhabited subjectively by the human participants in these relations at a particular site. Of course a proper understanding of real processes (as in the practical logics of located practice) must entail the indissoluble and dynamic interrelation of the real and the symbolic, but for analysts they need to be separated in thought in order to understand the complex and variable nature of their final unity.

Second, the piss take and the put-on are about the validation and enactment of a set of symbolic understandings different from the dominant power-based ones, a validation of an alternative "regime of truth" not based on power but subject to it.

The piss take is the more general and prevalent form. It operates to provide a continuous reminder that there is another way of looking at things, a way different from the dominant managerial view. In shop-floor culture, black can be white, at least for a time. Time itself "a goin' by" can be made to pass variably. Morguelike monotony can be turned into surreal carnival. Polystyrene cushion filler can be potato chips or fruit segments. You can "mek your own greetin'," "mek your own job," and even make "doin' a job" not "doin' a job." Perhaps most importantly, shop-floor culture generally and the piss take in particular provide a meanings system and expressive code for mounting resistance to authority—from a general capacity to "tek no notice" (it's just a put-on) to insisting, sometimes, "that's bloody black, you can't make it white"; from a generalized system for baffling the rationalized exercise of managerial power (nothing is serious) to a specific form of refusal, "Are you taking the piss?" In general the piss take creates a tendency in shop-floor culture to deprive formal structures of the formal meanings and certainties they create and need in order to function, challenging the epistemological basis of the "right to manage." The piss take shows the human potential for inhabiting materially enforced "objective" conditions as *really* something else, finally changing them. Humorously inserting people into fictitious realities that they take as real teaches them that, in general, what others project as seriously real can be taken as fictitious, or at least judged from a relatively independent basis for its practical truth value. Here is a living metaphor practically applied, a symbolic apprenticeship put to material use, a symbolic form doing real work.

The fundamental form of the piss take is one of ironic relation. Irony is about being in two places at once, occupying two opposing "realities" with their separate meanings and definitions. The conventional joke hinges on, and is resolved by, a punch line that brings these two realities together, revealing one as false, stupid, or risible. The shop-floor piss take—which is, remember, a whole modality, not an interruption of something else—therefore indicates an *alternative* continuous reality that has not been officially named or sanctioned. In this reality, individuals are "stranded." They are abandoned in, trapped in, or projected into the shadowy "reality" (actually it doesn't matter which, for "after a bit it dawns on 'em all"; it is the formal duality that matters). This continuous lesson in "doubling" in a "split epistemology," along with extended practical living in the unofficial reality, demonstrates that capturing the body of the worker in the "discourse" of the capitalist labor process is not to capture the mind, consciousness, language, and all of the cultural forms of collective awareness and vigor that go with *human* bodies and their symbolic interactions.

To be more prosaic, shop-floor culture shows all the time that there are possible dispositions of the body different from those proposed by management regimes of truth and direction. There are ways different from the officially sanctioned ones of being and doing, even in the most controlled of situations: slower ways, more dignified ways, more amusing ways, pointless ways, lazy ways. These other ways are more humanized and riddled with counteruses of time and humor. As we shall see later, it is in these ways, not in the ways of capitalist ideology, imagination, and managerial rationalism, that production is actually ground out and value-adding time made to pass in the uncomfortable service of others' economic interests.

In particular, it is my argument that these general capacities of the piss take and the put-on function to teach young workers something profound about their own labor power: first, its variable nature, and second, the need to control its expenditure (and ways to control it) in the face of management regimes based on its exploitation—regimes that distill themselves relentlessly in order to concentrate the exploitation of labor power. Crudely, and as I was trying it out on Percy, learning not to be "put on" in the piss take or the fool's errand is also learning not to be put on really—literally to avoid having ever greater burdens placed on your back, partly by older men on the shop floor who are exercising patriarchal relations of power, but more importantly by older men in managerial relations of capitalist power. It is no accident that unreasonable demands on the shop floor and elsewhere are met with the response, "Are you tekin' the piss?" It is a vital defensive lesson in the face of capital's global and inexorable assault on labor in the continuous intensifying and speeding up of labor processes. It is also a significant source of, and medium for, processes of alternative, "creative" identity formation experienced and developed under the specific conditions of the attempted direct control of the body in different kinds of management regimes.

Some Marxist categories can help the analysis here. "Labor power," generally, has great importance in the Marxist system because it is seen as the only source of profit. This was the essence of Marx's advance over classical theorists who had seen profit arising from the simple fact of ownership of capital or land. Labor is the source of profit because it is unique in that you can get more out of it (its "use value") than it costs you to buy (its "exchange value"). You can also get more out of it by intensifying it and squeezing out the pores of rest, inactivity, or laziness it contains. Through the application of science and technology it can be made more productive, more or less without limit. Labor power as use value is, therefore, actually a living thing capable of remaking its cost many times over, depending on the type of productive relation it enters.

Crucially, though, labor power is bought and sold not as a variable capacity but as a fixed capacity. It is bought as a dead thing, as a commodity *like any other commodity* on the market. Once it is sold like a can of beans, it is up to the new owner what to do with it—within work hours. If the new owner can get the laborer to produce a hundred times more than the laborer cost, then so much the better for the owner. According to Marx, commodity fetishism, now applied by laborers to the commodity of their own labor power as well as to all other commodities, ensures that workers ask no questions about this. They have been paid a "fair day's pay"—the price duly paid for the only commodity the worker has to sell, labor power—and it is no business of theirs to criticize how the employer might go about extracting "a fair day's work" or to ask into what kind of wider productive and social relations their labor power is inserted. There are many additions and adjustments to be made to this classical model, but the essential point to understand here concerns the way in which labor power is bought and sold as a reified, fixed, invariant commodity but is actually used in a way ever more developed, if not perfected, to exploit its variable nature.

Now, to lean on but to depart from the Marxist analysis, we can understand the importance and significance of a lived resistance to, and partial overturning of, this classical labor model in the practices of the put-on. As Marx said, labor power is not a can of beans; it is a variable power and can almost endlessly produce ever more cans of beans for others. But it also contains human sensuousness and imaginative symbolic capacity, not least for irony and different joke forms. These are used, in practice, as a major preoccupation of shop-floor culture, pace Marx, enabling workers to "understand" and limit the upside of this variability—to at least partially defetishize the commodity-ness *of their own sense of* labor power under capitalism, to "penetrate" this form of capitalist ideology[3] Though not abstractly stated, these meanings are, I would insist, embedded in forms and practices of shop-floor culture. At last we see the force of Percy's insistent view that the put-on "hardens" young men to the ways of the shop floor: they all "catch on to it, and "it all works out." This is nothing but the hardening of their own labor power: the practical damping down of its infinitely variable nature, making it less elastic, less malleable, less likely to be "used up." Hardening is learning how to place and operate a selective, subjective "governor" over the objective, commodified side of their own labor power, to effectively control its expenditure, even while lodged in conditions designed and redesigned to maximally exploit its infinite variability.

Q.E.D.?

It is the dream of some ethnographers that their patterned and paradigmatic general explanations, their "Q.E.D.s," should form a template that nicely coincides with the lived experiences, expressions, and activities of their "subjects" in the field (for example, Geertz's cockfighters and funeral [1973]). For others, discrepancies are aligned through personal journeys of suffering and almost spiritual empathy-finding (for example, Rosaldo's headhunters [1993]). Percy allows no such option concerning my interpretation of the piss take or put-on as a form of training to limit exploitation. Actually Percy suggests this interpretation, or I think he does, but when I replay the possibility back to him, he rejects it and explains repeatedly that it is about the young worker's learning the ways of the factory—about "breakin' 'im in," "hardenin' 'im." When I press him, he repeats another version of the same thing.

What are we to make of this? How does it square with our attempts to find "history in person" when the "person" rejects the "history"? Can the circle be squared, or shall we just ignore or silence Percy, getting on with our senior common room chat, resuming business as usual in our detached contemporary social science. Or should we go all the way with Percy and junk the search for generalizable paradigms? As Dan Linger asserted during the seminar discussions, perhaps Percy is the best thing about my paper, and his descriptions of shop-floor life should just be left to stand alone.

My position on this is to accept, literally, that Percy and I are both right and are precisely speaking a "contra-diction." We are in this instance "speaking against" each other, but who is to say that two contrary statements cannot both be right? They often lead us to the pregnancy of third statements (see my comments later in this chapter on a cultural Darwinism): we are dealing with a "both-and" rather than an "either-or" situation. Two or more things can be simultaneously true of a cultural form. Percy is right, but equally I have to say, from my own situated practices, that there is a social literacy deficit in what he tells us. *Bang*, there you are! No prevarication. There is a social literacy deficit in what Percy tells us. Although subjects are to be believed in what they tell us, something has to be added that is not already there. Otherwise, the intellectual endeavor is dead, redundant.

How is Percy "right"? To start with, he rejects not so much my specific interpretation, which of course may be wrong or deeply flawed, as interpretation in general. He is simply trying to tell the tale about how you get "hardened" on the shop floor, and I keep interrupting him, obtusely telling him that it's something else (as well). What Percy is telling me is that all practices are equal at the cultural level. They fill up all available spaces for meaning. The meaning of the put-on is irrevocably alloyed to its practice. If it were "explainable," you could cut out all the cultural stuff and nonsense and simply send an economic telegram: "Watch out for exploitation!" In a word, Percy is insisting on the "rough ground," the fullness and irreducibility of culture. I agree with him, and this is my tune too.

Every act of presentation, still more so of interpretation (though every act of presentation is also one of interpretation), is an act of translation, taking meanings differently to new audiences. This act is always treason to the original, making it different, partial, smaller. There is nothing more to Percy's story than what it conveys on its own rough ground: he lives, stands, kneels, knows on that rough ground. I cannot claim to live his experience better than he. I cannot be him; he cannot be me. Most of the social is outside the surveillance mechanisms of cultural critique and social science. It is always to be found strangely at the edges, seeping in. There is an argument that the best accounts are simply unadorned transcriptions of what researchers have been told (Terkel 1974), but even in these there are mediations: the original choice of subject, the invisible questions, the editing, the unspoken presuppositions that drive the whole endeavor, the shift from the walked word in context to the wooden word in print.

Here I sit, typing this for an unknown future audience. I hear knocking from an adjacent garden, which bothers me; someone's repairing a fence blown down in a recent gale. It reminds me of my own broken fences, not least getting this revised article off to Jean Lave. I notice my hands moving over the keys, become self-conscious as if someone's secretly filming me. Light a cigarette, pause to reflect, back to the chain gang, which to choose from a chaos of bobbing words around me, the best tantalizingly submerged. I reach out for a lost scrap of paper, a raft where I think I might have scribbled it better. That last sentence was the raft, and now it's lashed into place, maybe to float long after my death, instead of dying immediately in the trash can. A moment's satisfaction. Suddenly the TV is unaccountably turned up in the next room and my small son is shouting; he's at home from school ill. But all that said, you, in a library, perhaps far away in time and distance, cannot know what I am doing here other than from reading these typed words in front of you; you'll never know about the commotion in the next room. There is always so much more in any cultural production or situation than any account or theory can provide. We need humility on the powerful side of the division of labor, that of the mental reconstruction and interpretation of others.

Perhaps humor is the most difficult of forms to represent and analyze out of context. It is a chimera to think that it can be explained by something else, especially by an economic determination. It has its own autonomy and life, its own logic. It is a universal form with arcane origins. As we have seen, there is a particular, hard form of it at play on the shop floor, but so there is in the locker room, the pool room, and the bar, too. Who is to say which borrowed from which? Perhaps the general purpose of humor is to defeat the boredom that is an omnipresent part of the human condition, and there is certainly plenty of boredom on the shop floor, compulsion at its "dullest." The monotony of production is the main "level-specific" and proximate "cause" of the piss take and the put-on. The lived accomplishment of which Percy speaks, the "uneasy evasion of monotony" (T. S. Elliot, *Vers Livre*), is comparable to the textual accomplishments of surrealism and Dada. The sustained flights of irony and "reality doubling" within supposedly old-fashioned, gritty, realist cultures of the shop floor make the most exuberant postmodernist texts look positively sincere. Here is a living art that deals with the whole relation of the symbolic order to the material order, ironizing this time the material rather than the symbolic and therefore achieving deeply social functions against the inert idealisms and floating aesthetics of the "transcendent" bourgeois forms. But it is the continuities with "Art" that I am stressing here, that irreducibility of symbolic form that we must respect absolutely, even as our attempts to re-present it are always flawed in fundamental ways. All this is specific, and it is evidence for Percy's case that shop-floor culture is its very own thing, that it imposes its own temporality and forms in always connected ways, that the piss take or put-on is umbilically connected to what locates it: It "learns you the factory," making you "catch on to it" and pick up "the shop-floor way."

The unity and irreducibility of cultural experience that I learn (or relearn) from Percy is shown and underwritten in another remarkable way by the general linguistic form of what Percy tells me.[4] All loose, counter, or unattached meaning is mopped up in what amounts to a hegemonizing (or counterhegemonizing) mythology of the reproduction of shop-floor life: "it all works out" in the end. Here I mean mythology not as falsehood but as popular meaning embedded in a whole practical and expressive system displaying recurrent themes and figures. The cyclical and repetitious form is part of this formation of meaning, no part of which can be separated.

The metaphor or allegory is a structure of the whole system of meaning, so in uncovering one bit of it you have no choice but to disclose all of it. Language is functioning, for Percy, in this disclosive way rather than in an analytic way, and so it is fundamentally at odds with my language use. In a way, Percy is telling me a folk narrative that is uncompressable. A story is a story and cannot have a moral or a summary. A myth has to be told in its entirety because it deals with how the world was constructed, and by the myth is that world reconstituted and reconstructed. The broad truth of the myth has no place for my narrow and disconnected "truths."

Percy speaks from, and describes, a subordinate social position and so has no ownership of or control over a public universe of signs and symbols, no opportunities to reconfigure their connotations in colonizing representations of his own mythology. Instead, he uses concrete examples from his practical experience, always pushing them out from the particular into the general, then using the general to illuminate the particular. His unique experience, "I learnt the hard way," becomes a universal "They do, they do," "It's life really that is, it's always been on the shop floor," which is then mobilized to explain the particular again: If a bloke like you "was to go on the shop floor." Of course Percy is usually involved in the practice of the piss take and the put-on in action, not in explaining them to an interloper whose agenda, interests, and framing of the interview remain something of a mystery to him. In the interview, he is reconstructing and representing rather than living his experience, probably not something he has done before. I am also forcing him to defend himself at the end of the interview, but he is not quite sure against what. This no doubt partly explains the repetition and circularity, but he is presenting no false or invented thing; he can be no other thing than himself, and he knows, at least, that I have witnessed some of what he describes. In fact, the (friendly) pressure I put him under acts not to sideline but to highlight and emphasize the nature and connection of the way in which he makes meaning in general. The abstract is demonstrated time and again by the concrete, and the concrete is used to prove the abstract. This is another marked feature of his disclosive use of language; truth inheres in immediate reality, not in an evaluation of a distant and secondary representation of it. The disclosure and the authorial "I" are projected onto the real world as "truths" inherent in it—another reason, incidentally, why the functions of the put-on cannot be recognized by Percy. Accepting "doubling" would contravene that mythic episteme which, ironically, supports it. Everything is condensed into an obvious reality: it is as if he had said, "See, hear, this is how it is, it's there, isn't it? It's always there." Percy's insistence shows us the logic of a practice of mobilization of subordinate myth making: concrete event, myth, concrete event, myth, and so on.

So Percy is "right." How does my "rightness" relate to his "right-ness"? First, not in displacing or denying it. In fact, I argue that I need his "rightness" to establish the fullest version of my "rightness." I certainly cannot claim that economic relations "determine" the contours of Percy's world, the located meaning and form of the piss take and the put-on. In that case it would certainly be better simply to send an "economic telegram." What I propose should be seen as an *addition* to, not a substitution for, what Percy says. Of course there could be many kinds of such "additions," and I hope I have given enough data, context, and "subject response" (how often do we get that?) to allow you, the reader, to make your own theoretical additions in relation to what interests you, in relation to what questions you might want to ask. This is no more than the "intellectual endeavor" I referred to earlier. For this is surely the point: what further questions are there to be asked that simply do not interest Percy? To try to answer these questions, it is unavoidable that something should be added to what he says. My questions are clear: Why are the piss take and the put-on so prevalent in shop-floor culture, and what light does this prevalence cast on the nature of the capital-labor relation at a cultural level, on the nature of the informal social relations of work, and especially on the puzzle (for me) of the manner of the "free" application of human labor power to "unfree" labor processes?

Of course the ethnographer in me must respect and try to re-present Percy's experience and "level-specific" autonomy, his "right-ness." I undertake my interpretive enterprise not to attempt to outdo Percy on his own "rough ground" but to get a better and more adequate basis for answering *my* questions. At bottom the nature of my enterprise is not to produce a better sense of Percy's world than Percy does but to make a textual intervention for theoretical purposes. This is my justification for undertaking the treason of translation; by contrast, the empiricist's endeavor is *really* treason for treason's sake. There is certainly an "openness" and "leakiness" about ethnography to which I subscribe and which does not quite fit a tight version of my case here. The ethnographer must pick up and record the fullest and richest data not only to "surprise" and disrupt prior theory but for a more open ambition to "surprise" (Willis 1992 [1980]). There is always more "in the field," especially in the form of "respecting Percy's truths," than can be explained by existing "answers." The ethnographic point is precisely to try to pick this up as the relevant material, always in excess, for possible (no guarantees) creative and unprefigured answers to crucial questions, in the reader's as well as the ethnographer's theorizing. But still I insist that this pursuit of the "open arts" of ethnography is undertaken not to outdo Percy but to discover materials of relevance to basic questions *of the ethnographer*. It is because such materials are to be discovered, and because *specific* theories are yet to be developed, that it is necessary to have the widest and loosest "hunch-driven" definition of "relevance"—not that there should be no questions or that "Percy's world" can in some way be directly presented.

Of course, there is a disingenuousness in the preceding formulations that has to be faced. I have reasons for preferring some questions over others; they are not all equal in my mind. We live in an era of intense change, structured by deep inequalities and a mystified "behind-the-back" and "hidden-hand" market system. Lived cultural forms may struggle for transparency in their articulations with their actual conditions of existence, but very few achieve it. Percy's cultural stage is real—no false consciousness here—but it is held up by props, and it props up other worlds, in ways that are crucial, in two-way action, to all its scenes, but this propping is not all on the stage. The complex relations of these props are not, for me, just another academic question. A changed relation of props will, and has, changed Percy's world, mostly for the worse. Increased transparency, some answers to my "questions," is a vital prerequisite, in my judgment, for the dialectical development and emancipation of "practical knowledge" and for its hopes of controlling more of what it seeks to understand. But even this reasoning should be understood not as a displacement of Percy's truths: it is my basis for thinking my questions worth asking (and there is always such a basis, usually unacknowledged) and for knowing, actually, that I can proceed only through Percy's truths.

We are still left with the $64,000 question. If not one of antagonism or displacement, what is the actual relation of Percy's and my truths? This is the most difficult of things to put into words, and I have been struggling with different formulations through all of my writings. How to pose a form of relation between levels of the social whole that is not one of mechanical determination but of the form "It is no accident that...."? The common ground between Percy and me that must be understood is that I do not look for an explanation in a reduction of the piss take or put-on to something else; I look for an explanation in how other purposes can be seen to be served through its very fullness and irreducibility. If the culture were not singing its heart out, singing its own songs burstingly, the piss take could not fulfill these other functions: the doubling of reality, the sensuous knowing and controlling of the special variable nature of labor power. A form that did not have its own kinds life, fullness, and history (including arcane causation) would not have the life to maintain itself as a possibility for doing other kinds of work to help it, finally, maintain its own conditions of existence.

EXPERIMENTING WITH A CULTURAL DARWINISM

For the first time I am going to use a new "raft of words"—namely, a Darwinian metaphor—to propose a notion of causation of the "it's no accident" kind, still respecting the autonomy of cultural forms. Let us say, just as Percy directs, that the piss take or put-on is itself and nothing else, sufficient unto its day and its song. But then let me add, on top of this, that it is so prevalent because it has been "selected for"—meaning nothing more than maintained in continued vigorous life, not dying out—because it fulfills other purposes, finds other "niches" of meaning relating to structural properties of the locating context, purposes that may not be conscious to its participants but that nevertheless make their lives more "survivable," compared with the alternatives, in a particular historical structure. This formulation has said nothing about selection's "determining" any aspect of the piss take, the internal form of which could be random or accidental, perhaps never known or understood. What is not accidental is the functions it finds it can perform through no prior purpose or design. So two things are true: the put-on is funny *and* a proletarian training. There is a structural space within the system for a "proletarian training," and any *effective* form could fill it—that much might be predictable, but not the "what" and "how" of that space-filling, that space referred to at the beginning of this chapter, the space between transgression and reproduction.

The first reason for the "selection" of the piss take is simply that it serves to defeat boredom. That is to say, the piss take and the put-on are more likely than nonselected forms to occur under conditions of monotony; they are more likely to be able to maintain humans in those conditions for longer periods of time, or for the same time with less suffering or distress, less motivation to get out of the situation. The second selection, a major, specific, and more interpretive one, is for the ability of the piss take and the put-on to generate and maintain an epistemological "doubling" of reality, the ability to enable humans to occupy material conditions as, up to a limit, something else. There are many subcategories of this ability: control of temporality, extension of alternative symbolic reality, provision of a meanings base from which to judge friends and enemies on the shop floor and to resist management regimes in a variety of ways.

The third selection, specifically the territory of the put-on, is for its ability to produce an inverse fusion (an inversely applied homology?) of the variability of symbolic "realities" and the (infinite) variability of labor power: an interchange between the material/sensuous and symbolic, *widening* the variability of shop-floor cultural forms (the piss take extends into the many varieties of the put-on) and *narrowing* the variability of labor power (providing sensuous and symbolic mechanisms for its control). This is the formal principle of inherent variability that, once learned and operated, is reapplied from the externally symbolic to the sensuous materiality and uniqueness of the productive and transformative powers of the self: same principle, opposite operationalization—impossible without the prior learning of variability.

I would argue that it is the enmeshed double lashings and lastings of these last two "selections" that fix the ironic forms of shop-floor culture so durably to its structured and material context, both "exposing" and "learning" nuanced and profound aspects of the nature of this context as well as making it more livable. There are no management philosophy manuals, guides, or experiments in how to develop and hold in place alternative and subversive "regimes of truth," simultaneously providing guides to the special nature of labor power and how to limit its subjective spending. Rather, they are all devoted to the reverse. No alternative, radical, or progressive formal system or training regime fills up this "empty space." Cultural forms step into the gap. If forms other than the piss take and the put-on could accomplish this invisible training more effectively, then they might have become dominant instead.

None of this is to take an inch from what Percy says. If there were any less in what he says, then some other forms would indeed have taken over. And these "selections" in no way "determine" what is selected— they only give them more chance to grow for themselves.

I have just argued that my "selections" do not exert a determination on internal forms, but only on their frequency and longevity. Yet there is a twist in my argument that considerably strengthens it. This is that selection operates not only on forms but on elements within them. This gives us more visible evidence. It is a "bend in the known" that is a guide to aspects of the unknown, in this case the manner of the nonreductive relation of levels within the social totality, along with the type and nature of the "structural niches" that remain to be filled. Remember the previous discussion of irony and how the joke form works, usually by bringing together dual realities in a punch line to "make people laugh." Percy points out that this may be so in a pub or a club, but is not so on the shop floor. I have seen and been perplexed by the way shop floors empty at the home-time hooter even in the middle of never-to-be completed jokes. Indeed, as is clear from the transcript, the punch lines of the piss take and the put-on are generally very delayed or never arrive. Why should this be so? Why should these forms differ in highlighting a different part of the joke equation: not a resolution to produce laughter (though this is important) but the maintenance of irresolution? I would argue that this feature of the piss take is "selected for" (not determined) precisely because of its efficiency in maintaining a permanent presence of the living possibility of dual (or more) definitions of the reality one shares (and creates). This restressing constitutes a selective process over time that precisely aids the "doubling" and "labor power learning" functions of the piss take and put-on, which are forms that rely more on the "epistemological splitting" of the irony form than on its resolution in laughter. The longer the punch line can be delayed, the more effective is the work supplied to maintaining and understanding variability: the symbolic "doubling" of reality, the real control of sensuous labor. Of course, Percy says in that section of the transcript that the purpose of humor is to make time go faster, and this must be respected. But it does not deny "doubling": it is an aspect *of it,* one of the living forms of my analytical category.

Another specific feature of the shop-floor joke form and the way it differs from other jokes is also relevant here: "stranding," the extended abandonment of projected identities in alternative realities. This is a feature that distinguishes the shop-floor piss take from that described in the OED as "mockery" or "parody"—at the beginning of the chapter I described the piss take as "po-faced" mockery. Stranding can be seen as another selected-for internal feature that again highlights the extensiveness and durability of "alternative reality" (de-stressing "laughter") as an omnipresent form of shop-floor life. It is the other side, or the personification, of the principle of "doubling," and it further adds, especially in the put-on variety, to the effectiveness of the culture, *on top of whatever else it might be,* as *also* an effective proletarian training in the deflection of management regimes of truth and in the sensuous hardening of labor power. So selections in and on the joke form—frequency, stranding, de-stressing, and delay of the resolution—all help to reinforce what I claim are the *extra* and *social* functions of the piss take and the put-on. The meanings of these reinforcements, in my view, hang in the cultural air but require no consciousness and criticize no lack of consciousness in the particular participants in cultural practices. They require only that cultural practices be effective at increasing "survivability" on the shop floor. But this is the necessary specificity of how the put-on teaches the young worker the shop floor and hardens him to its ways. It is the "history in person."

A note of clarification is needed here to separate this nascent "cultural Darwinism" from social Darwinism. I am arguing for a "critical selectedness" that may not be in the best interests of the economic whole or of the economically dominant within it. In important ways it strengthens opposition and helps to prevent the weakest from dying out. Heresy! It is also collective, social, and symbolic, all in marked contrast to social Darwinism. So far as I know, it is the first time that the Darwinian concept of selection has been applied to a socially antagonistic relation to show how subordinate forces might be strengthened rather than weakened. Darwinism might allow through the back door of social analysis what has been kicked out the front door: subordinate collective logics and interests in relation to structural location.

Whether or not a cultural Darwinism can be developed—and all of the preceding arguments could be put in other words, including the "penetrations" formulations of *Learning to Labour* (the culture "understanding" structural "niches and properties," the "space to be filled" not supplied with conventional or official meaning)—a larger continuing purpose of mine is to develop *specific* understandings of *particular* sensuous/material mechanisms within the larger fabric of capitalist social formation. This becomes more urgent now, after the dislocations and free-floatingness of postmodern approaches, to one side, and, to the other, the collapse of asserted Marxist notions about some essential force of a homogeneous working-class culture resisting capitalist ideology. I want to find "class" or aspects of "classness" or "history in person" not through the application of general categories downward but in the recording and analysis of actual cultural practices at concrete sites. "Simple" determinations from capitalism must be seen not as full specifications but as highly abstract "first guesses" for the dialectical interdependencies of concrete sites, the quivering symbols and practices of which must be given their full scope.

Of course there is a continuous flow of meanings and forms between sites, not least, for instance, the forms of humor inherited by the shop floor, and it is a mindless task to imagine that everything can be traced around from site to site, making causal additions for every one. Nevertheless, it is not unreasonable to believe that there are some privileged sites of cultural fixing and formation—if you like, for cultural "speciation" (work sites still among them)—where something of the mechanisms that might operate more variably and invisibly elsewhere can be understood and that export, so to speak, more than they import. Percy's shop-floor culture, I would argue, has been a particular source and mechanism for the reproduction of a certain male, working-class humor and characteristic way of thinking and acting. Though this is a topic for another time (see Willis 2000), it may be that these "exports" and self-reproductions of meaning (which reproduce themselves especially by reifying aspects of the mythological form) are not always as relevant to their new sites of deployment as they were to their development at the "privileged" sites. There may be anachronisms and what we could term "anaculturalisms" where meanings resources survive but are misapplied in the context of their time, place, or structure. Perhaps, more correctly and to continue with the Darwinian metaphor, there may be new "selections," new creative uses of what has been inherited, which also blindly carry over (because we are not dealing with anything approaching "determination") an awkward or negative, indivisible baggage. Forms such as the masculine "hardening" of labor power that become indivisibly bound up with shop-floor culture may be carried over to sites where they are less relevant. The creative bonding of the material and the sensuous ("labor power") with the symbolic (the variability of irony) at one site is unselfconscious and, once transferred, may result in physical/symbolic unravelings or new articulations with less benign effects.

I would certainly argue that there is deployed on many sites of working-class experience a double ability to recognize formal reality and its codes and expectations, on the one hand, but also, on the other, to recognize the informal plane beneath: the boiled-down actual minimum conditions to be met; the understanding and practice of a wealth of human forms and terms for meeting and dealing with these minimum conditions on acceptable human scale. This simultaneous double ability is a fundamental feature, historically, of the many lived forms and varieties of working-class culture, as is the associated humor and often cruel wit through which the second level is differentiated, enacted, and sometimes enforced.

This double ability colors all of life and has great influence on individual styles and sensibilities. It might be suggested that this is the basis for continuing, widespread middle-class suspicions that, despite specific compliance with formal or expected roles and rules, workers (usually male) often hold something substantial back, have whole continents of meaning in reserve even while respecting demarcation lines. They will laugh at you once your back is turned. There is an otherness, an "unclubability," a distance, a detachment, a separateness, an indefinable refusal to fit in with your view of them that comes across often as "ignorance" or "lack of education" now that class is not a fashionable or allowable category of explanation. Generally, role behavior cannot be read as role compliance, and role compliance cannot be read as role commitment, which in turn cannot be read as role belief. These disjunctions indicate the space for a practice of social learning that may have neither language nor iconographic form but that is evidential in ways of being, in cultures that are lived in both within and beyond their conditions of existence. There will always be other knowings, other visions, other ways of showing, saying, and so forth, that will wriggle around the stolidity of what *is* and arrive at some version of what *might be.*

In general and among all classes, and among women as well as men, developing conflicts, potential fight scenarios, situations in which someone feels he or she is being pushed too far can be punctuated with a defining, escalating moment, "Are you taking the piss?"

Just as class difference and class cultural forms are dismissed as old-fashioned, meaningless, or redundant, many hitherto middle-class or professional occupations are actually being proletarianized as the speed-up and intensification of labor processes become, in turn, part of their management regimes of control and direction. Even where Japanization of management ideologies seems to offer job ownership, job enrichment, and meaningful consultation to employees, it is to be expected that some specific working-class forms such as the piss take and put-on will become much more prevalent in the lived cultural relations of supposedly middle-class groups. As proletarianized and intensified working conditions have swept through the British university system in recent years, common-room culture is changing apace.

To continue the Darwinian metaphor, but in an economic and less optimistic mode, and to expand on the larger theme of irony, another crucial "selection" of shop-floor forms, the piss take and the put-on, is that they may well help, after their own fashion, to meet some wider and fundamental conditions necessary for the maintenance of capitalist production. Despite their immediate resistances and autonomies, the piss take and the put-on have a countervailing balance of reproductive effects and involvements. These mechanisms are defensive and protective; they do not provide alternatives. Just as they prevent maximization of exploitation, they also naturalize acceptance of a minimum. The "alternative" reality has its own notions of what is fair, necessary, and legitimate. These can correspond to, and sometimes informally police and enforce, quite high levels of production. Time passes "quickly" in culture, but at the same regular accumulating pace for capital. Moreover, that these are essentially symbolic forms, suffused also with symbolic forms of masculinity, means that conflicts can be displaced from the economic sphere and resolved in the symbolic sphere. Often as expert as the shop-floor Percys in the swordplay of badinage, banter, and piss-taking, foremen can settle disputes through and in practices that exercise and respect shop-floor prowess and masculinity—uncapping again the bottomless well of power in human labor. The resistances and pleasures of shop-floor culture may be strangely congruent with areas of silence and what can be yielded, as well as what must not be given up, in what they seem to oppose.

More generally, there may be a wider social weakening rather than strengthening of solidarity and social connection through the piss take and put-on. In any symbolic plane or activity, anyone can be taken as target or perpetrator of the piss take, unjustly or not. Social life can be riven and patterned by hard streams of intimacy (sharing the joke, so to speak), by bitter streams of undeserved victimization, and by acid streams of paranoia in which people question any motive or intention that might be deemed to be about "taking advantage."

Percy also illustrates the efficacy of the piss take for reproducing the mental-manual divide. He will not relate the piss-take or put-on to the *real* put-on, so he certainly will not stretch it to a wider relevance in the critical understanding of capitalist relations. Cultural forms are so replete with meaning that they push out what seem to be alien, "noncultural" mental forms. Mythic forms and their projection onto "natural truths" embedded in reality further delegitimate forms of mental knowledge. This can produce intrinsic suspicion of all abstraction everywhere, which is effective and the only defense in many situations but which is also strangely and strongly reproductive of the (mental-manual) architectural divisions that capitalism needs for its continuance.

Percy is in a time capsule from perhaps the last great age of at least some autonomy and control in English working-class culture. The "structure of feeling" has shifted somewhat now in England, along many dimensions: the decline of working-class institutions; the deradicalization of politics; a deepening inequality mediated less through labyrinthine cultural forms and more through cynicism and coercion (still trading in different ways on detachment and indifference); and the rise of commodity culture, displacing both traditional/folk and legitimate/high forms of culture. But, mutatis mutandis, the relations we have looked at still hold great relevance. The approach, methodology, and analysis used here are more apposite than ever. There are many continuing streams of working-class forms of life, culture, and knowing, even if they have been split off from, or are no longer tributaries of, one main (formerly often imagined anyway) river. It is now more necessary than ever to specify the specific sites, concrete relations, and sensuous mechanisms of this continuing "classness," since an assumed historical essence and mission are no longer available to classify and supply automatic meanings (nor were they ever, according to my work—a reason for its renewed timeliness). Beneath the ideological gloss of the "new" human resources management, benign Japanization, "worker empowerment and involvement"—the management attempt, if you like, to "fill up" the structural space occupied by shop-floor culture—lies the reality of the speed-up and intensification of labor processes. Even the unemployed face worklike discipline and regimentation from the state, no longer "Mother State" but (disciplinary) "Father State." Whole swathes of formerly semiprivileged middle-class professions, along with the new and expanded service industries, are undergoing profound processes of proletarianization of their own working relations and conditions. Globalization, as labor threat rather than commodity promise, helps to drive all this, handing to controlling elites some of their best-ever sticks, alibis, and justifications. There are and will be multiple and chaotic informal responses to these unfolding developments, responses that will color, often in unrecognized ways, the fabric of all of our daily lives. Percy supplies something of a model and a template for understanding some of this.

He won't be the last to ask, "Are you tekin' the piss?"

Notes

Phil Corrigan made long written comments on this chapter and discussed it at length with me. Although he is not responsible for its faults and difficulties, it is hard to separate his words from mine in several passages of the chapter. I have also benefited from insightful comments and suggestions from my colleagues Marcus Free and Darek Galasinski.

1. This and other issues are explored in Willis (1992 [1980], 2000).

2. Key to transcript:

[ ]	Background information
...	Pause

(...)   Material edited out

3. Penetration is a concept I first used in *Learning to Labour* (1977) to designate a process through which "the lads" of the counterschool culture "saw through" the limits and contradictions of individualisitic and meritocratic ideologies in educational provision as they experienced it.

4. The following linguistic points of analysis were suggested to me by Darek Galasinski.

7

The Identity Path of Eduardo Mori

Daniel T. Linger

Anthropologists tend to think of people as living "in" culture or "in" history. Here I shift perspective to reveal, as the title of this book promises, "history in [a] person." I highlight the ways in which Eduardo Mori, a Brazilian of Japanese descent, engages and transcends social facts.[1] In doing so, I seek to complicate our vision of the relation between persons and history.

Eduardo Mori was born in Brazil to Japanese immigrants and grew up among Brazilians of many races and ethnicities. He now lives and works in Toyota City, an auto-manufacturing center near Nagoya in central Japan, where I met him in late 1995.[2] The combination of Japanese descent, Brazilian upbringing, and Japanese residence is a recipe for identity quandaries. My account, an example of person-centered ethnography (Hollan 1997), focuses on Eduardo's doubts and deliberations about his ethnic affiliation. From his vantage point, history presents itself as personal experience, grist for the mills of consciousness and action.

Person-centered ethnography offers a corrective to anthropology's long-standing tendency to fetishize sociological abstractions (Sapir

1917). Such abstractions, taking on spurious lives of their own, can render persons inert and their perceptions, thoughts, and feelings theoretically dispensable. Anthropologists thereby run the risk of losing themselves in "fantasied universes of self-contained meaning" (Sapir 1949 [1939]:581)—the beautiful, seductive social theories that are our most highly valued professional commodities.

The problem lies not in theories of the social per se but in theories of the social that usurp the personal, pretending to speak for experience. Instead, social and personal viewpoints should complement each other. In studies of identity, the need for a double perspective is compelling. Seen as collective phenomena, identities are categories ground out through sociohistorical processes. But it is wrong to imagine that society fills those categories with individuals who adopt them as personal identities.

For the selves inferred from discursive formations are virtual: public representations do not manufacture subjectivities.[3] Person-centered ethnography reveals the slippage between social category and personal appropriation. It illuminates how people apprehend, reinterpret, and qualify categorical ascriptions, how they navigate among them, and how they sometimes invent new ways of seeing themselves and others. From afar, Eduardo Mori appears, like everyone else, to live in a world he did not make. Up close, we learn that Eduardo makes of the world his particular life.

Shifting the focus to Eduardo Mori compensates for the sociocentric tilt in theory, but it raises new and perplexing issues, hard to formulate in the usual terms of the human sciences but equally hard to ignore. I refuse to reduce Eduardo Mori to a social product. But neither do I consider him a psychological product, a psychodynamically or cognitively driven automaton. During conversations with Eduardo, I was struck by his critical, creative presence. Such idiosyncratic aliveness presents a challenge to deterministic social and psychological theories. I do not dismiss the search for explanatory social forces or mental operations—the pursuit is, in the last analysis, a matter of philosophical preference—but I do wish to underline the fluidities in Eduardo's reflections. They suggest to me that we should theorize people with caution, rendering forthrightly their moments of uncertainty and equivocation.

Eduardo's move from Brazil to Japan has an ironic counterpart in his tentative, fitful passage from Japanese to Brazilian. The latter trajectory is what I term his identity path—his sequence of identifications with various national and ethnic categories.[4] I believe that Eduardo's identity path could have followed a different course and that its future direction is uncertain. The unpredictability is a sign not of Eduardo's postmodern insubstantiality but of his gravitas. Eduardo occupies the liquid moments. Our own discussions were such moments, in which he used his playful, nostalgic, and painful reflections to think about who he had been, who he was, and who he might become.

Eduardo was not, is not, and will not be, in the words of James Baldwin (1985 [1955]:15), "a deplorable conundrum to be explained by [social] Science." His identity path is, I propose, an obstinate singularity —the intricate, irreducible product of his accommodations to and attempts to fly from what Baldwin calls the "cage of reality" (1985 [1955]:20–21).

BETWEEN JAPAN AND BRAZIL

Many Japanese-Brazilians have made a journey like Eduardo's, with similarly disruptive and generative consequences for identity. Let me sketch the general circumstances under which the current geographical movements and identity shifts are taking place.

In the decades before World War II, with the blessing and assistance of a Japanese government eager to jettison citizens it could not feed, nearly 200,000 Japanese crowded into boats bound for Brazil.[5] Those immigrants *(isseis)* worked as field hands on the coffee and cotton plantations.[6] Nearly all stayed on and made lives in Brazil. Most settled in the state of São Paulo, not far from where they had landed. Some went to neighboring Paraná. Still others ranged farther afield, into the central plains and on to Amazonia. Eventually, many bought farms or set up small businesses. Their children *(nisseis)* and grandchildren *(sanseis)* grew up speaking Portuguese, eating rice mixed with beans and manioc flour, and rubbing elbows with those of different colors and cultures, even as they linguistically distinguished themselves *(japoneses)* from those whom they called *brasileiros,* or *gaijin* (strangers). Many attended prestigious universities, entered the professions, and married "Brazilians," raising *mestiço* children.[7] At one and a half million, the country's current *nikkei* (Japanese-descent) population is the largest in the world, and by the usual standards—education, income, job status—Brazilian nikkeis as a group have done well.[8]

Brazil, however, has not. Brazil remains a nation of unrealized promise, afflicted with a troubled polity and a precarious economy. In the meantime, Japan pursued a disastrous war and achieved a spectacular recovery, becoming an industrial power of the first rank. By the late 1980s, the prewar surplus of unskilled rural labor was a distant memory; Japanese capitalism now suffered from a deficit of unskilled factory labor. A 1990 change in immigration law, prompted by Japanese industry's desire for a flexible, low-cost, and culturally tractable labor force to do the industrial dirty work abjured by Japanese citizens, for the first time permitted nikkeis to live for extended periods in Japan (Oka 1994).[9]

The effect was immediate. Salaries in Brazil, even in its wealthiest regions and even for highly skilled positions, remain low, and future employment and business prospects are uncertain. Japanese wages have proved a powerful attraction for those wishing to save money for a new house, a child's education, or a small shop or factory in Brazil. Despite Japan's astronomical prices, a worker's wages, judiciously spent, permit a reasonable standard of living.[10] Moreover, the move to Japan, where the streets are safe at all hours, offers an escape from the climate of fear in Brazilian cities, where both crime and punishment are out of control. There are also less tangible rewards. Rather than consuming international sophistication at a distance, through imported movies, music, and clothing, one can now become—almost—a bona fide first-world cosmopolitan. Finally, the journey to Japan has, for nikkeis, intensely personal dimensions. A Japan hitherto an inner landscape, an anachronistic shadowland assimilated uncertainly into the self, promises to materialize before one's eyes. These various considerations carry different weight for different people, but together they offer a strong incentive for many to make the trip.

The risky odyssey that took many weeks for the isseis has become, for their descendants, a boring 24-hour glide in the reverse direction. Nikkeis enter Japan as legal migrant workers *(dekasseguis)*, laboring mainly in so-called 3-K (or 3-D) factory jobs *(kitanai, kitsui, kiken*—dirty, difficult, dangerous) that pay them many times what they can earn in most white-collar occupations in Brazil. Brazilian residents of Japan now number close to 200,000, and many more have made the circuit through Japanese workplaces back to their homes in Brazil.[11] Often the circuit becomes a circle. With Japanese savings exhausted and Brazilian prospects discouraging, or afflicted by the so-called returnees' syndrome (*síndrome de regresso*) and unable to readapt to Brazil, ex-dekasseguis again board the airplanes headed for Tokyo and Nagoya. Over the years, some go back and forth repeatedly, in a slow-motion, long-distance commute.

The to-and-fro movement of Brazilian nikkeis differs from most cases of temporary labor migration in that it has elements of a "return." But where is the point of reference, the "home"? Whether a Brazilian nikkei is part of a Japanese or a Brazilian diaspora (or neither) depends on her perspective. Some nikkeis are globally minded, others provincial, and a few protean, readily trading an old Brazilian self for a new Japanese one. In the most general terms, Brazilian nikkeis find themselves suspended between Japan and Brazil, making unique lives from incongruous parts of themselves.

Most nikkeis hail from southern Brazil, home to an impressive array of immigrant ethnic groups and to the multihued descendants of Africans, Europeans, and indigenous Brazilians who inhabit all regions of the country. Many feel both a deep affinity with multiracial, multicultural Brazil and a sentimental attachment to insistently Japanese Japan, having grown up in families that emphasized the distinctness and even superiority of Japanese culture and blood.[12] But until recently it was rare for a Brazilian nikkei to have set foot in Japan. One learned and reaffirmed Japaneseness through family and community assertions of identity, consumption of traditional foods and celebration of traditional festivals, rudimentary Japanese language classes, and the complementary recognition of difference, sometimes with overtones of prejudice, by "brasileiros." A grandparent might recount the Japanese migration to South America, an ethnohistory of suffering and redemption. That myth has now gained an unfinished postscript: the current "reverse migration" (Oka 1994) to Japan.

Those nikkeis who have crossed the Pacific typically find themselves shuttling in company vans between clockwork factories and narrow apartments. They must fill out documents they cannot read and obey instructions they cannot understand. All but a few descend into a state of illiteracy or, at best, semiliteracy, learning to recognize just enough ideographs to negotiate their daily routines.[13] There is little time or energy available for systematic study. Dekasseguis typically work six days a week, sometimes 10 or 12 hours a day, with virtually no paid vacations. When not at work, people make the rounds of the supermarket, the department store, the Circle K, the pinball parlor, the video shop, the Brazilian restaurant.[14] They catch up on sleep. On a free day, one might travel to Tokyo Disneyland with the children, or to the next prefecture to visit a brother or sister. Brazil remains distant, but the telephone provides an intermittent (albeit costly) link with family and friends, the Portuguese-language newspapers carry articles from home, and ethnic shops rent copies of the soap operas, talk shows, and tabloid news programs aired on TV-Globo last week. Thus overseas nikkeis can, after a fashion, participate in everyday Brazilian life, but only with electronic prostheses that seem increasingly artificial as time melts away in the routine of the workplace and the isolation of the company-owned dormitory room or the public housing project.

The dekasseguis' Japan—opaque, rich, demanding, aloof—bears little resemblance to a father's or grandmother's faded prewar recollection. It assigns Brazilian nikkeis to a controlled, stigmatized margin. Japanese descent is the price of admission to the country, but it is hardly, in the case of South Americans, a source of distinction. Whereas Japanese typically expect and accept cultural incompetence from a non-nikkei North American or European, South American nikkeis receive criticism for minor lapses in behavior and language. Cultural and linguistic imperfections stigmatize them as defective Japanese, and as Brazilians they lack the redeeming first-world origins and fluency in English of Japanese-Americans or Japanese-Canadians. Japanese acquaintances occasionally charge them with having abandoned the country and having failed to participate in its postwar reconstruction. And whereas many Japanese accord North American and European civilizations attention and a certain respect, if not necessarily admiration, most seem to imagine Brazil as a hodgepodge of jungles and slums and Brazilianness as at best a mystery, at worst a sad third-world affliction.

Not surprisingly, in the collision with this shockingly new old world, nikkei selves made in Brazil get remade in Japan. Their own

"Japaneseness," formerly a taken-for-granted cornerstone of self, comes into question, as does their evaluation of its meaning. Nikkeis do not all respond the same way to their encounters with Japan, but often they seem jarred into reflecting at length upon who they are, reformulating themselves continually as the months in Japanese limbo stretch into years.

INTERVIEWING EDUARDO

My main objective is to show how, as he engages these historical circumstances, Eduardo Mori rethinks himself. In what follows, I present excerpts from two interviews conducted in September 1995.[15] A person-centered interview explores someone's subjective world, attending closely to particularities of thought and feeling. The passages highlight four moments when Eduardo seemed to consolidate different identities. Eduardo's identities vary in duration and degree of emotional commitment. Strung together, the moments constitute an identity path.

At the time, Eduardo and I were recent acquaintances. He had responded a few weeks earlier to a notice I had posted in our apartment complex, appealing for participants in a study of Brazilian dekasseguis. Eduardo knew I was an American anthropologist with experience in Brazil, understood that I was interested in issues of identity, and, I believe, saw me as a prospective friend.

I began with general questions that invited Eduardo to discuss issues of self and identity. I followed up with improvised interventions, pursuing lines of thought that he himself had broached. Such an exchange is far from a "normal" conversation. It makes strong demands on the interviewer, who must attend closely to what is being said and how it is being said without putting the interviewee on the spot. One tries to engage the person sympathetically, accompanying the intellectual and emotional flow and tactfully exploring key topics as they emerge.

The abridged transcripts constitute a first-order account—a close-to-the-ground report of a specific ethnographic encounter. I have arranged them in a simple, low-level organizational scheme: moments of identity. Even as edited they preserve subtleties, ambiguities, and contradictions easily lost or suppressed when memories substitute for records made at the moment, or when an author's words replace those of others.

Because of their complexities and uncertainties, person-centered interviews resist theoretical predetermination. Instead, they push one to question presuppositions. The following passages are susceptible to multiple higher-order ("theoretical") construals. Eduardo's identity path is neither a social construction nor a product of his own agency— rather, *it is both at once*. The transcripts condense more information than any of the conflicting interpretations that can be placed upon them. I take up these issues explicitly following presentation of the interview material.

EDUARDO'S IDENTITY PATH

Eduardo Mori's parents immigrated to Brazil from Hokkaido, Japan's northernmost island, during the peak period of Japanese immigration in the 1930s. The youngest of nine siblings, Eduardo was born in 1965 in the central Brazilian state of Goiás. He briefly studied economics in college. Just before coming to Japan he had worked in Brasília, the country's capital, as a computer operator for a state-run telecommunications company, earning about $100 per month.

In 1989, a friend suggested to Eduardo that he might make a better life for himself in Japan. He thought it over and finally contacted a broker *(empreiteira)* who specialized in placing nikkeis in Japanese factories. Eduardo left Brazil in April 1990, two months before the change in the immigration law, entering Japan on a tourist visa. The broker sent him to Homi Danchi, a public housing complex in Toyota City, where he still lives, and put him to work at an auto-parts plant. Since then he has visited Brazil only once, for several months in 1991, when he married Elene, a non-nikkei from Rio de Janeiro. They returned to Japan, where Elene also took a factory job, eventually trading it for less demanding employment in a Nagoya nightclub.

Without further ado, here are the interview excerpts.

Moment 1 (before 1990): Japanese in Brazil

EDUARDO: When I got here, the first thing I saw was that Japanese culture had been very much influenced by the West, it had already been transformed, transfigured. I was shocked by this. Really, many things have changed. If my parents came to Japan, they would be very surprised at the difference.

DANIEL: Could you talk a little more about [your parents']
image of Japan?

EDUARDO: Well, I can tell you exactly how it is. It's a photograph. Once you've found the place, you take the photograph.
And whatever's registered in the photograph will last for a long
time. That was the image that my parents brought, only it was in
a time when Japan was Japan. Traditional Japan, without mixture, without living alongside, maybe practically without contact,
without foreigners. So there was a time when posters were distributed in Japan, with a glorious map of South America, and
standing before this map was a young woman pointing her finger precisely at South America. And then there was a great
movement in which many, many boats went to Brazil, carrying
immigrants to a better life, who knows. And my father, he went
alone to Brazil, and he went practically just out of curiosity. And
when he arrived in Brazil, getting off at the port of Santos, he
began working in the fields.

He started working on a cotton plantation. You had to pull
out the cotton early in the morning. Since it was still covered in
dew, [the fieldworkers] would be soaked from the waist down,
and their hands became callused because you had to break the
husk and pull out the cotton.

And soon afterward came his parents. Then came my aunts,
my father's sisters, and so began an orderly life, it was Japan carried to Brazil, the Japanese colony within Brazil. Some things
from that time still remain today, precisely from that [ancient]
tradition. I learned that Japan had been abundant in rice but
lacked other foods, vegetables, fruits, which were very expensive.
[There was also] the cultural image, that was the pride of Japan,
the seriousness, honesty, the duty, the obligations, and it was
always this that I received, and always respected. So it's a very
beautiful image that I projected, really, all of this I still, always
venerated.

My upbringing was rigid, and my father always lamented that
he hadn't given us a more comfortable life, because during this
whole time we worked a lot. It was a tradition, since I was small,
if a family is made up of nine brothers and sisters, all nine would

have to work. Later on, with respect to school, my mother was more rigid than my father, studying was a duty, an obligation. Without the understanding that was in school, you could never have a better life. Education was always rigid, rigorous. That's the image engraved on me, I haven't erased that image from the photograph. I know that in Japan this type of life, this type of culture really still exists, without being influenced by Westernism.

There was in Japan, there still is in Japan, when there's a large family, the parents get everybody together and say, "Please, when you go out to work never dishonor the name of the family." This was also used in Brazil. In...the jobs I've worked, the programs [and] trade unions in which I've participated, I've always carried with me this...this word, try never to dishonor the name of the family.

DANIEL: Did [your parents] talk about their youth in Japan?

EDUARDO: No, because their memory couldn't recover their adolescence, just a few points that marked it. [I remember once] when my mother asked my grandmother to buy bananas, and my grandmother said that she would not have had this opportunity in Japan.

Before I left for Japan I asked my mother if she'd like to come. She said no, she didn't have any desire, maybe one day she'd come on a holiday, but to stay, she didn't want to stay here. Now I know exactly why. She comes from a very rural family here in Japan, so she always wanted a comfortable life, and in Brazil she discovered that this life really exists, and that what isn't lacking at home are fruits....Bananas, oranges, which she eats in great quantities, without worrying about tomorrow. I asked her, what's the memory she had of Japan. There's a peculiar word, to say "cramped," it's *semai.* Japan is very cramped. It seems like she imagined that in the future she could go to a country where she could breathe.

Maybe she wouldn't want to return to the place where she used to be, but she would want to see exactly what Japan transformed itself into after the scarcity of fruit, after the scarcity of food.

And so I'm making exactly the reverse journey that they made, they went to Brazil and I'm returning [to Japan]. Who knows, maybe it's a source of pride for them that in Brazil a seed grew and this seed is returning home. Clearly, I'm not going to stay here long, but I only want to bring the message that Japanese people are fine over there, just as they're fine here, so there should be a link between Brazil and Japan. Yes, this link, very great and very strong, exists.

Moment 2 (1990): Gaijin in Japan

EDUARDO: As soon as the airplane took off, I felt a certain fear about what was going to happen here. I had hope for [a positive] change, but I was afraid of what was going to happen. Maybe a moment when things could get out of control. You're a little lost here, not knowing how to say anything, not knowing how to write, or ask for help.

DANIEL: Describe your first days here, if you remember.

EDUARDO: I remember the first day. I landed at Narita airport [in Tokyo]. But look, for me it was...it was really frightening, because there were a lot of Japanese people [*amused*]. I had to wait, me and...four Brazilians. I sat there lost in the airport, and then came...the person [from the broker], and this brought me a little feeling of security.

I was one of the pioneers. And when I...was sitting there dazzled by the new world, with so many people who were different, even though I belonged to the [same] race, for me it was a terrific scare. I went into Tokyo...never had I seen a megalopolis like that, it frightened me a lot. And...just when I was going to get out of the van, the Japanese man asked me to wait inside. I saw him go into an office, talk with four people, and one of them looked out, through the window, and approached more closely. Then he said a word that I knew well, "*Muito prazer* [pleased to meet you], my name is Onoda." In Portuguese. So I saw that he was a Brazilian, and this made me feel more calm. We then went to Yokohama, [where I] stayed for a day and a half.

It was a dormitory for Brazilians who were arriving, and so it was, today you go to Yokohama, you go to Nagoya, they were distributing people. I asked myself, What will I be doing? Where am I going? And I was selected to come to Nagoya.

DANIEL: Everything was already—

EDUARDO: Already determined. So I came here to Homi. I arrived on the eighteenth of April, 1990. There were so few Brazilians here that it was very common for the Japanese to stop and stand there looking, stand there whispering among themselves, right? Stand there observing you, like you were an alien.

DANIEL: But how did they know?

EDUARDO: Ah, precisely by your style of dress, by your posture. Brazilians gesticulate a lot with their hands when they talk, they talk a little louder, laugh loudly. I felt like I was a, a spectacle, walking around Homi, because wherever I went people stopped. They inhibited me, they made me nervous. But you get used to it, and...I'm no longer reticent or afraid of the things I used to be....Maybe with all this time I've been here, it's helped me to control a certain fear I had, a terror of things going out of control.

DANIEL: But at the beginning, not knowing anything—

EDUARDO: I was illiterate, I couldn't read, I couldn't write, I couldn't speak...so I was practically an expert in silent movies, like Chaplin. But little by little I learned the language, I learned their customs, I kept on learning and, today, here I am.

When I arrived here, I saw myself as a foreigner, I couldn't tell if I was a Brazilian or an American or an Italian, at that time I was a foreigner. I was different. Because when someone just arrives here, at that time, when people would stop and look at you, sometimes you would feel so strange that you couldn't exactly remember your nationality.

Moment 3 (1991): Japanese in Japan

EDUARDO: I was thinking [in May 1991] that if I went back to Brazil and if the economy had gotten better maybe I would stay there. The good-bye party here, it's, let's say, even in Japan, you leave here and go to a neighboring city, some people feel, uh, a friendship, that it will be a while before you meet again. But I was going back to Brazil, which is nineteen thousand kilometers from here, so they would never see me again. Maybe some even gave thanks to God for that [*both laugh*], that I was going away—

DANIEL: I doubt it [*both laugh*].

EDUARDO: Well [*laughs*], so, the *hanchō* [group leader] went, the foremen, and some Japanese [workers] that I knew. But some were there [just] because all the leaders were there. Some Japanese who didn't talk to me much went because it was a good-bye party. Of the people I felt closest to, there was the hanchō, it's usual for [the hanchō] to give a speech, and Japanese people, when they give a speech [because] someone is leaving, the first thing they say is, "Anta no karada wa, ki o tsukete," meaning, Take care of your body. People say, "Be careful, take care of yourself." That's how they talk. [*Clears throat.*]

At that moment I stopped being a Brazilian who was leaving, I was a Japanese, it was like a group of friends who would never be separated. At that moment I felt I was a Japanese. At that moment I had a very strong desire to stay. I felt very good to be treated like that, it's as if during all the time I'd been there, [I'd] been a negative point, but at that moment you think, Hey, I always thought no one was paying attention, but everyone's paying attention now. Everyone knows that you really exist. That's what I was thinking. And so I began to understand that there are certain situations in which you are pushed to the side, but this doesn't mean that you're no longer being watched by them, that is, it doesn't mean that when you're sitting at the table, you don't exist for them.

DANIEL: So on that occasion you became a Japanese?

EDUARDO: Yes, it was at that moment, I think it was only at that moment. That day. It seemed that the differences were put aside, it seemed that you were no longer a Brazilian, so everyone treated you really like…like a…friend. And so it was at that moment that I really no longer felt like a stranger.

DANIEL: When you say that you felt Japanese at that moment, you're saying what exactly?

EDUARDO: That there was no difference at all. There had been this barrier that I talked about. [But this was a group] without rank. I mean, there was neither a general nor a captain nor a colonel. Everyone there was, was…a worker. There was no distinction of hierarchy.

At that moment I didn't feel strange, I didn't feel different. You're an American, a Brazilian says, "We're friends," there doesn't exist anymore either an American or a Brazilian, it's like that. There were neither Japanese nor a Brazilian there, everybody was the same.

DANIEL: Was it that you felt Japanese or was it that you felt, let's say, a human being—

EDUARDO: Right.

DANIEL: —among a group of human beings.

EDUARDO: Human beings. So for me at that moment there didn't exist a table full of…only of Japanese.

DANIEL: Mm-hmm.

EDUARDO: It existed, yes, but it didn't exist, everybody was united, right, there was no difference at all, nobody, at that moment, nobody treated you like…a person of a different color. You were the same color as them.

DANIEL: Yes, but, but you *are* the same color as them.

EDUARDO: I'm their color. I'm yellow. [*Laughs.*]

Moment 4 (1992–present): Brazilian in Japan

EDUARDO: With the [June 1990 change in visa regulations] the great mass of Brazilians started to come. I also took advantage of this [change] to see what Japan is like, to get to really know the culture, the food, only it left me wanting certain things. Relations in Japan, Japanese people, they're very cold, and that's something my father, he, he, maybe, I don't know if he was afraid to say anything but he hid that part, the coldness. For you to have contact with a Japanese you have to win him over first, and in that winning him over you have to hide your feelings a little. You have to never think about going home, you've got to just think about work. And Brazilians are very different, because a Brazilian thinks about things at home, the family, his parents. In some situations, you can't see inside [Japanese people], it's a very thick wall, so I can't manage to visualize them. That's what makes them cold.

Sometimes they're really rude, sometimes they're really serious, but I think all that's normal here. The older Japanese were accustomed to this, it was a custom to speak in a loud voice, to yell. But sometimes this doesn't bother me, what's important is that the Japanese have a certain vision, I won't say whether it's correct or not, but it's a different vision, and I for my part am still…quite Brazilian. I like human warmth [*calor humano*], I like people who are responsive.

…

EDUARDO: Today I'm a Brazilian. I managed to identify myself. After two or three years, you finally can identify yourself. You manage to recover your identity. So I am Brazilian.

DANIEL: I never expected that, no. That in the beginning you simply feel like a gaijin, a gaijin from any old planet or country or something—

EDUARDO: Or from the world beyond.

DANIEL: From the world beyond, right, and so with time, instead of becoming Japanese you became more—

EDUARDO: Brazilian.

DANIEL: Brazilian. Ah, why that, huh? Why do you think you didn't become more Japanese?

EDUARDO: With time I had to…know exactly where I came from, right? The [Brazilians] were all saying, "The first thing you should never hide from anyone is that you are a gaijin, you are a dekassegui, you are a Brazilian." No one ever said to me, "You have to be a Japanese. You have to be like them, you have to behave like them." Even if they told me I had to be [Japanese] I think I wouldn't accept it.

DANIEL: Why not?

EDUARDO: Mmmmm...I'm very much a patriot, I'm very proud. In Brazil, it's funny, in Brazil I feel Japanese....In Brazil, [nikkeis always] say, "You're Japanese."

[There] I tell myself, You're Japanese. And in Japan now I tell myself that I'm a gaijin, I'm a *burajirujin* [Brazilian, in Japanese]. Maybe with their help saying that I'm a burajirujin, I recognized myself as a *brasileiro* [Brazilian, in Portuguese]. So I think I never identified myself with [being Japanese], only by my features, they're traces that my parents didn't manage to hide [*amused*].

DANIEL: And when you go back to Brazil, you'll again be—

EDUARDO AND DANIEL: Japanese.

EDUARDO: I'm like a person without a country in Brazil. But I've grown accustomed to that. If I really thought that here I'm Japanese, and there I'm Japanese, and if here I wasn't accepted as a Japanese and there I wasn't accepted as a Brazilian, then I'd, I'd...I'd feel pretty hopeless. But I'm Brazilian here, and Japanese there. Maybe a Brazilianized Japanese, as people say. But over there in Brazil I'm going to have a lot of human warmth [*calor humano*], even being Japanese.

DANIEL: How to say it. Well. Now you're a Br—

EDUARDO: Brazilian.

DANIEL: Brazilian in Japan, right. And before you were a Japanese—

EDUARDO AND DANIEL: In Brazil.

DANIEL: And it might be that in the future you'll again be—

EDUARDO AND DANIEL: A Japanese in Brazil.

...

EDUARDO: Like that time [I went back to Brazil, in 1991], really I felt Japanese here, but I thought to myself, Why be Japanese, why would a Brazilian try to be Japanese here in Japan? Is it really going to change anything in my life? Maybe I could keep being Japanese, a Brazilian naturalized Japanese, but I'm not going to have my own life, it's going to be a limited life, it's going to be a completely closed life...maybe it wouldn't have much charm [*graça*], maybe it wouldn't have much feeling. Things here, I've noted that people do things...because of obligation, and I...really I couldn't make my identification some years from now, I couldn't...establish challenges here, to stay here ten years, fifteen years. Now, however much they might one day want me to stay, I'll respect [their wish], but I won't accept [it], because it's a...it's a different universe. Your behavior is gaijin. They want you to be a *nihonjin* [Japanese]. Well, I as a Brazilian, I'm not going to pass the rest of my life eating sushi, and maybe *misoshiru* [miso soup], *yakisoba* [fried noodles].

A PERSPECTIVAL ILLUSION

Suppose we set out to build a second-order account—a theoretical explanation—on the evidence just presented. Is Eduardo's identity path the product of a changing conjuncture of historical forces? Or does Eduardo make his own path?

Both these claims seem right, like incompatible perceptions of an optical illusion. One can, for example, tell Eduardo's story in a passive mode, emphasizing his enmeshment in temporally specific situations that are clearly beyond his control. He is buffeted by global economic forces, by discursive constructions, and by the influence of those with whom he must have direct, face-to-face dealings. The story might go like this.

Eduardo's Identity as a Product of History and Discourse

Eduardo's identity path is an effect of the changing requirements of global capitalism, as administered by national governments. In the early twentieth century, Japanese rural poverty and Japanese govern-mental policies gave rise to several waves of emigration. South American countries were eager recipients of Japanese surplus labor, and, especially after the United States enacted an exclusionary immi-gration policy in the 1920s, Japanese migrants, including Eduardo's parents and relatives, flooded into Brazil, where plantation workers were in demand.

Thus Eduardo was born to native Japanese parents who inculcated in him a sense of Japaneseness. They recounted tales of their own pas-sage to Brazil, variations on a general nikkei myth, and instilled in Eduardo a compelling sense of obligation. They linked this value to Japanese identity, such that, for Eduardo, maintaining family honor and conscientiously carrying out responsibilities became essential markers of his Japaneseness. Moreover, drawing on a system of ethnic categories dominant in Brazil during this period, non-nikkei Brazilians reinforced Eduardo's identity boundaries by referring to him as "Japanese." Hence Eduardo grew up conscious of being a nikkei, a Japanese in Brazil rather than a generic Brazilian. Being a nikkei meant having specifically Japanese qualities worthy of respect by other nikkeis and having an image that drew ambivalent but unmistakable attention from other Brazilians.

In the late 1980s, world economic forces once again directly inter-vened in Eduardo's personal history. The possibility of an advantageous move to Japan opened up. Even before the change in Japanese law, agents began to contract nikkei workers for Japanese factories. Eduardo, locked into a low-paying job in a stagnant Brazilian economy, was a prime candidate. He placed himself in the hands of an employ-ment broker, who organized his trip down to the last detail. Upon his arrival in Japan, the broker dispatched Eduardo to Toyota City, having arranged a job for him at an auto-parts factory and an apartment at Homi Danchi. In the housing complex, his strangeness became the object of curiosity and commentary. This gawking by Japanese residents who were unfamiliar (and uncomfortable?) with foreigners produced in Eduardo a kind of denationalization, even a deracination. In the fac-tory, he received less overt but equally unsettling treatment: an unas-similable stranger, owing to the significance in Japan of the Brazilian nationality he had acquired at birth, he was either considered a "negative point" or ignored, rendered invisible. Following Japanese custom, however, his factory workmates threw him a party as he was departing for Brazil in 1991, giving him brief recognition as an equal that momentarily fostered in him novel feelings of connectedness, of shared Japaneseness, even of biological sameness.

But such feelings of solidarity could be generated only in the quintessentially transitory setting of a customary rite of passage. When Eduardo returned to Japan with Elene, Brazilians were no longer rare spectacles. Dekasseguis had by late 1991 become a major presence in industrial regions, with a growing sense of themselves as a distinct group (a Brazilian diaspora?) rather than simply strangers. Other Brazilians he met admonished Eduardo never to pretend to be Japanese or to deny that he was Brazilian, reinforcing his own sense of Brazilianness, which received additional validation from the "Brazilian" to whom he was married. Still denied acceptance as a Japanese, he now found his Brazilianness affirmed. In attributing "human warmth" to Brazilians and a lack of "human warmth" to Japanese, Eduardo is simply acknowledging the group membership ascribed to him within his present historically specific discursive environment.

But I would suggest that the story can be told another way, in a more active mode. Eduardo is in this view a grappler and a decision maker. Here is an example of such a story.

Eduardo's Identity as a Product of Personal Agency

Throughout his life Eduardo has shown a marked tendency toward introspection and a readiness to rethink his situation and himself. Although his parents tried to instill in him both a sense of Japaneseness and the value of obligation, their attempt partially failed. In light of his own experience, Eduardo revised (even in some cases reversed) the ideas they proposed and the self they tried to build for him. He now sees their Japan, for example, as a faded snapshot of the past, a representation of a place that no longer exists. When he finally encountered Japan in person, one of his first realizations was that the people around him were "different," despite their racial sameness. They were frightening precisely because they *were* "Japanese." This realization made it impossible for him to regard himself any longer as a substantial product of blood descent.

Eduardo consequently suffered a loss of identity, coming to view himself as an alien. But the ridicule and invisibility associated with that category, which he felt as a sense of exclusion, were difficult to bear. When given the chance, he grasped at a fleeting Japanese identity, but almost immediately began to question the viability of such an identity for himself. Upon his return to Japan from Brazil, he rejected all his previous conceptions of self—the no-longer-tenable Japanese-Brazilian identity, the alienating gaijin nonidentity, and the pointless Japanese nouveau identity—in favor of a more satisfactory option: a strengthened sense of himself as a Brazilian.

All these identity reconfigurings involved active reworkings of meaning. For example, the Japaneseness he experienced at the farewell party had little in common with the Japaneseness he learned as a youngster. Before his trip to Brazil, Eduardo had come to construe Japaneseness as inclusion in a group, in contrast to foreignness, which meant exclusion. Moreover, the idea of Brazilianness had ceased to have positive content. But upon his return to Toyota City in 1992, he assigned both Brazilianness and Japaneseness new meaning.

His increasing familiarity with Japanese people and Japanese ways moved him to reassess what he had been taught as a child. He came to view "obligation," so important a part of his feelings of Japaneseness in Brazil, in a somewhat negative light, as associated with an overly serious attitude, a lack of responsiveness, a coldness. He contrasts Japanese coldness with "human warmth," a quality he now values highly and which he feels to be emblematic of Brazilianness. Through reflection and introspection, he has come to see both Japaneseness and obligation as largely foreign to his sense of who he is, and Brazilianness and human warmth as central. By virtue of his life choices and particular sensibilities, Eduardo has remade himself, albeit uncertainly, into what he now calls a "Brazilianized Japanese."

It is clear that the radically new situations in which Eduardo found himself importantly conditioned his revisions of self. But after all, Eduardo *resolved* to travel to Japan, deliberately confronting hazardous and alien situations. He put his own identity in play the moment he stepped onto the plane in São Paulo, recognizing that things might well go "out of control."

THEORETICAL ENIGMAS

Other interpretations of the interview material are possible, with different balances struck between social construction and personal agency. As elsewhere in social science, anthropological theories generally utilize the metatheoretical framework "actor-in-a-field." That is, a given theory identifies a "field" (a cultural system, a social structure, a discursive universe) and an "actor" (a person, a class, an ethnic group) located within it.

Depending on the constraining power attributed to the field, the actor has more or less freedom of movement. At the deterministic end of the continuum, actors are creatures of the field. All change inheres in the immutable dynamics of the system. The universe unfolds; the future is immanent in the present, which was immanent in the past. At the opposite extreme, actors are existentialists. Their actions, undetermined by their surroundings, cannot be explained.

Deterministic and volitional extremes violate most social scientists' deeply held, if inconsistent, notions of why things happen in the human world. Surely it cannot be all cause and effect; the idea of conscious choice has experiential force. Yet surely it cannot be all conscious choice, because choices are evidently constrained. Hence, credible theories strike a compromise, shunning (at least rhetorically) deterministic and volitional extremes. The strategy of middle-ground theories is to carve out an area, bounded by constraints, within which an actor exercises a degree of autonomy.

Eduardo Mori challenges us to confront the limitations of such theories, which are shot through with theoretical vacillations and dubious rhetorical strategies. Anthropologists have often described action in evocative terms—as "orchestration" (Holland 1997), "authorship" (Holland, this volume; Parish 1994), and the ubiquitous "practice."[16] My own discussion of "meaning-making" (Linger 1994) strikes me, in retrospect, as an attempt to declare the fact of agency without venturing to specify its precise characteristics. Recourse to theoretical imprecision and suggestive metaphors signals our unease over determinism, difficulty in theorizing agency, and inability to let go of either. We seem to be at a conceptual and philosophical impasse.

Vacillation is not all bad—better to hesitate at an impasse than to charge ahead heedlessly. This paper's strategic retreat from theory, its presentation of detailed, relatively unadorned ethnographic evidence, is a reminder that the world makes its own claims. Ethnography cannot be wholly innocent, but in paying close attention to what others are saying and doing, it can avoid merely illustrating a generalizing account. In the diversity of plausible second-order readings that they invite, the transcripts remind us of the frailties and inadequacies of theory. They offer rich, multifaceted, irreducible accounts of human behavior.

Person-centered ethnography has, like the variety of fiction advocated by James Baldwin, a paradoxical, sober, potentially liberating indeterminacy. In a scathing attack on the formulaic "protest novel," Baldwin wrote:

> [The human being] is not, after all, merely a member of Society or a Group or a deplorable conundrum to be explained by Science. He is—and how old-fashioned the words sound!—something more than that, something resolutely indefinable, unpredictable. In overlooking, denying, evading his complexity —which is nothing more than the disquieting complexity of ourselves—we are diminished and we perish; only within this web of ambiguity, paradox, this hunger, danger, darkness, can we find at once ourselves and the power that will free us from ourselves. It is this power of revelation which is the business of the novelist, this journey toward a more vast reality which must take precedence over all other claims. What is today parroted as his Responsibility—which seems to mean that he must make formal declaration that he is involved in, and affected by, the lives of other people and to say something improving about this somewhat self-evident fact—is, when he believes in it, his corruption and our loss; moreover, it is rooted in, interlocked with and intensifies this same mechanization. (1985 [1955]:15)

On a more personal note, Baldwin, a black man and a gay man all too aware of the repressive effects of normalizing discourses, described with precision the "disquieting complexity" of identity-making:

> We take our shape, it is true, within and against that cage of reality bequeathed us at our birth; and yet it is precisely

through our dependence on this reality that we are most endlessly betrayed. Society is held together by our need; we bind it
together with legend, myth, coercion, fearing that without it we
will be hurled into that void, within which, like the earth before
the Word was spoken, the foundations of society are hidden.
From this void—ourselves—it is the function of society to pro-
tect us; but it is only this void, our unknown selves, demanding,
forever, a new act of creation, which can save us—"from the evil
that is in the world." With the same motion, at the same time, it
is this toward which we endlessly struggle, and from which, endlessly, we struggle to escape. (1985 [1955]:20–21)

I believe that Eduardo would echo these thoughts. In his own disquieting, complex struggle to forge a personal accommodation with
historical circumstance, he concretely does so.

TRUCE-SEEKING

Like Baldwin, I am unwilling to reduce human realities to fantasies
of exhaustive explanation or to wishful, but likewise mechanistic,
polemics. The novel offers an alternative; perhaps attentive ethnography, focused on the extraordinary specificities of human lives, does too.
Both novels and ethnographies can be crude, clumsy, pinched, self-
serving, self-defeating. Never can they, in good faith, guarantee liberation, and when they pretend to do so, perhaps they imprison us still
further. Yet certain ethnographies, like certain novels, can refrain from
reducing us to types by recognizing the complex particularities of our
struggles in a world we did not create. As Baldwin wrote, characterizing
his own efforts to come to terms with being a black man in the United
States: "Truce…is the best one can hope for" (1985 [1955]:5).

An adequate rendition of human truce-seeking currently lies
beyond our grasp. Just discerning it is a challenge. If our abstractions
are not to ensnare us, dulling awareness and sensibility, we must strive
to see beyond them, into what Sapir called "the nooks and crannies of
the real" (1949 [1939]:581). For this difficult enterprise we need not
more theory but the openness required to witness the uncommon, the
unknown, the unexpected. To close this essay, then, let me advance,
albeit gingerly, yet another metaphor, as a spur to the imagination.

Once I asked Hiroshi Kamiōsako, a Japanese friend who is a Kyoto painter and kimono designer, to take me to a temple he liked that was off the tourist track. We visited a small Zen temple in the city's northern suburbs. The temple had a garden of raked gravel, rocks, and clipped bushes, behind which was an earthen wall and a vista of Mount Hiei in the distance. In the middle ground, just beyond the wall, cedars rose on either side of the far-off peak. The garden's elements were primordial earth-stuff, vegetation, an ancient nonhuman landscape. In such a garden, the careful choice, placement, and framing of natural materials produces a subtle yet stunning effect. I am not educated in the esoteric meanings of Zen gardens. For me, an effective Zen garden has a visceral impact, an earthy, almost tactile specificity.

In such gardens, material and artist are inseparable: one would certainly not want to describe a Zen garden as a product of nature, nor as solely a human creation, nor again as, say, 50 percent natural and 50 percent human. A Zen garden depends for its effect, for its very existence, on the contrast between human engagement with nature and nature's nonhuman intransigence. Subtract either element and you destroy the garden.

Similarly, a person must make a self, and a life, from obdurate materials—the conditions of one's birth and the vicissitudes of one's journey through the world. Lives are not aesthetic creations, but they share with some such creations the important fact of irreducibility. The idiosyncratic apprehension, use, and ordering of unalterable circumstances make persons absolutely unique, despite their immersion in what is, in a gross sense, the same world.

And perhaps, as the effect of a Zen garden cannot easily be captured in language, such human creations as selves and lives also escape our attempts to couch them in terms of consequence or volition, the most readily available linguistic resources for the description of human action in the world. Some Zen gardens resemble one another, as do some lives, generated as they are out of similar materials and under similar constraints. But in an important sense, a particular life, like a particular Zen garden, is an obstinate singularity. To be fully appreciated, it must be taken on its own terms.

I do not wish to push the aesthetically freighted analogy too far. Too often the materials from which selves must be formed are unyielding, unpromising, unsatisfactory, even alien and painful. Selves are often the products of urgent necessity (Wikan 1995); alternatively, they may have a tentative, nostalgic, or longing quality. And selves, unlike scrupulously planned and carefully preserved gardens, are haphazard, subject to accidents, and always unfinished.

But occasionally a self achieves a state of suspended tension, a point of abeyance, suggestive of a Zen garden. If home is, especially in these days of transnational lives, less a physical space than an existential truce, then perhaps Eduardo will someday find a home in the world. I close with a fifth moment in Eduardo's identity path, an imagined opening to the future strongly tinged with yearning (cf. Malkki, this volume).

Moment 5 (the Future): Brazilian in Brazil?

DANIEL: Is it more…comfortable, let's say, to be a Brazilian in Japan or to be a Japanese in Brazil? Do you understand the question?

EDUARDO: Mm-hmm. It would be easier for me to be a Brazilian in Brazil.

DANIEL: Brazilian in Brazil.

EDUARDO: In Brazil.

DANIEL: Is that possible?

EDUARDO: It's possible. Eh…In Brazil…I never had anything like…anything as rigid as it is here. What hurts you a lot is this very great rigidity. So, a Brazilian, he lives a more unruly life, without any rules, but to be sure with a certain limit. A Japanese, he's got rules. Because I think I'm not much for rules, I'm, I'm really Brazilian, and so I think I feel comfortable at home, in Brazil. I would really prefer that…Japan understood Brazil a little better. Right? That [Japan] understood why the dekasseguis are here. Maybe they would open certain doors for us. Right? Because in Brazil…mmm, in Brazil we've got Japanese, we've got Germans, we've got Italians, we've got Americans, we've got Vietnamese, Chinese. So there, a Brazilian, when he meets a

Chinese friend, he'll never fail to say, "Hi, how are you doing, how's everything?" I really miss that here. That intimacy, that really comfortable thing in the sense of saying, "Hi, how's it going, how are things, how's your family?" And a Japanese person no, a Japanese only says "Good morning," a "good morning" like, of the factory, really forced. It's that obligatory greeting. With us it's different, we ask with warmth.

I miss that, I miss Fridays, when we leave work and head for a bar, that's the usual thing. Drink a beer, relax a little. There was always a person to sing a samba, samba is also a product of Brazil, it corresponds to a certain human warmth that's also a thing of Brazil. I miss Brazil, so I think what I'd rather do is really to go to Brazil, to be a Brazilian in Brazil instead of a Japanese here in Japan.

I only have the feeling that one day I'm going home, whether I'm Japanese or Brazilian at home, of this I have complete certainty.

Notes

Nancy Chen, Diane Gifford-González, Judith Habicht-Mauche, Peter Knecht, Chieko Koyama, Gene Kumekawa, Arkadiusz Marciniak, Steve Parish, Joshua Roth, and the editors of this volume read my essay with care and provided perceptive commentary. Thanks also to Peter Stromberg for a 1993 conversation in Montreal (at the Society for Psychological Anthropology meeting) that set me thinking in these directions. I presented versions of this paper at colloquia at Nanzan University and the University of California, Santa Cruz, and would like to thank colleagues at those institutions for their comments. Though I delivered a different paper at the Santa Fe advanced seminar—I was then in the midst of the Japan fieldwork—I thank the participants for provocative discussions that enabled me to formulate the present argument. The Japan Foundation and the University of California, Santa Cruz, sponsored my research.

1. All names are pseudonyms, except that of Hiroshi Kamiōsako.

2. I did fieldwork in the Nagoya-Toyota area from June to August 1994 and from July 1995 to July 1996.

3. Thanks to Don Brenneis for the epigram "virtual identity." The most vul-

nerable works are those that draw a sharp contrast between an egocentric Western self and a sociocentric non-Western self on the basis of ideologies (e.g., Dumont 1980; Geertz 1984 [1974]). See Spiro 1993 for a comprehensive critique.

4. For Eduardo and many other Japanese-Brazilians in Japan, the question of ethnic identity moves forcefully into awareness. Although conscious grappling with nationality is the topic of this chapter, ethnic identity is not always, or in all respects, fully conscious. See Kumekawa 1993.

5. From 1908, with the arrival of the first boatload of immigrants from Japan, through 1942, 188,986 Japanese entered Brazil, the vast majority arriving after 1924. Immigration then tapered off, totaling 53,849 in the postwar period (Folha de São Paulo 1995; data provided by the Japanese Consulate General in São Paulo).

6. Many Japanese words have entered the everyday Portuguese of Brazilians living in Japan. Portuguese renditions of such words, though inconsistent, occasionally differ in spelling and inflection from the romanizations familiar to English speakers. In spoken Japanese, for example, *issei* is both singular and plural; Brazilians generally say *isseis,* pluralizing the word in the Portuguese manner. (But *gaijin,* "foreigner," sometimes does not change in the Portuguese pluralization.) In the usual romanization, *nisei* denotes the child or children of an immigrant Japanese; in Portuguese romanizations, for phonetic reasons the singular is written *nissei* and the plural *nisseis.*

7. Rates of *mestiçagem* are, among nisseis, 6 percent; among sanseis, 42 percent; and among *yonseis* (fourth-generation descendants), 61 percent (Bernardes 1995a, citing data from a 1988 study by the Centro de Estudos Nipo-Brasileiros).

8. Bernardes 1995b. According to a Datafolha survey conducted in August 1995 and cited by Bernardes, 80 percent of nikkei families residing in the city of São Paulo had incomes of 10 minimum salaries or more. (The legally established monthly minimum salary in Brazil is approximately $100.) Bernardes noted that a 1994 survey by the Fundação Sistema Estadual de Análise de Dados (Seade) found that only 30 percent of all families in metropolitan São Paulo had salaries that high. Similarly, 53 percent of nikkei adults had university educations, versus 9 percent of all residents.

9. The law offers nisseis three-year visas, and sanseis, spouses, and dependent children one-year visas, all renewable. Immigration officials have some flexibility in determining the duration of such visas.

10. Male factory workers I knew in Toyota typically earned in the neighborhood of $3,000 per month, including overtime. Women earned about one-quarter less.

11. The Japanese Ministry of Justice, Department of Immigration, reports 168,662 Brazilians resident in Japan as of June 1995 (*International Press* 1995). This figure does not include approximately 20,000 Brazilians of dual nationality (Klintowitz 1996:28).

12. According to a Datafolha poll of nikkeis residing in the city of São Paulo, 59 percent stated that "Japanese" were prejudiced against "Brazilians," whereas only 35 percent thought that "Brazilians" were prejudiced against "Japanese" (Folha de São Paulo 1995:11). The same poll showed that 67 percent of São Paulo nikkeis said they preferred Brazil to Japan, versus 22 percent who said they preferred Japan to Brazil.

13. Japan uses four scripts, three phonetic (*hiragana, katakana,* and *romaji*) and one ideographic (*kanji,* or Chinese characters). Scripts are combined when writing, though kanji are the most important elements of written Japanese. Few Brazilian nikkeis I know have competence in kanji, sometimes humorously described as *pés de frango*—chicken feet.

14. For an ethnographic discussion of one such restaurant in Nagoya, see Linger 1997.

15. We had tape-recorded conversations, in Portuguese, on September 9 (one hour) and on September 23 (two hours). I have abridged the transcript but I did not alter the sequence of exchanges. Glosses and clarifications are bracketed.

16. One of the most striking of such "practice" images is that invoked by Parish (1994), drawing on the work of Shirley Brice Heath (1983). Parish compares human actions, from ritual enactments to moral careers, to "raising a hymn" in certain African-American churches. His point is that all concrete action is complex, dynamic, unfolding, unique. "Raising a hymn" is infinitely more complicated and alive than any cultural or discursive account of a hymn can suggest.

Part Three

Futures in Contest

8

Class and Identity

The Jujitsu of Domination and Resistance in Oaxacalifornia

Michael Kearney

Among the most enduring struggles in world history is that of indigenous peoples of the Americas against nonindigenous peoples and their institutions and against forms of identity that arrived in the Western Hemisphere after 1492. This chapter examines the sociocultural dynamics of the contemporary phase of this long saga for indigenous peoples from the state of Oaxaca in southern Mexico, with special attention to the growth and actions of an organization that represents them, the Frente Indígena Oaxaqueño Binacional, often referred to as the Frente.[1] My basic questions are these: Why do many Mexican indigenous peoples, such as those represented by the Frente, continue now, at the beginning of the twenty-first century, to endure as distinct identities within the greater Mexican nation-state? And why are some such identities now becoming more intensely lived and more extensively organized?

Until recently, the great master narrative of modern Mexican nationalism was one of the leveling of residual postcolonial cultural differences as indigenous and nonindigenous peoples presumably melded into an emergent modern, mestizo nation. But two trends are notable in the present moment. One is the resurgence of indigenous identities at a time when indigenous peoples' "assimilation" into "modern" national societies and cultures was widely assumed to be inevitable. Now, however, after almost five centuries of this "civilizing project" in Mexico, such differences are still deep, and indeed, new politicized cultural differences are emerging along the divide of indigenous and nonindigenous identities. The most noteworthy is the uprising of the Zapatista National Liberation Army, or EZLN, in the Mexican state of Chiapas in 1994, in which the Zapatistas presented themselves primarily as a movement of indigenous peoples rather than as peasants or workers (Harvey 1998). Indigenous peoples thus have a contemporary prominence in national and international political arenas at a time when many anthropologists and others had predicted their demise.[2] In addition to the Oaxacan case and that of the Zapatistas, there are numerous other examples of such emergent indigenous presences throughout the Americas (Kearney and Varese 1990; Van Cott 1995; Warren 1998, this volume).

Another notable feature of the present conjuncture is that the Mexican state, after a long-term policy of nonrecognition of indigenous peoples and of incorporating them into the national mainstream, is now, in significant ways, reversing this policy. Through various constitutional reforms and policy initiatives, the Mexican state appears to be supporting the viability of indigenous communities and cultural institutions even as it seeks to contain them by doing so. One way of regarding such a policy shift is to see it as a capitulation to the politics of multiculturalism. However, the analysis presented here suggests that it is instead a subtle means of reproducing class inequality in Mexican society, albeit an inequality that manifests itself as ethnic differences.

In brief, I argue that the resurgent expression of ethnicity (a form of *identity*) in the Oaxacan case is largely a cultural expression of and a proxy for a partial consciousness of subaltern *class* positions in fields of unevenly distributed value. Class consciousness has proved a poor basis for mobilization in postrevolutionary Mexico and, indeed, in most of contemporary Latin America and elsewhere. But a recent deterioration of living standards for millions of Mexicans, associated with neoliberal reforms and a falling peso, has stimulated a variety of protests that have taken the form of "new social movements"—NSMs—the first of which exploded onto the political scene in the wake of the great 1985 Mexico City earthquake (Escobar and Alvarez 1992; Foweraker and Craig 1990). Most of the theorists and activists discussing NSMs in Mexico see them as viable alternatives to class-based politics. But whereas NSMs tend to be formed around specific issues and identities—such as urban services, the environment, debtors' rights, women's needs, and gender politics—ethnicity as a base of mobilization tends to encompass a broader range of political objectives.[3] Even though ethnicity has the potential to bring together multiple issues, however, its potential social base is limited by the sociocultural specificity of its membership. Nevertheless, indigenous peoples who present themselves as such may have the power to enlist broad support from other groups and sectors, and often from ones abroad (Brysk 1996).

The second part of the thesis is that once ethnicity is out of the bag, so to speak, the state must seek to limit its oppositional potential with "strategies of containment," but it does so with only partial effectiveness, because such strategies also in part constitute the "enduring identities" that they seek to contain. This chapter thus speaks to a central theme of this volume, namely, the "endemic" nature of certain struggles. It examines a perverse dynamic whereby the more that subaltern people struggle "in person" against oppression, the more they have to. This leads us to suspect that struggle and resistance are themselves implicated in the reproduction of culturally based class differences that are the necessary condition of inequality. Such self-defeating dynamics are forms of what we can refer to as "jujitsu politics," in which subjects' best efforts at self-defense serve to bring them down. We are thus dealing with an inherent contradiction that results from people's building solidarity by constructing a self-conscious subaltern identity that in turn serves as the difference upon which oppression feeds, in a perverse dialogic of cultural and class differentiation.

THE AREA AND THE PEOPLE OF THE FRENTE

The main groups represented in the Frente are various communities and organizations whose members are identified as and who identify themselves as "indigenous peoples"—Zapotecs of the central valleys and the Sierra Juárez of Oaxaca, Mixtecs of the Mixteca region in the western one-third of the state, Triques, who are an enclave in the

Mixteca, and others of the 16 groups of indigenous people also present in the state. The case of Oaxacan communities is exceptionally complex, owing to the presence of tens of thousands of Oaxacan migrants in northwestern Mexico and deep into the United States, especially in California (fig. 8.1). This great border area is a "third space" that in some ways transcends the political and cultural spaces of both Mexico and the United States and that is sometimes popularly referred to as "Oaxacalifornia" (Kearney 1995; Rivera-Salgado 1999a, 1999b, 1999c). Clearly, the sociocultural and political dynamics occurring in this vast transnational field are too complex to be fully addressed in a single chapter. I therefore concentrate on the relationship between indigenous peoples of Oaxacalifornia, as represented by the Frente and some other organizations, and the Mexican state.

According to comparative data on income and other indicators, Oaxaca is among the poorest states in Mexico, and the Mixteca is the most economically depressed region of Oaxaca. Lack of employment and the prevalence of family farming that does not meet household food and income needs have provoked migration from the Mixteca for many generations.[4] Most of this migration since the 1960s has been to seek work in corporate agriculture in the states of northwestern Mexico and in California. On the basis of a 1993 survey, it was estimated that in peak summer months there were about 50,000 Mixtecs in California, representing more than 200 communities in Oaxaca (Runsten and Kearney 1994). This number has most likely grown in recent years, and a much larger number is present in agricultural enclaves in the Mexican states of Sinaloa and Baja California (Garduño, García, and Morán 1989; Wright 1990; Zabin 1992). There are also thousands of Oaxacans—mostly farmworkers—dispersed in Oregon, Washington, Florida, North Carolina, and elsewhere on the East Coast. Some tens of thousands of Mixtecs and lesser numbers of Zapotecs also live in *colonias* of the Mexican border cities of Tijuana, Mexicali, Nogales, and Ensenada. Whereas Mixtecs migrants tend to be located in rural areas of the United States, the greatest concentration of Zapotec migrants north of the border is in Los Angeles, where there are some 40,000 by most estimates.

An understanding of the history of the Frente must take into account its diverse antecedents.[5] In a long tradition of Mexican

FIGURE 8.1.

Oaxacalifornia.

migrants, Mixtecs and Zapotecs in northwestern Mexico and the United States began in the 1960s to form hometown migrants' associations to provide mutual support to the migrants and to channel economic support to their hometowns. Also, many migrants have participated in a wide variety of progressive labor union activities that challenge the hegemony of official, state-run labor unions and "popular" organizations that are organized by the Mexican government but do not well represent the interests of their members (Kearney 1988).

In the 1980s, leaders of Oaxacan village organizations and farm labor leaders representing large numbers of Mixtec and Trique farm-workers in Mexico began to form organizations of organizations. Some of these took the form of nongovernmental organizations (NGOs) concerned with community and regional development, whereas others concentrated on cultural projects having to do with maintaining "traditional" regional and village forms of music and dance. The detailed history of how these organizations combined, split, and regrouped in different combinations, and how their missions evolved, is too complex to recount here (see Velasco Ortiz 1999). Suffice it to say that the Frente has slowly and steadily emerged as the major coalescence of such organizations in their diverse forms, both in Mexico and in the United States.

DIALOGIC STRATEGIES OF THE FRENTE

In retrospect, it is apparent that the Frente has deftly carried out several subtle strategies that have empowered it in its confrontation with agencies of the Mexican state and other adversaries. These strategies can be seen as forms of dialogism, the essence of which is the interplay between the forms and meanings of the interlocutors of a dialogue—in this case Oaxacans and agents and agencies of the Mexican state. As Holland and Lave (this volume) note, dialogism has to do with "the generativity of the cultural genres through which people act upon themselves and others." Here I am extending this concern with genres to the formation of selves—of new self-identities—that form out of the dialogic in which "indigenous peoples" challenge the state, which in turn responds with its own images and programs for the organizational constitution of "indigenous peoples," to which people respond, thus provoking further riposte by the state, and so on in a process of sociocultural differentiation that is imminently dialogic.

The Frente has deployed three general dialogic strategies vis-à-vis the state that are apparent: we may refer to them as *displacement, consolidation,* and *reappropriation.* Each of these strategies has provoked agencies of the Mexican state to respond with corresponding counter-strategies, which, together with the moves of the subalterns, result in a dialogism out of which "indigenous identity" is formed. Discussing each of the three strategies of this dialogism in turn, I begin with the moves made by the Frente and then examine countermoves by the official agencies.

Displacement

In the theory of practical anthropology, displacement is any intentional or unintentional movement that relocates subjects into geographic or social spaces such that their constructed identities as political beings are altered (Kearney 1996a:70).[6] In the case of the Frente, the extensive migration of its members and leaders from Oaxaca to northern Mexico and California has constituted a series of basic geographic displacements of people into different cultural and political spaces. The first of these displacements was from the hegemonic domain of local community and regional *caciques* (political bosses) and entrenched power holders in Oaxaca to regions in the north beyond their political reach. Migration to northern Mexico also relocates the migrants beyond the territorial domain of the official central powers in the state of Oaxaca, although they then come into domains of official and unofficial power in the north and also remain within the territorial realm of the Mexican federal government. But further displacement from domains of official and unofficial Mexican power has been effected by movement across the border into the very different socioeconomic, political, and cultural spaces of the United States, where Mexican agencies and Mexican corporate power are not hegemonic. In this way, political displacements are nurtured by spatial displacement via migration (Kearney 1996a:175–176).

These geopolitical and cultural displacements have changed the social fields in which the Frente and its members organize and face the Mexican state, and they have deeply affected the construction of identities and their positions in fields of value. For example, the formation of the Frente in 1992 and its incorporation as a not-for-profit organization in California have given it a form, status, and legal identity quite unlike anything it could possibly have in Mexico, much less in the more limited domain of Oaxaca (see Lestage 1998). The growth of the Frente as a transnational organization has also seen parallel changes in its multiple missions and their displacement to new political fields. The antecedent forms of the Frente in Mexico struggled primarily with issues involving peasants, urban employees, farmworkers, and low-income urban dwellers, and with problems of intercommunity conflict. These are all fields of struggle in which the state and conservative power brokers are organizationally and ideologically hegemonic and well able to contain subaltern opposition by controlling the leadership, resources, and definition of mission of popular organizations that are supposed to defend subaltern interests. But the Frente was able to significantly alter this conjuncture by, first, presenting itself as genuinely autonomous and as truly representing peasants, workers, and migrants and, second, displacing these issues to the more inclusive ones of human rights and environmental issues (Kearney 1994; see also Kearney 1996a:182–185). But the most significant displacement effected by the Frente was to recast all of the issues just mentioned as concerns of *indigenous peoples*. Previously, *indigenismo* in Mexico had been basically a project promoted and managed by the state and limited basically to issues of community "development" and "modernization" within an ideology affirming the construction of a homogeneous mestizo nation. The Frente, however, began to assert a profoundly different indigenous project that was predicated on the continuity and indeed the strengthening of indigenous peoples as separate cultural and political identities within a pluricultural Mexican nation.[7]

Consolidation

Organizationally, the Frente is unique in the history of Mexican indigenous peoples because of several notable features. First, as a political project it has been able to bring together a number of Oaxacan corporate rural communities. Oaxaca is notorious for intercommunity conflict. Indeed, there is good reason to assume that agencies of the Mexican state and of the state of Oaxaca have allowed such conflicts to endure and have even fanned them as a way of inhibiting the formation of regional grass-roots opposition to official state and federal power (Dennis 1987). Leaders of the Frente have been successful in bringing leaders of some of these feuding communities together on several occasions to reduce tensions, and they continue such efforts as a step in creating a sense of regional identity and solidarity. This project has been feasible only in the deterritorialized space of Oaxacalifornia, where members of different warring communities find that they have much more in common as Mixtecs, Zapotecs, or Triques and also primarily as *indígenas* vis-à-vis Mexicans and "gringos."

In sum, the consolidating projects of the Frente lump innumerable specific local issues formally defined as problems of individuals, communities, peasants, or workers. The Frente redefines them not just as matters of the appropriate jurisdictions but as cases of concern within the broader context of systematic violations of human rights of indigenous peoples and of regional environmental and social problems.[8] These consolidated issues are thus strategically displaced from those political fields in which the state and traditional power brokers hold most of the cards to the very different transnational field of public opinion and the world of NGOs.[9]

Reappropriation

Holland and Skinner (this volume) describe, per Bakhtin, how subalterns may reappropriate the language that others use to describe them, inverting it and in effect turning it into positive symbolic capital useful in their own defense. Furthermore, such borrowed language is more than just symbolic capital, for such reappropriation involves fashioning a more agentive sense of themselves—a more powerful and positive identity.

This taking of negative symbolic capital that has been applied to a social identity and actively, intentionally revalorizing it and using it to construct a new self-identity can energize the redefinition and reorganization of the subaltern group.[10] The main instance of such reappropriation in the case of the Frente is the intentional use of terms such as indígena, Zapotec, and Mixtec. All of these terms were virtually absent from the language of self-identification of Oaxacans prior to their massive circular and permanent migrations to the north, beginning in the 1960s. In great measure these terms were responses to the negative labels and epithets they encountered in the north, where, on both sides of the border, they were often seen as undesirable outsiders by Mexican mestizos and Chicanos, who often referred to them as *indios* and *oaxacos* (Kearney 1988). In the border area, as throughout Mexico, *indio* is a term of opprobrium that reflects a racialized prejudice against indigenous peoples and that conveys the sense of "dumb Indian." And *oaxacos* is a derogatory epithet that is a corruption of the correct *Oaxaqueños;* it implies backwardness and lack of civilization. It was to offset such slurs that the migrants began to identify themselves with pride as Mixtecos or Zapotecos and by the more inclusive Oaxaqueños and *pueblos indígenas*. And it is of course precisely such collective terms that are necessary to forge the broad, multifaceted organizational project of the Frente.

STRUGGLE AND VALUE, CLASS AND IDENTITY

A fundamental distinction in this chapter is that between class and identity. The position taken here is that political struggles are at base contentions over the distribution of forms of value available in a community and, more specifically, over who produces, appropriates, and consumes value in its different forms. Briefly, the theoretical stance is that value is unevenly distributed among different *class positions* located in a field in which value is unevenly produced, exchanged, accumulated, and consumed. Indeed, class is defined by such positionality and relationships of uneven production, consumption, and exchange in fields of value.[11] It is both a *position* in a field of value and a *relationship* of uneven exchange with other positions. Class, so defined in terms of value, thus has an objective basis. But given the abstract and generalized nature of value, class does not enter much into popular self-consciousness as a dimension of personal, much less collective, makeup. Even though uneven value exchange—that is, class relationship—is the most important relational dimension among persons and groups, it is only in rare historic moments that it serves as a basis for a sense of personal and collective identity, as, for example, when workers actually do unite as a class.

In contrast to class position and relationships within fields of value, identities are culturally constructed and are thus more apparent as dimensions of personal and collective selfhood. Whereas class positionality and relationships defined in terms of value are too abstract to enter much into everyday consciousness of self and other, identities, as cultural constructions of personal and collective selfhood, are readily cognized, reified, and habitually embodied. Contrary to much contemporary anthropology and sociology, identity as I define it has a phenomenal nature different from that of class. Whereas class is defined in terms of value—its uneven production and consumption by and

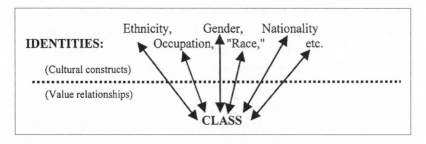

FIGURE 8.2.

Relationship between identities and class.

unequal exchange among persons—identity is always a culturally constructed aspect of the person and the group.

Class relations become possible only when disparate identities have been constructed, allowing their bearers (e.g., boss and employee, lord and peasant, husband and wife) to come together in the uneven exchange of value—such uneven exchange constituting a class relationship. Thus the relationship between class and identities is one not of either-or but of both-and (fig. 8.2).[12]

The main point is that the process of inequality that matters is the process of class inequality—that is, the uneven production, consumption, and exchange of forms of value, especially forms of value that enable one to accumulate net economic value that another has created. That other person may be an employee, a spouse, a slave, or someone more distantly related to one via chains of uneven exchange, such as the person who harvested the lettuce in one's salad in exchange for an exploitatively low salary that lowers the price paid for the salad. Because humans are all one species, such systematic class differentiation of persons much be based in nonnatural—that is, culturally constructed—diacritics that add up to and cohere as cultural *identities* arrayed in fields of unevenly produced, consumed, and exchanged value.

CLASS AND CLASSIFICATION

In looking at the history of ethnic differences in Mexico, the anthropological question that arises is not only why does cultural difference persist, but why is it created de novo in forms of expression that are so eminently political? The answer that I propose and explore in this chapter is that the reproduction and, indeed, the creation of much of the cultural difference that arises within and that is maintained within communities and between communities in contact lies not in the realm of culture but in that of class, of which cultural differences are a necessary dimension.[13] Such cultural differences are necessary because class as a form of difference has no natural basis, and in modern nations no legal basis, and must therefore have some artificial diacritics, some constructed marks that are inscribed on the bodies and in the dispositions and cultural repertoires of persons who have come to exist in class relationships, that is, in relationships of unequal exchange with each other.

Most analyses of domination and resistance take difference as a given and then proceed to describe projects intended to bring about redistribution of value and so to level it. But deep penetration into the resilience and persistence of domination over resistance requires a displacement of analysis to the genesis of the difference upon which economic inequality in its manifold forms is based, that is, to the most basic social dimension of difference, namely, class.[14] Furthermore, in tracking down the social origins of class difference, priority must be given to the most fundamental aspect of class, namely, its classificatory nature. Class is first and foremost a system—a dynamic—of class-ification.[15]

I thus propose to join the economic senses of class used in political economy with the concerns with classification in cultural anthropology in order to look at the formation of class identities—that is, social classification—as a process that is both cognitive-habitual and political, because it takes place within complex political fields in which identities are constructed, embodied, and situated and so gain and lose forms of value. The concept of "class" as used here is taken more as a verb than as a noun—that is, more as a process than as a quality. Thus, social classification is the process whereby different cultural identities are created in relationships of unequal exchange—class relationships—such that net economic value flows from some to others.[16]

The resilient persistence of class difference suggests that its amelioration is perhaps best advanced by analysis of its genesis and perpetuation. In other words, we must inquire into why embodied cultural differences, which are the necessary resources for class differentiation, are constantly created and re-created. My working hypothesis is that struggle itself is implicated in the perpetuation of class difference, which, by the definition I employ, is synonymous with a differential distribution of value.[17]

The current recrudescence of indigenous identities in Oaxaca, as elsewhere in the Americas, thus raises questions about the efficacy of struggle, confrontation, and resistance to oppose oppression. I return to this issue in the final section of the chapter, but to set this discussion in perspective it is useful to review theories of difference and domination that attend to cultural mechanisms, not forgetting of course that cultural forms of domination are typically backed up by police, military, and other forms of physical coercion. But such coercion is usually accompanied by a dialogic process of classification. As used here, and following Bakhtin's general meaning, *dialogic* is taken to refer to forms of interaction that promote difference between the parties in dialogue. Dialogic processes may thus be contrasted with dialectic ones in that whereas the latter eventually annihilate difference in a synthesis of antithetical forms, dialogic processes often spawn and perpetuate difference. My main concern in this chapter is to apply Bakhtin's insights regarding dialogic processes to class differentiation, especially as it is mediated by ethnogenesis.

JUJITSU THEORIES OF CULTURAL DOMINATION

What I refer to as jujitsu theories of domination (Kearney 1996a:156) can be considered a fourth generation of theories of cultural domination.[18] Jujitsu is an apt designation for such theory in that it is a weaponless system of self-defense. The master of jujitsu waits for an opponent to strike and then deftly redirects the blow in order to trip or throw him. The modern martial art and sport of judo is based on jujitsu principles such that each opponent attempts to use his adversary's own strength and momentum against him. This analogy can be applied to the politics of cultural domination. In contrast to the cultural dynamics of top-down domination, jujitsu forms of domination mobilize the active efforts and momentum of subjects in their own self-defense to bring them down and keep them down. The subalterns' own best efforts at self-defense and resistance provide the energy deployed in their subjugation. Such a theory smacks of blaming the victim, but

these victims are often quite creative and adroit in defending themselves, even though such efforts are, in the larger scheme of things,
counterproductive in that they promote the cultural differences on
which class processes depend.

A brief review of the development of jujitsu theories—I have identified four of them, which I label "rituals of rebellion," "resistance,"
"distinction," and "partial penetrations"—is in order to introduce the
particular variant, the fifth, that is the focus of this chapter. All of the
five varieties of jujitsu theories are at work in the case of Zapotec and
Mixtec differentiation and domination. In all cases the jujitsu in question is a sort of pas de deux in which the contestants make use of the
initiative and momentum of opponents to defeat them.

Max Gluckman (1954) revealed how, in southern Africa, certain
institutionalized rituals reenacted social tensions in burlesque form,
serving to discharge the pent-up hostility and resentment of subalterns
toward their social superiors. Even though these rituals seemed overtly
to accentuate and challenge the social order, they actually promoted its
continuity. This is what I call the "rituals of rebellion" theory of jujitsu
domination.

James Scott (1985, 1990) has written much about "resistance" by
subalterns who employ multiple forms of it to alter their presentation
of self in order to minimize the extraction of value from them and to
minimize abuse by those who have power over them (Kearney
1996a:154–158). Resistance is a form of jujitsu, first, in that the kow-
towing, pulling of the forelock, shuffling, and other subaltern styles
associated with it perpetuate the diacritics of class difference in the
process of accommodating to it. Furthermore, resistance is used not
only against class superiors but also against class equals. Resistance not
only diffuses opposition among myriad small sites, thus corroding subaltern class solidarity, but it also reproduces the distinct class-based cultural identities that are necessary for exploitation.

The "distinction" theory arises from the work of Pierre Bourdieu
(1984), from whom we have a good sense of how a system of class identities is reproduced by the active effort of subalterns and others to
accrue forms of symbolic capital—that is, distinction within a preexisting hierarchy of accepted agreements about the value of different cultural forms. In Bourdieu's model, subalterns willingly and creatively

participate in the reproduction of the class system that oppresses them. Although Bourdieu presents a penetrating analysis of the reproduction of class differences, notably absent from it is any concern with the primary Marxist issue in class analysis: the way in which economic value is unevenly produced and consumed in class society such that there is a transfer of value upward in the class system. Indeed, Bourdieu tells us little about how upper classes accumulate wealth from lower classes. Also lacking from Bourdieu's work is much concern with struggle or resistance—that is, explicit practical applications of his analysis (although some can be derived).

Paul Willis, in *Learning to Labour* (1977) and in his contribution to this volume, presents a jujitsu model that, in its focus on resistance, goes beyond the models of Scott and Bourdieu. There is a dialogic component to Willis's work whereby resistance is integral to the reproduction of class difference. Furthermore, Willis's model of class resistance and reproduction is directly relevant to the main theme of this volume—history in person. For there is in his work a personal dimension of such struggle, by which I mean the perverse reproduction of difference due not only to the institutions of inequality (the state and its agencies, etc.) but also to the habitual actions of persons in their resistance to such structured inequality. In *Learning to Labour,* Willis describes how English working-class boys rightly perceive that schooling did not prepare their fathers and other older male relatives to avoid dead-end working-class jobs. This insight is an intellectual penetration into how the educational system does not serve their needs, and they therefore resist it by cutting classes and adopting anti-intellectual attitudes. But when they are older and wish to marry and settle down, they realize that they are unqualified for any other work except that which they sought to avoid. Thus, in the larger scheme, their accurate understanding is, in Willis's terminology, only a *partial penetration* into the dynamics of class reproduction, and especially into the way they are mobilized to actively participate in their own subjugation.

Compared with Bourdieu, Willis presents a more dynamic jujitsu theory in his concern with the efforts of subjects to resist what they perceive as class inequities. Thus, the "piss take" (Willis, this volume) is comparable to the class-perpetuating dynamics—the dialogic—of distinction, but it is different in that the reproduction of difference is motivated by working men's enjoyment of their solidarity and their resistance to their class superiors. The point is that by so promoting a culturally based solidarity, they actively participate in the reproduction of the difference that is a sine qua non of their subjugation.

In the case of contemporary indigenous politics in Oaxacalifornia, a fifth jujitsu theory of domination and defiance is called for. It begins with the conscious, intentional construction of difference as a way of amassing social and symbolic capital to oppose oppression. But this intentionally constructed difference is the very difference that under-girds the inequality and exploitation that are being opposed. We can refer to this fifth form of jujitsu domination as "strategies of contain-ment," a term I have taken from Frederic Jameson (1981; see also Horne 1989), but with modified meaning, as elaborated in what follows (see also Kearney 1996a:61–69).[19]

More specifically, I am concerned with how cultural struggle is mobilized by a perverse dialogic of inequality to participate in the reproduction of the identities that are the basis of that inequality. Whereas other jujitsu theories take unequal identities as givens, con-tainment theory seeks to uncover how the identities of inequality are formed—are constructed—in the first place, thus making possible the reproduction of the relationships of inequality. The elaboration of Zapotec and Mixtec ethnicity to oppose the state and inequality in gen-eral is a prime example.

As in all other active strategies of class defense, there is an inherent dilemma in elaborating ethnicity as a means of defending class inter-ests. The dilemma resides in the fact that exploitation rests on differen-tiation of identities. Thus any strategy of self-defense that rests upon the construction of a unique subaltern identity as a basis for solidarity in the service of defense runs the risk of doing the dirty work of exploitation by promoting the very difference upon which it is based. What is distinctive in this Oaxacan case of the emergence of ethnicity out of a dialogic of defense and domination is that it takes place to a large extent in legal fields in which there is a struggle over the formal, explicit dimensions of social class-ification—that is, the *cultural construction* of indigenous identities that are *socially constituted* as actual class positions. Only when such identities have thus been constructed and constituted do the dynamics of extraction of value from persons at such class positions and their defense of it come into play.[20]

A BRIEF HISTORY OF SOCIAL CLASSIFICATION IN MEXICO

The state—admittedly somewhat reified as used here—is uniquely able to invent and reify, that is, to *class*-ify (to construct and constitute), identities. It is instructive to review briefly such classificatory policies in Mexican history.

The Spanish colonial project of the sixteenth century was informed by mercantilist theory concerning the need of great nations to have external sources of wealth. At the base of the system of colonial production and accumulation were the indigenous populations that provided the labor for colonial agriculture, mining, and other enterprises. In this arrangement, local communities of indigenous peoples were primary sources from which economic surplus was extracted. They were, at least on paper, assured of sufficient land, water, woods, and other resources to be self-sufficient, and they were protected from excessive predations that could undermine their self-sufficiency as sources of labor power and other resources upon which the colonial project was based.[21] A major justification for these policies was that they served to "civilize" the indigenous peoples. Indigenous peoples as such were originally brought into being as social identities in New Spain by being thrown into contrast with Europeans at the time of the conquest. Throughout the subsequent colonial period, the distinctions between "whites," "indios," and other categories were inscribed in a series of caste laws that officially specified the biological nature of such identities and gave them legal status.

The formal, legal caste distinctions between Indian and non-Indian were swept away in the mid-nineteenth century by liberal political reforms that sought to modernize independent Mexico and to meld its diverse regional, "racial," and ethnic communities into a single biologically and culturally homogeneous, modern, mestizo nation. Postrevolutionary Mexico is notable in having one of the most stable systems of governance in modern history in association with extreme disparities in wealth. If we take wealth differences as indicators of class differences, then the question that arises is, What forces or conditions have muted the disruptive pressures of class difference that have erupted so frequently in virtually every other Latin American nation? Much has been written about "the Mexican system," which is usually seen as combining stability with great inequality by means of a powerful bureaucratic state that has had enormous capacity to co-opt weak oppositional leaders and to repress others. Subaltern class opposition has also been deftly controlled by the state's ability to channel organizational forms of political expression into official, state-run labor unions, peasant organizations, and popular associations (Hamilton 1982).

Throughout most of the twentieth century, indigenous peoples, who occupy the lower socioeconomic levels of the Mexican class system, participated in the Mexican political system not primarily as "indígenas" but as "peasants" or "workers." And throughout this period the federal government advanced the previously mentioned assimilationist policy whereby indigenous peoples were to have been melded into the modern mestizo nation-state. Thus, no mention of indigenous peoples was made in the 1917 Mexican Constitution, which, still in force, is the most enduring one in contemporary Latin America.

Yet this assimilationist policy has to a great extent failed, as is evidenced by the large and growing numbers of peoples and communities identified as indigenous that not only remain outside of the national cultural and social mainstream but also exist in conditions the Mexican government designates as "extreme poverty." The modernist project in which the state was a central actor has not led to the full incorporation of indigenous peoples into a modern, culturally homogeneous Mexican nation. Instead, indigenous identities and the political projects of indigenous peoples have emerged as major issues in contemporary Mexican politics.

Elsewhere (Kearney 1991), I have proposed that modern nation-states such as Mexico must constantly manage a structural contradiction that is inherently unstable. On one hand, they must promote and preserve national unity based on nationalist sentiments and a sense of common identity. On the other hand, the state is responsible for the smooth reproduction of the national society, its institutions, and its economy, including its social classes. In a nation-state such as Mexico, the challenge of reproducing a common national culture under conditions that also perpetuate wide social inequality is enormous. To do so, the state must contain class conflict within the bounds of national unity.

Such containment failed dramatically when the pressures of class inequalities erupted in the 1910 Revolution. But the postrevolutionary Mexican state soon developed the single most successful and enduring record of national stability with extreme inequality in modern history.

After the Mexican Revolution, the new corporate state became a major force promoting the assimilation of indigenous peoples into mainstream mestizo society. But as I discuss next, the liberal policies and programs that the state enacted actually promoted class differentiation. In order to prevent the rebellion and revolution that such inequalities would otherwise provoke, the state also took measures to weaken potential opposition from the disadvantaged sectors. Official rhetoric did this in part by promoting a common national cultural identity, an imagined community of "Mexicans." Furthermore, this cultural project has been accompanied by effective strategies of containment whereby subaltern identities are first formally constructed and then incorporated into official organizations. These organizations give social life to the identities so created, by enabling them to be incorporated, lived, and experienced.

THE NEOLIBERAL STATE AND INDIGENOUS PEOPLES

Until recently, low-income rural Mexicans were for the most part extensively mobilized into a plethora of state-run labor unions and peasant associations that effectively constructed proletarian and peasant identities in order to contain potentially disruptive political energies.[22] In the 1980s and 1990s, these forms of containment were elaborated within a more general program of neoliberal free market and free trade reforms that were intended to stimulate a rising tide of prosperity for all Mexicans (Barkin 1990; Barry 1995; Otero 1996; Warnock 1995). During this program of structural adjustment in the 1980s, poverty increased, and it has remained high into 2000. There are some 12 million indigenous people in Mexico, of whom 56 percent have been defined as living in "extreme poverty" (Warnock 1995:184). Furthermore, it is primarily in areas with high percentages of indigenous peoples, such as Oaxaca, that exteme poverty is the highest.[23]

A basic tenet of Mexican neoliberalism is a "market rule" form of capitalist development, which typically is assumed to promote assimilation of ethnically diverse groups into the national mainstream. But in the present conjuncture, the neoliberal Mexican state is promoting free-market-based and free-trade-based development while also making certain concessions to indigenous communities. How are we to understand this apparent contradiction? From the work of James Ferguson (1990), Arturo Escobar (1991), and others, we have come to understand how rhetorical ploys and institutional forms that seemingly promote development actually function to promote de-development— that is, to perpetuate disparities in levels of development between regions, or what we could call regional class differences. This suggests an examination of the history of capitalist development in Mexico.

The liberal projects of the eighteenth century were ostensibly aimed at reducing differences by privatizing Indian communal lands and modernizing the nation. These policies in fact resulted in the deep socioeconomic inequalities that provoked the Mexican Revolution of 1910. Similarly, the movements of indigenous self-assertion of the 1990s can be seen as having been provoked by the neoliberal reforms put in place in Mexico in the 1980s. In both periods, liberalism was touted as the means to build a culturally unified, modernized nation. But there is a certain contradiction in Mexico's neoliberal reforms as a force of modernization. On one hand, they promote a diminishing of the autonomy and power of the nation-state as power bleeds upward from the state to supranational entities such as the North American Free Trade Agreement (NAFTA) and multinational corporations that operate in supranational spaces. On the other hand, the current architects of Mexican neoliberalism are meanwhile negotiating the dispersal of power downward to state and municipal governments and various forms of regional autonomy in a process referred to as "the new federalism." But these regions are in great measure defined in ethnic terms, which could reinforce cultural differences between "indigenous" and "non-indigenous" regions, thus in effect reapproximating the colonial system of communities defined in terms of "castes." Also, as part of the neoliberal project, Article 27 of the Mexican Constitution was altered in 1992 to permit the privatization of collectively and communally held agrarian lands. These changes were widely perceived as another blow by the forces of neoliberal restructuring against basic social contracts protecting small rural producers from the ravages of the market economy.

Now, at the beginning of the twenty-first century, the capacity of the Mexican state to contain economic inequality and cultural differences is again being severely tested. The most dramatic expression of this testing is the ongoing uprising of indigenous peoples in Chiapas who have declared the autonomy of pluriethnic regions and forced the federal government to negotiate with them (Barry 1995; Collier 1994; Ross 1995). One of the most notable features of this remarkable movement, which is embodied in the EZLN, is that its leaders and members, rather than presenting themselves as "peasants" or "workers"—the identities deployed by most radical political movements in postrevolutionary Mexico—have presented themselves as "indigenous peoples."[24]

By certain measures, the Zapatista indigenous movement has achieved far greater national and international support than any other proletarian or peasantist movement in modern Mexican history. Indeed, massive Mexican and global public opinion in support of the Zapatistas has prevented them from being crushed by the military superiority of the federal government. Certainly, the strength of both the actual mobilization and the ensuing public support lies in some large part in presentation of the Zapatistas as indigenous peoples.[25] This achievement is due largely to the displacement of the site of confrontation by the Zapatistas from those fields in which the state is hegemonic—namely, agrarian and peasant issues—to the field of indigenous politics, where it is far less so. Indeed, the appearance of the Zapatistas, the Oaxacans, and other groups on the international stage as "indigenous peoples" has caused the state to scramble to regain hegemony in the field of indigenous politics.

Consequently, the state's contemporary strategy of containment has entailed significant alterations in the assimilationist policy that had prevailed since the mid-nineteenth century. Among these is the Mexican Senate's ratification of the International Labor Organization Convention 169 and its signing by President Salinas in 1990. This treaty put Mexico on record as being a pluricultural nation in which indigenous peoples have basic cultural rights. Article IV of the Mexican Constitution was subsequently modified to make it conform with the spirit of the ILO Convention, although the implementing legislation has not yet been enacted.

More recently, the state has signed agreements with the EZLN in

Chiapas that recognize the presence of "pluriethnic autonomous regions," as well as another agreement that opens dialogue between indigenous leaders, representatives of the federal government, and intellectuals. The goal is that these talks will lead to the formation of such regions in other areas of Mexico with large populations of indigenous peoples (Kearney 1996b).

What we see in the dynamics of the autonomy issue is that the state actually participates in this dialogic relationship with regard to classification. The possibility of gaining some form of regional autonomy presents a dilemma to indigenous organizations. On the one hand, it is a route to possible greater independence and power. On the other, it is also a means whereby such greater difference, now also juridical in nature, is inscribed on indigenous identities and territories and is potentially at the service of exploitation, which depends on such difference. Such was the case in colonial Mexico, and thus the present movement toward the formation of autonomous regions presents the possibility of a certain perverse repetition of history.

These constitutional changes can be seen as concessions to the innumerable popular groups throughout Mexico whose mobilization had the potential to become politically disruptive. But these concessions by the state also, to some degree, channel subaltern political energy into political terrain that is not without contradictions and limitations for popular political projects. Grass-roots leaders who opt to build political strategies based on indigenous identities and autonomy must calculate the potential loss of political and cultural capital not invested in other modalities such as "proletarian," "peasant," or "urban" organizations. An even worse scenario is that they could be participating in the creation of a two-tiered society in which pluriethnic autonomous regions become the de facto Mexican equivalent of Indian reservations in the United States. The worse case scenario is that indigenous politics could serve to reproduce impotent "indigenous peoples" who, as a legal social category, are once again marginalized from mainstream society and left without the political and cultural resources to defend their bottom-line class interests. Such a scenario would be one of successful containment. But at present, the dynamic between containment and active indigenous construction of relatively autonomous identities is more balanced.

The great danger that indigenous leaders of the Frente face is that the promotion of indigenous political and cultural projects might reinforce the reproduction of the very subaltern class identities that they are intended to surpass. But what are the alternatives? A recourse to the overtly class-based strategies and projects that have already failed? The focused, single-issue-oriented politics of the new social movements? As for party political strategies at the national level, they were effectively blocked by the hegemony of the ruling Institutional Revolutionary Party (PRI), which dominated Mexican national politics from 1930 until it lost the presidency to the National Action Party (PAN) in 2000. The possibility that new political spaces may open up in the PAN administration is uncertain. And meanwhile, the PRI continues to dominate party politics in the state of Oaxaca. Clearly, ethnicity provides a basis for a broad-spectrum political project with potential for mass mobilization, but a project not without contradictions.

THE EMERGENCE OF OAXACAN ETHNICITY IN OAXACALIFORNIA

For hundreds of thousands of Mexicans, many of them indigenous people, a response to the declining incomes and living conditions in Mexico is permanent or circular northward migration in search of work. The great majority of Oaxacan indigenous people who migrated from the 1970s through the 1990s went to northwestern Mexico and to California. In few cases, however, was migration of Oaxacans to California little more than a palliative for their problems in Oaxaca (Besserer Alatorre 1999a, 1999b; Zabin 1992), for California was experiencing comparable negative economic conditions in this period. Like the depression-era refugees depicted in Steinbeck's *The Grapes of Wrath,* the Mixtecs and Zapotecs coming to California in the 1980s arrived at a time of economic downturn and deplorable living and working conditions that paralleled those in Mexico (Cornelius and Martin 1993). Anti-immigrant sentiments in California were aggravated by the post–cold war restructuring of the defense and aerospace industries, which provoked an especially strong statewide economic downturn in the late 1980s. The political reaction was comparable to previous scapegoatings in California directed at Mexicans and other foreigners (Galarza 1977; McWilliams 1939).

There is a certain irony to this antimigrant reaction in California, especially in the case of Mixtecs, who work primarily in agriculture, the state's primary industry. The health of California agribusiness has always depended heavily on exploitable foreign peasant workers like the Mixtecs, who are typically fleeing poverty in their home communities. For a number of reasons having to do with increasing competition from foreign producers, an oversupply of farm labor, and conservative political dismantling of protections for farmworkers, living and working conditions for California farmworkers were deteriorating at precisely the time Mixtecs were starting to come into California agribusiness in large numbers.[26] Juan Vicente Palerm (1989) documented how farmworkers in this period were marginalized from mainstream society in California by being shunted into Mexican enclaves of rural poverty that effectively inhibited cultural and social assimilation. Indeed, this enclavement was similar to the segregation and isolation of Mixtec farmworkers in the labor camps of Baja California and Sinaloa (Garduño, García, and Morán 1989; Kearney 1988; Nagengast and Kearney 1990).

Whereas Mixtecs migrating to California go mainly into agricultural work, Zapotec migration to California since the 1970s has been directed mainly to the Los Angeles area, where Zapotecs have moved into a variety of urban economic niches (Klaver 1997). Owing to high degrees of circular migration and especially to social, cultural, and residential enclavement, comparable to the rural enclavement of Mixtecs, Zapotecs, too, have been little prone to assimilation to Anglo California culture and society, despite being deeply integrated into it economically. This enclavement and marginalization of Mixtecs and Zapotecs has been reinforced by the growing antimigrant sentiments directed against "illegal aliens," which have taken such forms as the 1995 California ballot proposition 187, which sought to deny illegal immigrants access to public education, public health, and social services and to impose more vigorous surveillance and apprehension of "illegals." Such conditions augment anxiety about apprehension and expulsion and drive migrants farther underground. Thus they reinforce the segregation and enclavement that impede assimilation and acculturation but promote ethnic differences.

Whereas emergent indigenous identity in Mexico is being constructed in large part by a neoliberal state caught in the contradictions of its own policies, in the United States the construction of emergent Oaxacan identity is being driven by the restrictionist migration policies of California and the federal government. While the Mexican state is coming to officially recognize—that is, construct—Mixtec and Zapotec peoples as "indígenas," they are being officially constructed in the United States as "illegals" and "aliens." In the dialogic of ethnicity in Oaxacalifornia, emergent indigenous identity is being doubly determined, fomented by both the policies and laws of the Mexican state and counterpart processes in the United States at the federal and state levels. The thesis that thus presents itself is that the class-related conditions that indigenous peoples are experiencing are provoking mobilization in an ethnic mode. This mobilization has been taking place in a transnational social and cultural space that transcends the U.S.–Mexican border and constitutes the third space of Oaxacalifornia —an environment conducive to the emergence of ethnicity (see Kearney 1995; Rivera 1999b).

THE DIALOGIC OF ETHNICITY: STATE AND INDÍGENA

There are many ways in which a dialogic process of ethnic differentiation is effected. A mestizo curls his lip at an indígena, putting him in his place with a sneer that the recipient interprets as meaning, "You are indígena." The federal government designates communities as *pueblos indígenas,* and they respond as such.[27] What concerns us in the rest of this chapter are the dialogic relationships that began in the mid-1980s between Oaxacan indigenous peoples and the Mexico state in greater Oaxacalifornia.

As I argued earlier, indigenous ethnicity is in large part a refracted consciousness of class. As such it is doubly threatening to the national project of the Mexican state: first, as class consciousness (albeit refracted), and second, as a cultural project that undermines national cultural solidarity. What is notable about the present moment is how the state itself is now involved in this contradiction. Once ethnicity is abroad, agents and agencies of the state must confront it and seek to contain it. They do this with strategies of containment, which, as I have discussed, are always dialogic in nature.

Agents and agencies of the state thus create ethnic categories and communities that are proxies for class in order to contain subalterns in their class positions. The state's strategy advances the dialogic by constructing ethnic identity in order to contain the expression of class consciousness upon which it is based. But such ethnicity is only a permutation of the original contradiction. By the same token, subalterns avail themselves of the social and symbolic capital (ethnic identity) so constructed, employing it to mobilize the communities that are so defined. The social and symbolic capital created in this process serves as currency for a development of the collective identity so formed. Then, at some point the state becomes concerned to contain not only class but also the ethnicity that has been unleashed by the underlying class differentiation and the state's efforts to contain it.

But ethnicity both unites and divides subalterns and results in an erratic pattern of organization and coalition building, factionalism and disunity. By creating solidarity in one sphere, it promotes conflict in another. This dialogic thus organizes a complex cultural-political field in which the more visionary grass-roots leaders in Oaxacalifornia are trying to forge larger coalitions of *los pueblos indígenas* while the state seeks to channel ethnicity into a disorganized kaleidoscope of *grupitos*.

It was Bourdieu's (1984) great contribution to show how the diacritics and habitus of class are constantly formed by the creative acts of subalterns attempting to define themselves and gain distinction within their own social spheres. Bourdieu's model of the differentiation of cultural markers of class can be likened to Bakhtin's dialogic processes in that signs that become positive marks of distinction and solidarity within the subaltern group also become negative subaltern capital within the larger process of sociocultural differentiation. But what the case of Oaxacan indigenous ethnicity also demonstrates is that such creative acts of distinction acted out within specific class factions are not only shaped by dialogic processes operative between classes but also consolidated by a dialogic operative between agencies of the state and popular organizations.

Another important dimension of this complex field is Oaxaca's heavy dependence on the tourist industry. It is based in large part on the appeal of the "traditional" cultural resources found in the state's indigenous communities, their crafts, and their cultural activities, many of which have become commercialized—especially those in and around Oaxaca City and the other major tourist enclaves in the state. It is in this development strategy based on the promotion of "traditional cultures" tourism that agents and agencies of the state again enter into a major contradiction. The state that has so long been dedicated to modernizing traditional cultures out of existence now finds itself promoting them as valuable commercial resources. Nowhere is this contradiction more apparent than in a type of Oaxacan festival known as the *guelaguetza*.

GUELAGUETZA FESTIVALS

In Oaxaca City, the guelaguetza is a large, professionally choreographed celebration of ethnic dance and music representing the "seven regions" of Oaxaca. It is staged repeatedly every summer by the state government in a large amphitheater in Oaxaca City and is aimed mainly at promoting the state's tourist industry (Nagengast and Kearney 1990). Historically, most of the dances performed in the guelaguetza derive from colonial times, when they were promoted by Dominican friars as a means of converting Native Americans to Christianity. But soon after the institutionalization of these dances, they and their music developed into regional and town forms and became a means of promoting town solidarity and autonomy. They have survived as such into the present.

In recent years, a series of annual alternative guelaguetzas has appeared in California, where the festivals are organized and performed by grass-roots Zapotec and Mixtec migrant organizations of the Frente and attended primarily by Oaxacan migrants in Los Angeles and elsewhere in California. As developed in California, the popular guelaguetzas can be seen as a cultural variant of guerrilla warfare, according to a principle by which subalterns "liberate" arms and other resources from their more powerful adversaries and then use them against those same foes. The moral justification for this strategy is that the value contained in these resources was obtained by exploitation of the subaltern community and is therefore being returned to its rightful owners. In this sense, the official guelaguetza can be seen as having been created out of popular resources that were repackaged and commodified for commercial interests. The popular guelaguetzas reappropriate this cultural resource and put it to work for the benefit of its rightful owners.

Each spring and summer, some six to eight guelaguetzas are organized and presented in Los Angeles and elsewhere in California. Those in attendance, ranging from a few hundred to around 5,000, are predominantly Oaxacans. The main items on the programs of these popular guelaguetzas are performances of Oaxacan folk dances by groups elaborately costumed in "traditional" village and regionally specific attire. Most of the costumes are made in California, where the dance groups are also formed, and live musical accompaniment is provided by "traditional" village brass bands formed in California. Each of the dance groups and bands is formed by a specific village association based in California. Some of these dance groups and bands also travel to Oaxaca to perform in their hometown fiestas, imparting to them a richness of "traditional" culture that would not exist were it not for the high rates of emigration from these communities to California.

Some rivalries and political differences among Oaxacan leaders and associations have been played out in the politics of organizing the guelaguetzas. These tensions center on intercommunity conflicts in Oaxaca that are extended into California. They also arise from competition between Mexican political parties, in that different towns and their associations tend to have different party affiliations. Some town-based organizations—mainly Zapotec ones from the Sierra Juárez region and the central valleys of Oaxaca—have been most involved in developing the guelaguetzas as cultural events that enhance town pride and solidarity, and they have received financial support in doing so from the government of Oaxaca, which is dominated by the ruling PRI. Some Mixtec and Zapotec leaders and associations oppose acceptance of such support, which they see as a form of co-optation. They instead develop a cultural politics that is more oppositional to the dominant political forces in the government and more aligned with the rival Party of the Democratic Revolution (PDR). Representatives of the Oaxacan government, federal agencies, and the Mexican Consulate General in Los Angeles, as well as commercial interests, have entered into these frays.[28] By granting support to the more conservative organizations, some of these entities have fueled divisions between those organizations and the more progressive ones, thus weakening the formation of a unified indigenous Oaxacan front. At the same time, this support has promoted the preservation and indeed the creation of indigenous Oaxacan identity among the diasporic Oaxacan community that has nurtured all of the Oaxacan transnational organizations. Thus has developed a dialogic in which some organizations and their leaders are co-opted by being subsidized, which underwrites the development of a generalized Oaxacan indigenous identity, which in turn fuels the cultural and political projects of all the Oaxacan organizations.

The guelaguetzas thus offer an example of how the dialogic between state and grass-roots projects operates. The state is caught in a contradiction in which its policy of assimilating indigenous peoples to the mainstream is undermined by (1) its efforts to exploit the symbolic capital of indigenous culture to promote the tourist industry and (2) its efforts to co-opt certain Oaxacan organizations, which also nurture those organizations and promote indigenous Oaxacan identity in general. The guelaguetza became a site of this dialogic when grass-roots organizations reappropriated it to promote their solidarity and autonomy. The Mexican state, in association with commercial interests, responded with its own U.S. version, seemingly doing so in order to co-opt factions within the Frente and to promote division within the U.S.-based Oaxacan community. At the same time, the official guelaguetzas promote a general indigenous identity in the greater transnational space of Oaxacalifornia.

At present the guelaguetzas in California are vibrant and mostly independent from government and commercial control. But the political field in which they exist is crosscut with tensions and contradictions, and it remains to be seen whether the festivals will continue to nurture independent grass-roots organizations of Oaxacans and of the Frente or whether the energy, creativity, and identity that is invested in them becomes channeled into reproduction of difference in the service of the status quo.

CONCLUSION

Mixtec and Zapotec ethnicity, as it is elaborated in its dialogic exchange with the state, is a two-edged sword. Even as it is a modality (identity) in which to mobilize "indígenas" in projects of self-expression and self-determination within the Frente, so does it serve as a form of negative symbolic capital that is the basis of discrimination and exclusion in the greater society. A great challenge to indigenous leaders and their advisers is to constantly moderate the dialogic process so that the forms of capital—cultural, social, symbolic, and economic— that are formed and accrued by indigenous peoples participating in this process have maximum positive value (as resources promoting pan-ethnic solidarity) and minimal negative value (as signs of "indios" and markers of specific group identities defined in opposition to others). The contradiction inherent in this situation is that the dialogic processes in which the leaders are involved inevitably produce both kinds of symbolic capital.

The promotion of indigenous ethnicity as a strategy for creating solidarity has limitations similar to those of the "piss take" that Willis describes elsewhere in this volume. In other words, even as it promotes subaltern solidarity, it also promotes social class diacritics that become marks and habits essential to the distinction of subalterns within a system of class differences that depends on such diacritics of difference. This dynamic is illustrated by the guelaguetzas, which reveal a form of dialogical jujitsu in which impulses of self-definition work in tandem with forces of containment to reproduce subaltern identity within a greater system of inequality.

Like the custom of the piss take, the identity of the indígena may be a vehicle that is inherently incapable of carrying forward a viable political-cultural project. Indeed, it is perhaps but another popular identity that is conflated with and occludes the dynamics of subaltern class formation within the greater heteroglossia of transnational capitalist society. But there are two sides to this dynamic, for the Oaxacan organizations and their leaders are also using a kind of jujitsu on the state—an appropriate metaphor, since jujitsu is designed to be used in self-defense by the weak against the powerful. Basic to such jujitsu as practiced by the Oaxacan organizations has been a geographic displacement of the sites of confrontation with the state to non-Mexican territory within greater Oaxacalifornia. The first phase of this displacement, owing to transnational migration, was territorial. But the ensuing relocation of Oaxacan politics beyond the borders of Mexico in turn displaced the dynamics of class and ethnicity into a new transnational field in which both new forms of domination and new possibilities for struggle have opened up.

Notes

1. In addition to valuable comments made by fellow participants at the SAR seminar, this chapter also benefited from valuable discussions with and comments and editorial guidance from Dorothy Holland, Jean Lave, Carole Nagengast, and Jane Kepp.

2. A central intellectual project of Mexican and U.S. anthropology in the twentieth century was the study of the leveling of cultural differences, which was seen as an inevitable historical process. Indeed, historical particularism as practiced in both nations was the painstaking study of the acculturation of tribal peoples and immigrants into the national melting pots. This was a kind of anthropology that mestizo and assimilating first- and second-generation immigrant anthropologists were disposed to embrace and elaborate as they participated in the construction of their respective national identities.

3. Escobar and Alvarez (1992:5) make a distinction between "resource mobilization" and "identity-centered" theories of new social movements; the political dynamics of the Frente basically fit the latter type.

4. Regarding migration as it relates to economic conditions in the Mixteca, see Cederstrom 1993, Kearney 1986, and Stuart and Kearney 1981.

5. We are now fortunate to have two excellent Ph.D. dissertations available that deal with the Frente and other Oaxacan transnational organizations—those of Gaspar Rivera (1999b) and Laura Velasco Ortiz (1999). I am drawing on these sources as well as on notes taken while serving as adviser to the Frente, and also on previously published work (Kearney 1986, 1988, 1994, 1995, 1996b; Nagengast and Kearney 1990). I am also indebted to innumerable individuals who have been primary sources of information, most notably Bonnie Bade, Federico Besserer, Lucas Cruz Fentanes, Rufino Domingo, Juan Lita, Sergio Méndez, Emilio Montes, Algimiro Morales, Arturo Pimentel, Gaspar Rivera, and Laura Velasco.

6. As a political strategy, displacement is often a response to *containment.* For a fuller discussion of containment—which consists of construction and constitution—see Kearney 1996a:61–69 and passim, which develops an analysis of what in effect is a dialogic relationship between containment and displacement.

7. Numerous other popular Oaxacan organizations are active in both California and Mexico, and most of them are or have been affiliated with the Frente, perhaps most notably the Organización Regional Oaxaqueña (ORO), which is based in Los Angeles and is made up of a number of Zapotec community-based organizations.

8. An earlier approximation of this consolidating process was presented in Kearney 1988, written before the formation of the Frente. In it, I characterized the process as "dialectical," in contrast to what I now consider to be a "dialogic" process.

9. Here, consolidation by the Frente also involves a displacement into the transnational world of NGOs, for not only is it incorporated as a not-for-profit organization in California and in Mexico, but also some of its member organizations are NGOs. The Frente has also developed relations with and receives support from a number of secular and religious NGOs. As Alcida Ramos (1994) noted, such involvement of indigenous peoples in the world of NGO politics is not without potential pitfalls. See also Brysk 1996 regarding the pros and cons of such a strategy.

10. Such reappropriation and inversion of negative symbolic capital to promote collective self-pride and organizational solidarity were also seen in the building of the "black is beautiful" politics of the 1960s in the United States.

11. "Value" as used here is comparable to, yet more general than, what Bourdieu (1986) meant by "forms of capital" (see Kearney 1996a:136–170, 1988). One difference is that in my definition of value it is continuous with "power" in its physical, agentive, and symbolic senses. Examples of diverse forms of value-power are money, calories, prestige, authority, symbolic capital, property, and knowledge. Fuller discussion of this concept of value-power appears in Kearney n.d.

12. This distinction between and symbiosis of class and identities is elaborated in Kearney 1996a and is intended to foreground class analysis, but to do so in a way that avoids what Hale (1994:12) referred to as "the persistent economic reductionism of the Left, its alienating doctrine that class analysis is sufficient to understand identities, determine programs and devise strategies for a multicultural America."

13. One of the theoretical objectives of this chapter is to ground "identity" primarily in political economy, rather than in the realm of culture, as is common in the literatures on identity politics and in American cultural studies. Such cultural approaches, in rightly recognizing that class provides little basis for collective action, fail to distinguish the two senses of class identified by Marx: class-in-itself versus class-for-itself. In rightly observing that classes fail to mobilize for themselves, they jump to the fatal conclusion that class as a dimension of identity is theoretically and politically unimportant (see Kearney 1996a:172–174).

14. Sex, based in biology, is perhaps more ontologically robust than class,

but it is not central to this case.

15. The hyphen is used here to call attention to the way in which the formation of all social class identities and relationships is inseparable from cultural classification, such that social class formation is simultaneously a cultural construction of the difference upon which class identities qua identities are based. Hereafter, mention of social classification implies this double sense of the term as both cognitive categorization and social class differentiation.

16. Value, as considered herein, is convertible to power, and vice versa, such that it is more accurate, if less conventional, to refer to "value-power" (see Kearney 1996a:151–152, 162–168).

17. A differential distribution of value is a difference that makes a difference. In other words, difference, which is the basis of struggle and resistance, is implicated in the genesis of the very difference it seeks to ameliorate. Moreover, such a dynamic is imminently dialogic, per Bakhtin (1981).

18. Early theories of cultural domination basically took class difference as given and sought to explain how it was reproduced by being naturalized in everyday consciousness. A first generation of such analysis was developed mainly by Marx and Engels (1976), who identified how *ideology*—created by the mental work of elite intellectuals—naturalized the status quo as ordained by, for example, "the will of God" and other such ideas that become insinuated in everyday worldview. A second generation of theory explored how such ideas become *hegemonic* by becoming more deeply naturalized—that is, detached from the class origin, as defined in the foregoing sense of ideology—and thus more uncritically accepted as commonsensical (Gramsci 1971; cf. Comaroff and Comaroff 1991). Foucault's analysis of the pervasiveness of forms of surveillance that induce subjects to *discipline* themselves is a third generation and transitional to jujitsu theories in that forms of discipline derive primarily from the state (top down) but mobilize the active compliance of subjects, in contrast to the more passive nature of ideological and hegemonic forms of cultural domination of subalterns that originate from the dominant class(es).

19. The theory of containment was previously applied to another constructed identity, namely, "the peasant" (Kearney 1996a:65).

20. For example, in Mexico, membership in state-administered "peasant" and "worker" unions is a legal status, just as in the United States membership in Indian reservations is determined by criteria of the federal government.

21. Regarding the colonial project in Mexico and in Oaxaca, see Wolf 1957, Pastor 1987, Chance 1978, and Whitecotton 1977.

22. The Mexican political system is notable for its extensive corporate organization whereby different sections of the population are highly organized into a multitude of unions and associations dominated by the federal government (see Hamilton 1982).

23. Regarding the widening of income disparities in Mexico, see Alarcón González 1994.

24. A precursor of the Zapatistas' and the Oaxacan transnational organizations' deployment of indigenous identity as a basis for collective political action was the mobilization of the municipality of Juchitán, in the Isthmus of Tehuantepec in eastern Oaxaca, which in 1981 became the first independent leftist municipality in Mexico since the 1920s. The organization mainly responsible for this extraordinary movement is COCEI (Coalición Obrero Campesino Estudiantil del Istmo), which effectively mobilized its political project as a revival of indigenous isthmus Zapotec culture and society (Campbell 1994; Campbell et al. 1993; Stephen 1996). Concerning comparable contemporary indigenous movements for autonomy elsewhere in Latin America, see Díaz Polanco 1996, Kearney and Varese 1990, and Van Cott 1995. For more on Mexico, see Sánchez 1999 and Burguete Cal y Mayor 1999; for Guatemala, see Warren this volume and 1998. For cautions and concerns about this path, see Ramos 1994.

25. In massive, broad-based public demonstrations throughout Mexico in support of the Zapatistas, the predominantly mestizo demonstrators chanted, "We are all indigenous people."

26. Runsten and Kearney (1994) estimated that approximately 40,000 Mixtec migrant farmworkers were in California in 1993, with many more cycling in and out. See Zabin 1992 and Zabin et al. 1993 regarding living and working conditions of Mixtec migrant workers in California.

27. See Linger's chapter in this volume for a similar response by Eduardo Mori, who is also perceived as an exotic foreigner.

28. Among such entities are the governor of Oaxaca and personnel of his office who attend to the Oaxacan community in Oaxaca and abroad, the consul general of Mexico in Los Angeles, several dozen Mexican consulates elsewhere in California, representatives of the Bank of Mexico, and a federal research and aid program for Mexican farmworkers, Jornaleros Agrígolas, as well as a number of other state and federal agencies.

9

Getting to Be British

Jean Lave

> In short, what individuals and groups invest in the particu-
> lar meaning they give to common classificatory systems by
> the use they make of them is infinitely more than their
> "interest" in the usual sense of the term; it is their whole
> social being, everything which defines their own idea of
> themselves.
>
> —*Pierre Bourdieu,* Distinction, *p. 478.*

The port wine trade includes firms bearing names such as
Cockburn, Croft, Dow, Graham, Warre, and—all in one firm—Taylor,
Fladgate, and Yeatman. These firms make port wines with names like
"Queen's Ruby," "Club Port," "Captain's," and "Imperial"; the port
served at in-house luncheons is often labeled "Founder's Reserve."
British merchants and their descendants have been a presence in
Porto, Portugal (a city of two names, called Oporto by the British),
overseeing family firms for more than a century—some claim as many
as 300 years. Today, the privileged position of the old port families in
the British enclave in Porto is in question. The contribution of the port
trade to the Portuguese economy has declined sharply since 1974,[1]
when the Portuguese Revolution opened the country to a vast influx of
European Union funds and multinational corporations. The latter
bought most of the port firms, turning the port trade into a tiny sub-
market of the worldwide "alcoholic beverages industry."

The social production of port families' lives in the British enclave
in Porto is undergoing transformation as well. Deep struggle marks
divisions over whether the community should continue to be acclaimed

(from within and without) as a "300-year-old port wine trading enclave" or instead take on the character of an extranational base for multinational corporate managers. Changes are taking place in the specifics of old conflicts in which national and class identities were made and by which they were lived. Participants in the enclave, acting in the name of conflicting ways of being British, battle each other over the future trajectory of changes in the enclave that each needs in order to produce, confirm, and sustain comparative power and privilege.

The British port gentry families have become less able to sustain the little-challenged cultural-political supremacy to which they have been accustomed and the old community institutions that they nonetheless are still able to control. This has led them to engage in practices of concession to other social groups in the enclave and to modify practices of social exclusion focused on relations of class, nationality, and gender. Port gentry families are now fashioning and living distinctively different anticipations of future resolutions of these tensions as they try to provide for the next generations. Thus, local contentious practices are both shaped by and implicated in the question of how, after many generations of residence in Porto, families continue to get to be British—a lifelong, highly engaging problem for those who aspire to it. In this chapter I address some of the complexities of local practices of struggle, and I examine the making of identities that have kept the British port families in Porto and that give urgency to their efforts to keep on being British.[2]

BACKGROUND

The first British buyers seeking wine in Portugal in the mid-seventeenth century were a motley assortment of travelers, interested in wines of the Alto Douro region east of Porto (figs. 9.1, 9.2), who ventured over from England and Scotland to trade in whatever was available. Later, merchants "came out" to live in Portugal, the better to acquire sufficient quantities of good port year after year from wealthy Portuguese proprietors or small vineyard keepers in the Alto Douro. They bought and sold other things besides port wine: coal, salt cod, beaver hats.[3] Still later (1790–1880), in a lengthy but dizzying spate of shifting partnerships, the British established the port houses that later yet (about 1950 [see Robertson 1987]) wrested control of the fermen-

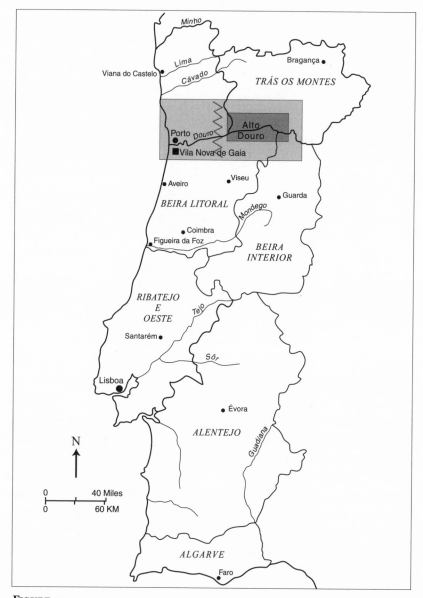

FIGURE 9.1.

Regions of Portugal.

tation and blending of the wine from the many small Alto Douro wine producers. Their more recent involvement in the trade, unlike their mixed commerce in earlier times, has provided the British port families

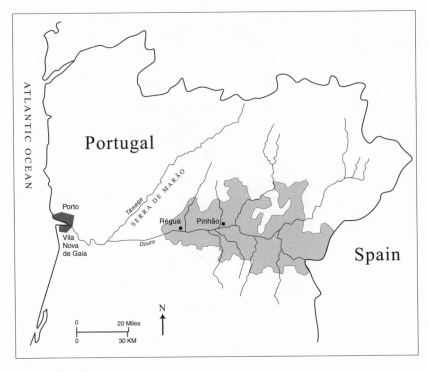

FIGURE 9.2.

The port region.

in Porto with increasingly convincing-looking grounds for extrapolating backward, however erroneously, a noble and harmonious history, that of a community dedicated to a single elite enterprise. This has enhanced in the British community in Porto the legitimacy of the "old port families" to define traditions, a "soul" or "spirit" of the enclave (a port family scion's term), and the privileges accreting thereto.[4]

Since the mid-1960s (see Bradford 1978), but accelerating after the revolution in 1974, many old family firms (both Portuguese and British) have been sold to multinational corporations—British (e.g., Harvey's, IDV), French (Allied Domeq), Canadian American (Seagrams), and Portuguese (SOGRAP). Not all of the old firms, however, have fallen into multinational corporate hands; some that have not are Churchill Graham's, a British family firm; Wiese and Krohn, a Portuguese family firm; and the Symington group, now a unique multigeneration family holding company. Some members of old British port families have stayed on in leadership positions in their firms: George Sandeman, Peter Cobb, Bruce Guimaraens, Gordon Guimaraens, Robin Reid, Alistair Robertson, and Huyshe Bower, to name a few. But the multinationals employ increasing numbers of Portuguese managers; jobs for the next generation of British port families are in doubt. Port family men are in danger of becoming most useful and used as gentlemen salesmen: British "gents" with splendidly tailored suits, old school ties, and exquisitely educated "noses," remnants of a historic past increasingly done up in museum exhibits to attract tourists for the tours each firm offers of its aging, blending, bottling, and tasting facilities in Vila Nova de Gaia.

Under the circumstances, it would be easy to imagine struggles over class and cultural differences between British and Portuguese participants in the trade that would end, and shortly, with the demise of the British enclave in Porto, either through the repatriation of British subjects "home," as they persist in referring to England, or through "deanglo-saxonisation" (the Australian sociologist J. P. Bailey's term [1976], referring to the British in Argentina).[5] Indeed, the decreasing significance of the port trade in the larger scheme of things, and with this, the shrinking of the economic base for port families, has in part led to an opening up of the British colony's institutions, especially the Oporto British School (OBS) and the Oporto Cricket and Lawn Tennis Club (OC&LTC), once potent means for sustaining distinctions of nationality (often confounded with class) through the exclusion of Portuguese participants. At present the club and school could not survive without their preponderance of (paying) Portuguese members. Struggles go on behind the scenes all the time to keep control of these institutions in British hands.

But not just any British hands. Rather than experiencing a quick demise of the British presence in Porto following the revolution of 1974, the dimensions of living, contending diversity in the British community have changed. Several hierarchically arranged groups clash over their different interests and stakes in the community. They particularly fight over the Oporto British School, where the old port wine merchant families, through their long-term residence in Porto and their claims as founders of club, school, hospital, consulate, Anglican church, and Factory House (the 200-year-old port merchants' club) as well as the port firms, oppose the new corporate managers and their families who have been brought in to supervise the many British and other multinational companies moving into northern Portugal. The major question concerning the British community in Porto may not be whether the community will disappear but whether it will, for the foreseeable future, continue to be a venerable community of port shippers who graciously extend an egalitarian welcome to three-year contract managers during their "short stay" as visitors—gracious so long as the visitors do not try to disrupt or change the order of things while they are there.[6] Or is the community to become a transient series of managers in a variety of industries, from a variety of North American and northern European countries, for whom the principal significance of residence in Porto is encompassed in their desire to move on quickly to a more prestigious office in a faster-track country? From this perspective, the British enclave in Porto is a community whose historical involvement in the port trade furnishes a quaint past but not a vital trajectory into the future.

"The British colony" as self-characterization emphasizes the bounded, exclusive character of British residence in Porto, but it hides the wider political significance of the British presence.[7] The British are ambiguously immigrants from Britain. Many have stayed over numerous generations, but they still "go home" to Britain and "come out" to Portugal (as they did to India and Africa), whereas they simply "visit" France or the Netherlands. They take great pains to sustain British citizenship. But they have difficulty placing themselves within British class and culture when in England. British-Portuguese relations in what might be called the "postcolonial enclave" are undergoing transformation as the mode of living in Porto seems increasingly to involve three-year stints by managers engaged in transnational migration for multinational corporations.[8]

Yet there are continuing, significant *differences* of nationality and class in the deepest long-term conflicts in the trade. These are to be found among an overlapping cast of characters, institutions, issues, stakes, and activities in struggles in British-dominated circles in the social life of Porto as well. The economics of the trade is insufficient to explain the salience of "being British in the port trade" in Porto. We must address in broader terms of cultural practice the initial question about what makes the British in Porto British.

BEING BRITISH IN THE ANTIPODES

The British who have lived in Porto over many generations have sustained British national identities in good part through the density of their common social existence in an enclave bounded in national terms. In spite of their quite different composition and purposes, the practices of day-to-day life in the colony in Porto have precedents in colonial enclaves at the antipodes, the far reaches, of the British empire, in colonial government enclaves, military outposts, merchant entrepôts (or "factories"), and missionary stations (e.g., Allen 1976; Bailey 1976; Comaroff and Comaroff 1991; Farrell 1978; Orwell 1934; Scott 1977; Tanner 1964, 1966).[9] At the same time, the British enclave is not easily visible. It is not a walled compound with managers' houses up and down the hill reflecting their ranks, like the old Coats and Clarke property on the other side of the Douro River in Vila Nova de Gaia. Instead, participants in the British enclave travel up and down the Campo Alegre and through the streets of an exclusive seaside neighborhood called Foz ("mouth"—of the river) to meet most of their collective social obligations (fig. 9.3). Because it is fashioned more as a matter of practice than of proximity, the enclave is produced in spatial terms as it is woven through daily rounds of activity concretely sheltered and made possible in a cluster of institutional settings that draw people across broad reaches of the city. It may be helpful to describe some of the practices within those settings, especially the ones that make those institutions interdependent.

Spatial Production of the Enclave

The eastern edge of the community is marked by St. James Church and its graveyard (hard won only after a century's battle against the Catholic Inquisition, which required heretics to bury their dead beyond the tide line in order not to "pollute" national soil; the first churchyard burial finally took place in 1788).[10] The church, hidden behind a high wall, was built according to the plans and dimensions of the ballroom in the Factory House in Porto (Delaforce 1982). The old family *quintas*—large homes with extensive gardens, generally walled—

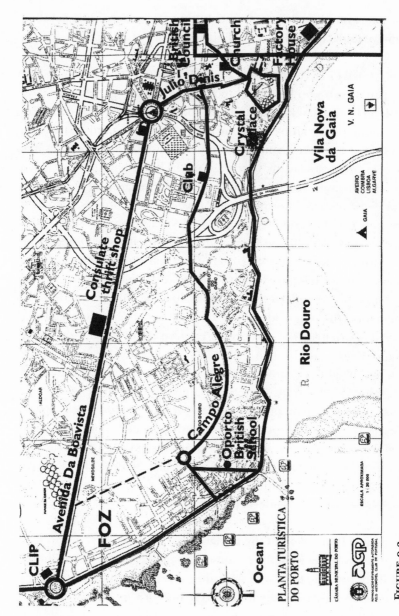

Figure 9.3.
Western Porto and the British enclave.

were clustered around what is now the Crystal Palace gardens and down the Campo Alegre toward Foz. The British Council, a recent addition and more peripheral part of the community, lies just beyond the church, but outside the area marked by the church at one end and the ocean at the other. In their heyday, the quintas perched on the bluff overlooking the river were convenient to the Factory House and the port "houses," or firms, in Vila Nova de Gaia. This triangle marked the concentrated focus of the community. Now, a high-rise apartment building on the Campo Alegre, built where one of these quintas once stood, is home to at least one couple active in church and club. On down the Campo Alegre is the Oporto Cricket and Lawn Tennis Club— via a long driveway whose entrance is a gap in the row of Portuguese retail businesses that line the street.[11] In an apartment building a block up the street on the same side is another high-rise where the church maintains an apartment for the Anglican priest, just opposite the computer center for the University of Porto, renowned for its ugly red exterior and graceless industrial design. It stands where the Perkins family home used to be. There is a fairly long stretch after that—several long blocks, with the university on one side and residences on the other. At the far end, starting down toward the ocean and Foz, the occasional apartment building houses a British family.

Meanwhile, roughly parallel to and only a few blocks from the Campo Alegre is the Avenida da Boa Vista—a decidedly Portuguese thoroughfare that stretches from the Rotunda da Boa Vista, surrounded by international shopping malls, past commercial chain hotels and international businesses to a long row of large and ornate nineteenth-century mansions set apart in spacious grounds. These mansions, built by wealthy Porto merchants after the style of the English, now house banks, clubs, and wealthy Portuguese families. The Hilton Hotel, the main landmark on the Boa Vista, occupies what used to be the Symington family quinta. None of the British families lives directly on the Boa Vista, although one mansion is the residence of the British consul and his family—a gift to the British consular service from the last heirs of a British port family some years ago. It contains in its extensive gardens a small outbuilding, now the British Hospital Thrift Shop, which has been maintained by the St. James Church Ladies' Guild for many years—indeed, from the time when there was a British hospital in Oporto. The shop collects donated clothes, shoes, and small household items and then sells them cheaply to poor Portuguese families. The substantial proceeds are given, with other Ladies' Guild contributions, to local charitable causes. Some of the apartments and houses a few blocks away from the Avenida da Boa Vista on either side are occupied by scattered British residents. The Campo Alegre arrives at the southern end of Foz, the Boa Vista at the northern end. The Oporto British School (OBS) is just south of the Campo Alegre; the new, rival Colegio Luso-Internacional do Porto (CLIP) is just north of the Boa Vista. In between is the major concentration of port merchant and other British families and the Portuguese provisions shops they have patronized over several generations, since the first of these shops moved from the area near the Factory House in the Rua dos Ingleses out to Foz as the families moved too.

When the community moved west, the Factory House lost its place as the day-to-day hub of an exclusive social life among the port shipping families. This imposing three-story club building, with its huge library, billiards room, dining rooms, kitchens, caretakers' quarters, reception rooms, and ballroom, built in 1790, stands empty much of the time. It still is the scene, however, of elegant weekly luncheons held by the heads of the founding family firms and their guests (men only; dessert and port are served after all remove to the second dining room, arranged exactly as the first) and of occasional fancy dinners and balls by invitation of the members—a mixture of commercial and convivial occasions. It continues to exert its power to mark exclusive social standing in the community (Lave 2000).

The OC&LTC, "the club," has become a different kind of social center to a different kind of British community, more numerous and heterogeneous than in the past. In 1992 it had a membership roll of 511 families. Of these, 188 families were members (only British citizens were eligible), slightly outnumbering the 174 associates, which included (in separate categories) 146 Portuguese families and 28 "Other Foreign Nationals." Overseas corresponding members and other miscellaneous categories made up the rest. This membership composition suggests some of the changes that have taken place in the community since the late 1960s, accelerating after the Portuguese Revolution of 1974.

The British community in Porto owns a surprising amount of collective property, conceded over the centuries by the Portuguese to the

British through their consul. While old British port merchant families and their allies manage, oversee, and maintain this property, paradoxically, ownership is ill defined. This gives a concrete embodiment to "the British community" that seems amazingly difficult to undo, because it is unclear who owns the collective property. Further, a propertied foreign enclave is an anomaly with respect to the housing of its public functions. There is no proper civic entity to own schools or maintain courts on behalf of the enclave. This ambiguity in property holding makes "the British in Porto" together—but not as a legally defined entity—the owners of the school, club, church, consulate, and (for a much smaller, more clearly defined group that is nonetheless not a legal entity) the Factory House. All of the enclave's "institutions" were founded by British heads of family firms—in the case of the church, on land conceded by the Portuguese government. The Factory House is a special case, tied up in the changing politics of the port trade and of British imperial policy (e.g., at the beginning of the nineteenth century, when Britain's trade factories abroad were officially abolished). The Factory House land was purchased by the consul, using funds raised by the exporters, in the name of the British Factory; the church, likewise. The school was started by a specific group of families but is not owned by them. The club space was bought by selling the site of a former club. Who owns it? This is unclear, but the port families who started the previous and current clubs hold claims to autochthonous privilege, if not deeds and titles to the buildings and grounds. The consulate was donated on behalf of the British port community to the British government to house the British consul (a unique arrangement, for Porto's British community is the only one currently in existence to support its own consul, and it clearly would not have one otherwise). All of this maintains a material base of collective existence that seems impossible to dissolve, since it is impossible to define. At the same time, it makes palpable the "founders" position of the port families and the exclusively male character of those "founders," in part because they act as proprietors.

Daily Practice

Though the enclave is much less visible than it was 20 years ago in Foz or a century ago in Campo Alegre, it is sturdily and tightly woven together in the activities of the families who make it up.[12]

The British in Porto speak British English as their first language. Those born and brought up in old port families speak Portuguese, too, but with a strictly British cadence and accent. You would never mistake one of these (skilled) Portuguese speakers for anything but British.[13] British residents out on three-year contracts—and often even longer— do not learn Portuguese and speak only English. I was sitting on the terrace at the club one warm June Sunday afternoon watching a cricket match and talking with a British couple, long-term residents of Porto. I asked the woman if she spoke Portuguese. Like many others of whom I asked this, she said no, and then expressed regret that she had not learned. "Why not?" I asked. "Well, we lived a long way out of town, and there was only one other British family nearby. So of course we came in to the club all the time, so I was never around Portuguese people enough to make it worth learning."

Growing up in British port family and club life is a potent source of resources for being British in Portugal; there are others. After breakfast in the morning men go to work in the port houses in Gaia; young children go the Oporto British School. Older children are away in boarding schools in England. Their still older brothers and sisters are in university or secretarial school or are working in England, or they are marrying and returning to Porto to live. When young couples are about to have a child, they now go to England for the birth, to ensure British citizenship for the child.[14] For children and adults, play after school or work, relaxation, and social time are coordinated through and at the club.

Women with free time have lunch at the club, as do elderly members and often men with their business associates in the trade. The Anglican priest eats there regularly. There are two-day-old British newspapers and the weekly *Anglo-Portuguese News* available in the lounge, a video club of British films, and a dusty library of donated English paperback books. The young mothers' exercise group meets several mornings a week, and the quilting group convenes one morning a week. Monthly meetings of the St. James Church Ladies' Guild are held at the club. Theme dinner dances are held at least once a month (including a St. Andrews Ball, a St. Patrick's Day Ball, etc.), in addition to a fancy buffet luncheon each Sunday after church and a constant round of tennis and squash tournaments. Cricket is a regular Sunday event in the summer, with both local and interclub matches. The cricket pitch at the club is imposing, with a rustic tea pavilion at the far end of the field (devoted to comradely drinking during the match, but in the past also devoted to elaborate teas, brought by the port wives, at the interval). A great deal of bridge is played at the club (including the Ladies' Guild's Wednesday afternoon bridge club), and there are private parties, the annual general meetings, governing board meetings, and fund-raisers (e.g., the Ladies' Guild Christmas bazaar takes over the club for one day in the middle of December).

Attendance at St. James Church is semi-mandatory for the consul and the OBS headmaster. Indeed, priest and headmaster used to be one and the same, and since the school headmastership was separated from the priest's duties, it has been difficult to find retired British priests content to do nothing but minister (for a low wage) to the congregation. The congregation is for the most part elderly and dwindling, with weekly attendance ranging between 20 and 75 persons. Only 64 British families were on the church roll in March 1994.[15] There is a constant tussle between the priest, who is a bit hard of hearing and would prefer that the congregation sit close to the front of the church, and members, several of whom insist on sitting in the pews their families have occupied for several generations at the back of the church.

The church celebrates an annual harvest festival service in which the church is decorated by the OBS children with ropes of ivy, fruits and vegetables, and cans of food they have brought to be donated to the Salvation Army. But the harvest decorations are punctuated by boxed bottles of port donated by several of the port firms (a peculiar sight protruding from the festoons of ivy). The Douro Singers, led by the music teacher at the OBS (many of the members sing in the choir at the church), do a special Christmas carol service at the church (reproved by the priest, who opposes Christmas celebration with the argument that Easter is the true high point of the Christian calendar). The evident struggle of the church to continue to exist suggests what the school and the club—both robust and relatively prosperous—would be in for if paying Portuguese participants were not in the majority. But the Catholic Portuguese cannot be invited into the Anglican church community.

The Oporto British School has grown from the handful of boys with which it started, sons of the British port shippers who founded the school in 1894. It was headed by the priest from St. James and met in a house in Foz. Today the school has sizable grounds that include, in addition to the playing field and ball court, the original house, a number of small buildings, and a large, two-story classroom building that also houses the library and offices of teachers and the headmaster. There is a junior school and a senior school. The upper age range has been in contention for years. The school admitted girls in 1931; in 1933 it extended admission to children with one British parent, so long as no school of the non-British parent's nationality existed in Porto, thus excluding all Portuguese children. This policy continued until about 1960. The vicissitudes of school admissions policies, and the practical events to which they were in part responses, offer a starting point from which to seek greater comprehension of community struggles. The language of instruction, most of the teachers, and the curriculum were, and are, British prep school fare, so that students prepared to take the Common Entrance Exam, seeking admission to boarding public schools in England from age 13.[16] Who does not take the exam, why, and what they do instead are questions that reveal tensions in the community.

In 1994 the school had an enrollment of about 225 children, of whom a preponderance were Portuguese. Headmasters these days are professionals hired from the headship of a public school in England or of a British school abroad (most recently from such a position in Colombia). The teachers have for many years been divided among British teachers hired with the help of an overseas teachers' hiring agency in London, port wives who take part-time jobs working at the school, and Portuguese teachers hired to teach primarily Portuguese language and history. This list still reflects a hierarchy of pay and prestige, although the school has become more egalitarian under the leadership of the most recent head. The school's governing committee has been carefully organized, behind the scenes, to reflect and represent the interests of the old port families. They seem to view the school as composed of families rather than as an institution for the purpose of educating the community's children. Given that it has always carried the burden of volunteer work, this committee has taken extraordinarily detailed control of the daily workings of the school. Continual dis-agreements highlight relations between governing committee and headmasters; the turnover in headmasters has been notably frequent since the mid-1970s.

In sum, participants' lives in the enclave are interwoven as their activities sustain and create interdependencies among both organiza-tions and participants. The British in Porto find each other, are able to be or become British citizens, get a British education and religious training for their children, and entertain themselves after a fashion. For the most part they marry other British citizens, both in Porto and by importing spouses from England.

LOCAL CONTENTIONS AND SOCIAL PLACE

The focus in this chapter is on those who grew up in British port wine gentry families, of whom several generations have resided in Porto. This small group of families engages in a particular way of becoming British. But other participants in the British enclave in Porto do it differently. British families who have grown up in the United Kingdom and come to reside in Porto for a few years simply *are* British through social trajectories that produce them as such, without requir-ing them to make concerted, direct, and intentional efforts to produce those trajectories. Some other British residents in Porto have come from long years, occasionally lifetimes, in former European colonies, British and Portuguese, in southern Africa. For them, being British is something else again. Part of understanding what it means for the port gentry to "get to be British in Porto"—if in fact they do "get to be British"—is voiced in the heterogeneous life histories and social rela-tions in the enclave.

To address this issue, we must ask where they find the resources of "Britishness" that are implicated in such practices. They say of them-selves, and their doings predictably invoke the same from British visi-tors, that they are "more British than the British." This requires elucidation, for it is clearly not the same thing as being British, though it may be closely related to the object of analysis of this chapter, "getting to be British in Porto."

Stuart Hall (1995:7) has insisted that we "not forget that retention characterized the colonizing cultures as well as the colonized. For if you look at the Little Englands, the Little Spains and the Little Frances that were created by the colonizers, if you consider this kind of fossilized replica, with the usual colonial cultural lag—people are always more Victorian when they're taking tea in the Himalayas than when they're taking tea in Leamington—they were keeping alive the memory of their own homes and homelands and traditions and customs."

In Porto, further, the port families feel themselves to have (had) an important part in the production of a distinctive emblem of British culture—all that surrounds the drinking of port wines.[17] They have suffered none of the violent ruptures Hall points to as constitutive of historical relations for the colonized (frightening though the 1974 revolution may have been). They "stayed on"—though what they stayed on "after" is not well defined. The British in Porto are both like and unlike "Caribbean people of all kinds, of all classes and positions, [who] experience the question of positioning themselves in a cultural identity as an enigma, as a problem, as an open question" (Hall 1995:8). For the British port families, their national (and class) identity is emphatically not in question, or at least it should never, ever be seen as doubtful, despite the enormous effort it takes to produce "British" national/class identity in their location in Porto.

There are far more British residents in Porto than the small number of families who claim descent from eighteenth- and nineteenth-century participants in the port trade from England. Yet formulations of that history and its promulgation by the port firms in Vila Nova de Gaia, made concrete in the monuments they have built to the trade diaspora, give "the British enclave in Porto" a collective identity more vivid, romantic, and distinctive than the antecedents many other British communities in the antipodes claim as their own. Oporto is the oldest British factory in Europe, and it is the last still in existence. This enclave has been responsible for centuries, to hear its members tell it, or to hear others tell it on their behalf, for the production of a notably elite commodity.

Claims to community distinction are a potent argument for the distinctiveness of identities—identities of relative inclusion and relative exclusion alike. In this case they have something to do with manly mirages of empire, privileged social classes, totally domestic women, and vintage port (*with* cigars and *without* "ladies"). Claims to distinction emerge in the life trajectory requirements for a certain kind of "organization gentleman" (and "gentlewoman"). There is concrete evidence for claims of high distinction for some in the port trade buildings erected between 1790 and 1840. The Factory House, the port houses, the church, the graveyard, and the consulate now have a certain impact on arguments about the value of the past and its relations with future economic and cultural transformation. The buildings, the billboards, the concentration of port houses in Gaia are also evidence for claims to community distinctiveness, as are, ironically, the advertising efforts of the multinational corporations that fly banners on the *quai* in Gaia proclaiming the venerable age of old (often British) family port firms. In sum, the British community is a hierarchical enclave of diverse identities whose relations are given in the acceptance by all that this is an "old port merchant enclave." It would be organized quite differently if it were not British and were not deeply connected with the port trade.

Practices of Exclusion

At the same time, it is the constitutive divisions, the heterogeneous social fractions and their relations, that inflect the cultural practices day to day in the British enclave. At the social apex are those families with powerfully influential positions in port firms who are still or newly wealthy and the old port families with whom they are intermarried, or with whom they grew up, and who still have strong claims on the privileges of autochthony. There may be two, a dozen, or perhaps two dozen such families, depending on the exclusivity of the criteria operating on a given occasion.

Who is not accepted? Portuguese families who applied to the OBS were given a cold reception until about 1960. Even then they were told without apology of the quota system, such that only after all British children were accepted would places be selectively available for Portuguese children.[18] Should a fundamental issue concerning the school arise at the annual general meeting, only British parents can vote on it (the 1989 articles say that only British persons may vote on the sale of land or property, the amendment of the articles, or the disbanding of the association). And, lunching often at the OC&LTC, it would be difficult not to notice that British members occupy the strip of desirable tables next to the windows; Portuguese families more often sit at the inner row of tables. British members hop from table to table, talking with friends and family, but only to tables with other British lunchers. Portuguese members tend to stay at their tables. The membership roll of the OC&LTC is divided, as mentioned earlier, into members (British) and associates (divided further into "other nationalities" and "Portuguese"). The distinction is more serious than its connotations of less than full membership; associates pay equal dues but do not have voting privileges in the most serious decisions affecting the governance of the club.

After reading classical accounts of British colonial club life in the antipodes, such as George Orwell's *Burmese Days* (1934) and Paul Scott's *Staying On* (1977), one might, on the one hand, think it extraordinary that non-British people are allowed in the club at all. On the other hand, it is clear that without the participation of the Portuguese members, the club could not survive financially. So British members of the club exercise polite tolerance along with visible exclusion. There are a few Portuguese members of St. James Anglican Church. They report being ignored or snubbed by the rest of the membership. The wife in one such couple has been elected to the church board, but women are not expected to contribute ideas or initiative at the board meetings, she told me. One Portuguese woman from a prominent church family is treated with a nervy oscillation between politeness and condescension. She regularly organizes Ladies' Guild activities, but always in a way segregated from other guild activities, which are organized by British women.

The picture of the British families that emerges here helps to confirm the view that this is not a community self-sufficient enough to continue to close its doors to the "native" population around it. The picture is a more complex one of mild seduction and firm rejection, of reluctant invitations followed by renewed distinctions.[19] A Portuguese family holding a large, private christening party might dominate social activity in the club on occasion, but regular club events—the balls, cricket matches, and tournaments—are British in intent, organization, and attendance.[20]

If Portuguese families are merely tolerated, there are more subtle ways in which other participants in the British enclave (defined in terms of the spaces, organizations, and activities described previously) are positioned in a social hierarchy, in between the most prominent and sought-after families and the Portuguese. There are two further categories of the unequal, both British. These are "pillars" and "manager families on contract."

The pillars are British citizens, high-level managers for British companies in and around Porto and their wives. They are sometimes from old port families but have worked all their adult lives for companies that do something other than make port wine. In some cases they arrived in Porto as adults to take up managerial positions in port firms. More often they moved from southern Africa or other parts of the former British (or Portuguese) empire where their companies have manufacturing plants or offices. They expect to stay in Porto until they retire or even for the rest of their lives. They are highly respected, in part because of their positions and long-term residence, in part because of their colonial credentials, and in part because of their hard work on behalf of the community. They are to be found on governing boards, often as secretary or treasurer, as organizers of major community events (such as the recent centenary celebration of the OBS), or on the hiring committee to choose a new headmaster or priest. Very occasionally they are not British but of "other nationalities," that is, northern European or American. The labor they contribute is necessary to establish a substantial position in the community; it is never enough to achieve full acceptance by the old port families. But they are pillars of the community in one further sense as well. They defend the enclave as a venerable and special one, whose current generation of influential port families carries the history and the spirit of the community and whose desire that life should not change, at least neither rapidly nor radically, is fully justified and appropriate. They defend the port families and their agenda against the families of British managers of multinationally owned industrial enterprises in Porto.

The managers, on three-year contracts, are on average a bit younger than the pillars. The manager families are seen by port families and pillars as troublemakers. By definition, this would include anyone making suggestions about changes in the community who has not established long residence and contributed labor to community activities. As either old port family members or pillars characterize them, stereotypically, they just sweep in and want to change things without any respect for those who have made the community what it is today and who are responsible for it. Then they leave. Those who stay steadily on have to pick up the pieces and deal with the inevitably negative consequences of the thoughtless dissatisfaction of short-term residents.

In sum, the old families exclude others; pillars take a good deal of prestige from their fairly close association with old families and translate for them, while in speaking on their behalf they appear to be of them. These highly respectable British men also do much of the community's "executive" work. The Portuguese, excluded within the community, remain a puzzle. It seems likely that it is in their relations with Portuguese families who are not members of the club and do not send their children to the OBS that Portuguese club members derive some advantages, by a sort of contagion of British superiority. In short, the British families who claim kinship in the port trade do not maintain the social superiority of their position by themselves. The Portuguese finance it, as do the others, including manager families on contract. The pillars defend the old port families, and the manager families on contract give service to the community, seek friends in it, send their children to the OBS, attend church, and depend on the club for their social life.

Class relations, given in national terms, are urgent matters in the enclave. But divisions of gender are also deeply felt and practiced, if not subject to public struggle. Young British wives from the United Kingdom do express shock at the expectations that suddenly circumscribe their lives when they move to Porto. Wives of men engaged in the port trade raise children and provide the labor that keeps enclave institutions going, but they do not take up careers in the port trade, though some are discerning and knowledgeable about the wine and the trade. They dare not seek or expect employment or a substantial economic position or the independence from their husbands this might imply. They are expected to be available to help create the illusion that the port firms are still old family affairs as they assist in entertaining clients. They are explicitly excluded, according to a centuries-old rule of the Factory House, from attending the weekly luncheons held by the members.[21]

Women do most of the community's work without acknowledgment—certainly without influence equivalent to their contributions. As volunteers, they finance and run the church. They attend the church they finance, but its services and its executive committee are permeated with sexist dismissal of women. The Ladies' Guild runs the thrift shop, a complex operation that raised nearly $10,000 a year in 1992–1994. They manage the school requirements to find, negotiate rent on, clean, furnish, and maintain housing for British teachers at the OBS. They organize the enormous Christmas bazaar each year and make most of the items sold there.

Given starkly contrasting possibilities (of which most were aware) for women's life paths in the United Kingdom and Portugal as compared with the enclave, and given other resources for resisting enclave practices that exploit, disacknowledge, or exclude women and their contributions to the futures in which all have high stakes, it is surprising that struggles over gender inequality took no overt form in the enclave. No groups, no discussions, no critique of gender relations surfaced in the social lives of the women I came to know well. This, too, was part of getting to be British in Porto.

CONCESSIONS

No matter how pervasive those practices of exclusion and their incorporation into the intimate identities of the British port family heads and members, they are not uncontested, even in the practices of the British port families themselves. Instead, at least where nationality and class are concerned, they are tempered and muffled in contradictory relations by which concessions are made to those on whom the families long practiced more definite exclusions. This can be seen in several ways. First, concessions are implicated in what seems an unusual facility on the part of the British to continue reproducing their position as arbiters of class culture in the international ambience of Porto. Thus, in contentious local practice in the enclave, access to the OBS and to the club have been gradually and reluctantly conceded to those whom the port merchant families have long struggled to exclude, but neither the agenda of activities nor control over these institutions has changed hands.

The term "concession" also suggests the carnival sideshow, where hawkers sell chances and appearances. The purveyance of British class culture at the antipodes has something of this quality about it and seems a vital mode of survival for "old British port families." The effects of ambiguous ownership of club, church, and school were discussed earlier. Other ambiguities concerning property are tied up with patronage exercised in a fashion that makes possible specific concessions that advance the battle to conserve British port life. Part of the way the port shippers insinuate a luxurious gentleman's standing with respect to clients of their businesses and guests of all kinds (including peripheral participants in the British enclave) is to play on confusion between their family ties and (formerly family) firms. As they entertain at the port houses and Factory House and at the firms' quintas in the Alto Douro, they blur lines between "the old homestead," or family country home, and what are basically small hotel–guest houses owned and run by the multinational firms. In some cases the British family members do have memories of going up to a family (firm) quinta as children, before the firms were sold. In other cases they simply inhabit proprietarily, when engaged in their duties as business hosts, luxurious spaces that are not their own. These claims to historical, if not current, ownership stand in contrast to the custom in Porto whereby almost all the families have long rented their houses and apartments.

These practices offer opportunities for patronage within but also beyond the port business. One or another of the firms offers an annual day outing for church members and friends to a company quinta (to visit company headquarters in the Alto Douro, the guest house, the business office, and the fermenting and wine storage facilities). They also help to raise funds for the church by hosting port tasting evenings at the club once or twice a year. The small group of non-port-connected church members and visitors is thus treated to a glimpse of the historic trade and to samples of elegant brew. At the same time, the key role of port in the enclave and its identity is affirmed. Finally, in a more minor vein, port house resources are brought to bear in community activities as the port firms are continually called upon to sponsor, contribute funds to, and lend tables and chairs for community social affairs of various kinds. They donate the port served after church each Sunday (St. James is the only Anglican church in the world that serves port after the service, members like to tell visitors) and provide institutional support for active members of the community's church, club, and school boards, who thus are able to serve *their* community "for free."

All of this helps to underwrite the position of the port shipping families in the enclave. They exude and, further, might be said to purvey British class and cultural practices compounded through processes described earlier: by creating a common and vivid history; by asserting claims to the privileges of originating the wine, the trade, and the enclave; through contagion from the "noble wine" they make and sell (to hear community members talk); and through the attenuated but real effects of the (no longer formal) British empire on a global international hierarchy of national class cultures. All this helps to account for the resilience of the economically no-longer-salient British enclave in its present hierarchical and differentiated state. The participation of the Portuguese families whose collusion is essential is another facet of the same resilience.

Although they are distanced in both time and space from the (national) class culture that others wish to appropriate, the British in Porto are not without resources of connectedness with signs of the British upper class—royalty, nobility, and influential politicians. They import those connections for consumption in Porto: Queen Elizabeth and Prince Philip visited the Factory House in 1957, and reminders of their visit are prominently displayed there. More recently, Margaret Thatcher opened the new building of the OBS. John Major stayed at a Symington quinta for his summer holidays in 1993. And one hears an interminable series of stylized conversations, often with a slight competitive edge to them, about "the royals" and accounts of "the time the duke was here," none with any specific content except to remind listeners of the speaker's classy connections.

British culture capital may be itself a commodity sought after around the world. There seems to be a worldwide class/national cultural hierarchy not only reflecting the globalization of trade (older and newer) but also existing as part of that trade itself. In the present case, British enclaves like the one in Porto purvey their class culture to the formerly or the semi-colonized or, in this case, to the informally colonized in return for the opportunity to reproduce their own immediate social position and its social significance within the confines of antipodal enclaves. This chapter is, indeed, an attempt to describe how the British in Porto manage to muster resources of Britishness in order to sustain themselves across generations, at long distance from their "homeland." The dilemma for the Portuguese participants, and the advantage for the British, is that to the extent that the Portuguese challenge the prestige and position of the British, the less valuable or less available becomes the British cultural formation the Portuguese are seeking for their children. Some such exchange also lies in relations between the remaining British participants in the port trade and the multinational corporations that own the port firms.

EXCLUSION, CONCESSIONS, AND IDENTITY DILEMMAS

The scions of the port trade respond diversely to the dilemmas they share. Three prominent figures in the trade are fashioning, in practice, three different trajectories into the future of the enclave. One scion of a very old port family and firm married an American woman and lived in the United States for many years as an employee of the multinational firm that bought the family firm from his father. He was sent to Porto by the corporation to head his family's former firm in 1990. His marriage at an end, he lives at the far end of Gaia in a faceless new apartment block and has nothing to do with the social life at the club, church, or school. He has since married a Portuguese employee of his firm. He appears to have joined his career with the corporation, having recently been seconded for a stint at multinational European headquarters in Paris. But he seems torn, claiming that his principal loyalty is to the family business.

The second scion twits the first about being merely a contract-manager interloper (perhaps as an ironic gesture toward his own family's late [-nineteenth-century] arrival in Porto). The second port shipper's father before him bought several of the British family firms and fashioned a family holding company in which one male offspring of each male collateral in each generation is promised employment in the trade. They have prospered and are among the wealthiest in the enclave. The current head of the clan takes a central place in enclave affairs and maximal identification with and responsibility for it. He is married to a woman from a British family in Lisbon, and his adult children are deeply concerned with reproducing their trajectories for their children and maintaining the enclave as the old port families' fiefdom.

The third scion retired recently as manager of a major British family firm (now multinationally owned). He is dismayed and depressed by public opinion that attributes to Portuguese colleagues what he feels was his own role in starting an imitation medieval fraternity designed to enlist wealthy, prestigious patrons of, and experts on, port wine, the Confradia do Vinho do Porto. He is married to a Portuguese woman, thinks the British are fools not to see the inevitable "Portuguese tide" washing over them, and is angry at the mismanagement and loss of historical records that might leave behind clearer traces of the British port family firms.

These three reflect in their lives and their outlooks alternative fates for the British enclave as well as for their families and themselves. They and their children can try to become nondistinctive participants in new global management trajectories. They can fight to sustain the enclave as it is, even if eventually its boundaries are reduced to those of the families themselves, and it becomes something other than a community. Or they can succumb to that "Portuguese tide." Whatever their differences, these trajectories all involve a riveting focus on getting to be British—or not—in Porto. The stakes are wealth, position, precedence, and the pleasures of acting with a consciousness that one's actions have a historical significance beyond the immediate. The dangers include the possibility that they will be left behind as nothing but troglodytes (as one of their unrepentant offspring who lives in London dubbed them), only to find their identities of British privilege dissolved one day.

None of these "futures" represents the possibility of "returning" to England. It would be difficult to do so because of a variety of inflationary effects of life in the enclave, both economic and social, and the ironic incommensurability of class-cultural practices in Great Britain and Porto after all these years.[22] The incommensurability is captured in the notion that the British in Porto are more British than the British, which is fatally different from simply being British in Great Britain. In short, the practical means demanded by their struggles to be British in Porto anchor them in specific, practically situated ways. They *are* "at home"; they cannot *go* home. In this sense, long-occupied enclaves of colonizers who "stay on" are indeed diasporic societies (Hall 1995). The irony is that whatever they are peddling in the antipodes, it is not British in comparison with contemporary upper- and upper-middle-class practices at the metropole.

The cost of sustaining supremacy socially in the enclave may have resulted from, or may be resulting in, the shrinking of the contexts in which the port families and pillars are leading actors. In the early 1800s, the port firms and their hand-picked consul helped to design major institutions of civic life in the city of Porto. At the beginning of the twentieth century, British companies were furnishing the know-how to build the utilities, trolley lines, and banks of Porto. By contrast, today they have little impact on the city. These days it is the Association of Exporters of Port Wine, which includes all the port firms without regard for nationality, that represents "the port trade" to the state body that regulates the port trade (the Port Wine Institute), to the national legislature, and to high government. The British in Porto are notoriously ignorant about the political, social, and cultural life of Portugal (a hallmark of British enclaves; see note 16), thus insulating themselves from important contexts of their own lives. It is as if they are seducing and excluding themselves out of relevance to the world around them. This cultivated oblivion is convenient to their own position, part of the practice of exclusion that gives others the desire to "get in."

STRUGGLES OVER ENCLAVE IDENTITY AND FUTURES

It should not be too surprising that of the three future histories-in-person of the port scions, it is the second family head and his children, successfully in control of access to participation in their port companies for generations to come, who have invested enormous energy and concern in preserving the community as it is, was, or might have been. This family composes one of the poles around which the community in its hierarchical social aspect seems to revolve (Lave 2000).

The port families have grown up British very much in the dispersed colonial mode of the empire. They are struggling to sustain their lives and the significance of the enclave for themselves. Other participants have a variety of other stakes. Change in community identity matters deeply to members of the enclave because all of them have stakes in their children's future. Schools, then, must often be key places in which struggles that inform all aspects of social existence surface as active debates over the imperatives of children's life trajectories (identities in the making). Some of these may be glimpsed in two events in the spring of 1994 and in excerpts from the brochure of a new school that styles itself as a rival to the OBS.

The first of the two events was a painful, unexpected fight, according to the new headmaster, at the annual general meeting of the Oporto British School (held at the club), in which parents of students in the school and the school governing committee had argued over, then voted down, the headmaster's appeal to change the name of the school from the Oporto British School to the Oporto British International School. He was surprised at the heat generated by such a small, obviously appropriate change that would reflect the changing student composition and new school priorities, for the OBS had recently, after a decade of debate, initiated something called the International Baccalaureate (IB) degree. The heat in this example was generated in intersecting, deeply related conflicts reflected more specifically in the examples that follow. The next event begins to show how the school is caught up in the ongoing struggles over getting to be British in Porto.

At the annual general meeting of St. James Anglican Church (held at the club) shortly thereafter, there was tense debate between elderly members of old port families and the newly arrived manager of a British manufacturing plant in Portugal. He and his wife were energetic, responsible, and eager to take part in community activities. Both sang in the choir, and their children attended church with them. The debate was about moving the altar and changing the church service to make it more informal and to make the church more welcoming to children. The most vociferous opponent, the widow of the head of an influential family port firm, finally said, "I don't want it to change; I remember how church services have been all my life and I want them to stay that way."

At the club on Sunday a couple of weeks later, I joined the elderly woman for lunch. In between greeting other churchgoers who were dining at the club, this woman described wrathfully a disagreement she had had with this same man during the hospitality hour that morning. The discussion was about whether children should or should not be sent to boarding schools in England for their education. The man had said he wouldn't dream of sending his children. The woman exclaimed with indignation, "I asked him if he knew of [name of a public] school and he hadn't even heard of it. I'm not a snob! But anyone who hasn't heard of the school is simply not on my list!"

The third glimpse into the debates over children's futures comes from CLIP, a Portuguese-sponsored, English-language international school in Porto that opened in 1986 with a Portuguese-American head, formerly from Cambridge High and Latin in Cambridge, Massachusetts. The school had a glossy brochure, with bright, elaborate graphics and many color photographs of children at the school, entitled "CLIP: Colegio Luso-Internacional do Porto"—that is, reading from front to back in one direction, in Portuguese. Turn the brochure upside down and backward, and the English version was called "CLIP: Oporto International School." A number of its claims were intended as challenges to the OBS:

- The governance of CLIP is based on a democratic model for decision making, as articulated in its Charter. CLIP recognizes the preeminent role of parents, teachers, and students in the educational process.

- Teaching methods and subject syllabuses are drawn from English speaking educational systems with careful note and consideration given to the programmes of work existent in the present Portuguese system.

- CLIP's pupils share the love of learning and intellectual ability so necessary to the attainment of academic excellence. They differ, however, in most other aspects. Coming from different national and ethnic backgrounds, and speaking a motley of languages, CLIP's pupils give to the Colegio the right mix for its success as an international school.

- Criteria for Admission include: 1. All applicants to CLIP will be considered regardless of their race, religion, sex, or national origin....4. A lottery system will be used when the number of candidates who have met the Standard of Admission exceeds the number of slots available....6. Prior knowledge of English, even though preferable, is not a condition for admission.

These conflicts within and about the schools reflect the cross-currents of political, economic, and cultural globalization in which the British enclave in Porto is caught up in all aspects of its daily existence. The OBS, at its founding in 1894, was embedded in relations of empire just as much as the mercantile practices of the port traders.[23] It is the intentions of parents and the effects on children of being removed from their families to boarding schools in England (total institutions that have traditionally replaced personal roots in family with old school loyalties of a more abstractly nationalistic sort) that principally express the peculiar concerns over life trajectories of old port family members.[24]

The "old port families" view the OBS as a preparatory school for children who will attend public schools in England from the age of 13. By contrast, managers in multinational firms with branches in Portugal who come to Porto for three years on contract anticipate a peripatetic existence. These families favor a full international school with an International Baccalaureate curriculum available all over the world. The Portuguese families who eagerly send their children to the school (and without whose financial support the school would cease to exist) want a British education for their children, but they must decide for themselves whose version of "British education" best fits their needs.

The International Baccalaureate (in effect, a curriculum for a high-school diploma and a program of international supervision to guarantee the certification of the program in specific schools) has its origins not in England but in that center of worldwide capitalist neutrality, Switzerland. It is intended to make possible a continuous curriculum, at a coordinated pace, across international secondary schools, thus enabling transnationally migrating managerial families to secure a single standard educational trajectory for their children without sending them to metropolitan boarding schools. It is an English-language program and to a great extent is built on British educational traditions. But it is in English primarily because the global language of business today is English, not because of direct historical roots in pre–World War II relations of empire.

This description of the International Baccalaureate program is my own—it does not reflect precisely the way it figures in debates at the OBS. The headmaster's charge in 1993–1994 was to build a high-quality school. His loyalty lay first with this professional project rather than with the insertion of the degree in local political struggles. He argued that the IB offered a high-standard educational plan from which students at the OBS could benefit greatly. He saw it as a way to expand the school to a full high-school degree without having to start from scratch, and as the only way to cultivate a professionally esteemed reputation for the school.

It takes resources to build such a program. The fights were over whether putting resources into this project would take them away from the junior school, which prepared primary-school-aged children to take the Common Entrance Exam for British public schools. The old port families were still intent on this mission for the school and opposed the IB program. The program was instituted in the early 1990s, but its continued existence is still an unresolved matter of conflict.

The IB program fit the interests of various constituencies of the OBS besides the manager families on contract. It met the needs of poorer British families who lacked the means or desire to send their children to England (e.g., several families of missionaries and teachers).[25] For Portuguese families who sent their children to the OBS for primary school, it avoided the incommensurate curricula and organizational differences their children faced when switching to the Portuguese school system. The OBS, as a feeder prep school, had published a clear vision of the proper trajectories of education for boys, but there were no comparably clear purposes stated for the education of girls. Discussions about the admission of girls and "other nationalities," especially Portuguese children, were couched in terms of favors to these constituencies; they had to fight to get themselves included and their wishes upgraded to equally important and legitimate concerns. The conflicts I have described were not played out in the name of gender issues.[26] They engaged people in arguments about whether the OBS was to support trajectories of character and class positioning of those boys (and without obvious public concern, girls) who would spend their adolescence to young adulthood principally in the United Kingdom.

CLIP is located in the restored former Porto trolley line power station at the opposite end of the oceanfront community of Foz from the OBS. The project commenced as the effort of a former OBS headmaster in collaboration with a group of Dutch and Scandinavian parents. Command of the project was soon taken over by a small group of wealthy and influential Portuguese businessmen in Porto (each with professional educational training in the United States). The oppositional character of the CLIP school surely had its roots in part in the Portuguese businessmen's experience sending their children to the OBS. The exclusion of Portuguese parents from voting about the most vital school issues, parent meetings conducted exclusively in English, and the visible hierarchy among teachers by nationality, among other things, eventually led them to withdraw their children from the OBS and concentrate their efforts on the international school. The latter undercuts OBS fees and promises an auxiliary language school and shortly a college associated with the secondary school. CLIP pays its teachers higher salaries and has succeeded in hiring teachers away from the OBS. The senior head teacher was formerly at the OBS. The head teacher of the junior school was formerly head of the junior form at the OBS and is the wife of a young manager in a port firm. The school emphasizes nationality-blind admissions, the equality of pay and standing among all teachers, equal opportunity for all parents to participate, and above all the equitably international (rather than British) character of the school.

The competitive, potentially life-and-death struggle between the schools helps to make visible relations between the old port firm families, contract managers, and Portuguese families with stakes in the British enclave. Fights over schooling are part of the interconnected shifts toward multinational corporate political-economic relations and clashes between old and new political-economic relations. British expatriates are caught up in them in different ways and are engaged in different and changing relations with the Portuguese families who involve themselves in school and club and who are themselves negotiating their stakes in postrevolution political-economic changes.

It is possible to reiterate this in another way in summing up the struggles over educational trajectories: It should be clear that putting the Oporto British School's resources into the IB degree conflicts with the educational agenda of the old port families. With the IB degree (which CLIP does not have and perhaps could not get a license for, given the OBS program so close by), the OBS serves the interests of the

British contract-managers' families at the same time that it does not discourage the continued presence of a large group of Portuguese children at the OBS. Moreover, so long as the hierarchy of the OBS offers some assurance of the value of a specifically British education to some Portuguese families, their presence is assured, and it gives an important affirmation to the value of British class culture. This could subtly strengthen the hand of the old port families with respect to the managers on contract,[27] which is important because mass desertion from the OBS to CLIP by either contract managers or Portuguese families would destroy the OBS. CLIP makes appeals to both. Affirmation of the more equitably international character of CLIP challenges the rightfulness of the claims of the old port families to "their" school and its mission to educate their own children first and only incidentally children other than their own. To further complicate the picture, the IB is necessary to keep a high-quality headmaster, and a headmaster in favor of the IB is going to push for increasing international and egalitarian control of the school.

It seems that the port families must capitulate, and the British enclave shed its identity as the old port wine merchants' colony. And yet resistance, while it may be the weapon of the weak, is the weapon par excellence of the wealthy and the conservative: port families continue to struggle to maintain the OBS in its old form. Their coordinated action so far carries the day. A port family head recently offered a desperately needed loan to the OBS, but on condition that he be given control over appointments to the school governing committee for some years to come. There is strong resistance among the members to a more professional relation between the committee and the headmaster, who ordinarily would assume the day-to-day management of the school. And so it continues. I recently received a letter from Porto saying that the IB is again in jeopardy and a fight is in progress over whether it will continue.

With all the partially discontinuous layers or arenas in which transformations of relations play out, the notion of a clear outcome to local contentions and the enduring struggles of which they are a part probably makes little sense. These are, after all, lifelong, life-shaping endemic struggles that in part consist of their participants. These struggles must affect who participates in the future in the port trade, and how, and with what kinds of views of their role in the trade, of national identities and relations between Portuguese and British farmers, firms, and multinational companies, and of the importance of continuity and tradition however contrived. They affect intergenerational relations. Exploring such struggles raises questions about whether and on what terms old British port families will continue to participate in the trade and about what changes will emerge in the trade in years to come.

CONCLUSION

"How do you get to be British?" is evidently a polysemic question. In one sense it is about growing up, "becoming British." In another sense it is about participation in daily practices, "being British" day by day. And in a third sense it is about privilege: how is it that some are entitled to "be British," but not others? These questions should not be separated. Keeping them together is one way to refuse to draw a line between being British and learning to be British, between life trajectories that are part of everyday practice and the struggles of everyday life practices whose contradictory complexities help to forge many varieties of lives (and identities) in the making.

There is a fourth meaning to the question "How do you get to be British?" One could read into it doubt about the outcome. This is no longer a trade enclave in the age of empire, influential, confidently dominant, and strongly buttressed from "contamination" by "the natives." The enclave's problems are not those of wine merchants in an informal colony of Great Britain, going about their business with the arrogance of the self-affirmed "superior" and with the support of political, economic, and diplomatic forces very much to their advantage. The descendants of those merchants live now as an enclave in a country with which they share membership in the European Union. The British "colony" has no official status, and the premises on which old British families in the enclave seem to operate are not so easily concealed or as acceptable as they might have been a century or even 50 years ago. So getting to be British today in Porto is a privilege under challenge and imperiled.

For "old port families," two kinds of local processes of practical struggle, each with internal contradictions, reflect the precarious character of present arrangements, taking substance from the larger clashes between lingering merchant and aggressive multinational capitalist forces that are restructuring the port trade. The first local struggle, which creates the context for the second, is found in the families' attempts to grapple with potential fates of erasure and dissolution of their identity within a unique port wine community, of their place of privilege in a community defined to their specifications, and of their intimate sense of unique, privileged, and historically significant selves. These are fears and fates of superannuation—of becoming irrelevant, of becoming fossils, of being dissolved, of being erased from history and memory, of being viewed as ridiculous or quaint. At the same time, there are palpable fears of pollution (perhaps just a different kind of fear of superannuation) through contaminating contact with Portuguese people of all kinds and a variety of differentiated but robustly British others.

The sites for this first struggle are surely those where futures are made—schools, principally, but club and church as well. Struggles to control the significance of social divisions and at least equally to dominate claims about social solidarities make such sites places where reifications of "community" are lived and believed and to which they accrete. Such sites are also the signs of a community—social congregations that are experienced as more than the sum of the families that compose them—at the same time that they are battlegrounds for factions, families, men and women, and other constituent fractions. They matter because capturing the flag of future community identity is so obviously a means of cultivating a place, a future, and even an honorable past for one's "own" (a more powerful stake than for "oneself" to patriarchal British men, women, and children) and of staking out advantageous grounds for ongoing enduring struggles.

They may be quite similar, but struggles to escape superannuation and pollution are often at cross-purposes with one another. In concrete terms, there are various contradictory practices that involve gathering up allies while trying to avoid being overcome by them—simultaneously courting and rejecting "other" British and susceptible Portuguese families through practices of concession and practices of exclusion. So "old port family" exclusions of Portuguese and of contract-managers' families are about staying uncontaminated as well as about maintaining privileges that depend on exclusivity. Attempts to

keep Portuguese children out of the OBS and their parents from intimate participation in the governance of school, church, and club; the
dangers of speaking Portuguese too well; the avoidance and second-
ranking of Portuguese club members and teachers at the school—all of
these express, create, and sustain fear of contamination or, ultimately,
mistaken identity. To be taken for Portuguese would amount to being
taken for a native, an inferior.

It is possible to join the new managerial forces—to join the
enemy—but preserve the living edge of one's existence, and possibly
power and resources comparable to present ones. But then pollution is
inevitable. To fight superannuation may entail trying not to compromise or recruit allies. Safe from polluting ties, one may be true to one's
heritage, one's being, one's way of life—and lose it. Or one may give
up, accepting the (apparently) inevitable. The three scions' visions of
the future reflect different varieties of these uneasy, unsatisfactory ways
to resolve, but not solve, the dilemmas as they see them. A few men may
be successful at moving into multinational management, a way of
accepting superannuation with cheering compensation. Comparatively
less romantic, more humdrum possibilities await those who retire to
become odd antipodal British residents in London or Edinburgh.
Alternatively, there are a variety of trajectories, rare and more radical
than geographic removal, for moving into Portuguese social spheres
and family life. Though such trajectories are close and convenient
(their danger), they involve cutting social ties and refusing British views
of national, racialized inferiority. The various levels at which seduction
and rejection operate together in concessions made by the British are
ways of protecting the community from contamination under circumstances in which it is increasingly difficult to avoid contact, much less
interdependence. Most common is uneasy and vaguely defeated exit by
young men and women to the United Kingdom, where they try to
blend in and plan to stay.

The second internally contradictory process concerns the unintended, paradoxical effects of *struggling* to get to be British in Porto. In
this struggle, the meaning of "getting to be British in Porto" does not sit
still: The old port families and, to the extent that they control its popular identity, "the British community" end up getting to be "more British
than the British"—which is definitely not the same thing. The local and

relational character of processes by which intimate interiors are made in everyday social life comes into focus in the tensions, disagreements, battles, and near mayhem in which "the" British mix it up with each other. They are quite heterogeneous in class, life experiences, positions, and perspectives on being British in Porto. These differences help to make each of them complexly "British." Interior dialogues surely involve a variety of confusing us/others with different claims on Britishness.

Various kinds of alters, various kinds of voices (some present, some absent), contribute to the varied trajectories of the "old British." I have tried to show in this chapter some of that variety—old port families, pillars, contract managers, British visitors from the United Kingdom, Portuguese workers who are "not British," upper-middle-class families who also do not make it as British, and so on. If the "I-for-itself" for long-term British residents in Porto is British-in-Porto, then the "not-I-in-me" is in part "real British." There is deep uncertainty about the authenticity of that which they find most crucial to defend against all comers: that they are *not* Portuguese but *British*. These uncertain dialogues of nationality in persons and in practice must contribute to the (more than UK-British) intensity with which national identity is in question in Porto.

Being "more British than the British" is usually considered a signature problem of enclaves, which are seen as somehow falling into a frozen language, culture, or history. To repeat Stuart Hall's (1995:7) sketch of former colonists: "If you consider this kind of fossilized replica, with the usual colonial cultural lag—people are always more Victorian when they're taking tea in the Himalayas than when they're taking tea in Leamington." Some visitors to Porto would agree. But social fossils are surely made rather than left over, and these "Victorian" scenes are made in practical struggles. On the ground, being "more British than the British" seems to me a matter of present struggles concerning the future, in circumstances in which that future is in grave doubt. I have argued that "old port families" fight for their future by homogenizing a disparate past and claiming 300 years of continuity that are belied by the changing history of British participation in the port trade (see Duguid 1995). And I have argued that they are engaged in practical processes involving bartering a certain British class culture in return for a continued privileged position in the enclave and other complicated concessions as well—not to keep things as they were but to produce the privileges of being British into the future.

If this chapter seems riveted on national identity, perhaps I should underline in closing the ways I see this as a matter of class, gender, and race. I have been discussing these throughout, actually: Old port families attempt to draw class lines between themselves and the contract managers, who in general have more education than the "old port families" but probably similar class standing to those same families when they first set foot in Porto years ago (something they are generally careful to ignore). Gender relations have been touched on as I tried to create a sense of the way deeply sexist, limiting, and repressive practices of male domination were so widely *not* recognized, discussed, or addressed. For women to raise gender issues would be taken as a further sign of their insufficient grasp of what's "really important," namely, the riveting struggle to sustain British national identity and its due privileges, laid out in patriarchal terms. To my American ear, issues of nationality were couched in a language of race, of blood inheritance, of the possibility of contamination through intermarriage, and of the gendered difference in the meaning of receiving blood and citizenship through a male or female parent. It seems to me that relations between long-term British residents and the Portuguese who work for them or try to join community institutions are as much a racial phenomenon of a particular historical variety as they are a conflation of class and national cultural practices (Stoler 1995).

The chapter is entitled "Getting to Be British," whereas the discussion has concentrated on the British enclave in Porto. I suspect that there are many other British enclaves around the globe, as well as postcolonial enclaves (whether British or not) and enclaves constituted perhaps along quite different lines, in which local practices of struggle are closely similar to those described here. Struggling against superannuation and pollution, erasure and loss of distinction are common human issues, as changing power, fortunes, life circumstances, and conditions of social existence threaten human stakes in all kinds of futures and pasts. I also recognize that in other times and places, struggling over community identity is significantly a process of trying to imprint an advantage on future struggles. And these in turn must help to guarantee the changing character of local and global struggles. Using homogenized and romanticized histories in pursuing specific futures and attempting to simultaneously seduce and reject salient "others" are broadly practiced efforts to establish social distinctions— the social distinction of one's own and distinctions between one's own and the "other." Any and all such efforts seem to me in the end humdrum local struggles that hold global historical and political-economic struggles in sustained, mediated, moving interconnection with daily, intimate uncertainties of identity.

Notes

The Luso-American Foundation for Development and the National Endowment for the Humanities generously provided support for this research. I am very grateful to my co-researchers on the Port project, Paul Duguid and Shawn Parkhurst, for their long and deep contributions to my work in general and this chapter in particular. Susan Shepler made vital contributions to the conception of the paper and to its practical development as well. It has been a great inspiration to work on this SAR seminar and book with Dorothy Holland.

1. Consumption of Portuguese wine in the British Isles can be traced back at least to the thirteenth century. In the following centuries, uncertainty over the supply of French wines and favorable Anglo-Portuguese treaties in 1654 and 1702–1703 enlarged the importance of Portuguese wines to England. Diminishing colonial revenues made the trade an increasingly significant source of foreign currency for the Portuguese state. See Shillington and Wallis 1907. Conceição Andrade Martins (1990:238) put the contribution of port to Portuguese foreign earnings at 25.9 percent by the end of the eighteenth century. Today it is less than 2 percent.

2. This inquiry into the sustenance and transformation of British class culture in the enclave of port wine exporters is part of a collaborative anthropological-historical investigation of the port wine trade and its families entitled "Producing Families, Trading in History: An Ethno-Historical Investigation of the Port Trade of Northern Portugal." My colleagues include the historian Paul Duguid, who has for the last several years been investigating the restructuring of the port trade in the period of the Portuguese civil war (1830s). Anthropologist Shawn Parkhurst's doctoral dissertation explores ways in which the Alto Douro, the demarcated region of port viticulture, is constituted in the dense, day-to-day

relations of class, nationality, and gender in and between Portuguese villages of small vineyard keepers. We are engaged in a collaborative, interdisciplinary, multiperspectival attempt to illuminate the enduring struggles in the trade that shaped the lives and fortunes of all concerned. My field research included a year in Porto (August 1993–August 1994), two months (June–July) in 1996, and June 1999.

3. For example, Graham's, a well-known port firm, was founded in 1808 in Lisbon. This family firm started shipping port in 1822. In 1875 it opened a cloth printing and dye works in the south, and in 1888, spinning and weaving mills in Porto.

4. The firms in Porto are also acting fairly successfully (and increasingly) as a cartel. They speak with one voice in the newspapers, concealing their differences. In public, they appear to accept their competitive relations in the spirit of schoolboys (and often say, "Well, we compete, but certainly that's a very long way from here, where port is sold, not in Gaia").

5. Philip Curtin (1984) has argued that distinctive cross-cultural trade enclaves must eventually disappear as traders either return to their "home" countries or move into the host population.

6. R. E. S. Tanner noted: "The writer lived in small European communities in Burma and Tanganyika from 1945 to 1960 and was struck not only by the similarity of behavioural patterns in these two widely separated countries but by an historical similarity between such modern communities and European communities in India and Burma described in autobiographical and fictional works from 1860 onwards" (1964:319; see also Tanner 1966). There are obvious differences among such communities and their purposes, activities, sources of legitimation, and trajectories in relation to the history of global imperialism. At the same time, many of the aspects of social life described by Tanner are strikingly similar to those in the British enclave in Porto in the mid-1990s.

7. Stanley Chapman (1922:13) argued that "the British empire was not built up simply as a tool of international diplomacy or as the opportunity for offloading surplus manufactures; it is to be seen rather as a long-term and continuous aspect of the strategy of British mercantile capitalism."

8. Carol Breckenridge and Peter van der Veer (1993:1) wrote: "We can therefore speak of the postcolonial period as a framing device to characterize the second half of the twentieth century. The term postcolonial displaces the focus on postwar as a historical marker for the last fifty years....To call this postcolonial is to...bring to our attention the relation between colonialism and

nationalism in the politics of culture in both the societies of the ex-colonizers and those of the ex-colonized." In many cases, ex-colonizers have "hung on." Stripped of their colonizing positions, they move into corporations that increasingly replace the exploitive political economics of colonialism with the exploitive political economics of multinational corporatism.

9. Robin Reid, a Factory House member in Porto, pointed out that many of the books in the Factory House library are about other British Factory Houses around the globe. Contemporary members of the community have relatives in, and have themselves lived in, other such enclaves—for example, in the Portuguese colonies in Africa, in Argentina and Chile, in Sri Lanka, in India, and so on. The consul and the headmaster have spent their professional lives traveling from one of these enclaves to another; the young head history teacher at the OBS and his lawyer wife plan to live their lives in movement every few years from one to another. They recently left Porto for three-year jobs in Singapore.

10. In 1603, merchants in Lisbon circulated a petition for religious freedom, but not until 1654 did a treaty gave British Protestants the right to a cemetery. It was 1753 before the Portuguese king ordered a "new" British cemetery, and the site was finally purchased in 1787 (Delaforce 1982).

11. George Orwell (1934) wrote: "In any town in India the European Club is the spiritual citadel, the real seat of the British power, the Nirvana for which native officials and millionaires pine in vain." Similarly, see Allen 1976; chapter 9 describes the club in Anglo-India.

12. "Neighbours in Jane Austen are not the people actually living nearby; they are the people living a little less nearby who, in social recognition, can be visited. What she sees across the land is a network of propertied houses and families, and through the holes of this tightly drawn mesh most actual people are simply not seen. To be face-to-face in this world is already to belong to a class. No other community, in physical presence or in social reality, is by any means knowable" (Williams 1973:166).

13. British citizens who have been raised in Argentina, according to Bailey (1976), speak fractured English, although their Spanish has an English accent. Isabel Allende (1985) has written similarly of the British in Chile (see note 16).

14. There was a much-discussed case recently in which a woman whose baby was about to be born took the risk of staying on in Porto to help her mother-in-law, who was ill. She could not make it to England in time for the birth. The baby is "technically" Portuguese, because the parents' grandparents

were born in Porto. A legal case was immediately instituted by the father to gain British citizenship for his son.

15. Corporate subscribers included C. J. Chambers Ltd., Cockburn Smithes, Compania de Linha Coats and Clarke, Croft/Delaforce, Ernst and Young, Garland Laidley SARL, Martinez Gassiot, Rawes (Peritagens), SIKA Industria Quimica, Taylor, Fladgate and Yateman, and W. and J. Graham. That is, of the 11 corporate subscribers, 5 are port firms, and a sixth (Chambers) belongs to an old port family.

16. In Isabel Allende's *The House of Spirits* (1985), the twin sons of Clara are sent to a British boarding school near their home in Chile. There has recently been a horrible earthquake that has nearly destroyed the country. "They went to see the twins at school. It was the first time they had all been together since the earthquake, and they were surprised to find that the only part of the country unscathed by the disaster was that ancient institution, where the event had been ignored completely. The country's ten thousand dead had gone unmourned and uneulogized while the boys went on singing English songs and playing cricket, moved only by reports that reached them, three weeks late, from the British Isles. The women were astonished to discover that these two boys, whose veins flowed with Moorish and Spanish blood, and who were born in the farthest depths of the Americas, now spoke Spanish with an Oxford accent, and that the only emotion they were capable of expressing was surprise, raising their left eyebrows. They had nothing in common with the two energetic, lice-infested boys who spent their summers in the country. 'I hope all that Anglo-Saxon phlegm doesn't turn you into morons,' Clara said as she bade her sons goodbye" (p. 167, paperback edition).

There is much in Allende's fantasy of the British at other antipodes. In Porto, it invokes complaints by the Portuguese (and by British residents about themselves) that the British pay little attention to the world around them, in part because they hope to remain unscathed by political upheavals (e.g., the port firms at the time of the revolution, when some private companies were nationalized). They get their news from the BBC and now Sky television, and they eschew local media and thus local events. They speak Portuguese with a distinctly British accent; they play cricket with intensity at the Oporto Cricket and Lawn Tennis Club. They maintain a prep school to prepare their boys (and now girls) for boarding schools in England. I don't know about "Anglo-Saxon phlegm."

17. Some Porto-British contributions have become part of British

myth/culture/literature in the UK. Port wine figures in various ways, as in the ceremonious laying down of supplies and imbibing of port at Oxford and Cambridge colleges. Port is enshrined in novels—for instance, George Meredith's *Evan Harrington* (1861). The plot involves an upright squire who is impelled by the seductions of a couple of cases of fine port wine to marry off his daughter against her will.

18. The school charter of 1894 begins, "First Resolution re: Scholars, Clause I: That the School be exclusively for British subjects [meaning boys] of the age of six years and upwards provided they can read and write." As late as 1989 the first article of the OBS charter simply copied a declaration brought along through many official revisions of the charter: "The Oporto British School is an educational association, formed by the members whose names appear in the corresponding register and whose object is to maintain a school to administer instruction and education to the children of British subjects, in order to prepare them for the entrance examinations to British schools, up to the 13 plus level. The principal, after consultation with the Board of Governors, may accept non-British pupils as long as the number of pupils from countries where the common language is not English does not prejudice the normal school programme." The articles of the charter revised in 1957 stipulate that students who come from foreign countries cannot compose more than 20 percent of the students.

19. It seemed surprising, then, that members emphasized that membership in the club implies a commitment to an egalitarian ideology. Tanner (1964) reported a strong ideology of equality in clubs in administrative enclaves in British East Africa, while at the same time there was intense preoccupation with establishing social hierarchy within the community, especially the club. Susan Ostrander (1993:18) commented that there is "a particular kind of presentation of self to which upper-class people are typically raised. They are taught from a very early age social graces that set them apart from others but do so in a way that, on the surface, conveys an impression that they are like others." In *Old Money*, Nelson Aldrich (1988:86) characterized the ability of his own class to put others at ease and make them feel good about themselves as a "gift: that the upper classes could close, even as they marked, the social distance between themselves and others." He described how upper-class social graces convey, on the one hand, the message "Why, you're as good as I am!" (p. 85). On the other hand, this acquired demeanor, this "sense of composure, as though they were perfectly integrated" also brings out in others a sense of being unable to achieve

this kind of natural, effortless, easy, confident sense of oneself (p. 83). There are resonances here with port families' practices.

20. Stuart Hall (1995:8) discusses the signatures of diasporic societies, which include "the profound process of assimilation, of dragging the whole society into some imitative relationship with this other culture which one could never quite reach." And "one of the complexities of the independence movement—certainly in the British Caribbean islands—is that, in the early phases of those movements, so-called political independence from the colonial power occurred, but the cultural revolution of identity did not" (p. 9). In Portugal, nothing so clear-cut as a national independence movement has informed the process with respect to the Anglo-Portuguese alliance. But Hall's analysis nonetheless speaks to the situation of the British in Porto, who, being "never quite [able to] reach" British metropolitan culture, and thus able only to be more British than the British, have an imitative relationship with it. Why this should be so invites further analysis.

21. I argue elsewhere (Lave 2000) for the crucial importance of the Factory House in establishing the boundaries of the port gentry and anchoring major social divisions in the enclave. The exclusion of women is one of these and has a history (at least) as old as the Factory House itself.

22. Social inflation comes about in part because they occupy positions of high standing in a very small community. In Great Britain, their "exile" at the antipodes would have the opposite effect. Several port family members told me poignant stories about their disastrous attempts to live in England for extended periods of time.

23. J. A. Mangan points out that historians of empire on the whole do not touch on education, nor do historians of education touch on imperialism, and he introduces one of his edited volumes with the proposition that "one fact emerges with great force[:]…the close and continuing association between British imperialism and the public school system" (1988:6). The network of private preparatory schools, of which the OBS is an example, is, according to Mangan (1988:13), "a mid-to-late Victorian manifestation. Its raison d'etre was to be found largely in the expanded public school system of the second half of the nineteenth century. As it grew, so the 'preparatory schools' grew, serving the public schools as 'feeders.'…They taught the housemaster's credo of king and country." The prep schools were a form of socialization into public schools, and the public schools, a form of socialization for upper-middle-class boys into the civil and military branches of imperial expansion. The boys were inculcated with

chauvinism, racism, and bigotry. Their ethnocentricity applied to "the Continent as well as the Kaffirs" (Mangan 1986:27). In many respects the port family sons must have felt at home in the public schools they were sent to in Great Britain; in other respects, being in no obvious way part of the great project of empire (the trade colony in Porto was not a project of British government directly), they may have felt uninteresting and may have suffered from the "anti-commerce elitism" of the public schools as well (Mangan 1986:30).

24. I am grateful to Peter Gow for this speculation.

25. By Ann Stoler's analysis (e.g., 1991), impoverished British residents represent a threat within the enclave, raising the possibility of less clear lines of exclusion and the specter of contamination.

26. A marathon performance of "highlights of a century of the OBS" (and the port community in Porto), presented by children and adults from the enclave at the school's centenary celebration in June 1994, was notable for its port- and British-centricity, its perfunctory nods to Portuguese history, its principally American popular music (lukewarm applause for the Beatles, a standing ovation for a Frank Sinatra imitation), and the uniquely derisive commentary by two fathers, the masters of ceremony for the occasion, on the senior girls' skit about Sylvia Pankhurst and the suffrage movement.

27. I am grateful to Susan Shepler for this point.

10

Figures of the Future

*Dystopia and Subjectivity in the Social
Imagination of the Future*

Liisa H. Malkki

Since the early 1980s, anthropology, history, cultural studies, and other fields have seen a great deal of groundbreaking work on nationalism and its relationship with history and historical consciousness (e.g., Anderson 1991 [1983]; Comaroff and Comaroff 1991; Hobsbawm and Ranger 1983; Spencer 1990). Much challenging, innovative work has also been done on history making, struggles over history, and history and narrative (e.g., Cohen 1994; Coronil 1997; Dirks, Eley, and Ortner 1994; Donham 1990, 1999; Pemberton 1994; Rosaldo 1980; Sahlins 1985; Schoffeleers 1985, 1987; Wright 1985). The relationship between nationalism and ethnic absolutism (Gilroy 1990), on the one hand, and historicity and memory, on the other, also became the cornerstone of my own work among Hutu refugees from Burundi exiled in Tanzania (Malkki 1995). I explored the ways in which the lived circumstances of exile were transforming people's sense of history and belonging, and how a particular refugee camp had become an intensified site of memory in which experiences, memories, nightmares, and rumors of violence converged to make and remake categorical enmities. I tried to understand how the social categories Hutu and

Tutsi had become (and were constantly becoming) interchangeable in so many ways with the moral categories good and evil.

Since the field research for that earlier project was completed in 1986, Burundi, like Rwanda, has seen massive new violence that is aptly described as genocidal in its logic. Numerous studies of the 1994 genocide in Rwanda and the massive violence of 1993 in Burundi (and all the violence since) exist already (e.g., African Rights 1994; Destexhe 1994; Guichaoua 1995; Jefremovas n.d.; Lemarchand 1994; Newbury 1998; Newbury and Newbury 1994; Prunier 1995; Reyntjens 1994; Vansina 1998; Wagner 1998). The political struggles and violence are still going on in both countries as of this writing. People in Burundi and its exiled populations in surrounding countries are fighting a shockingly underreported civil war.

It was in the historical context of this continuing political violence and its accompanying bitter struggles over truth and history that I took exploratory steps toward a new research project among Hutu exiled in Montreal, Canada, by going to talk with people about whether research among them might be possible. The project is still in its initial phases. I spent one month, from August to September 1995, in Montreal and was able, in that time, only to formulate a better understanding of some of the research questions that would be meaningful and worthwhile to pursue in coming years. In this chapter, I cannot yet present "findings." My purpose, rather, is to offer reflections on a project only just begun. This seems to me worth doing because the insights that the preliminary conversations with the Hutu refugees in Montreal produced seem particularly timely and important at this moment—in the Central African political context and in a global context where millennial fears, predictive management, and the projection of future scenarios tend to interject themselves into people's lives with a heightened intensity.

Since the preliminary fieldwork trip to Montreal, I have corresponded with a number of people I met there, and I sent this chapter for circulation and comment by those among them who, I thought, might be interested in reading it. Their comments are still coming in; here I quote extensively from only one person, Melchior Mbonimpa, a professor of theology and philosophy at a Canadian university and a Hutu exile from Burundi.

The Montreal conversations opened up for me new fields of vision into questions of subjectivity and the social imagination of the future. It became particularly clear that while linkages between nationalism and history have been extensively and well studied in anthropology, history, cultural studies, and other fields, links between visions of the future and transformations of national consciousness (or other forms of categorical thought) have been much less examined as yet.

Perhaps part of the explanation for the relative inattention to visions and narratives of the future in the study of national identity and national thinking can be found in our accustomed uses of the concept of history. It might be suggested, in a preliminary way, that the category "history"—usually understood in practice as that which has in one manner or another become part of the past—tends to artificially truncate the narrative emplotment of the (individual or collective) subject's trajectory into past, present, and future and to weight these terms in such a manner as to make the past most decisive or formative. The past shapes things with determinant force, whereas the future is an open question. Or so we tend to assume (at least when thinking with a conceptual apparatus that depends on linear, progressive time).

There is perhaps yet more to the theoretical and analytical invisibility of the future. It is common to see the imagination of the future dismissed as daydreaming, fantasizing, or merely indulging in crackpot schemes; imagined futures deemed insufficiently "realistic" are likely to be classed as utopian. The term "utopia," deriving from the Greek word for "no place,"[1] is often understood to refer to a pleasant fantasy with little purchase on "real life." History, on the other hand, presents itself as real: it has "already happened," we can give testimony about it, we can study how it comes to be made or narrated, silenced or monumentalized, struggled over or legitimated. We recognize that different categorical actors have different histories or different versions of history and its truths. But of the future we can say with certainty only that it does not yet exist—at least not empirically and tangibly. Anthropologists and historians are (as they should be) uncomfortable in the role of prophets or seers (even in cases where their long study of a social context or culture region gives them a special insight into likely scenarios). Thus, the past and the future have long ago been placed in a stable and commonsensical opposition to each other, like truth and fabrication, reality and fantasy.

These oversimple dualisms do a disservice not only to the conceptualization of the future but also to the concept of history. History, of
course, is not just "what happened." History involves continuous
processes of social production (Cohen 1994), invention (Hobsbawm
and Ranger 1983), imagination (Anderson 1991), and subversion, just
as the future does. And futures, like histories, are constrained and
shaped by lived experience that must be taken into account. If the two
are different, it is not because one is real and the other imagined—both
are imaginative constructions built out of people's perceived realities.
Both visions of the past and visions of the future depend on discursive
production, on certain kinds of narrativity. Both can serve as powerful
vehicles for social critique, subversion, and transformation. Finally, discourses of the past and discourses of the future feed off of one another;
indeed, they are often only different chapters of the same narrative
story, informing and justifying one another. That people struggle so
mightily over narrative visions of the past and the future and over what
the categorical, historical subjects of such stories shall be means generally that theirs are histories for use—for the present and for the future.
Once we start looking, it becomes clear that much of our political
energy and cultural imagination is expended in personal and collective
efforts to direct and shape (and, sometimes, to see) the future.

The future can be as implicated as the past in the narrative emplotment of a collective subject's trajectory. Different political factions, for
example, may well set themselves apart not just with different versions
of history but with different future-stories. Thus, versions of history
and versions of the future can both be meaningful, formative cosmo-
logical—or perhaps more accurately, cosmopolitical (Balibar 1994:6)—
stories. This is what appears to be happening among the people with
whom I have begun conversations in Montreal. But before I can present my sense of the possibilities of that research, it is necessary to lay
out a few more theoretical connections.

I suggested earlier a link between the social imagination of the
future and utopian thought. This connection seems warranted; the
imagined futures that people produce depend heavily on what for
Ernst Bloch was "the principle of hope."[2] He thought that utopia
expressed the principle of hope that is basic to humanity, and he was
eloquent in his recognition of the ways in which visions of the future

may form the lived present. "The future dimension," he wrote, "contains what is feared and what is hoped for" (Bloch 1986, vol. 1, p. 4). George Orwell (1970:274) also wrote of "the dream of a just society which seems to haunt the human imagination ineradicably and in all ages, whether it is called the kingdom of heaven or the classless society, or whether it is thought of as a Golden Age which once existed in the past and from which we have degenerated."[3]

There are two aspects of the concept of utopia that are especially useful to draw out here. First, the "imaginary societies denoted by the term 'utopia' are all presented as better than any existing society" (Emerson 1973:458), because of the virtues, alternatives, and possibilities that are imagined to characterize their social order. They are not only virtuous imagined societies, but they exist in implicit relation to actual societies.[4] Second, key to the idea of utopia is the idea of a whole society. The claim of any given utopia is that *the whole society* could be organized along different principles than it is now. Thus, a utopia is not just a matter of hope in general, or of an individual person's saying, "My life could be better"; it is a social matter entailing the imagination of a whole social collectivity, as William Morris did in *News from Nowhere*, for example.[5]

Many of the future visions best known today were written in an early and mid-twentieth-century Europe that had been torn apart and traumatized by two world wars.[6] There were utopias, but also dystopias —texts that entertained sinister and frightful visions of the future. What if the direction of history is not upward but downward? What if we are traveling toward a nightmare of hellish proportions? Orwell's *Nineteen Eighty-Four*, for example, was published in 1949. Huxley's *Brave New World* (1932) and Koestler's *Darkness at Noon* (1941) also posed painful questions about the future as a totalitarian world with no escape routes or breathing spaces. But other future-stories dealt with more optimistic scenarios. One of the most famous of the utopian writers must be H. G. Wells. He was ridiculed by Orwell for his "rigmarole of the World State" (Kumar 1987:387). Wells had written a great deal about the need for a world government in the course of his long life, and in 1940 he was a member of a team of scientists and intellectuals that worked to draft a "Declaration of Human Rights." He died before he could see the declaration—penned in part by him—adopted "in all its essentials" by the United Nations General Assembly in the 1948 Universal Declaration of Human Rights (Kumar 1987:387; cf. Showalter 1992).

It seems appropriate to have spent a few paragraphs on the questions of utopia and dystopia in Europe in the era of the two world wars because there, too, an almost unimaginable violence and horror inhabited peoples' life-worlds for many years. That kind of extended, apocalyptic horror is the present situation, and the recent history, in the Great Lakes region of Central Africa. The citizens of Rwanda and Burundi (and also many in Congo [formerly Zaire] and in other neighboring countries) seem to be at an impasse, cruelly trapped in structures of fear and violence out of which no just, secure, peaceful social order looks likely to come for the foreseeable future.

There were several hundred exiles from both Rwanda and Burundi in Montreal, Canada, and among them were Hutu and Tutsi. These two categories of people lived in mostly separate social spheres there, and yet both surely inhabited this apocalyptic world, if only at a remove.[7] Their circumstances were intimately tied to the lives and fortunes of those still living in the Great Lakes region in Africa. They might, many of them, be citizens of Canada legally, but their hearts and minds were constantly traveling back and forth, closing the distance between Bujumbura and Montreal, Kigali and Ottawa, Goma and Quebec.

All the people in these Central African societies and their quickly spreading diasporas are living in a world where no one can ignore the gruesome inventory of violence and loss. A genocide of at least 500,000 (and perhaps as many as 800,000) people recently occurred in Rwanda. A "selective genocide" that killed between 100,000 and 250,000 was visited on Burundi in 1972; some 20,000 died there in 1988. Mass killings of at least 100,000 people were carried out in Burundi in 1993, and the death toll from fighting and state violence has kept rising since then. Amnesty International and the United Nations have long been warning that genocidal violence is likely to begin again in Burundi, and in the meantime, the country is engulfed in a civil war. Mass displacements of people and the brutalization of ever fresh generations occur with each new violence. The two categories of people locked in agonistic opposition to each other over these years have been the Hutu and the Tutsi. (Both Rwanda and Burundi are usually described as having the same demographic map: 85 percent of the population of each country is Hutu, 14 percent Tutsi, and 1 percent Twa. I have discussed the political uses of these categories and population statistics elsewhere [Malkki 1995]. See also Vansina 1998:38.)

This prolonged social relationship to death and violence is probably the most important aspect to keep in view in the social landscape in which I hope to work in Montreal. This is a context in which people are living in the aftermath of one great period of genocide, tracking ongoing violence and human rights abuses scarcely reported in the North American media and living in fear of things to come. In these circumstances, one set of questions rapidly became more salient than others: In this diasporic, transcontinental society so largely produced because of violence, how did people conceive of possible or desirable futures? What alternatives did they see to the current status quo of fear and oppression? What could be done? What did they hope for?

I had not expected people to produce sunny, optimistic scenarios of a better future. But I have to admit I was still unprepared for the bleak absence of Bloch's "principle of hope." Europe's violent early twentieth century produced both dystopias and utopias. What I began to see in Montreal was the apparent *absence* of collective or personal visions of utopia in the hopeful sense. Descriptions of what a Burundian or Rwandan society at peace would look like, and discussions of what it would take to get people (Hutu and Tutsi) to trust each other and live together again, proved hard to come by. As one Burundian exile said, it will *not* be all right again: "the country is ruined," and all the Hutu can do is to clear their name as Hutu by exposing the "truth" that the worst violence and the most cunning machinations were carried out by the Tutsi category. Where people contemplated the future in discussions with me, the vision was starkly dystopian. Significantly, however, markedly different dystopian scenarios emerged. Of course, these dystopian predictions and anticipatory rumors occurred in the thick of a social life that I hope to be able to explore carefully during the project.

THE HUTU COMMUNITY IN MONTREAL

There were in 1995 about 100 Hutu men, women, and children in Montreal, about 50 in Quebec City, and about 20 in Ottawa. These groupings were growing rapidly due to births and immigration. The men (still more numerous than women) generally came first, whether as refugees or as students or both. They tended to be more highly educated than the women, who in many cases came to Canada in order to marry a particular man. There had been several arranged marriages that involved someone's finding a suitable fiancée for a young man in Canada and helping him to establish a correspondence with her by mail. It was at such a wedding in Montreal that I was first introduced to this community. I also attended a baptism for a baby of Hutu parents where I met most of the community again. These events, as well as personal introductions, allowed me to meet the bulk of the men living in Montreal and many of the women. I spent the month in large part just explaining to people what research I had done in Tanzania among the Hutu refugees there, and what I hoped to do in Canada. I was frequently asked to translate orally sections of my book into French.

In *Purity and Exile* (1995), I explored processes of the historical imagination of enmity, violence, and nationness, and the effects that the lived experience of exile might have on these processes. As mentioned earlier, I found that the political cosmology of the Hutu refugees was premised on a moralizing, categorical logic that tended to see the Hutu-Tutsi opposition as an opposition between good and evil. Preliminary conversations in Montreal suggested that the political cosmology I had traced among the Hutu refugees in camps in Tanzania had traveled to Canada as well.

Most people I talked with had experienced great sorrow and loss, and everyone (Burundian and Rwandan alike) appeared to be deeply affected by the 1994 genocide in Rwanda—whether because of the deaths of family members, the dispersal of friends and family into the vast then-Zairean and Tanzanian refugee camps or into other countries, or the difficulty of belonging to the category Hutu now that it was no longer possible to frame it as a category of "pure" victimization; for many, it now carried with it a suggestion of guilt for the genocide of the Rwandan Tutsi. In some respects, matters were more straightforward for the Hutu community in the aftermath of the 1993 mass killings in Burundi, when the country erupted in violence after the assassination of its first democratically elected president, Melchior Ndadaye. In that case, the Hutu could see themselves more unequivocally as victims: an elected Hutu president had been brutally assassinated, and the Tutsi-dominated Burundian military had butchered tens of thousands of people, most of them Hutu, though it should be noted that many thousands of Tutsi were also killed. After 1994, being a "Hutu" became very difficult. Taunts and suspicion sometimes tormented people at their workplaces in Montreal. One soft-spoken man described how, at the height of the television coverage on Rwanda, his coworkers at an auto plant called out to him in jest: "Eh, you Hutu! Are you gonna come and kill me with your machete?"

People also had stories of harsh and discriminatory treatment in Canadian immigration procedures. It was claimed that if a Hutu refugee fleeing political persecution in Burundi was applying for asylum, he or she might be rejected on the basis of ethnicity, since it was the Hutu ethnic category that had committed the bulk of the violence in Rwanda. People also told of Hutu refugees applying for asylum in Canada who tried to pass themselves off as Tutsi. In one case, a woman reportedly almost got through but then was turned back because the physiognomy of one of her children gave her away as Hutu. (I have studied this "anatomy of enmity" elsewhere [Malkki 1995]).

These immigration difficulties seemed to be but one dimension of current forms of racism in Canada, forms that made it difficult for the Hutu exiles to get jobs of any kind. Many of them tried to prolong their student status for as long as possible so that they could keep receiving stipends and not have to become unemployed. Unemployment rates among the exiles were very high. (One man who held a doctorate in philosophy from the University of Rome had ultimately found work at a car wash. He worked 12 hours a day and, having lost his wife to cancer three months before I met him, had to leave the eldest of his three daughters, a girl of 14, to care for the two younger ones after school).

Here, it should be noted that the Hutu were not alone in facing immigration or employment problems in Quebec. Melchior Mbonimpa (who wrote extensive comments on this paper) rightly noted:

> After the genocide against the Tutsi in Rwanda, it is probable that some Canadian immigration agents might have had a tendency to reject Hutu, even Burundians, on the simple criterion of ethnic belonging. But for those who have been admitted into Canada, and who have obtained Canadian citizenship, I think

that the difficulties of finding good jobs are not related to the fact that they are Hutu. It is more credible to underline other motives for discrimination, for example, *the fact of being an immigrant, and, also, the fact of being Black.*[8]

The people from Burundi and Rwanda who were exiled in Canada were closely tied to their homelands through memory, biography, and kinship. Yet Hutu and Tutsi individuals seemed to have little or nothing to do with each other even when coming from the same country, whereas Hutu, whether from Rwanda, Burundi, or Zaire, all appeared to know each other. Citizenship was evidently secondary to ethnic category and to the social imagination of race. This applied also to Canadian citizenship; many of the adults with whom I spoke had recently been granted Canadian citizenship, but they never seemed to consider that this fact alone could diminish their belonging to Burundi or Rwanda.

In the small but highly factionalized Hutu community in Montreal, different political actors set themselves apart not only with different versions of history but also with different future-stories—different scenarios of events and of possible or desirable social orders in the future. Most obviously, different futures were built into the array of political parties, community organizations, and social clubs that had formed in recent years among the Hutu in Montreal. The lack of consensus among this small population was striking. In future work, I will trace in more detail how the different Hutu political parties and groups in Canada try to impose their vision of the political alternatives and strategies.

For now, it is perhaps prudent simply to suggest the range of different positions. There were proponents of an extreme "ethnic absolutism" (Gilroy 1990) that precluded envisioning a common peace shared by Hutu and Tutsi; in this vision, national liberation meant a complete, definitive Hutu victory. Others were trying, with uneven success, to forge a coalition that would be at least formally non- or multiethnic. Many were only too aware of the need to win legitimacy in the international arena and knew that an ethnically pluralist party would be given more attention than a monoethnic party.

There were discernible factions and established institutional forums within which political action and debate took place, which I will explore more systematically in the course of the project. On the basis of preliminary work, it appears that differences in political opinion were markedly gendered; it seemed easier for Hutu women to explore new affiliations and alliances and to argue against the categorical logic of essential difference between Hutu and Tutsi. In several cases, women also spoke of their efforts to affiliate with, and work with, transnational women's organizations, and they were already quite knowledgeable about the protections for women and children established by the municipal and national governments in Canada.

There were also individual persons whose views and versions of the future failed conspicuously to fit into the dominant scenarios that saw the future as defined by the enmity between Hutu and Tutsi. Among them were people who expressed very strongly noncategorical, antiwar positions and spoke of "working for peace." One person who felt distinct social ostracism from other Hutu in Canada because of her views emphatically stressed the necessity of coexistence between Hutu and Tutsi. She said (and I paraphrase on the basis of my notes from our conversation): "Hutu have to learn to coexist with Tutsi and vice versa. You cannot just chase them out. And the Tutsi need to realize they are a minority. The example of South Africa shows that it is possible to have such a peace. We do not have to like each other, only coexist."

In sum, even in this very small community of people, there were marked differences in political visions of the future. There was, it seems, much more consensus about what had already happened than about things to come. People did not appear to argue about the correct interpretation of past events. But the future was another matter. What is to happen? What is to be done? What will become of us? These were fraught questions.

DYSTOPIAS

Again, it is hardly surprising that in the aftermath of genocide, and in the face of ongoing regional violence and repression, visions of the future would be dystopian. Some of these dystopias appeared farfetched, even paranoid. But it is worth remembering that very farfetched, sinister, horrifying things have repeatedly happened, and are happening now, in Rwanda, Burundi, Congo, and the Great Lakes region as a whole. It would therefore be unwise to jump to early conclusions about where the line between fantasy and reality, fact and rumor, might lie. Indeed, it might be helpful to suspend the search for such a line altogether. For the question, "Is it fact or fantasy?" may not be the best question that could be put to this material. To give up tracking that familiar line is not, of course, to suspend all judgment or to abandon empirical observation. But it seems to me that the first empirical questions to ask are, rather: What kinds of work do these dystopias do in contemporary social life (in Montreal, in Central Africa, and elsewhere)? How do they grow out of historical narratives of the nation, or out of the collective narration and memorializing of violence? How do they shape people's thinking or their sense of what could or should be done? And how do they define who can do what is to be done? How do these dystopias shape people's ideas of who the actors or subjects of history are?

Dystopia 1: A Tutsi Dynasty and the Extinction of the Hutu

Many Hutu in Montreal were convinced that the Tutsi in both Rwanda and Burundi, and also in the Congo and Uganda, were strengthening their regional alliances with a view to taking over the whole Great Lakes region, making a Tutsi empire, and ultimately decimating the majority Hutu population. President Yoweri Museveni of Uganda, who was said to be "ethnically Tutsi" and who is known to have supported the Rwandan Patriotic Front (RPF) over the years, was often called "the Hitler of Africa." One tract I was given in Montreal asserted: "The *Tutsi dynasty master plan* is similar to that of Hitler. Museveni may have red [*sic*] "mein Kampf" [*sic*]. After Czechoslovakia, Hitler's troops invaded Poland and so on. Likewise, Museveni invaded Rwanda. Soon he will be in Burundi, then Zaire and so on."[9]

Documents written by several Hutu exiles in North America and elsewhere were seeing active circulation among Hutu in Montreal. There was one document in particular that I was given by several different people on separate occasions: a 1994 issue of the *UDC Newsletter* (Uganda Democratic Coalition).[10] The first two pages claimed to reproduce a "Tutsi dynasty plan." Commenting on these rumors of empire, Mbonimpa noted: "'The Tutsi Dynasty master plan...' The expression seems odd to me. In French, I have always heard it spoken of as the 'Plan de l'Empire Tutsi,' which would be translated into English as

'The Tutsi Empire...' This would be more consistent because at issue is not, in reality, a dynasty, but a sort of federation of countries dominated by the Tutsi, who have no desire to create a single country."[11]

Although by no means everyone in Montreal in 1995 subscribed to these views of a regional Tutsi empire to come, it was evident that people were worried about their future as a categorical, collective subject, as "Hutu." One woman observed: "They are in the process of making a racial purification" in Burundi. She was referring to the fact that in the past few years, Hutu had been spatially segregated from Tutsi in Burundi and sometimes massacred in the process. Now Tutsi tend to be concentrated in cities, where military bases are also located, so that the military can easily give them protection. Hutu, meanwhile, are increasingly concentrated in the countryside, and neighborhoods of Bujumbura, the capital, that used to be Hutu or mixed have been systematically cleaned out through terror tactics. As Chris McGreal (1997a:5) reported:

> Burundi's Tutsi-led military government has forced hundreds of thousands of Hutus into camps dotted across the country. The authorities call it "regroupment" aimed at separating the majority Hutu peasant population from rebels battling the overwhelmingly Tutsi army and targeting civilians. Critics...call them concentration camps....In military terms, regroupment has borne fruit. In many areas the rebels are no longer able to shelter among the population or rely on it for support....And with whole communities driven out, the military embarked on a scorched earth policy, destroying homes and crops, and killing those who remained outside camps.[12]

As for Rwanda and the Congo, the recent actions of Tutsi-led forces in these regions have made the dystopia of a Tutsi dynasty appear less fanciful than it did some years earlier. In another report, McGreal (1997b:5) wrote: "The admission by Rwanda's defense minister and vice-president, General Paul Kagame, that his largely Tutsi army led Laurent Kabila's rebellion in the rechristened Congo has reinforced suspicions that his soldiers also played a leading role in the systematic murder of Hutu refugees—remnants of the 1 million Rwandans who fled into then-Zaire in 1994." These refugees were hunted down "across

1000 miles of then-Zairean territory through the eight-month war" (McGreal 1997b:5). The killings "were so widespread and systematic that they can be considered crimes against humanity and possibly geno-cide," according to a United Nations report (McGreal 1997a:5).

The Hutu woman in Montreal who spoke about contemporary practices in Burundi as "ethnic purification" was not alone in her worry. But there were other ways of envisioning the end of "the Hutu" as a cat-egorical subject. Another person, a university-educated researcher in the biological sciences, also had a vision of categorical extinction, but for him the future hinged on questions of culture and consciousness:

> One does not have confidence in our culture....Wherever one goes, one gets accustomed very easily....One forgets one's own culture and one's own history....*One suffers from acculturation.*
>
> Etymologically, the word "hutu" means slave. We accept it.... They have psychologically transformed us to accept that we are serfs....There is a fear now....Now the Hutu [in Burundi], they say, "We do not speak about politics" [they do not want to get into trouble]....If they do not become conscious now, this will be the end of a people [*s'ils ne prennent pas conscience actuelle-ment, ça sera la fin d'un peuple*]....We could be irretrievably exter-minated [*sans retour*]. [Emphasis added.]

The tortured categorical relationship between Hutu and Tutsi became one of the key themes of my earlier research. It would be important to trace in as much detail as possible how the social inferior-ity of the Hutu category is constructed—not just by Tutsi elites but by Hutu themselves (cf. Warren 1989). This question of subjectivity (and subjection) (cf. Balibar 1994) must be a vital issue in the social imagi-nation of the future. For if Hutuness cannot constitute a historical sub-ject in its own right, if it is condemned always to be a negative reflection of Tutsiness, then the Hutu category cannot be a producer of future-stories any more than it can produce authoritative versions of history. An interesting comparison comes from James Ferguson's work on the Zambian Copperbelt. In the wake of the collapse of the urban econ-omy, many Zambians were deeply pessimistic about the future and the possibility that it might bring anything better. "There was the powerful sense here that a progressive moral trajectory could only come from outside. Indeed, it proved extremely difficult to elicit from most informants any morally positive images at all of a Zambian-made future" (Ferguson 1997:146). When queried about the future, one mine worker answered with sadness: "'We black people are unable to speak of the future. We can only talk about the past'" (Ferguson 1997:146; and see Ferguson 1999).

The foregoing fragments strongly suggest that the Hutu as a categorical or collective subject was believed to be threatened—by subjection, but also by annihilation. What does it mean to tell a story about your own end as a collective entity, to envision the future without you or "your kind" in it? One had the sense that here were people on the brink not of a new age but of an imagined extinction. People in Montreal had evidently found occasion to contemplate a world without Hutu in it, to face the possibility that they as Hutu might cease to exist. One can imagine, all too clearly, that people of the category Tutsi in Montreal (and elsewhere) have had to face similar possibilities in recent years.

Dystopia 2: The War between Anglophony and Francophony

Some people insisted that the events in Rwanda could be explained only by reference to a plot to anglicize Central Africa, to make it all anglophone. One person specifically advanced a conspiracy theory about an RPF-USA alliance: "They want to take over and anglicize the whole Central African region." Here, it is necessary to know that the Tutsi-led Rwandan Patriotic Front took shape in exile, in anglophone Uganda, whereas Rwanda and Burundi are generally francophone. Many of the victorious Tutsi who swept into Rwanda therefore spoke English. People in Montreal noted with frustration that this made them better able to communicate their views to the English-speaking world, especially to the United States, while the French-speaking Rwandan Hutu could not get their side heard.

The notion of a transnational conspiracy to anglicize the Great Lakes region of Central Africa sounded farfetched to me, and I asked what would be gained by such a plan. Why would anyone care? The only explicit answer I got was that the anglophones (comprising "the Americans, the English, and the [anglophone] Canadians") wanted "to promote their language" and to establish anglophony, an anglophone sphere of influence.[13]

> There is a war between the French and the anglophones. The
> Hutu-Tutsi problem is there already. They used this as a bridge
> to make war between the francophones and the anglophones.
> They utilized the Tutsi of Uganda to destabilize Rwanda. The
> Americans *want* Central Africa. In order to really have it, they
> want to favor the minority. They prefer the Tutsi to us. They
> think that the Tutsi are more beautiful, more capable…

It was striking to trace this theme in people's conversations at that particular moment because the politics of francophony versus anglophony among Quebecois happened to be a flashpoint, a key terrain for contestations over national identity, as Quebec approached the referendum of October 30, 1995, in which voters would decide on the sovereignty of Quebec from the rest of Canada. Struggles over language and culture were prominent in Montreal during that summer of 1995. On several occasions, people casually met on the street made a point of explaining to me, a foreigner, the virtues of a sovereign, "French" Quebec.

But the theme of a neocolonial or imperialist war of languages in the Hutu exiles' conversations should not be yoked too directly to events in Quebec, for two important reasons. First, as Mbonimpa points out:

> Between the Hutu and the Quebecois, there is not a "linguistic"
> solidarity that would translate into a "political" solidarity. The
> Hutu [in Montreal] are fiercely federalist because they believe
> (rightly or wrongly) that in an independent Quebec, they
> would suffer from an even greater discrimination. The Hutu,
> like the great majority of the "immigrants" residing in Canada,
> would more readily call themselves "Canadians" than
> "Quebecois."[14]

Second, in the wake of the 1994 genocide in Rwanda and recent events in Congo (Zaire), the international press has frequently reported on the perceived stakes involved in the contraction of francophony in Central Africa. "French concern over losing ground to English-speaking forces in Africa led Paris to support Rwanda's former Hutu Government in its fight against [English-speaking] Tutsi rebels"

(French 1996:A5), and the French government reportedly also has deep interests in the Congo rebellion. Although Zaire was never a French colony, it has long been francophone, and with a population of 46 million, "Zaire is the world's second-largest French-speaking country, after France itself, and the third-largest country in Africa" (French 1997:A3). A *Los Angeles Times* correspondent reporting from Kinshasa in December 1996 wrote: "In a country that feeds on rumors, the fact that only France among Western nations stands in apparent support of Mobutu's regime in its hour of need has spawned a siege mentality and countless conspiracy theories. Some here, for example, accuse the Clinton administration of secretly supporting the rebels in a diabolical plot to foist the English language on this Francophone nation" (Drogin 1996:A10). The "tensions of empire" manifested here are startlingly salient and current, and obviously not at all safely sealed in the colonial past (cf. Cooper and Stoler 1997:33).

To return to the theme of subjectivity, it is evident that "anglophony" is a subject different from "the Tutsi" and that this transformation can be consequential for people's understandings of current events and their predictions of the future (and also that it can reconfigure their narratives of the past). Transformations between "the Hutu" as subject and "francophony" as subject would be similarly important to explore.

Dystopia 3: The Designs of the International Community

The third dystopia cast *all* Burundians (and Rwandans), whether Hutu or Tutsi, as mere pawns in the invisible games and strategies of the world powers—the United States, France, Belgium, the West. There was a sense that the whole region has been had, and that no one cared about Africa. To paraphrase one person, "We are left there killing each other because it suits them."

Even a cursory review of the historical record reveals with frightening clarity that this region has indeed been abandoned time and again when international attention and assistance might have been called for. The readiest explanation is indifference: "it suits them" to do nothing. Noam Chomsky and Edward Herman (1979) have documented the extent of the indifference of the United States toward Burundi and Rwanda. René Lemarchand (1994:xiii) wrote of Burundi: "Few other countries have had a lower priority status on the diplomatic agenda of the State Department; fewer still received so little high-level attention in the face of massive human rights violations."

Much has been written about the anatomy of this indifference in the wake of the catastrophic violence in Rwanda and Burundi, whether in newspapers and weekly news magazines or in scholarly journals. In one news article, "Why the World Let Rwanda Bleed," a U.S. State Department official was quoted as saying: "What happened in Somalia has frankly made the American military gun-shy....I don't know how many times I've heard American officers say, 'These people are not worth one American life'" (Dahlburg 1994:A8). The same journalist noted that "Rwanda—this small, landlocked country plagued by its own murderous politics and ethnic hatreds, lacking strategic importance and anything to offer the world but coffee—fell victim to 'donor fatigue'" (Dahlburg 1994:A8).

In Montreal, people's recognition of this structural indifference was reflected in comments such as, "All they want from us is raw materials," and "We are a market for arms for them" (cf. Smyth 1994). The importance of the raw materials and the arms served to highlight the insignificance of the human populations in the region. The powerful nations of the world, it was understood, placed no value on the region's people.

But sometimes the indifference of the international community was refracted into another dystopian landscape. On one occasion, I was attending a baptism dinner at an inn on the St. Lawrence River. I sat with a man who told a story he had heard somewhere. I paraphrase from notes written from memory immediately following the dinner:

> The Western countries have a master plan to depopulate the entire region of the Great Lakes by fomenting war there. They will do this because they find the climate agreeable and they would like to build hotels and holiday houses there; but they cannot because it is already so densely populated. So they have to kill most of the people. Once they have done that, they can develop further tourism, and the survivors can work as porters and waiters in the hotels.

When he first heard this rumor, our dinner companion said, he had thought it farfetched, but now he was not so sure. It seemed to explain so many things that he had begun to think there was something to it. One of the things it would explain was the incredible indifference of the international community in the face of the political catastrophe in the region. It had not escaped notice, either, that many industrial countries have enriched themselves by arming the combatants in the region (see Mbonimpa, as cited in Malkki 1995; Smyth 1994).

Another refraction of the indifference of the international community comes from the Virunga National Park in Rwanda, world famous for its mountain gorillas. In the midst of some of the most intense fighting and killing in Rwanda, research scientists were sounding the alarm about the gorillas endangered by the fighting. An "emergency airlift" was even proposed at one time for the gorillas (Malkki 1995:295). The gorillas, "a flagship species," had to be "saved from extinction" while the genocide was going on. The horrible irony of this situation was not likely lost on the inhabitants of the region. It certainly was not lost on the Hutu exiles who lived in Montreal. One person said, sipping his coffee thoughtfully, "The gorillas have more value than Burundians or Rwandans." He thought it was entirely consistent with the plans for development of Western tourism in the region that the gorillas be protected.

Different dystopias (or visions of the future in general) have different political implications. Different dystopias give different answers to such questions as, Who is the enemy? What political course of action is called for? What will happen to us as a people? Who are the people? Are they the citizens of a state or its ethnic groups? In this third set of dystopic visions, "the Hutu" as a category are hardly a subject at all, hardly even pawns in the larger plans of powerful outsiders. And at times, all Africans in the region are collapsed into the same insignificance; they are just "wretched Africans" (cf. Ferguson 1999).

For most Hutu people in Montreal, the future as an object of knowledge and imagination was worrying, even fearsome. But there was wide disagreement over what the collective historical subjects should be in these two violence-ridden countries. Was it possible for Hutu and Tutsi to live together now? Some people said clearly, yes, it is necessary to make alliances across the divide and to coexist. Other versions of the future looked different. One man, talking with me at a

Dunkin' Donuts coffee shop in Montreal, said—his expression tinged with what I thought might be embarrassment—that the Americans and the French had been discussing plans for redrawing the territorial borders of Rwanda and Burundi and creating two new countries: a Tutsiland and a Hutuland. He seemed to tacitly acknowledge the nightmare quality of the future-stories that he was discussing and added: "These are things that are circulating among us. We are not dreaming them up [*on ne les rêve pas*]."

Mbonimpa responded to these themes as follows:

> Have you noticed that often one speaks of theories of conspiracy in order to avoid seeing and admitting conspiracies that are all too real? The discreet but very efficacious and consequential intervention in the Great Lakes region of Africa by the Anglo-Saxon powers does not depend on "theory." The role of the United States and Great Britain in the rise to power of Museveni; in the victory of the RPF [Rwandan Patriotic Front]; in the enthronement of Kabila at Kinshasa; and later in the endeavour to get rid of Kabila (an endeavour that has degenerated into a vast regional war implicating Angola and Zimbabwe on the side of Congo-Zaire, against Uganda, Rwanda, and Burundi)—all this depends not at all on a "conspiracy theory": these are verifiable facts on the ground, facts that can be abundantly documented, facts that even the powers who set them in motion no longer seek to deny....You are right on one point: it is not essentially for "linguistic" or sentimental reasons that the United States and Great Britain support *de façon indefectible* Museveni, Kagame, and Buyoya. It is for "strategic" reasons: these "warlords" [*seigneurs de guerre*] of Africa of the Great Lakes are "employees" of London and of Washington for [these reasons]: the "containment" of the "Islamic menace" that the Sudan represents; the conquest of the immense natural riches of Zaire.[15]

There are obviously very real strategic politics going on in Central Africa, even if one doubts the reduction of these politics into a single grand conspiracy on the part of "the anglophones." And one cannot help but be struck by the fantastical dimensions of even the most soberly recorded historical "facts" about the political history of the region. The widely documented and researched history of the region is riddled with hideous, dreamlike, but all-too-real conspiracies. The murders of Patrice Lumumba and Dag Hammarskjöld are but two examples.

The following account of the circumstances of Lumumba's death appears in the register of reputable fact now, many years after the events:

> Evidence of direct Belgian government complicity in the execution of the Congolese leader Patrice Lumumba must be made public and those implicated questioned, a historian demanded last week. Ludo de Witte, a Flemish expert on Africa, called for a parliamentary commission of inquiry to hear testimony under oath from former officials involved in the 1961 killing of one of Africa's most charismatic post-colonial leaders....Lumumba— popular, articulate, and a hero of the anti-colonial struggle— was just 36 when he became the first prime minister of the independent Congo in June 1960. But within a month a war erupted, provoked by the attempted secession of the copper-rich Katanga province, led by Moise Tshombe. Tshombe recruited Belgian, French, and South African mercenaries to fight the government....Lumumba was deposed and an unknown colonel called Joseph-Desiré Mobutu took control of the country, renaming it Zaire. He remained a faithful friend of the West until his overthrow in May 1997. The United States saw the militant nationalist Lumumba as a communist sympathiser; CIA involvement in plans to kill him has long been established by senate hearings and declassified documents. (Black 2000:7)

The article goes on to explain that Belgian officers were directly responsible for Lumumba's assassination. On January 17, 1961, Mobutu's forces, on orders from Belgium, took Lumumba to Katanga on a Sabena airplane. "He was assaulted in the presence of Belgian officers and tortured in a villa guarded by Belgian troops, before being shot by an execution squad supervised by a Belgian captain. His body was exhumed by a Belgian police commissioner, Gérard Soete, and dissolved in acid" (Black 2000:7).

And what happened to Dag Hammarskjöld, the Swedish secretary general of the United Nations, whose strange death in a 1961 plane crash in Central Africa has been the object of speculation for decades? As part of the proceedings of South Africa's Truth and Reconciliation Commission, its head, Desmond Tutu, reported receiving evidence that Hammarskjöld's death might have been orchestrated by a conspiracy between the United States, Great Britain, and South Africa. The evidence suggested that the intelligence services of these countries (the MI5 and the CIA, together with their South African counterparts) might have installed a bomb in the airplane that transported Hammarskjöld on a United Nations mission in Central Africa. The plane exploded as it was making a landing in Zambia (then Northern Rhodesia) (cf. Fabian 1996:131). The evidence unearthed by the Truth and Reconciliation Commission consisted of eight letters. One of them said: "There is a feeling that Hammarskjöld should be removed"; another, undated letter mentioned that "Allen Dulles is of the same opinion and has promised the full cooperation of his people."[16] Dulles was the U.S. Central Intelligence Agency's director from 1953 to 1961 (Mykkänen 1998:C5). The secretary general had been active in negotiating the political crisis between the Congo and Katanga Province.

Historical memories and rumors about both of these murders have recently been examined by Fabian (1996) and others. Careful study of the material discussed here highlights the obvious fact that political events in Central Africa need to be researched in a broad, longitudinal, regional and transcontinental frame. But more to the point in the present context, the material reveals the frightening thinness of the line between "fact" and "paranoia," "evidence" and "rumor," in the region's histories. All of these registers of knowledge and imagination have a dreamlike quality. All of them emit a sinister sense of unreality. And all make it clear that what is known is embedded in vast zones of what is not known, or even imagined. This sense pervades the Hutu exiles' accounts in Montreal. It also haunts the research conducted on Central African struggles over histories, truths, and the social imagination of the future, and it poses formidable challenges to the anthropologist concerning the ethics of knowledge production and one's very will to knowledge (cf. Bernault 1998; Newbury 1998; Vansina 1998; Wagner 1998).

CONCLUSION

I obviously cannot conclude with "findings" at this very preliminary stage of the envisioned research project in Montreal. But even
now the material suggests that historical structures of fear and enmity
need to be studied instead of just dismissed as paranoia or extremism
and thereby prematurely silenced. For it is they that are always already
projecting forms and structures into the future, as shadows dancing on
a wall. Even the most paranoid-sounding of future-stories can be as
important as any national history in shaping the present and political
alternatives for the future. One cannot easily rekindle Bloch's "principle of hope" without first taking account of the structures of fear, and
without examining the enormous losses that people have suffered on
all sides.

Notes

1. Emerson (1973:458) suggested that "utopia" derives from *two* Greek
words that mean "no place" and "good place."

2. Bloch's three-volume work, *The Principle of Hope* (1986), was written
between 1938 and 1947 as *Das Prinzip Hoffnung*.

3. Cited in Kumar (1987:2, and see 425n1).

4. Cf. Mannheim (1985 [1936]:203), who quotes Lamartine as follows: "Les
utopies ne sont souvent que des vérités prématurées" [Utopias are often only
premature truths].

5. I would like to thank James Ferguson for valuable discussions on the
topic of utopia. As he has suggested, modern utopias tend to involve a "planner's-
eye-view" of society and to depend on the category of the social that was itself
invented at some point. The social imagination of "a society" is not synonymous
with, and is probably culturally and historically more specific than, the social
imagination of "a world." A similar point is made by Owen Daniel and Moylan in
their preface to *Not Yet: Reconsidering Ernst Bloch* (1997:viii).

6. The whole experience of industrialization (the dark Satanic mills, etc.)
in Europe produced backward-looking utopias such as William Morris's *News
from Nowhere* (1966 [1890]), Samuel Butler's *Erewhon* (1934 [1872]), and Edward
Bellamy's *Looking Backward* (1982 [1888]). These were utopias that looked to the
past to create a better world, in the process recording aspects of the malaise that
characterized the period. The twentieth-century dystopias have more often dealt

with war, science, social engineering, and the totalitarian state. Cf. Clarke (1966); Kumar (1987); Baczko (1989).

7. My planned research will take place only among the Hutu exiles in Montreal, as did my earlier research. Given the histories of enmity and mistrust that characterize the relationships between Hutu and Tutsi, it would unfortunately be difficult (perhaps impossible) to work with both social categories.

8. Melchior Mbonimpa, personal communication, 4 January, 2000. Emphasis in the original. This and all other quotes from Mbonimpa have been translated from the French by the author.

9. *UDC Newsletter,* June 1996, p. 7.

10. *UDC Newsletter,* June 1994, vol. 4, no. 3.

11. Mbonimpa, personal communication, 4 January, 2000.

12. McGreal further reported in the same article that the government claimed that 300,000 persons had been thus interned, but that outside agencies quoted double the figure.

13. Whereas French colonial and postcolonial expansion operated on such a notion of francophone culture, English-speaking imperial plans have not usually been phrased in quite this way. The person interviewed here also said: "The Americans do not want Catholics in Rwanda." Religion is an important dimension to be pursued in this project.

14. Mbonimpa, personal communication, 4 January, 2000.

15. Mbonimpa, personal communication, 4 January, 2000.

16. Mykkänen (1998:C5), translated from the Finnish by the author.

References Cited

African Rights

1994   Rwanda: Death, Despair and Defiance. London: African Rights.

Ahearn, Laura

1991   The Emergence of Cultural Meaning in a Nepali Women's Songfest.
          Paper presented at the South Asia Annual Meeting, Madison, WI,
          November.`

Alarcón González, Diana

1994   Changes in the Distribution of Income in México and Trade
          Liberalization. Tijuana, Mexico: El Colegio de la Frontera Norte.

Aldrich, Nelson W., Jr.

1988   Old Money: The Mythology of America's Upper Class. New York:
          Vintage.

Allen, Charles, ed.

1976   Plain Tales from the Raj. London: Futura. (Originally published by
          Andre Deutsch and the BBC, 1975.)

Allende, Isabel

1985   The House of the Spirits. New York: Knopf.

Anderson, Benedict

1991   Imagined Communities: Reflections on the Origin and Spread of
[1983]   Nationalism. London: Verso.

REFERENCES

Appadurai, Arjun
1998   Dead Certainty: Ethnic Violence in the Era of Globalization. Public
          Culture 10(2):225–247.

Aretxaga, Begoña
1993   Striking with Hunger: Cultural Meanings of Political Violence in
          Northern Ireland. *In* Violence Within: Cultural and Political Opposition
          of Divided Nations. Kay B. Warren, ed. Pp. 219–255. Boulder, CO:
          Westview Press.
1995   Dirty Protest: Symbolic Overdetermination and Gender in Northern
          Ireland Ethnic Violence. Ethos 23(2):123–148.
1997   Gendered Violence: Nationalist Women and Political Subjectivity in
          Northern Ireland. Princeton, NJ: Princeton University Press.

Ariès, Philippe
1962   Centuries of Childhood: A Social History of Family Life. New York:
          Knopf.

Aronowitz, Stanley
1990   The Crisis in Historical Materialism. Minneapolis: University of
          Minnesota Press.

Baczko, Bronislaw
1989   Utopian Lights: The Evolution of the Idea of Social Progress. New York:
          Paragon House.

Bailey, John P.
1976   The British Community in Argentina. Ph.D. dissertation, Department of
          Sociology, University of Surrey.

Bakhtin, Mikhail
1981   The Dialogic Imagination: Four Essays by M. M. Bakhtin. M. E.
          Holquist, ed. Caryl Emerson and Michael Holquist, trans. Austin:
          University of Texas Press.
1986   Speech Genres and Other Late Essays. Caryl Emerson and Michael
          Holquist, eds. Vern W. McGee, trans. Austin: University of Texas Press.
1990   Art and Answerability: Early Philosophical Essays. Michael Holquist and
          Vadim Liapunov, eds. Austin: University of Texas Press.

Baldwin, James
1985   Notes of a Native Son. London: Pluto Press.
[1955]

Balibar, Etienne
1994   Subjection and Subjectivation. *In* Supposing the Subject. Joan Copjec,
          ed. Pp. 1–15. New York: Verso.

Ball, Patrick, Paul Kobrak, and Herbert F. Spirer
1998   State Violence in Guatemala, 1960–1996: A Quantitative Reflection.
          Electronic document. AAAS and CIIDH.
          http://hrdata.aaas.org/ciidh/qr/english/qrtitle.html.

Barkin, David
1990   Distorted Development: Mexico in the World Economy. Boulder, CO:
          Westview Press.

Barry, Tom
1995   Zapata's Revenge: Free Trade and the Farm Crisis in Mexico. Boston:
          South End Press.

Barth, Fredrik
1991   Ethnicity Revisited. Paper presented at the annual meeting of the
          American Anthropological Association, Chicago.

Behar, Ruth
1993   Translated Woman: Crossing the Border with Esperanza's Story. Boston:
          Beacon.

Bellamy, Edward
1982   Looking Backward, 2000–1887. New York: Penguin.
[1888]

Benjamin, Paul
1989   Local Organization for Development in Nepal. Ph.D. dissertation,
          Department of Anthropology, University of North Carolina at Chapel
          Hill.

Bennett, Lynn
1979   Tradition and Change in the Legal Status of Women. Kathmandu:
          Centre for Economic Development and Administration, Tribhuvan
          University.
1983   Dangerous Wives and Sacred Sisters: Social and Symbolic Roles of High-
          Caste Women in Nepal. New York: Columbia University Press.

Bernardes, Betina
1995a   Brasil já possui quinta geração. Folha de São Paulo (October 19):
          Especial 2.
1995b   Comunidade de japoneses formam elite em São Paulo. Folha de São
          Paulo (October 19): Especial 10.

Bernault, Florence
1998   La communauté africaniste française au crible de la crise Rwandaise.
          Africa Today 45(1):45–58.

Besnier, Niko
1992   Reported Speech and Affect on Nukulaelae Atoll. In Responsibility and
          Evidence in Oral Discourse. J. H. Hill and J. T. Irvine, eds. Pp. 161–181.
          Cambridge: Cambridge University Press.

Besserer Alatorre, Federico
1999a   Moisés Cruz: Historia de un transmigrante. Culiacán, México:
          Universidad Autónoma de Sinaloa. Mexico City: Universidad Autónoma
          Metropolitana, Unidad Iztapalapa.

1999b   Estudios transnacionales y ciudadanía transnacional. *In* Fronteras
          Fragmentadas. Gail Mummert, ed. Pp. 215–238. Zamora, Mexico:
          Colegio de Michoacán.

Bista, Khem Bahadur
1969   Tij ou la fête des femmes. Objets et Mondes 9:7–18.

Black, Ian
2000   Belgium Accused of Killing African Hero Lumumba. Manchester
          Guardian Weekly, January 20–26, p. 7.

Bloch, Ernst
1986   The Principle of Hope. 3 vols. Oxford: Basil Blackwell.
[1938–1947]

Bloch, Maurice
1989   "Anthropology since the Sixties" Seen from across the Atlantic. *In*
          Author Meets Critics: Reactions to "Theory in Anthropology since the
          Sixties." CSST Working Paper 32. Sherry Ortner, ed. Pp. 1–14. Ann
          Arbor: University of Michigan.

Bondi, Liz
1990   Feminism, Postmodernism and Geography: Space for Women? Antipode
          22:156–157.

Bouillier, Veronique
1982   Si les femmes faisaient la fête: A Propos des fêtes feminines dans les
          hautes castes indo-nepalaises. L'Homme 22:91–118.

Bourdieu, Pierre
1977   Outline of a Theory of Practice. Richard Nice, trans. Cambridge:
          Cambridge University Press.
1984   Distinction: A Social Critique of the Judgement of Taste. Richard Nice,
          trans. Cambridge: Harvard University Press.
1986   The Forms of Capital. *In* Handbook of Theory and Research for the
          Sociology of Education. J. B. Richardson, ed. Pp. 241–258. New York:
          Greenwood Press.
1990   The Logic of Practice. Richard Nice, trans. Stanford, CA: Stanford
          University Press.
1991   Language and Symbolic Power. Cambridge, MA: Harvard University
          Press.

Bourque, Susan C., and Kay B. Warren
1982   Women of the Andes. Ann Arbor: University of Michigan Press.

Bradford, Sarah
1978   The Story of Port: The Englishman's Wine. Rev. ed. London: Christie's
          Wine Publications.

Breckenridge, Carol A., and Peter van der Veer, eds.
1993   Orientalism and the Postcolonial Predicament. Philadelphia: University of Pennsylvania Press.

Brintnall, Douglas E.
1979   Revolt against the Dead: The Modernization of a Mayan Community in the Highlands of Guatemala. New York: Gordon and Breach.

Brownlee, Brid
1985   Strip-Searching Is an Unnecessary Violation. Fortnight, March, 3:17.

Brysk, Alison
1996   Turning Weakness into Strength: The Internationalization of Indian Rights. Latin American Perspectives 23(2):38–58.

Bullard, Robert D.
1990   Dumping in Dixie. Boulder, CO: Westview Press.

Bullard, Robert D., ed.
1993   Confronting Environmental Racism: Voices from the Grassroots. Boston: South End.

Burguete Cal y Mayor, Aracely, ed.
1999   México: Experiencias de autonomía indígena. Copenhagen: Grupo Internacional de Trabajo sobre Asuntos Indígenas.

Burton, Frank
1978   The Politics of Legitimacy: Struggles in a Belfast Community. London: Routledge and Kegan Paul.

Butler, Judith
1993   Bodies that Matter: On the Discursive Limits of "Sex." New York: Routledge.

Butler, Samuel
1934   Erewhon. New York: Limited Editions Club.
[1872]

Cairns, David, and Shaun Richards
1988   Writing Ireland: Colonialism, Nationalism and Culture. Manchester, UK: Manchester University Press

Campbell, Howard
1994   Ethnic Politics and Cultural Revivalism in Southern Mexico. Albuquerque: University of New Mexico Press.

Campbell, Howard, Leigh Binford, Miguel Bartolomé, and Alicias Barabas
1993   Zapotec Struggles: Histories, Politics, and Representations from Juchitán, Oaxaca. Washington, DC: Smithsonian Institution Press.

Cancian, Frank
1965   Economics and Prestige in a Maya Community: The Religious Cargo System in Zinacantán. Stanford, CA: Stanford University Press.

Carlsen, Robert S.
1997   The War for the Heart and Soul of a Highland Maya Town. Austin: University of Texas Press.

Carmack, Robert
1973   Quichean Civilization: The Ethnohistoric, Ethnographic, and Archaeological Sources. Berkeley: University of California Press.

Casaús Arzú, Marta Elena
1992   Guatemala: Linaje y racismo. San José, Costa Rica: FLACSO.

Castañeda, Quetzil
1996   In the Museum of Maya Culture: Touring Chichén Itzá. Minneapolis: University of Minnesota Press.

Castells, Manuel
1989   The Informational City. Cambridge, MA: Blackwell.

Cederstrom, Thoric N.
1993   The Potential Impacts of Migrant Remittances on Agricultural and Community Development in the Mixteca Baja of Mexico. Ph.D. dissertation, Department of Anthropology, University of Arizona, Tucson.

CEH (Guatemalan Commission for Historical Clarification)
1999   Guatemala: Memory of Silence Tz'inil Na'tab'al. Electronic document. <hrdata.aaas.org/ceh/report>

Chance, John
1978   Race and Class in Colonial Oaxaca. Stanford, CA: Stanford University Press.

Chapman, Stanley
1922   Merchant Enterprise in Great Britain: From the Industrial Revolution to World War I. Cambridge: Cambridge University Press.

Chomsky, Noam, and Edward Herman
1979   The Washington Connection and Third World Fascism. Boston: South End Press.

Clark, Katerina, and Michael Holquist
1984   Mikhail Bakhtin. Cambridge, MA: Belknap Press of Harvard University Press.

Clarke, Ignatius Frederick
1966   Voices Prophesying War, 1763–1984. Oxford: Oxford University Press.

Cohen, David William
1994   The Combing of History. Chicago: University of Chicago Press.

Cojtí Cuxil, Demetrio
1994   Políticas para la revindicación de los Mayas de hoy. Guatemala: Editorial Cholsamaj.

1995   Ub'aniik Ri Una'ooj Uchomab'aal Ri Maya' Tinamit: Configuración del pensamiento político del pueblo Maya. Vol. 2. Guatemala: Seminario Permanente de Estudios Mayas and Editorial Cholsamaj.

1997   Ri Maya' Moloj pa Iximulew: El movimiento Maya (en Guatemala). Guatemala: Editorial Cholsamaj.

Collier, George, with Elizabeth Lowery Quaratiello
1994   Basta! Land and the Zapatista Rebellion in Chiapas. Oakland, CA: Institute for Food Development Policy.

Comaroff, John, and Jean Comaroff
1991   Of Revelation and Revolution: Christianity, Colonialism, and Consciousness in South Africa. Chicago: University of Chicago Press.

COMG (Consejo de Organizaciones Mayas de Guatemala)
1995   Construyendo un futuro para nuestro pasado: Derechos del pueblo Maya y el proceso de paz. Guatemala: Editorial Cholsamaj.

Community for Justice
1987   Strip-Searching: A Moral Issue. Eight-page pamphlet published in Northern Ireland.

Cooper, Frederick, and Ann Stoler, eds.
1997   Tensions of Empire: Colonial Cultures in a Bourgeois World. Berkeley: University of California Press.

Cornelius, Wayne, and Philip L. Martin
1993   The Uncertain Connection: Free Trade and Mexico–U.S. Migration. San Diego: University of California, Center for U.S.–Mexican Studies.

Coronil, Fernando
1997   The Magical State: Nature, Money, and Modernity in Venezuela. Chicago: University of Chicago Press.

Crapanzano, Vincent
1986   Waiting: The Whites of South Africa. New York: Vintage Books.

Curruchiche Gómez, Miguel Angel
1994   Discriminación del pueblo Maya en el ordenamiento jurídico de Guatemala. Guatemala: Editorial Cholsamaj.

Curtin, C., H. Donnan, and T. Wilson, eds.
1993   Irish Urban Cultures. Belfast: Institute of Irish Studies, Queen's University of Belfast.

Curtin, Philip D.
1984   Cross-Cultural Trade in World History. Cambridge: Cambridge University Press.

Dahlburg, John-Thor
1994   Why the World Let Rwanda Bleed. Los Angeles Times, 10 September, pp. A1, A8.

Danielson, Michael N., and Jameson W. Doig
1982   New York: The Politics of Urban Regional Development. Berkeley: University of California Press for the Institute of Governmental Studies.

Das, Veena
1995   Critical Events: An Anthropological Perspective on Contemporary India. Delhi: Oxford University Press.

Das, V., and A. Nandy
1985   Violence, Victimhood and the Language of Silence. Contributions to Indian Sociology 19(1):177–195. London: Sage Publications.

Davis, Mike
1990   City of Quartz: Excavating the Future in Los Angeles. New York: Verso.

de Certeau, Michel
1984   The Practice of Everyday Life. Berkeley: University of California Press.

Delaforce, John
1982   Anglicans Abroad: The History of the Chaplaincy and Church of St. James at Oporto. London: SPCK.

Dennis, Philip
1987   Inter-Village Conflict in Oaxaca. New Brunswick, NJ: Rutgers University Press.

de Paz, Marco Antonio
1993   Maya 'Amaaq' xuq Junamilaal: Pueblo Maya y democracia. Guatemala: SPEM/Editorial Cholsamaj.

Destexhe, Alain
1994   Rwanda: Essai sur le génocide. Brussels: Editions Complexe.

Díaz Polanco, Héctor
1996   Indigenous Peoples in Latin America: The Quest for Self-Determination. Lucia Rayas, trans. Boulder, CO: Westview Press.

Dirks, Nicholas B.
1992   Castes of Mind. Representations 37:56–78.

Dirks, Nicholas, Geoff Eley, and Sherry Ortner
1994   Culture/Power/History: A Reader in Social Theory. Princeton, NJ: Princeton University Press.

Donham, Donald
1990   History, Power, Ideology: Central Issues in Marxism and Anthropology. New York: Cambridge University Press.
1999   Marxist Modern: An Ethnographic History of the Ethiopian Revolution. Berkeley: University of California Press.

Drogin, Bob
1996   Zaire's Hopes Ride on Dictator's Return. Los Angeles Times, 16 December, p. A10.

Duguid, Paul
1995   Negotiating Change: Town Country Relations in the Twilight of the
        Companhia Geral. Paper presented at the sixth annual ICGP
        Conference, Durham, NH.

Dumont, Louis
1980   Homo Hierarchicus. Chicago: University of Chicago Press.

Duneier, Mitchell
1993   Slim's Table. Chicago: University of Chicago Press.

Eley, Geoff
1992   Nations, Publics, and Political Cultures: Placing Habermas in the
        Nineteenth Century. *In* Habermas and the Public Sphere. Craig
        Calhoun, ed. Pp. 289–339. Cambridge, MA: MIT Press.

Elshtain, Jean Bethke
1987   Women and War. New York: Basic Books.

Emerson, Roger
1973   Utopia. *In* Dictionary of the History of Ideas. Philip Weiner, ed. Pp.
        458–465. New York: Scribner.

Enslin, Elizabeth
1998   Imagined Sisters: The Ambiguities of Women's Poetics and Collective
        Actions. *In* Selves in Time and Place: Identities, Experience, and History
        in Nepal. D. Skinner, Alfred Pach III, and D. Holland, eds. Pp. 269–299.
        Lanham, MA: Rowman and Littlefield.

Escobar, Arturo
1991   Anthropology and the Development Encounter: The Making and
        Marketing of Development Anthropology. American Ethnologist
        18(4):658–682.

Escobar, Arturo, and Sonia Alvarez, eds.
1992   The Making of Social Movements in Latin America: Identity, Strategy,
        and Democracy. Boulder, CO: Westview Press.

Esquit Choy, Edgar, and Carlos Ochoa García, eds.
1995   Yiqalil Q'anej, Kunimaaj Tziij, Niman Tzij: El respeto a la palabra.
        Guatemala: Centro de Estudios de la Cultura Maya.

Fabian, Johannes
1996   Remembering the Present: Painting and Popular History in Zaire.
        Narrative and paintings by Tshibumba Kanda Matulu. Berkeley:
        University of California Press.

Faligot, Roger
1983   Britain's Military Strategy in Ireland: The Kitson Experiment. London:
        Zed Press.

Falla, Ricardo
1978   Quiché rebelde: Estudio de un movimiento de conversión religiosa, rebelde a las creencias tradicionales, en San Antonio Ilotenango, Quiché (1948–1970). Guatemala: Editorial Universitaria de Guatemala.

Farrell, James Gordon
1978   The Singapore Grip. London: Weidenfeld and Nicolson.

FAA/NYSDOT (Federal Aviation Administration and New York State Department of Transportation)
1996   The Port Authority of New York and New Jersey JFK International Airport Light Rail System: Written Evaluation/Technical Report on Changes to the Proposed JFK Airport Access Program. New York: FAA/NYSDOT.

Feldman, Allen
1991   Formations of Violence: The Narrative of the Body and Political Terror in Northern Ireland. Chicago: University of Chicago Press.
1994   On Cultural Anesthesia: From Desert Storm to Rodney King. American Ethnologist 21(2):404–418.

Ferguson, James
1990   The Anti-politics Machine: "Development," Depoliticization, and Bureaucratic Power in Lesotho. Cambridge: Cambridge University Press.
1997   The Country and the City on the Copperbelt. *In* Culture, Power, Place: Explorations in Critical Anthropology. Akhil Gupta and James Ferguson, eds. Pp. 137–154. Durham, NC: Duke University Press.
1999   Expectations of Modernity: Myths and Meanings of Urban Life on the Zambian Copperbelt. Berkeley: University of California Press.

Fischer, Edward, and R. McKenna Brown, eds.
1996   Mayan Cultural Activism in Guatemala. Austin: University of Texas Press.

Folha de São Paulo
1995   Brasil Japão 100 anos. Caderno especial, 19 October, 12 pp.

Foster, John W.
1991   Colonial Consequences: Essays in Irish Identity and Culture. Dublin: Lilliput Press.

Foucault, Michel
1979   Discipline and Punish: The Birth of the Prison. New York: Vintage Books.
1980   The History of Sexuality, vol. 1: An Introduction. New York: Vintage Books.

Foweraker, Joe, and Ann L. Craig
1990   Popular Movements and Political Change in Mexico. Boulder, CO: Lynne Rienner.

Fox, John W.
1987   Maya Postclassic State Formation: Segmentary Lineage Migration in Advancing Frontiers. Cambridge: Cambridge University Press.

Fraser, Nancy
1989   Unruly Practices: Power, Discourse, and Gender in Contemporary Social Theory. Minneapolis: University of Minnesota Press.

French, Howard
1996   Zairian Crisis Part of Broad Web of African Subversion and Revolt. New York Times, 23 November, pp. A1, A5.
1997   France Fears Anglo-Saxons Are Usurping It in Africa. New York Times, 4 April, p. A3.

Friedlander, Judith
1975   Being Indian in Hueyapan. New York: St. Martin's.

Galarza, Ernesto
1977   Farm Workers and Agribusiness in California, 1947–1960. Notre Dame: University of Notre Dame Press.

Garduño, Everado, Efraín García, and Patricia Morán
1989   Mixtecos en Baja California: El Caso de San Quintín. Tijuana, Mexico: Universidad Autónoma de Baja California.

Garzon, Susan, R. McKenna Brown, Julia Becker Richards, and Wuqu' Ajpub'
1999   The Life of the Kaqchikel Language: Maintenance, Shift, and Revitalization. Austin: University of Texas Press.

Geertz, Clifford
1973   The Interpretation of Cultures: Selected Essays. New York: Basic Books.
1984   From the Native's Point of View: On the Nature of Anthropological
[1974]   Understanding. In Culture Theory: Essays on Mind, Self, and Emotion. Richard A. Shweder and Robert A. LeVine, eds. Pp. 123–136. Cambridge: Cambridge University Press.

Gilroy, Paul
1990   Nationalism, History, and Ethnic Absolutism. History Workshop Journal 30:114–120.

Gluckman, Max
1954   Rituals of Rebellion in Southeast Africa. Manchester, UK: Manchester University Press.

Goodman, James C.
1981   Shiva's Scarlet Women. ASIA (Sept.–Oct.):20–25.

Gossen, Gary
1984   Chamulas in the World of the Sun: Time and Space in Maya Oral Tradition. Prospect Heights, IL: Waveland Press.

Gramsci, Antonio
1971   Selections from Prison Notebooks. Q. Hoare and G. Nowell Smith, trans. and eds. New York: International Publishers.

Guichaoua, Andre
1995   Les crises politiques au Burundi et au Rwanda (1993–1994). Paris: Karthala.

Guzmán Böckler, Carlos
1996   Ri Okel Nqetamaj pa Iximulew: Cuando se quiebra los silencios, lo que todos debemos saber sobre la historia de Guatemala. Guatemala: Editorial Cholsamaj.

Hale, Charles R.
1994   Between Che Guevara and the Pachamama: Mestizos, Indians and Identity Politics in the Anti-Quincentenary Campaign. Critique of Anthropology 14(1)9–39.

Hale, Charles R. , ed.
1996   Mestizaje. Journal of Latin American Anthropology 2(1).

Hall, Stuart
1992   Discussion. *In* Black Popular Culture. Gina Dent, ed. Pp. 85–91. Seattle: Bay Press.
1995   Negotiating Caribbean Identities. New Left Review 209 (Jan.–Feb.):1–14.

Hamilton, Nora
1982   The Limits of State Autonomy: Post-Revolutionary Mexico. Princeton, NJ: Princeton University Press.

Harvey, David
1989   The Urban Experience. Baltimore, MD: Johns Hopkins University Press.

Harvey, Neil
1998   The Chiapas Rebellion: The Struggle for Land and Democracy. Durham, NC: Duke University Press.

Heaney, Seamus
1983   An Open Letter. Derry, Ireland: Field Day Theatre Company.

Heath, Shirley Brice
1983   Ways with Words: Language, Life, and Work in Communities and Classrooms. Cambridge: Cambridge University Press.

Herr, Sheryl
1990   The Erotics of Irishness. Critical Inquiry 17:1–34.

Hill, Jane, and Judith Irvine, eds.
1993   Responsibility and Evidence in Oral Discourse. Cambridge: Cambridge University Press.

Hill, Robert M., and John Monaghan
1987   Continuities in Highland Maya Social Organization: Ethnohistory in Sacapulas, Guatemala. Philadelphia: University of Pennsylvania Press.

Hobsbawm, Eric, and Terence Ranger
1983   The Invention of Tradition. Cambridge: Cambridge University Press.

Hollan, Douglas
1997   The Relevance of Person-Centered Ethnography to Cross-Cultural
         Psychiatry. Transcultural Psychiatry 34(2):219–234.

Holland, Dorothy
1997   Selves as Cultured: As Told by an Anthropologist Who Lacks a Soul. *In*
         Self and Identity: Fundamental Issues. Richard D. Ashmore and Lee
         Jussim, eds. Pp. 160–190. Oxford: Oxford University Press.

Holland, Dorothy, William Lachicotte, Debra Skinner, and Carole Cain
1998   Identity and Agency in Cultural Worlds. Cambridge, MA: Harvard
         University Press.

Holland, Dorothy, and Debra Skinner
1995a   Contested Ritual, Contested Femininities: (Re)forming Self and Society
         in a Nepali Women's Festival. American Ethnologist 22(2):279–305.
1995b   Not Written by the Fate Writer: The Agency of Women's Critical
         Commentary in Nepal. Folk: The Journal of the Danish Ethnographic
         Society 37:103–133.

Holmberg, David
1989   Order in Paradox: Myth, Ritual, and Exchange among Nepal's Tamang.
         Ithaca, NY: Cornell University Press.

Holquist, Michael
1990   Dialogism: Bakhtin and His World. London: Routledge.

Horne, Haynes
1989   Jameson's Strategies of Containment. *In* Postmodernism/Jameson/
         Critique. Douglas Kellner, ed. Pp. 268–300. Washington, DC:
         Maisonneuve Press.

Huxley, Aldous
1932   Brave New World. London: Chatto and Windus.

International Press (Atsugi, Japan)
1995   Brasileiros formam terceira comunidade estrangeira no Japão. 17
         December, p. 1-C.

Jameson, Fredric
1981   The Political Unconscious: Narrative as a Socially Symbolic Act. Ithaca,
         NY: Cornell University Press.

Jefremovas, Villia
n.d.   The Rwandan State and Local Level Response: Class and Region in the
         Rwandan Genocide, the Refugee Crisis, Repatriation and the "New
         Rwanda." Unpublished manuscript.

Johnson, Richard
1987   What Is Cultural Studies Anyway? Social Text: Theory/Culture/Ideology
         16 (Winter):38–80.

Jones, Ann R., and Peter Stallybrass

1992   Dismantling Irena: The Sexualization of Ireland in Early Modern England. *In* Nationalisms and Sexualities. Andrew Parker, Mary Russo, Doris Sommer, and Patricia Yeager, eds. New York: Routledge.

Kearney, Michael

1986   Integration of the Mixteca and the Western U.S.–Mexican Border Region via Migratory Wage Labor. *In* Regional Impacts of U.S.–Mexican Relations. Rosenthal Urey, ed. Pp. 71–102. Monograph Series no. 16. San Diego: University of California, San Diego, Center for U.S.–Mexican Studies.

1988   Mixtec Political Consciousness: From Passive to Active Resistance. *In* Rural Revolt in Mexico and U.S. Intervention. Daniel Nugent, ed. Pp. 113–124. Monograph Series no. 27. San Diego: University of California, San Diego, Center for U.S.–Mexican Studies.

1991   Borders and Boundaries of the State and Self at the End of Empire. Journal of Historical Sociology 4(1):52–74.

1994   Desde el indigenismo a los derechos humanos: Etnicidad y política más allá de la Mixteca. Nueva Antropología (Mexico) 14(46):49–67.

1995   The Effects of Transnational Culture, Economy, and Migration on Mixtec Identity in Oaxacalifornia. *In* The Bubbling Caldron: Race, Ethnicity, and the Urban Crisis. Michael Peter Smith and Joe R. Feagin, eds. Pp. 226–243. Minneapolis: University of Minnesota Press.

1996a   Reconceptualizing the Peasantry: Anthropology in Global Perspectives. Boulder, CO: Westview Press.

1996b   La migración y la formación de regiones autónomas pluriétnicas en Oaxaca. *In* Coloquio sobre derechos indígenas. Coordinación General de Asesores del Gobierno del Estado de Oaxaca, eds. Pp. 634–656. Oaxaca, Mexico: Instituto Oaxaqueño de las Culturas.

n.d.   Reconceptualizing the Peasantry and Anthropology. 2d ed. Boulder, CO: Westview Press. Forthcoming.

Kearney, Michael, and Stefano Varese

1990   Latin America's Indigenous Peoples Today: Changing Identities and Forms of Resistance in Global Context. *In* Capital, Power, and Inequality in Latin America. Richard Harris and S. Halebsky, eds. Pp. 207–231. Boulder, CO: Westview Press.

Kilfeather, Siobhan

1989   "Strangers at Home": Political Fictions by Women in Eighteenth-Century Ireland. Ph.D. dissertation, Princeton University.

Kincaid, Dennis

1939   British Social Life in India, 1608–1937. London: George Routledge and Sons.

Klaver, Jeannie
1997   From the Land of the Sun to the City of Angels: The Migration Process of Zapotec Indians from Oaxaca, Mexico, to Los Angeles, California. Nederlandse Geografische Studies, no. 228. Amsterdam: University of Amsterdam.

Klintowitz, Jaime
1996   Nossa gente lá fora. Veja (April 3):26–29.

Koestler, Arthur
1973   Darkness at Noon. Daphne Hardy, trans. London: Hutchinson.
[1941]

Kumar, Krishan
1987   Utopia and Anti-Utopia in Modern Times. Oxford: Basil Blackwell.

Kumekawa, Eugene
1993   Sansei Ethnic Identity and the Consequences of Perceived Unshared Suffering for Third Generation Japanese Americans. *In* American Mosaic: Selected Readings on America's Multicultural Heritage. Young I. Song and Eugene Kim, eds. Pp. 204–214. Englewood Cliffs, NJ: Prentice-Hall.

Lachicotte, W. S.
n.d.   Intimate Powers, Public Selves: Bakhtin's Space of Authoring. *In* Power and the Self. Jean Mageo, ed. Cambridge: Cambridge University Press. In press.

Laclau, Ernesto, and Chantal Mouffe
1982   Recasting Marxism: Hegemony and New Social Movements. Socialist Review 12(6):91–113.

Lancaster, Roger N.
1997   Guto's Performance: Notes on the Transvestism of Everyday Life. *In* Sex and Sexuality in Latin America. Daniel Balderston and Donna Guy, eds. Pp. 9–32. New York: NYU Press.

Lave, Jean
2000   Re-serving Succession in a British Enclave. *In* Choice and Leadership in Elite Succession. Joao de Pina-Cabral and Antonia Pedroso de Lima, eds. London: Berg.

Lave, Jean, Paul Duguid, Nadine Fernandez, and Eric Axel
1992   Coming of Age in Birmingham: Cultural Studies and Conceptions of Subjectivity. Annual Reviews in Anthropology 21:257–282.

Lemarchand, René
1994   Burundi: Ethnocide as Discourse and Practice. New York: Woodrow Wilson Center Press and Cambridge University Press.

Lestage, Françoise
1998   Apuntes sobre los mecanismos de reconstrucción de la identidad entre los migrantes: Los Mixtecos de las Californias. *In* Encuentros Antropólogicos: Power, Identity and Mobility in Mexican Society. V. Napolitano and X. Leyva Solano, eds. Pp. 133–143. London: Institute of Latin American Studies.

Lévi-Strauss, Claude
1966   The Savage Mind. Chicago: University of Chicago Press.

Linger, Daniel T.
1994   Has Culture Theory Lost Its Minds? Ethos 22(3):284–315.
1997   Brazil Displaced: Restaurant 51 in Nagoya, Japan. Horizontes Antropológicos (Porto Alegre, Brazil) 5:181–203.

Lloyd, David
n.d.   The Conflict of the Borders. Unpublished paper.

Lovell, W. George
1988   Surviving Conquest: The Maya of Guatemala in Historical Perspective. Latin American Research Review 23(2):25–58.

Lutz, Christopher
1984   Historia sociodemográfica de Santiago de Guatemala, 1541–1773. Guatemala: CIRMA.

Malkki, Liisa
1995   Purity and Exile: Violence, Memory, and National Cosmology among Hutu Refugees in Tanzania. Chicago: University of Chicago Press.

Mangan, J. A, ed.
1986   The Games Ethic and Imperialism: Aspects of the Diffusion of an Ideal. Harmondsworth, UK: Viking.
1988   "Benefits Bestowed?": Education and British Imperialism. Manchester, UK: Manchester University Press.

Mannheim, Karl
1985   Ideology and Utopia: An Introduction to the Sociology of Knowledge.
[1936]   New York: Harcourt Brace.

Manz, Beatriz
1988   Refugees of a Hidden War: The Aftermath of Counterinsurgency in Guatemala. Albany: State University of New York Press.

Martins, Conceição Andrade
1990   Memória do vinho do Porto. Lisbon: Instituto de Ciências Sociais.

Marx, Karl, and Friedrich Engels
1976   The German Ideology. *In* Karl Marx and Friedrich Engels: Collected Works, vol. 5. Pp. 19–539. New York: International Publishers.

McGreal, Chris

1997a   Hutus Held Prisoner in Their Own Land. Manchester Guardian Weekly, 27 July, p. 5.

1997b   Truth that Lies Buried in Congo's Killing Fields. Manchester Guardian Weekly, 27 July, p. 5.

McHugh, Ernestine

1989   Concepts of the Person among the Gurungs of Nepal. American Ethnologist 16(1):75–86.

McVeigh, Robbie

1994   It's Part of Life Here…: The Security Forces and Harassment in Northern Ireland. Belfast: Committee on the Administration of Justice.

McWilliams, Carey

1939   Factories in the Fields: The Story of Migratory Farm Labor in California. Boston: Little Brown.

Meinhof, Ulrike Hanna

1986   Revolting Women: Subversion and Its Media Representation in West Germany and Britain. Women, State and Revolution. Essays on Power and Gender in Europe since 1789. Sian Reynolds, ed. Pp. 141–160. Amherst, MA: University of Massachusetts Press.

Meredith, George

1861   Evan Harrington. London: Bradbury and Evans.

Morales, Mario Roberto

1998   La articulación de las diferencias, ó, el síndrome de Maximón: Los discursos literarios y políticos del debate interétnico en Guatemala. Guatemala: FLACSO Guatemala.

Morris, William

1966   News from Nowhere. New York: Monthly Review Press.
[1890]

Mykkänen, Pekka

1998   Totuuskomissio: USA ja Britannia ehkä Hammarskjöldin "murhan" takana. Helsingin Sanomat, 20 August, p. C5.

Nagengast, Carole, and Michael Kearney

1990   Mixtec Ethnicity: Social Identity, Political Consciousness, and Political Activism. Latin American Research Review 25(2):61–91.

Nash, Catherine

1993   Remapping and Renaming: New Cartographies of Identity, Gender, and Landscape. Feminist Review 44:39–57.

Nash, June C.

1968   The Passion Play in Maya Indian Communities. Comparative Studies in Society and History 10:318–327.

National Council for Civil Liberties (NCCL)
1986   Strip Searching: An Inquiry into the Strip Searching of Women
        Prisoners at Armagh Prison between 1982 and 1985. Booklet. London:
        National Council for Civil Liberties.

Newbury, Catherine
1998   Ethnicity and the Politics of History in Rwanda. Africa Today
        45(1):7–24.

Newbury, Catherine, and David Newbury
1994   Rwanda: The Politics of Turmoil. African Studies Association Newsletter
        27(3):9–11.

Nordstrom, Carolyn
1996   Rape: Politics and Theory in War and Peace. Australian Feminist Studies
        11(23):149–162.

Nordstrom, C., and J. Martin, eds.
1992   The Paths to Domination, Resistance, and Terror. Berkeley: University
        of California Press.

Nordstrom, C., and A. Robben, eds.
1995   Fieldwork under Fire: Contemporary Studies of Violence and Survival.
        Berkeley: University of California Press.

Oka, Takashi
1994   Prying Open the Door: Foreign Workers in Japan. Contemporary Issues
        Paper no. 2. Washington, DC: Carnegie Endowment for International
        Peace.

OKMA (Oxlajuuj Keej Maya' Ajtz'iib')
1993   Maya' Chii': Los idiomas Mayas de Guatemala. Guatemala: Cholsamaj.

Ortner, Sherry B.
1995   Resistance and the Problem of Ethnographic Refusal. Comparative
        Studies in Society and History 135:173–193.

Orwell, George
1934   Burmese Days. New York: Harper and Brothers.
1970   Arthur Koestler. In The Collected Essays, Journalism and Letters of
        George Orwell, vol. 3. Sonia Orwell and Ian Angus, eds.
        Harmondsworth, UK: Penguin.
1981   Nineteen Eighty-Four. New York: New American Library.
[1949]

Ostrander, Susan
1993   Surely You're Not in This Just to Be Helpful: Access, Rapport, and
        Interviews in Three Studies of Elites. Journal of Contemporary
        Ethnography 22(1):7–27.

Otero, Gerardo, ed.
1996   Neoliberalism Revisited: Economic Restructuring and Mexico's Political
        Future. Boulder, CO: Westview Press.

Otzoy, Irma
1988   Identity and Higher Education among Mayan Women. M.A. thesis,
        Department of Anthropology, University of Iowa.

Owen Daniel, Jamie, and Tom Moylan, eds.
1997   Not Yet: Reconsidering Ernst Bloch. New York: Verso.

Palerm, Juan Vicente, ed.
1989   Latino Settlements in California. *In* The Challenge: Latinos in a
        Changing California. Pp. 127–171. Report of the University of California
        SCR 43 Task Force. Riverside, CA: University of California Consortium
        on Mexico and the United States.

Parish, Steven M.
1994   Moral Knowing in a Hindu Sacred City. New York: Columbia University
        Press.

Pastor, Rodolfo
1987   Campesinos y reformas: La Mixteca 1700–1856. Mexico City: El Colegio
        de México.

Pemberton, John
1994   On the Subject of "Java." Ithaca, NY: Cornell University Press.

Pigg, S.
1992   Inventing Social Categories through Place: Social Representations and
        Development in Nepal. Comparative Studies in Society and History
        34:491–513.

Pop Caal, Antonio
1992   Li Juliisil Kirisyaanil ut li Minok ib': Judeo-cristianismo y colonización.
        Guatemala: SPEM/Cholsamaj.

Prunier, Gerard
1995   The Rwanda Crisis: History of a Genocide. New York: Columbia
        University Press.

Ramos, Alcida
1994   The Hyperreal Indian. Critique of Anthropology 14(2):153–171.

Raxche' Rodríguez Guaján, Demetrio
1989   Cultura Maya y políticas de desarrollo. Guatemala: Coordinadora
        Cakchiquel de Desarrollo Integral, Departamento de Investigaciones
        Culturales.

Reyntjens, Filip
1994   L'Afrique des Grands Lacs in crise: Rwanda, Burundi, 1988–1994. Paris:
        Karthala.

Rivera-Salgado, Gaspar
1999a   Welcome to Oaxacalifornia. Cultural Survival Quarterly 23(1):59–61.
1999b   Migration and Political Activism: Mexican Transnational Indigenous
        Communities in a Comparative Perspective. Ph.D. dissertation,
        Department of Sociology, University of California, Santa Cruz.
1999c   Mixtec Activism in Oaxacalifornia: Transborder Grassroots Political
        Strategies. American Behavioral Scientist 42(9):1439–1458.

Robertson, George
1987   Port. London: Faber and Faber.

Rosaldo, Renato
1980   Ilongot Headhunting 1883–1974: A Study in Society and History. Palo
        Alto, CA: Stanford University Press.
1990   Culture and Truth. New York: Basic Books.
1993   Culture and Truth: The Remaking of Social Analysis. With a new intro-
        duction. Boston: Beacon Press.

Ross, John
1995   Rebellion from the Roots: Indian Uprising in Chiapas. Monroe, ME:
        Common Courage Press.

Runsten, David, and Michael Kearney
1994   A Survey of Oaxacan Village Networks in California Agriculture. Davis,
        CA: California Institute for Rural Studies.

Sahlins, Marshall
1985   Islands of History. Chicago: University of Chicago Press.

Sam Colop, Luis Enrique
1983   Hacia una propuesta de ley de educación bilingüe. Thesis for the
        Licenciatura en Ciencias Jurídicas y Sociales, Universidad Rafael
        Landívar, Guatemala.
1991   Jub'aqtun Omay Kuchum K'aslemal: Cinco siglos de encubrimiento.
        Seminario Permanente de Estudios Mayas, Cuaderno no. 1. Guatemala:
        Editorial Cholsamaj.

Sánchez, Consuelo
1999   Los pueblos indígenas: Del indigenismo al autonomía. Mexico City:
        Siglo Veintiuno.

Sapir, Edward
1917   Do We Need a "Superorganic"? American Anthropologist 19:441–447.
1949   Psychiatric and Cultural Pitfalls in the Business of Getting a Living. *In*
[1939]   Selected Writings in Language, Culture, and Personality. David G.
        Mandelbaum, ed. Pp. 578–589. Berkeley: University of California Press.

Scarry, Elaine
1985   The Body in Pain: The Making and Unmaking of the World. New York:
        Oxford University Press.

Scheper-Hughes, Nancy

1992   Death without Weeping: The Violence of Everyday Life in Brazil. Berkeley: University of California Press.

Schirmer, Jennifer

1998   The Guatemalan Military Project: A Violence Called Democracy. Philadelphia: University of Pennsylvania Press.

Schoffeleers, Matthew

1985   Oral History and the Retrieval of the Distant Past. *In* Theoretical Explorations in African Religion. Wim van Binsbergen and Matthew Schoffeleers, eds. Pp. 164–188. London: Routledge and Kegan Paul.

1987   Ideological Confrontation and the Manipulation of Oral History: A Zambesian Case. History in Africa: A Journal of Method 14:257–273.

Scott, James C.

1985   Weapons of the Weak: Everyday Forms of Peasant Resistance. New Haven, CT: Yale University Press.

1990   Domination and the Arts of Resistance: Hidden Transcripts. New Haven, CT: Yale University Press.

Scott, Paul

1977   Staying On. London: William Heinemann.

Shillington, V. M., and A. B. Wallis Chapman

1907   The Commercial Relations of England and Portugal. New York: E. P. Dutton.

Showalter, Elaine

1992   The Apocalyptic Fables of H. G. Wells. *In* Fin de Siecle/Fin du Globe: Fears and Fantasies of the Late Nineteenth Century. John Stokes, ed. Pp. 69–84. New York: St. Martin's.

Skinner, Debra

1989   The Socialization of Gender Identity: Observations from Nepal. *In* Child Development in Cultural Context. J. Valsiner, ed. Pp. 181–192. Toronto: Hogrefe and Huber.

1990   Nepalese Children's Understanding of Self and the Social World. Ph.D. dissertation, Department of Anthropology, University of North Carolina at Chapel Hill.

Skinner, Debra, and Dorothy Holland

1996   Schools and the Cultural Production of the Educated Person in a Nepalese Hill Community. *In* The Cultural Production of the Educated Person: Critical Ethnographies of Schooling and Local Practice. Bradley A. Levinson, Douglas E. Foley, and Dorothy C. Holland, eds. Pp. 273–299. Albany: State University of New York Press.

1998   Contested Selves, Contested Femininities: Girls' Production of
        Gendered Identities in and beyond a Nepalese Hill Community. *In*
        Sociohistorical Approaches to Selves, Persons, and Cultures in Nepal. Al
        Pach and Debra Skinner, eds. Pp. 87–110. Lanham, MD: Rowman and
        Littlefield.

Skinner, Debra, Dorothy Holland, and G. B. Adhikari
1994   The Songs of Tij: A Genre of Critical Commentary for Women in Nepal.
        Asian Folklore Studies 53:259–305.

Sluka, Jeffrey
1989   Hearts and Minds, Water and Fish: Support for the INLA in a Northern
        Irish Ghetto. Greenwich, CT: AI Press.

Smith, Carol
1993   Local History in Global Context: Social and Economic Transitions in
        Western Guatemala. *In* Constructing Culture and Power in Latin
        America. Daniel H. Levine, ed. Pp. 75–118. Ann Arbor: University of
        Michigan.

Smith, Carol, ed.
1990   Guatemalan Indians and the State, 1540 to 1988. Austin: University of
        Texas Press.

Smyth, Frank
1994   Blood Money and Geopolitics. The Nation, 2 May, pp. 585–588.

Spencer, Jonathan
1990   Writing Within: Anthropology, Nationalism, and Culture in Sri Lanka.
        Current Anthropology 31(3): 283–300.

Spiro, Melford E.
1993   Is the Western Conception of the Self "Peculiar" within the Context of
        World Cultures? Ethos 21(2):107–154.

Stephen, Lynn
1996   The Creation and Re-Creation of Ethnicity: Lessons from the Zapotec
        and Mixtec of Oaxaca. Latin American Perspectives 23(2)17–38.

Stoler, Ann L.
1991   Carnal Knowledge and Imperial Power: Gender, Race, and Morality in
        Colonial Asia. *In* Gender at the Crossroads of Knowledge: Feminist
        Anthropology in the Postmodern Era. M. di Leonardo, ed. Pp. 51–101.
        Berkeley: University of California Press.

1995   Race and the Education of Desire. Durham, NC: Duke University Press.

Stryker, Rachel
1998   Wee Girls or International Women: Strip Search and the Politics of
        Political Prisoners. Paper presented at the annual meeting of the
        American Anthropological Association.

Stuart, James, and Michael Kearney

1981   Causes and Effects of Agricultural Labor Migration from the Mixteca of
        Oaxaca to California. Working Papers in U.S.–Mexican Studies no. 28.
        San Diego: University of California, San Diego, Program in
        U.S.–Mexican Studies.

Tambiah, Stanley Jeyaraja

1996   Leveling Crowds: Ethnonationalist Conflicts and Collective Violence in
        South Asia. Berkeley: University of California Press.

Tanner, R. E. S.

1964   Conflict within Small European Communities in Tanganyika. Human
        Organization 23(4):319–327.

1966   European Leadership in Small Communities in Tanganyika prior to
        Independence: A Study of Conflicting Social and Political Interracial
        Roles. Race 7(3):289–302.

Taussig, Michael

1987   Shamanism, Colonialism, and the Wild Man. Chicago: University of
        Chicago Press.

Tedlock, Barbara

1982   Time and the Highland Maya. Albuquerque: University of New Mexico
        Press.

Tedlock, Dennis

1983   The Spoken Word and the Work of Interpretation. Philadelphia:
        University of Pennsylvania Press.

1993   Breath on the Mirror: Mythic Voices of the Living Maya. San Francisco:
        Harper San Francisco.

Terkel, Studs

1974   Working: People Talk About What They Do All Day and How They Feel
        About What They Do. New York: Pantheon.

Van Cott, Donna Lee

1995   Indigenous Peoples and Democracy in Latin America. New York: St.
        Martin's.

Vansina, Jan

1998   The Politics of History and the Crisis in the Great Lakes. Africa Today
        45(1):37–44.

Velasco Ortiz, Laura

1999   Comunidades transnacionales y conciencia étnica: Indígenas migrantes
        en la frontera México–Estados Unidos. Ph.D. dissertation, Centro de
        Estudios Sociológicos, Colegio de Mexico.

Vogt, Evon Z.

1969   Zinacantan: A Maya Community in the Highlands of Chiapas.
        Cambridge, MA: Harvard University Press.

Volosinov V. N.
1986   Marxism and the Philosophy of Language. 1st ed. Cambridge, MA:
[1929]   Harvard University Press.

Vygotsky, L. S.
1960   Razvitie vyshhih psihicheskih funktsii [Development of higher psychical
        functions]. Moscow: Izd. APN.
1971   The Psychology of Art. Cambridge, MA: MIT Press.
1978a   The Role of Play in Development. *In* Mind in Society: The Development
        of Higher Psychological Functions. M. Cole et al., eds. Pp. 92–104.
        Cambridge, MA: Harvard University Press.
1978b   Mind in Society: The Development of Higher Psychological Functions.
        M. Cole et al., eds. Cambridge, MA: Harvard University Press.
1987   The Collected Works of L. S. Vygotsky, vol. 1: Problems of General
        Psychology. Robert W. Rieber and Aaron Carton, eds. Norris Minick,
        trans. New York: Plenum.

Wagner, Michelle
1998   All the Bourgmestre's Men: Making Sense of Genocide in Rwanda.
        Africa Today 45(1):25–36.

Warnock, John
1995   The Other Mexico: The North American Triangle Completed.
        Montreal: Black Rose Books.

Warren, Kay B.
1989   The Symbolism of Subordination: Indian Identity in a Guatemalan
        Town. 2d ed. Austin: University of Texas Press.
1998   Indigenous Movements and Their Critics: Pan-Maya Activism in
        Guatemala. Princeton, NJ: Princeton University Press.

Warren, Kay B., ed.
1993   The Violence Within: Cultural and Political Opposition in Divided
        Nations. Boulder, CO: Westview Press.

Wasserstrom, Robert
1983   Class and Society in Central Chiapas. Berkeley: University of California
        Press.

Watanabe, John
1992   Maya Saints and Souls in a Changing World. Austin: University of Texas
        Press.

Whitecotton, Joseph W.
1977   The Zapotecs: Princes, Priests, and Peasants. Norman: University of
        Oklahoma Press.

Wikan, Unni
1995   The Self in a World of Urgency and Necessity. Ethos 23(3):259–285.

Williams, Raymond
1973   The Country and the City. Oxford: Oxford University Press.

Willis, Paul
1977   Learning to Labour: How Working Class Kids Get Working Class Jobs. Farnborough, UK: Saxon House.

1981a   Learning to Labor: How Working Class Kids Get Working Class Jobs. New York: Columbia University Press.

1981b   Cultural Production Is Different from Cultural Reproduction Is Different from Social Reproduction Is Different from Reproduction. Interchange 12(2–3):48–67.

1992   Notes on Method. In Culture, Media, Language: Working Papers
[1980]   in Cultural Studies, 1972–79. Stuart Hall et al., eds. Pp. 88–95. London: Routledge.

2000   The Ethnographic Imagination. Cambridge, UK: Polity Press.

Wilson, Richard
1995   Mayan Resurgence in Guatemala. Norman: University of Oklahoma Press.

Wilson, William J.
1987   The Truly Disadvantaged. Chicago: University of Chicago Press.

Wolf, Eric R.
1957   Closed Corporate Communities in Mesoamerica and Central Java. Southwestern Journal of Anthropology 13:1–18.

Wright, Angus
1990   The Death of Ramón González: The Modern Agricultural Dilemma. Austin: University of Texas Press.

Wright, Patrick
1985   On Living in an Old Country: The National Past in Contemporary Britain. London: Verso.

Zabin, Carol, coordinator
1992   Migración oaxaqueña a los campos agrícolas de California: Un diálogo. San Diego: Center for U.S.–Mexican Studies, University of California.

Zabin, Carol, Michael Kearney, Anna Garcia, David Runsten, and Carole Nagengast
1993   Mixtec Migrants in California Agriculture. Davis, CA: California Institute for Rural Studies.

Index

Central Africa: Anglicization of, 339; conspiracy theory in, 344; diaspora from, 330, 331; dystopias in, 342; genocide in, 331, 335, 340; human rights violations in, 342; strategic politics in, 344–45; tourism in, 343

Centre for Contemporary Cultural Studies, 12

Chetri, 123, 129n8; agricultural work and, 129n6; Tij festival and, 125, 130n10

Chiapas, agreement with, 268; uprising in, 267

Chomsky, Noam, 341

Christian Response to Strip Searches (CRSS), 53, 61n9

Christianity, Christ-centric sense of, 74; Pan-Mayanists and, 84

Citizenship, British, 292; Canadian/Hutus, Tutsis and, 334

civic associations, 143, 145

civil-religious hierarchies, 76, 91n9

civil rights organizations, strip searches and, 37

class, 16, 278n13; classification and, 257–59; conflict, 264; consciousness, 248, 271; cultural differences and, 258; differences in, 286; dynamics of, 276; identities and, 256–57, 257 (fig.), 278n11; national culture and, 317; relations, 21, 256, 300; sex and, 279n14; subalterns and, 272

class culture, 213, 302; British, 305, 312, 318n2; national, 303; in Porto, 301, 303–4; working class, 211, 212, 261

class differences, 213, 257; indicators of, 259, 263; persistence of, 258–59; reproduction of, 261; struggle and, 259, 285

class dispositions, 142, 168

class identities, 26, 282; formation of, 140–42, 258; political struggles and, 141–42

class inequalities, 248, 257, 265

CLIP. See Colegio Luso-Internacional do Porto

Coalición Obrero Campesino Estudiantil del Istmo (COCEI), 280n24

coalition building, 148, 272; community

activism and, 155; importance of, 149

COCEI. See Coalición Obrero Campesino Estudiantil del Istmo

Colegio Luso-Internacional do Porto (CLIP), 290, 310–11, 312; admission criteria for, 308; governance of, 308

Coleman, Barbara, 152, 156, 157, 163; on AGT, 167; on Airport Access people, 156; on East Elmhurst compromise, 166; situational constraints and, 167

colonial club life, accounts of, 298

colonial gaze, strip searches and, 54–57

colonialism, nationalism and, 319–20n8; political economics of, 320n8

colonias, 250

commodity fetishism, 199

common-room culture, changes in, 213

communities, 29, 168; punishment of, 56

Community Board 1, 157, 163; aviation committee of, 164

Community Board 3, 152, 163, 164; African Americans on, 144; Airport Access team and, 157; Aviation Subcommittee of, 154, 157; concerns of, 159; East Elmhurst trench and, 168–69; runway overrun and, 145

Community Board 12, 156, 163

community identity, changes in, 306; constructing, 140; struggle over, 317–18

community work, 75; women and, 289, 290, 293, 300–301

Compania de Linha Coats and Clark, 287, 321n15

concessions, 301–4; dilemma of, 304–6

Confradia do Vinho do Porto, 305

consolidation, 252, 254–55

containment, displacement and, 277n6; strategies for, 249, 265, 271

continuity narratives, 67

control, 27, 214; battle for, 38; sexualization of, 40

cooperative movement, 81, 82

Corona, 137, 138; Hayes and, 139; port authority and, 169

costumbre, Catholic Action and, 76

counterhegemonizing mythology, 203

counterinsurgency wars, 80–81

School of American Research
Advanced Seminar Series

PUBLISHED BY SAR PRESS

CHACO & HOHOKAM: PREHISTORIC
REGIONAL SYSTEMS IN THE AMERICAN
SOUTHWEST
  Patricia L. Crown &
  W. James Judge, eds.

RECAPTURING ANTHROPOLOGY:
WORKING IN THE PRESENT
  Richard G. Fox, ed.

WAR IN THE TRIBAL ZONE: EXPANDING
STATES AND INDIGENOUS WARFARE
  R. Brian Ferguson &
  Neil L. Whitehead, eds.

IDEOLOGY AND PRE-COLUMBIAN
CIVILIZATIONS
  Arthur A. Demarest &
  Geoffrey W. Conrad, eds.

DREAMING: ANTHROPOLOGICAL AND
PSYCHOLOGICAL INTERPRETATIONS
  Barbara Tedlock, ed.

HISTORICAL ECOLOGY: CULTURAL
KNOWLEDGE AND CHANGING
LANDSCAPES
  Carole L. Crumley, ed.

THEMES IN SOUTHWEST PREHISTORY
  George J. Gumerman, ed.

MEMORY, HISTORY, AND OPPOSITION
UNDER STATE SOCIALISM
  Rubie S. Watson, ed.

OTHER INTENTIONS: CULTURAL
CONTEXTS AND THE ATTRIBUTION
OF INNER STATES
  Lawrence Rosen, ed.

LAST HUNTERS–FIRST FARMERS: NEW
PERSPECTIVES ON THE PREHISTORIC
TRANSITION TO AGRICULTURE
  T. Douglas Price &
  Anne Birgitte Gebauer, eds.

MAKING ALTERNATIVE HISTORIES:
THE PRACTICE OF ARCHAEOLOGY AND
HISTORY IN NON-WESTERN SETTINGS
  Peter R. Schmidt &
  Thomas C. Patterson, eds.

SENSES OF PLACE
  Steven Feld & Keith H. Basso, eds.

CYBORGS & CITADELS:
ANTHROPOLOGICAL INTERVENTIONS IN
EMERGING SCIENCES AND TECHNOLOGIES
  Gary Lee Downey & Joseph Dumit, eds.

ARCHAIC STATES
  Gary M. Feinman & Joyce Marcus, eds.

CRITICAL ANTHROPOLOGY NOW:
UNEXPECTED CONTEXTS, SHIFTING
CONSTITUENCIES, CHANGING AGENDAS
  George E. Marcus, ed.

THE ORIGINS OF LANGUAGE: WHAT
NONHUMAN PRIMATES CAN TELL US
  Barbara J. King, ed.

REGIMES OF LANGUAGE: IDEOLOGIES,
POLITIES, AND IDENTITIES
  Paul V. Kroskrity, ed.

BIOLOGY, BRAINS, AND BEHAVIOR: THE
EVOLUTION OF HUMAN DEVELOPMENT
  Sue Taylor Parker, Jonas Langer, &
  Michael L. McKinney, eds.

PUBLISHED BY CAMBRIDGE UNIVERSITY PRESS

DREAMING: ANTHROPOLOGICAL AND
PSYCHOLOGICAL INTERPRETATIONS
Barbara Tedlock, ed.

THE ANASAZI IN A CHANGING
ENVIRONMENT
George J. Gumerman, ed.

REGIONAL PERSPECTIVES ON THE OLMEC
Robert J. Sharer & David C. Grove, eds.

THE CHEMISTRY OF PREHISTORIC
HUMAN BONE
T. Douglas Price, ed.

THE EMERGENCE OF MODERN HUMANS:
BIOCULTURAL ADAPTATIONS IN THE
LATER PLEISTOCENE
Erik Trinkaus, ed.

THE ANTHROPOLOGY OF WAR
Jonathan Haas, ed.

THE EVOLUTION OF POLITICAL SYSTEMS
Steadman Upham, ed.

CLASSIC MAYA POLITICAL HISTORY:
HIEROGLYPHIC AND ARCHAEOLOGICAL
EVIDENCE
T. Patrick Culbert, ed.

TURKO-PERSIA IN HISTORICAL
PERSPECTIVE
Robert L. Canfield, ed.

CHIEFDOMS: POWER, ECONOMY, AND
IDEOLOGY
Timothy Earle, ed.

PUBLISHED BY UNIVERSITY OF CALIFORNIA PRESS

WRITING CULTURE: THE POETICS
AND POLITICS OF ETHNOGRAPHY
*James Clifford &
George E. Marcus, eds.*